Wessex to AD 1000

A Regional History of England

General Editors: Barry Cunliffe and David Hey
For full details of the series, see pp. xii–xv.

Wessex
to AD 1000

Barry Cunliffe

Longman
London and New York

Longman Group UK Limited,
Longman House, Burnt Mill,
Harlow, Essex CM20 2JE, England
and Associated Companies throughout the World.

Published in the United States of America
by Longman Publishing, New York

First published 1993

ISBN 0 582 49279 3 CSD
ISBN 0 582 49280 7 PPR

British Library Cataloguing-in-Publication Data

A catalogue record for this book is
available from the British Library

Library of Congress Cataloging in Publication Data

Cunliffe, Barry W.
    Wessex to AD 1000 / Barry Cunliffe.
      p. cm. – (A Regional history of England)
    Includes bibliographical references and index.
    ISBN 0–582 49279–3 (cloth). – ISBN 0–582–
    49280–7 (pbk.)
    1. Wessex (England) – History. 2. Wessex (Eng-
land) – Antiquities. 3. England – Civilization – To
1066. 4. Man, Prehistoric – England – Wessex. 5.
Land settlement – England – Wessex. I. Title. II.
Series.
DA670.W48C86 1993
942.3 – dc20   92–12638
                            CIP
                            AC

Set by 3DD in 10/12pt Sabon Roman
Produced by Longman Singapore Publishers (Pte) Ltd
Printed in Singapore

Contents

List of plates

List of figures

General preface

England cannot be divided satisfactorily into recognizable regions based on former kingdoms or principalities in the manner of France, Germany or Italy. Few of the Anglo-Saxon tribal divisions had much meaning in later times and from the eleventh century onwards England was a united country. English regional identities are imprecise and no firm boundaries can be drawn. In planning this series we have recognized that any attempt to define a region must be somewhat arbitrary, particularly in the Midlands, and that boundaries must be flexible. Even the South West, which is surrounded on three sides by the sea, has no agreed border on the remaining side and in many ways, historically and culturally, the River Tamar divides the area into two. Likewise, the Pennines present a formidable barrier between the eastern and western counties on the Northern Borders; contrasts as much as similarities need to be emphasized here.

The concept of a region does not imply that the inhabitants had a similar experience of life, nor that they were all inward-looking. A Hull merchant might have more in common with his Dutch trading partner than with his fellow Yorkshireman who farmed a Pennine smallholding: a Roman soldier stationed for years on Hadrian's Wall probably had very different ethnic origins from a native farmer living on the Durham boulder clay. To differing degrees, everyone moved in an international climate of belief and opinion with common working practices and standards of living.

Yet regional differences were nonetheless real; even today a Yorkshireman may be readily distinguished from someone from the South East. Life in Lancashire and Cheshire has always been different from life in the Thames valley. Even the East Midlands has a character that is subtly different from that of the West Midlands. People still feel that they belong to a particular region within England as a whole.

In writing these histories we have become aware how much regional identities may vary over time; moreover how a farming region, say, may not coincide with a region defined by its building styles or its dialect. We have dwelt upon the diversity that can be found within a region as well as upon common characteristics in order to illustrate the local peculiarities of provincial life. Yet despite all of these problems of definition, we feel that the time is ripe to attempt an ambitious scheme outlining the history of England's regions in twenty-one volumes. London has not been included – except for demonstrating the many ways in which it has influenced the provinces – for its history has been very different from that of the towns and rural parishes that are our principal concern.

In recent years an enormous amount of local research, both historical and archaeological, has deepened our understanding of the former concerns of ordinary men and women and has altered our perception of everyday life in the past in many significant ways, yet the results of this work are not widely known even within the regions themselves.

This series offers a synthesis of this new work from authors who have themselves been actively involved in local research and who are present in or former residents of the regions they describe.

Each region will be covered in two linked but independent volumes, the first covering the period up to AD 1000 and necessarily relying heavily on archaeological data, and the second bringing the story up to the present day. Only by taking a wide time-span and by studying continuity and change over many centuries do distinctive regional characteristics become clear.

This series portrays life as it was experienced by the great majority of the people of South Britain or England as it was to become. The twenty-one volumes will – it is hoped – substantially enrich our understanding of English history.

Barry Cunliffe
David Hey

A Regional History of England

General Editors: Barry Cunliffe (to AD 1000) and David Hey (from AD 1000)

The regionalization used in this series is illustrated on the map opposite.

* already published

1. The Northern Counties
2. The Lancashire/Cheshire Region
3. Yorkshire
4. The Severn Valley and West Midlands
5. The East Midlands
6. The South Midlands and the Upper Thames
7. The Eastern Counties
8. The South West
9. Wessex
10. The South East

Acknowledgements

Anyone writing a book of this kind has to rely very heavily on the work of others. A glance at the bibliography will provide many of the names of those who have been, or still are, active in researching the early history of Wessex. But let me stress that the bibliography is highly selective – it could easily be four times the size without including trivia. In giving emphasis to the more up-to-date works I have done scant justice to the great pioneers of the eighteenth and nineteenth centuries whose work has laid the foundation for our understanding – people like Stukeley, Colt Hoare, Pitt Rivers, the Cunningtons and many others – they deserve a volume to themselves. So too do the leaders of the county societies which arose in the nineteenth century and have continued to this day to encourage local research and to publish it in their journals. A history of archaeological endeavour in Wessex would be a microcosm of the cultural and scientific evolution of the nation.

My debt to my fellow workers past and present is, I hope, self-evident, and my gratitude to them is deeply felt. More particularly I would like to mention individuals who have helped in specific ways: Mick Aston for providing a brilliant array of air photographs from which a selection has been made; Derek Roe, Nick Barton, Alasdair Whittle and James Campbell, who have read sections of the text and who, in the midst of busy professional lives, have readily offered their expert guidance to help improve its shortcomings; Gary Lock, who has advised on radiocarbon dating and has helped prepare the list in the appendix; Alison Wilkins, whose line illustrations enliven the text; and Lynda Smithson for her skill, patience and encouragement in preparing an immaculate typescript.

Finally I would like to thank the hundreds of people who during the last thirty years have helped me sift through the soil of Wessex in pursuit of its secrets. They are too many to list in full but the dedicated hard work and the good companionship of Cynthia Poole, Lisa Brown, Kathy Laws, Ian Brooks and Graham Barton have made our summers together on the Wessex Downs something always to look forward to. This book is for them.

The publishers would like to thank the following for permission to reproduce copyright material: the Trustees of the Dorset Natural History and Archaeological Society, Dorset County Museum for plate 7.2 and the Royal Commission on the Historical Monuments of England Crown copyright for plates 3.1 and 7.1.

Introduction

The 'Wessex' of this book is not a natural geographical entity nor is it the legally defined territory ruled by the kings of the West Saxons. 'Wessex' is a more diffuse concept – it is all things to all men. Thomas Hardy, responsible for reintroducing the word into everyday use, used it with delightful vagueness though to him the Dorset focus was all important. 'Wessex' has an undoubted charm about it due in no small part to Hardy's lively imagination. With its connotations of sweeping landscapes – the seed bed of our deeply rooted British culture – it has come to stand for stability, tradition and reliability. Thus in the telephone directory it is possible to find Wessex building societies, Wessex double glazing, Wessex used cars and even Wessex steam laundries! Advertising copywriters have much to thank Hardy for. Indeed so persuasive is the term that it has been used in this series of regional histories in place of the somewhat less emotive 'Central Southern England' which would have been a better match for the other titles.

For us, then, Wessex means the counties of Somerset, Avon, Dorset, Wiltshire, Hampshire and Berkshire. It is a region with a high degree of physical coherence dominated by the upland chalk massif of Salisbury Plain stretching east to end abruptly at the Weald, fingering down through Dorset to touch the sea in Weymouth Bay and extending sufficiently far north to create a defiant scarp overlooking the Vale of the White Horse and the Thames valley beyond. To the south the chalk cradles the younger softer rocks of the Hampshire Basin – mainly sands and clays – laid down in the Tertiary period. From the chalk rim spring water is carried across the Tertiaries in a series of rivers, the Frome, the Piddle, the Stour, the Avon, the Test, the Itchen and the Meon, to the lowest axis of the basin now occupied by the Solent. The coastline formed in these softer rocks has constantly changed as the sands and clays have been eroded by the sea and the loosened materials redeposited as spits and bars.

The chalk upland of Salisbury Plain is separated from the chalk of the Marlborough and Berkshire Downs by two wide valleys floored by clays and sands of differing geological ages. To the east, lying in a downfold in the chalk, are the younger Tertiary rocks of the London basin, similar in lithography and generating the same land forms as those of the Hampshire basin and eroded by a Thames tributary, the river Kennet. To the west is a narrower valley, the Vale of Pewsey, created by river erosion cutting down through the chalk and exposing the Upper Greensands and Gault clay beneath.

Westwards from the chalk the grain and texture of the landscape change dramatically. The dominant feature is now the north–south ridge of limestone of Jurassic age beginning, for our regions, in the Cotswolds and ending in the cliffs south of Bridport fringing Lyme Bay. The light calcareous soils, good building stone and ease of communications have created a narrow but continuous corridor across the region congenial to settlement and broken only by the valley of the Avon, which cuts a minor gorge through the ridge at Bath. The Jurassic spine is separated from the western scarp of the chalk by lowlands dominated by thick and tenacious Oxford clay. These include the Vale of the White Horse, the upper Avon valley, the Vale of Wardour and the Blackmore Vale, though at the southern extremity of the region, the two calcareous bedrocks are closely juxtaposed in the confused and broken landscape of west Dorset.

Beyond the Jurassic ridge the landscape faces westwards towards the Bristol Channel. It is a zone of contrasts but one dominated by the carboniferous limestone ridge of the Mendip Hills in the centre and the uplands of increasing altitude extending westwards from the Quantock Hills to Exmoor, a region more properly considered to be part of the south-western peninsula. Between lies the marshy lowland of the Somerset Levels drained, if inadequately, by the rivers Brue, Parrett and Tone.

The solid geology, so briefly described, has given structure to the region which has, in turn, dominated the way in which man has lived within and used it. The caves of Mendip offered shelter for Upper Palaeolithic hunters, the light sandy soils provided congenial camp sites for Mesolithic hunting groups, while for much of the later prehistoric period the calcareous soils of the chalkland were favoured as farm land: it was here that the ritual monuments and settlements of the Neolithic, Bronze Age and Iron Age abounded. With greater pressure on land and improved technology late in the Iron Age the heavier soils began to be systematically colonized and after the Roman interlude settlement positively favoured these richer soils as the downlands became increasingly exhausted.

The structure of the land imposed constraints on ease of communication. The chalk uplands enjoyed a palimpsest of tracks linked to the ridgeways which radiated outwards from the hub of Salisbury Plain providing easy and direct communication across hundreds of kilometres. Similar routes lay along the Jurassic spine. The clay vales and the Tertiary basins were, no doubt, less well provided with ways through but the main river valleys edged with gravel terraces would have been much in use, those of the Hampshire basin providing direct links from the chalk uplands to the harbours of the Solent so vital for cross-Channel trade. Two of these rivers were of particular importance. The Stour allowed easy access from the Solent shore through the heart of the Dorset Downs to the Jurassic ridge from which it was easy to reach the river Parrett and thus the Bristol Channel, while the Salisbury Avon led directly to the heart of the chalk plain and provided an easy route leading to the river Kennet and the Thames. Both Stour and Avon come together in Christchurch Harbour, a well-protected anchorage shielded by the mass of Hengistbury Head. Harbours of this kind were extensively used throughout the prehistoric period.

With the arrival of the Roman armies an entirely new communications system was imposed linking the major urban centres with direct and well-engineered roads. It was this system, focused as it was on London and largely oblivious of the constraints of landscape, that led to a reorientation in the socio-economic structure of the region. The survival of many of these roads throughout the Saxon period helped to maintain the dominant position of London albeit after an interlude.

These broadly sketched generalities should not be allowed to obscure the fascinating diversity of the Wessex region nor should they blind us to the fact that the landscape was constantly changing. In the distant past major changes took place over a considerable time scale as the ice sheets came and went. After about 10,000 BC the climate began to improve, though with a number of fluctuations of decreasing magnitude, until the present day. It was in the more recent period, from about 6000 BC, when Britain had finally been severed from the Continent, that man began to take a hand in shaping his environment, setting in train irreversible processes such as the development of heathland, the depletion of the once fertile loessic soils of the chalk downs, and the alluviation of the valleys. It is this interaction between man and his environment that provides one of the main themes of this book.

A second leitmotif is the growing complexity of society. Over the period which concerns us it is a fair generalization to suppose that population increased, though no doubt with minor fluctuations imperceptible in the archaeological record, until the middle of the Roman period. Man is a gregarious animal and from the beginning would have lived in groups. In the Palaeolithic period these would have been small bands hunting together. By Mesolithic times the foraging groups were probably larger and worked systematically in discrete territories. The introduction of domesticated animals and cultivated plants in the fifth millennium BC required a more sedentary existence which manifested itself in a blatant expression of territoriality, so evident in the massive monuments of the period. Soon after the middle of the second millennium the appearance of permanent fields and boundaries reflect a landscape rapidly filling. With more mouths to feed and greater aspirations to satisfy the productive base of society had to be expanded. By the beginning of the first millennium BC signs of stress appeared as the hillforts so vividly demonstrate. Attack, defence and warrior prowess are much in evidence in the archaeological record.

From about 100 BC the proximity of Rome began to make itself felt. The growing Empire's incessant demand for raw materials and manpower encouraged a lively trade which in time gave a new stimulus to the economy and began to change, irrevocably, the structure of society. This process was continued and enhanced during the brief period of Roman occupation but the early energy which followed the invasion was soon spent and in Wessex, by the end of the second century, the seeds of decay inherent in the Roman system began to take root. Population and prosperity peaked and decline began. It needed only the incursion of bands of Germanic immigrants from northern Europe to tip the unstable system back into a tribalism comparable with that in the third and second centuries BC. Even old hillforts were reoccupied.

Gradually new stability began to emerge as the tiny chiefdom coalesced and by the beginning of the eighth century Wessex was a united kingdom once more. Trade with the Continent began under royal patronage and with it came the growth of a market economy and the re-emergence of urban life. By the middle of the ninth century when Danish raids began the stability of Wessex was such that at first it could repel and later culturally absorb the intruders. The scene was now set for the development of medieval England.

In this brief prologue we have, in a breathless scamper, sketched the scene and outlined the plot: it remains now to let the play unfold but before it does those who wish to understand something of the intricacies of dating, so absorbing to archaeologists, might like to consult the programme note in the Appendix beginning on page 334. There is, of course, no compulsion to do so!

Chapter 1

The Formation of the Landscape and the Early Hunter-Gatherers

Most people have heard of the Ice Age and may be aware that it divides into several intensely cold *glacial* phases interspersed with warmer *interglacials*, but few, even professional archaeologists, find it easy to grasp the immensity of the time spans involved. Perhaps the simplest way to provide a perspective is to remind ourselves that the entire development of mankind in Britain, from the beginning of the Mesolithic period in the eighth millennium BC until now, could lie in the early stages of just one interglacial and that much of the British Isles could disappear beneath the ice once more as part of the cyclic changes of the next million years.

Our knowledge of the Pleistocene period, which began about two million years ago, has developed rapidly in recent times and as new data are accumulated concepts and terminologies change. The subtleties of it all, hotly debated and no doubt fascinating to the specialist, do not concern us here, but we need to establish a few widely accepted generalities against which to view the Wessex evidence (D. A. Roe 1981, Chapter 2). In the last half a million years Britain has experienced six glacial maxima (Fig. 1.1) known as the Thurnian, Baventian, Beestonian, Anglian, Wolstonian and Devensian glaciations interspersed by periods of temperate climate (interglacials) of which the Cromerian (between the Beestonian and Anglian glaciations), the Hoxnian (between the Anglian and Wolstonian glaciations) and the Ipswichian (between the Wolstonian and Devensian) are the most significant from the point of view of human settlement in Britain (D. A. Roe 1981). Research during the 1980s has shown that this widely used scheme is an oversimplification and it is now possible to define nineteen major climatic events covering the last 700,000 years, half of which are warm and half cold. Correlation with the traditional scheme is not easy and at some points there is no general agreement. Until the situation has been clarified it is simpler, for our purposes, to retain the more familiar nomenclature remembering that it is only an approximation to the truth.

The southernmost extent of the ice cap at the time of the glacial maxima is not easy to define with precision but it is generally accepted that during the

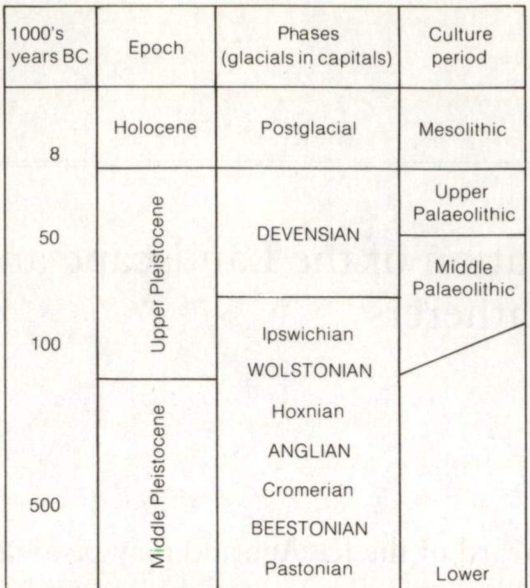

1000's years BC	Epoch	Phases (glacials in capitals)	Culture period
8	Holocene	Postglacial	Mesolithic
50	Upper Pleistocene	DEVENSIAN	Upper Palaeolithic
			Middle Palaeolithic
100		Ipswichian	
		WOLSTONIAN	
	Middle Pleistocene	Hoxnian	
		ANGLIAN	
500		Cromerian	
		BEESTONIAN	
		Pastonian	Lower Palaeolithic
		BAVENTIAN	
1000	Lower Pleistocene	Antian	
		THURNIAN	
2000		Ludhamian	

Figure 1.1   Diagram to illustrate the main glacial epochs

Anglian and perhaps the Wolstonian phases the edge of the ice sheet lay a little to the north of the Thames–Severn axis while in Devensian times it was significantly to the north. Throughout these long glacials the land of what was eventually to become Wessex was part of a vast expanse of Arctic or sub-Arctic tundra devoid of human life.

As the ice sheets receded so the land warmed up and the environment began to change. During each interglacial, tundra gave way to steppe and then began a cycle of vegetational changes which can be divided into four distinct phases (Turner and West 1968). The first, the *pre-temperate* period, saw the gradual colonizing of the steppe by closed forest dominated by birch and pine as temperatures changed from cold to cool. With the onset of warmer conditions, during the *early temperate* period, mixed oak forest prevailed to be modified in the *late temperate* period with late-immigratory trees such as hornbeam and fir. Then, as temperatures began to decline again, came the *post-temperate* period when once more birch and pine became the dominant tree species. With the onset of the next glacial episode trees disappeared altogether to give way first to steppe and then to tundra. This generalized cycle was true not only for the major interglacials but also for some of the interstadials which alleviated the long periods of intense cold, though not all of them reached fully temperate conditions.

6

Along with the changing vegetation came changes in fauna: first small creatures like wolf, marten and pig colonized the new environments and later, at the height of the warm period, horse, deer, wild cattle, rhinoceros, elephant and even on occasion hippopotamus were to be found indicating temperature maxima in excess of today.

As ice sheets receded, so land and sea-level readjusted through the interaction of two processes: the retreat of the ice allowed the land, previously depressed by the weight of the ice cap, to rise, while the greatly increased volume of melt water caused a considerable rise in sea-level. The two systems were in opposition and could at times lead to an equilibrium in the relationship of sea to land but at temperature maxima and minima considerable differences of sea-level could be experienced. During the Anglian glaciation sea-levels were probably only a little lower than today but during the Wolstonian and Devensian glaciations they fell to between 80 and 100 m below OD (Ordnance datum). In contrast during the Cromerian, Hoxnian and Ipswichian interglacials sea-level was *c.* 100 m, 40 m and 20 m above the present mean.

Although the processes outlined are a considerable simplification of a highly complex and still ill-understood situation, the albeit brief discussion serves to set the scene for a more detailed consideration of this period – the Pleistocene – in Wessex.

The Earliest Hunters

It is inevitable that the earliest periods are the least understood. This is particularly so in the Pleistocene period when successive ice ages have removed much of the evidence of preceding interglacials, virtually wiping the slate clean each time. Even so, valuable scraps of evidence survive such as the stratified deposit found in a cave above Westbury-sub-Mendip in 1969 as a vast quarry began to eat away the hillside (Bishop 1975; D. A. Roe 1981: 94–7). The cave was filled with sediment up to 20 m deep largely deposited during the Cromerian interglacial dating to the period between, very approximately, 700,000 and 400,000 BC. The complex and closely stratified deposits can be divided into three broad zones. On the limestone base were a series of sands and gravels. These were overlaid by a thickness of calcareous deposits which were sealed at the top with red silts. The lowest sands and clays produced a fauna dominated by hyena and rhinoceros, suggesting a temperate climate. The calcareous deposits were also laid down during temperate times. Remains of horse, deer, cattle, rhinoceros, bear, scimitar-toothed cat, wolf, jaguar and dhole were recovered. These accumulated as the result of deposits being washed in or more likely as prey carried into the cave by bears

7

or hyenas. The red silts at the top accumulated while the climate was cooling down with the approach of the Anglian glaciation. The environment was cool and damp with open forest prevailing. At this time birds of prey, probably owls, inhabited the cave, dropping the remains of water vole, shrews, moles, amphibians and birds onto the cave floor.

That the faunal assemblage is Cromerian is not in serious doubt. Where there is some uncertainty is the extent to which, if at all, man was represented. Throughout the calcareous deposits chipped flints have been found which are widely considered to be the result of human activity. The most convincing of these are two bifacially worked pieces, presumably general purpose cutting tools. These flints, if indeed they are humanly worked, are the only soundly stratified artefacts in our region which can be assigned to the Cromerian interglacial.

During the Anglian glaciation, the ice sheet penetrated as far south as the Thames valley and the Wessex area reverted to tundra gripped by permafrost. The melt water from the ice cap probably gave rise to the precursor of the Solent river system. Gravel terraces recorded at 70 m and 57 m above present sea-level are thought to belong to this development.

By about 300,000, the ice was once more receding with the onset of the Hoxnian interglacial. This was the period when crude flake tools, cores, choppers and large flakes – known as the Clactonian industry – made their appearance in East Anglia and the Thames valley. In Wessex the Clactonian is unrecorded except for a possible assemblage found at low tide, at Rainbow Bar, Hill Head, Hants. It is, however, unstratified and doubts have been expressed about its date (D. A. Roe 1981: 149–50). It was during this period of congenial climate that the large bifacial cutting tools known as hand axes, of Acheulian type, became comparatively common. Archaic forms of these tools (Fig. 1.2) have been found in river gravels at St Catherine's Hill, Christchurch and Corfe Mullen, Dorset (Calkin and Green 1949; D. A. Roe 1981: 189–90). Because of their crude appearance they have been called 'Earlier

---

Figure 1.2 Hand axes from Corfe Mullen, Dorset. (After Calkin and Green 1949: Figs 7–9)

Acheulian' but their exact geological position is uncertain. A little west of our area, at Kent's Cavern in Torquay, some of them were found in a cave in association with Late Cromerian or Early Anglian faunal remains.

Typical Acheulian axes of more developed kinds are extremely widespread in Wessex, the great majority of them coming from the gravel terraces of the major rivers, in particular the Test, Itchen and Avon with concentrations in the area from Christchurch to Poole and to a lesser extent the Salisbury region (Fig. 1.3). In Hampshire alone D. A. Roe (1968) has identified over 1500 sites, some of them most prolific and other find-spots have since been added. At Dunbridge 953 hand axes were recorded from a single gravel pit while from Barton-on-Sea 197 have been collected from the foreshore, fallen from the gravels that cap the cliffs. The problem with material of this kind is that most of it is redeposited, that is it has been washed out of its original context and incorporated in later river gravels. These 'secondary contexts' have relatively little information to offer about the people who made the implements: the tools were, for the most part, recovered from gravel-working in a casual manner and are thus without precise context. Accurate dating is extremely difficult. Hand axes were an extremely long-lived type and in Hampshire probably continued to be made throughout both the Hoxnian and Wolstonian phases and some groups may even have been made as late as the beginning of the Devensian (Shackley 1981: 6). To introduce some order into the material Roe (1976, 1981) has suggested a four-stage evolution beginning with the archaic forms, mentioned above, which are likely to be of pre-Hoxnian date. In stage 2 he places pointed hand axes partly flaked with bone or wooden hammers, while stage 3 is typified by more refined forms, including ovate (or cordate) axes. Stages 2 and 3 are tentatively assigned to somewhere within the Hoxnian to Wolstonian periods. The fourth stage, which includes finely pointed axes often of plano-convex shape, is thought to be later and belongs to the Ipswichian and Early Devensian periods. Five examples of the type have come from the Southampton area, for example at Warsash and at Highfield.

Although more than a thousand find-spots of hand axes are known in Wessex very few have been examined under careful archaeological supervision. Two sites, however, stand out as being of considerable potential: Knowle Farm, in the Kennet valley in Wiltshire, and Red Barns, on the south side of Portsdown Hill in Hampshire.

Knowle Farm Pit, Savernake, has produced perhaps a couple of thousand hand axes over the years. While it is clear that they come from several levels in a fluviatile deposit a significant concentration were found in a band of 'river silt'. This observation, together with their fresh, unrolled, condition, suggests that they may have derived from a working site close by (D. A. Roe 1969: 4–5). In 1977 a machine cut was made through the deposit to explore the stratigraphy (Froom 1983). In the 4½ m section exposed, three layers of gravel were identified separated by two layers of sand. Detailed observation

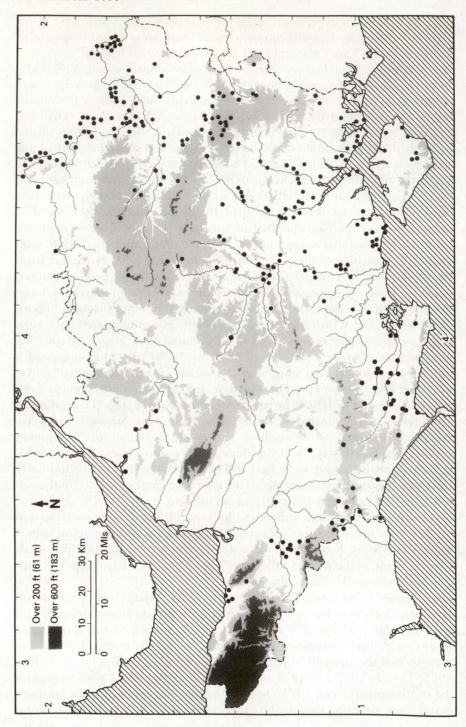

suggested that the accumulation represented a considerable period of time involving several processes all reflecting cold-climate conditions. Analysis of the 70 or so artefacts and waste flakes recovered, while confirming that working floors had existed nearby, strongly suggests that the collection does not represent a single industry but rather was derived over a period of time probably during the Wolstonian period from a variety of sources, perhaps of different ages. The Knowle Farm site exemplifies the problems involved in attempting to study deposits of this kind.

Red Barns, Portsdown, provides a far more satisfactory range of evidence. Here, at *c.* 30 m OD on the south side of a chalk ridge overlooking Portsmouth Harbour, excavation exposed a layer of grey soil sealed by a sludge deposit of broken-up chalk. The main collection of artefacts lay on the natural chalk bedrock towards the base of the soil. It consisted of waste flakes of all sizes together with a few unfinished hand axes discarded because of faults. Clearly, the Red Barns assemblage is one of the very rare examples of an *in situ* working floor where a hunting band, attracted by easily accessible chalk nodules from a nearby cliff, stayed a while to fashion tools. The site probably dates to the Wolstonian period, on the basis of its elevation in relation to a raised beach discovered nearby which represents a marine transgression reaching *c.* 37.5–38.5 m OD during the Hoxnian interglacial (ApSimon, Gamble and Shackley 1977). The Red Barns deposit, so clearly undisturbed by marine activity, must date to a period after the Hoxnian sea-level had receded.

There is little to be said, from the Wessex evidence, of the hunting and scavenging strategies adopted by early man. The animals killed and eaten during the temperate episodes included the straight-tusked elephant, rhinoceros, horse and deer together with a variety of fish and birds: the larger beasts were scavenged, the smaller hunted, but much of the diet would have comprised plant foods present in abundance in the forests which covered the landscape.

The Wolstonian glaciation came to an end about 130,000 BC and for about 60,000 years the Ipswichian interglacial prevailed – a period covering several minor climatic fluctuations. The major temperate phase can be dated to between 90,000 and 75,000 BC at which time the sea-level was at about 7.5 m OD. Raised beaches of the period have been noted at several coastal localities between Selsey (in Sussex) and Portland Bill (Shackley 1981: Fig. 2). During this time the characteristic tool type was the heart-shaped (cordiform) hand axe, also known in the continental terminology as the *bout coupé* hand axe (D. A. Roe 1981: 236–52; Tyldesley 1987). These axes belong to larger assemblages called Mousterian of Acheulian tradition, characteristic of the Atlantic part of Europe.

Figure 1.3 Locations producing Palaeolithic hand axes. Some of the individual find-spots have produced quantities of axes. (After D. A. Roe 1968)

Several significant deposits of this period occur in Wessex. Along the Solent coast, at Great Pan Farm, in the Isle of Wight, an assemblage was found in a river gravel and sand deposit which could be correlated with the 7.5 m raised beach (Shackley 1973). Among the 112 implements recovered were backed blades, knives, Levallois flakes (i.e. flakes struck from carefully prepared cores) and *bout coupé* hand axes. Similar assemblages or stray finds have been collected from Cams near Fareham, Warsash, Stone (Lepe) and Christchurch. Further inland, at Fisherton near Salisbury, a single *bout coupé* hand axe was found in a brick pit. The brickearth in which it was buried had been created in dry icy conditions as a fine dust, laid down in glacial melt water. In the same deposit were found the bones of mammoth, reindeer, muskox, marmot, lemming and arctic goose. Together the evidence suggests the onset of cold conditions coming at the end of the Ipswichian stage (Delair and Shackley 1978). Isolated examples of *bout coupé* axes occur from time to time on the chalk downs for example in the Basingstoke area, and at West Kennet (Holgate and Tyldesley 1985) and several have been found in the Bournemouth region.

It seems highly likely that the Mendip caves were used during this period but evidence is slight. However at a cave known as the Hyena Den at Wookey Hole, the contents of which were largely removed between 1859 and 1874, quantities of flint tools were found. A more recent study of the material, and of the cave itself, has suggested that two distinct industries were probably present, the earliest being typified by small bifacially worked hand axes characteristic of the Mousterian of Acheulian tradition (Tratman, Donovan and Campbell 1971). A single find of a small Mousterian hand axe came from the nearby Rhinoceros Hole but it is no longer thought to belong to an Ipswichian horizon.

During the Ipswichian phase the landscape began to take on something of its present basic form and already the main drainage pattern had been established, though there was to be one more major glacial episode to clothe the skeleton of the landscape with a further mantle of periglacial deposits. The marine transgression to 7.5 m OD disrupted the Solent river system by flooding the main valley and it may well have been at this time that the ridge of chalk joining Purbeck to the Isle of Wight was finally breached allowing the sea easy access to the soft rocks of the western part of the Hampshire basin.

Hunter-Gatherers of the Upper Palaeolithic Period

The last of the major periods of glaciation to which the land of Britain was subjected is known as the Devensian and lasted from about 70,000 BP until

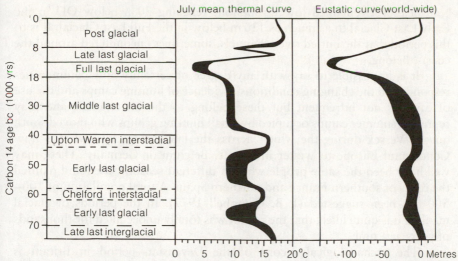

Figure 1.4 Diagram to illustrate temperature and sea-level changes during the last glacial. (After J. B. Campbell 1977: Fig. 83)

c. 10,000 BP. During this considerable span of time temperatures fluctuated. The pattern is complex but three major warm periods, or interstadials, have been identified: the Chelford Interstadial focusing around 60,000 BP; the Upton Warren Complex spanning the period from 38,000 to 25,000 BP; and a final brief interstadial, the Windermere Interstadial of about 13,000– 12,000 BP. Even at its maximum extension the Devensian ice cap did not approach Wessex. The most intense phase, the Full Last Glacial of the Late Devensian (*c.* 20,000–15,000 BP), saw ice reaching only as far south as the Wash though the Welsh Mountains were under permanent ice at the time (Fig. 1.4).

Throughout the long periods of glacial maxima the land of Wessex would have varied from being a lowland barrens covered with herbs and mosses, through a tundra to a lowland scrub steppe. With the retreat of the ice cap during the interstadials much of the region would have reverted to park land or forest, the July temperature at these times reaching 16°C, approximately its present day average. In the periods of intense cold Wessex lay within the periglacial zone and was subject to a frost climate which created a distinctive array of soils. Wind blowing of fine rock particles under cold dry conditions led to the formation of brickearths (redeposited loess) while solifluction and melt water activity produced coombe rock (chalky mud slides over permanently frozen subsoil), marl and gravels. All of these, under freeze/thaw conditions, were subject to cryoturbation (contortions and mixing). Deposits of this kind once blanketed the Wessex region and many patches still remain (Evans 1968).

13

Sea-level remained low throughout reaching 30 m below OD in the Early Last Glacial to as much as 130 m below in the Full Last Glacial. It is to this period that the buried river channels, sometimes encountered around the coasts, belong.

It is impossible to say with any degree of certainty how communities responded to the changing conditions. Evidence of hunting camps and the use of caves is not infrequent but these belong to the interstadials and may represent summer camps occupied by small hunting groups who moved south out of Wessex during the winter across the land bridge into what is now Continental Europe to winter in France, Belgium or Germany. These may well have been the same people who, in different seasons, used and painted the caves of southern France and northern Spain. A total population of 100–500 has been suggested (J. B. Campbell 1977). In the periods of glacial maxima it is quite likely that the region was totally unoccupied for thousands of years at a time.

The archaeological record of the Devensian period in Britain is dominated by a distinctive array of small flint artefacts usually made from carefully prepared blades, which includes such items as pen-knife-like backed blades, shouldered tanged points, burins, scrapers, awls and borers, representing a specialized tool kit designed for hunting and the working of such materials as bone, wood and leather. Less common are artefacts of bone, antler and ivory, including needles and awls, harpoon points, *bâtons de commandement* and occasionally ornaments. Under favourable conditions artefacts may be found stratified with faunal remains providing an indication of environment and hunting preferences. It is conventional at present to divide this material into two phases, the Early Upper Palaeolithic, emerging at the beginning of the Upton Warren Interstadial Complex (*c.* 36,000 bc*), and the Late Upper Palaeolithic, which did not begin until the climate started to ameliorate after the glacial maximum was past, *c.* 12,500 bc.

The Early Upper Palaeolithic is sparsely represented in Wessex except for a concentration of occupied cave sites in the Mendips (J. B. Campbell 1977). Four caves (Fig. 1.5), Badger Hole, Hyena Den, Soldier's Hole and Uphill Cave, have produced characteristic Early Upper Palaeolithic tools while at Pickens Hole undifferentiated Upper Palaeolithic flints have been found in a context, providing a radiocarbon date of 34,256 bp (BM-654). Pickens Hole also yielded human teeth and bones of arctic fox, hyena, lion, horse, woolly rhinoceros, reindeer and mammoth (Tratman 1964). At Badger Hole, the fauna included hyena, lion, otter, ox, brown bear, horse, reindeer and giant Irish deer. A similar assemblage was recovered from Soldier's Hole together with bison and a variety of birds such as teal, grey lag goose, whooper, swan, ptarmigan and grouse. A further indication of the cold open

* *Note:* bc means 'before Christ' but measured in radiocarbon years while bp means 'before the present' in the same units. Further subtlities surrounding the use of radiocarbon dates are discussed in the Appendix, pp. 334–5.

environment is provided by a pollen analysis from Badger Hole, which showed that the local vegetation was predominantly of grass sedges and ferns with trees and shrubs accounting for less than a quarter of the surviving pollen. The Mendip caves were clearly a preferred environment providing shelter and a degree of safety for the small bands of hunters who exploited the grassy uplands of the Mendip hills and the marshes of the Somerset Levels to the south as well as areas of now-submerged coastal plain. Cave sites in south

Figure 1.5 Mendip caves occupied in the Upper Palaeolithic period. (After Jacobi 1982: Fig. 2.2)

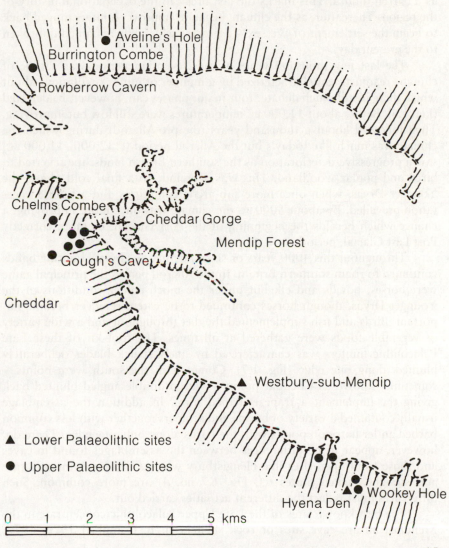

Wales, e.g. the Gower Peninsula, are in a comparable situation overlooking what is now the Bristol Channel from the north.

Elsewhere in Wessex few camp sites of the Early Upper Palaeolithic are known but isolated tools, which may tentatively be assigned to the period, have been found at Cameron Road, Christchurch, Fir Hill in the Nadder Valley (J. B. Campbell 1977: 150) and Seagry, near Chippenham (Tucker 1985). At best they are a reminder that open camp sites may once have existed in many of the Wessex river valleys.

The Full Last Glaciation, spanning the period 18,000–11,000 bc, was so severe that the hunting bands were driven south, leaving southern Britain as a barren tundra. This marks the last break in the occupational history of the region. Thereafter, as the climate began to improve, hunters moved back to begin the settlement of Wessex – a process which has remained unbroken to the present day.

The last few thousand years of the Devensian period was a time of climatic readjustment characterized by a number of minor oscillations about which there is still much debate: four major phases can, however, be detected (Fig. 1.6). Before about 11,000 BC temperatures were still low but improving. Then followed about a thousand years (the pre-Allerød) during which the climate was much like today's but the Allerød period (*c.* 12,000–11,000 BC) saw a progressive deterioration as the southern British landscape reverted to birch and poplar woodland. This was a prelude to a final cold phase, the Younger Dryas, when once more sub-arctic conditions and a tundra vegetation prevailed. By about 8000 BC the climate was once more improving, a change which heralds the beginning of the Post Glacial, or more correctly Post Last Glacial, period.

Throughout this 4000 years or so of fluctuating climate hunting bands continued to roam southern Britain. In the Allerød period the principal game were horses, bovids and elk but under the much colder conditions of the Younger Dryas, though horses continued to be eaten, reindeer became important. Birds and fish supplemented the diet throughout and a wide variety of vegetable foods were gathered at all times. The tool kit of these Late Palaeolithic hunters was characterized by finely struck blades deliberately blunted along one edge (Fig. 1.7). Common in the south were points – sometimes known as Cheddar points – with a double angled blunted back giving the implement a trapeze-shaped form. In addition the assemblage usually contained a variety of burins and scrapers together with less common barbed antler harpoon points with the barbs along only one edge. There do, however, appear to be differences between the assemblages found in caves and those from open sites like Hengistbury where Cheddar points are rare and straight backed pieces (cf. Fig. 1.7 no. 4) are more common. Such differences must reflect the different activities carried out.

The best known sites of the Late Upper Palaeolithic concentrate in the Mendips; all are cave sites or rock shelters (J. B. Campbell 1970, 1977;

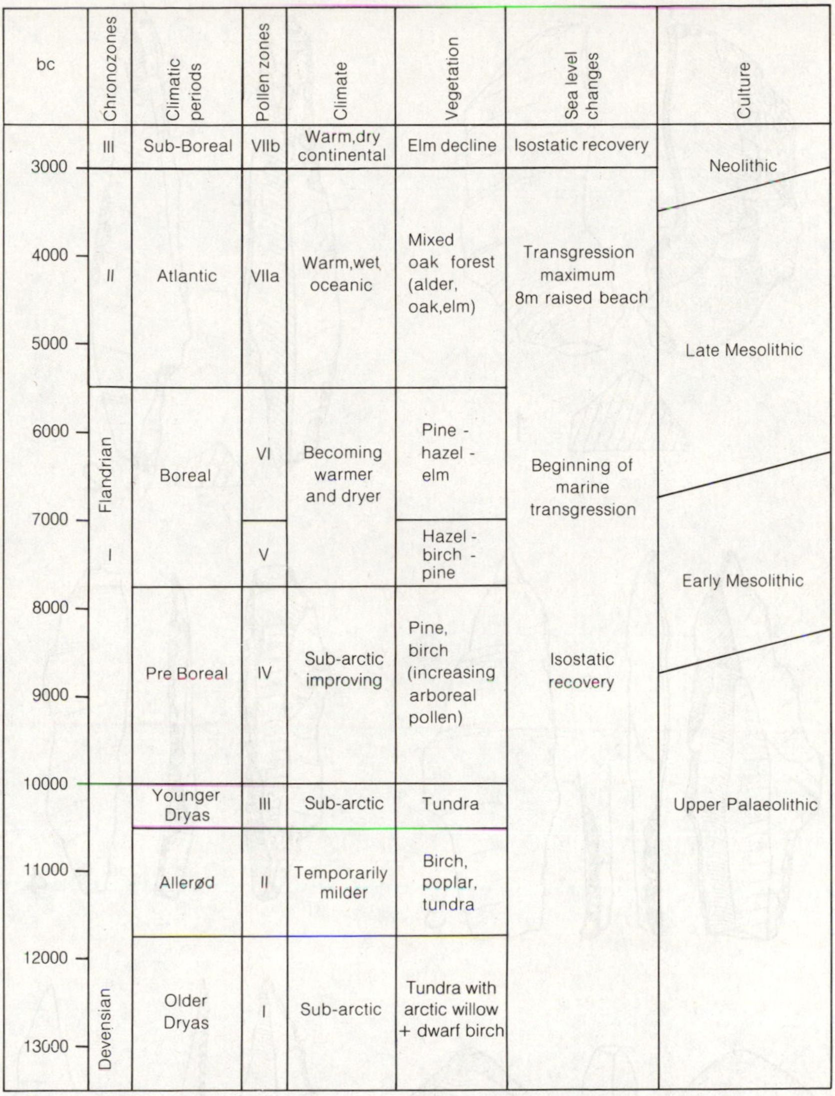

bc	Chronozones	Climatic periods	Pollen zones	Climate	Vegetation	Sea level changes	Culture
3000	III	Sub-Boreal	VIIb	Warm,dry continental	Elm decline	Isostatic recovery	Neolithic
4000	II	Atlantic	VIIa	Warm,wet oceanic	Mixed oak forest (alder, oak,elm)	Transgression maximum 8m raised beach	Late Mesolithic
5000							
6000	Flandrian	Boreal	VI	Becoming warmer and dryer	Pine - hazel - elm	Beginning of marine transgression	
7000	I		V		Hazel - birch - pine		Early Mesolithic
8000		Pre Boreal	IV	Sub-arctic improving	Pine, birch (increasing arboreal pollen)	Isostatic recovery	
9000							
10000		Younger Dryas	III	Sub-arctic	Tundra		Upper Palaeolithic
11000		Allerød	II	Temporarily milder	Birch, poplar, tundra		
12000	Devensian	Older Dryas	I	Sub-arctic	Tundra with arctic willow + dwarf birch		
13000							

Figure 1.6 Simplified diagram showing environmental change and the periodization for the period 13,000–3000 bc.

Jacobi 1982). Five of the caves in Cheddar Gorge were occupied in this period: others lie in the vicinity of Wookey and on the north side of Mendip in Burrington Combe. The most informative is Gough's New Cave in Cheddar Gorge, much of which was excavated earlier this century producing over 7000 pieces of flint and chert, including knives, scrapers and burins for working bone and antler, as well as human remains. Implements of antler,

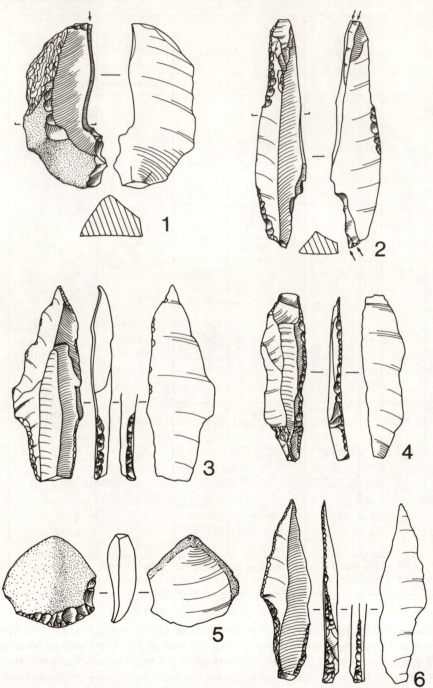

Figure 1.7 Upper Palaeolithic implements from Hengistbury Head, Dorset. (Scale ⅔.) (From Cunliffe 1978a: Fig. 5, after Mace 1959: Figs 5 and 9)

bone and mammoth ivory were also recovered, one of which, a bone point, was decorated with groups of notches reminiscent of a tally or measure (Tratman 1976). A small part of the original stratified deposit removed from the previous excavations was examined in detail in 1986–7 (Currant, Jacobi and Stringer 1989). Remains of at least three humans were recorded, two adults and a child. One fragment of frontal articulates with a piece found 60 years before (Stringer 1985). A series of radiocarbon dates for these remains focuses around 12,500–11,500 bp. Many of the human bones show knife cuts which hint at ritual dismemberment.

On the northern side of the Mendip massif, on the east side of Burrington Combe, is situated the rift cavern of Aveline's Hole. Although excavations have been extensive, the quantity of stone artefacts recovered is not great, only 31 utilized pieces from a collection of 250 pieces. Unlike Gough's Cave, where occupation was intensive and suggests a frequently used home base, Aveline's Hole is more likely to have been a transit site used by hunting bands exploiting the Yeo valley and the Failand Ridge. The presence of Mesolithic material as well makes interpretation difficult.

The communities using the Mendip caves for shelter had access to a rich variety of plant and animal life (Jacobi 1982). The upland landscape was probably a moss tundra broken by expanses of heather, bilberry and crowberry and occasional strands of dwarf birch and willow. Lower down the slopes and in more sheltered locations the trees would have been more dominant while the valleys and marshes supported grasses and sedges. Faunal remains typical of this varied landscape have been recovered from many of the cave deposits, most notably from Gough's Cave. Horse and red deer produced the greatest bulk of meat but smaller mammals like the mountain orarchi hare, pika and arctic fox, together with the occasional brown bear, may have varied the menu. Among the birds recovered were ptarmigan, willow grouse and peregrine falcon.

Elsewhere in Wessex fewer than ten open sites of Late Upper Palaeolithic date are known but only at Hengistbury Head has excavation of an adequate nature been undertaken. Here, on a high hill overlooking what was then a wide coastal plain and commanding the confluence of the Avon and Stour, a substantial base camp was established (Mace 1959; J. B. Campbell 1977; Barton 1992). Flint nodules, some from as far as 12 km away, were carried to the site to be worked into a variety of tools especially end scrapers, burins, backed blades or bladelets, and shouldered points. The site would appear to have been a residential hunting location for a band concerned to track migrating animals.

Other open sites broadly contemporary with Hengistbury have been identified at Rush Corner, Bournemouth, Long Island in Portsmouth Harbour, Crown Acres in the Kennet valley and more dubiously at Pilsdon Pen and on the Isle of Portland in Dorset. There is little yet to be said of their size or function but it is tempting to think of some of them as being the autumn and spring bases of hunting groups who in the summer months migrated with the deer and horses to the northern pastures, but interpretations of this kind must await the results of more properly planned excavations.

How long the Late Upper Palaeolithic assemblage of tools and weapons continued in use in Wessex is difficult to establish with any degree of certainty but a few radiocarbon dates from the Mendip caves offer tantalizing possibilities for interpretation. The date of 12,378 bp for a bone of a brown bear from Sun Hole, associated with a group of backed blades, is entirely within the expected range as are the series of dates from Gough's Cave ranging between *c.* 12,400 and 11,300 bp but the two dates for human bones from Aveline's Hole, 9060 and 9360 bp, are more problematical. If the human remains were contemporary with the Late Upper Palaeolithic tool horizon and not later intrusions from above, then we are forced to accept that in the Mendip region, hunting groups were practising traditional craft skills well into the Post Glacial period by which time more advanced hunting groups with a more developed technology (classified as Mesolithic) were already established in the lowland areas of our region.

Readjustment to the New Land

With the retreat of the Devensian ice cap, the Holocene or Post Glacial period began. In broad perspective two main trends can be seen, the violent oscillations of land and sea-level, experienced during the Full Glacial, began to even out, while the climate gradually improved to approach its present day averages. In detail, however, the picture of the crucial 5000 years, from 9000–4500 BC, is far more complex and these subtleties are directly relevant to our understanding of the human groups who, like the rest of the plant and animal communities, had to adjust to the fast changing conditions (Simmons, Dimbleby and Grigson 1981).

Sea-level changes are by no means easy to determine not least because different parts of Britain reacted in different ways to the removal of the ice sheet which had depressed it. To begin with the isostatic uplift seems to have proceeded at about the same rate as the sea-level rose in response to the great volumes of water freed from the melting ice, but towards the middle of the seventh millennium bc the sea-level had begun to rise faster flooding the land. It was during this time that the plain stretching from East Anglia across to Belgium and The Netherlands began to suffer inundation – a process further enhanced by the general down warping of the land comprising the southern North Sea basin.

The loss of this territory would have had a far-reaching effect on the hunting communities of the region. The vast expanse of lowlands broken by lakes, marshes and the wide meandering flood plains of the Thames and Rhine (the two perhaps flowing as one for the last hundred kilometres to the sea) must have been a virtual paradise for roaming bands of hunter-gatherers, the teaming wild life, abundant fish and swarms of migrating birds providing easy prey. There can be little doubt that this huge area formed a focus for man's food-gathering activities. But as these traditional hunting territories began to disappear beneath the inundations so the communities were forced to move to marginal lands where they had to adapt to less favourable conditions. Eventually, by about 7000 BC, the inundation was sufficiently advanced for the North Sea to join with the wide inlet of the English Channel, cutting Britain off from the Continent for the first time. Thereafter the hunting bands in Britain began to develop in relative isolation.

The marine transgression continued in the south of Britain until about 5000 BC and thereafter slowed considerably. By the middle of the fourth millennium more stable conditions were beginning to prevail. At Chesil Beach in Dorset the base of a peat layer representing a freshwater marsh developing immediately above estuarine clays of the marine transgression phase has produced a radiocarbon date of around 4400 BC and a comparable interface at Tealham in Somerset has been dated to roughly 4700 BC. Two further Somerset dates for phragmitic peat just above transgression silt of *c*. 4400 BC from Tealham and 4700 BC from Shapwick Heath add confirmation to the mid-fourth millennium date for the phase of stabilization in the south.

The period 9000–4000 BC saw massive vegetational changes in Britain the main phases of which are briefly summarized in Fig. 1.6. This sequence is based on the study of pollen zones recorded in peat sequences (Godwin 1940, 1956). Zones I–III belong to the closing stages of the Late Pleistocene while IV–VIIb span the period of readjustment considered in this section. The scheme presents a broad generalization of the trajectory of change rather than a closely dated sequence of universal applicability. Clearly altitude and latitude had a considerable effect on when the change from one zone to another took place at any particular locality but the scheme presented is broadly applicable to southern Britain. The system of chronozones (Turner and West 1968; Sparks and West 1972) is more useful for correlations over a large area.

The main trends in the vegetational history of the period are well established. The beginning of zone IV was marked by a dramatic decline in non-tree pollen as the forest of birch and pine began to take hold of the land. Hazel, appearing towards the end of zone IV, was the main colonizer in zone V but as the climate became warmer and drier, other trees like elm began to become significant. Zone VIIa (the Early Temperate of Flandrian II) was a warm wet period of Oceanic weather the beginning of which was marked by a considerable increase in alder pollen. In the more westerly parts of the country, alder was the dominant species but the climax vegetation of the period is best characterized as a mixed oak forest of oak, elm, ash, alder, lime and hazel. By the beginning of zone VIIb, warmer, drier, more continental conditions had returned, the most significant event in the vegetational history of the country being the rapid decline of elm, a phenomenon possibly enhanced by the advent of farming communities. This fascinating problem is one to which we shall return (p. 37).

The change from the steppe/tundra conditions of the Late Pleistocene to the developed mixed oak forest of the Late Temperate had a marked effect on fauna. The herds of large mammals which once roamed the steppe retreated north with the ice sheet, to be replaced by a more varied array of smaller creatures, though herds of deer, elk and wild cattle were still to be found in the forests. From the point of view of human hunting communities, the Flandrian forests, marshes, estuaries and sea shores presented rich environments in which specialist hunting and gathering strategies could evolve to provide food in plenty: in archaeological terms this is referred to as the Mesolithic period.

It is at present conventional to divide the Mesolithic into two broad periods: the Early Mesolithic from about 9500 BC to 7500 BC and the Later Mesolithic from 7500 BC to 4400 BC, the divide coming at approximately the point when Britain became an island. The Early Mesolithic shared much in common with contemporary cultures of the North European Plain but the Later Mesolithic communities, now cut off from the Continent, began to take on a decidedly insular aspect.

The Early Mesolithic

The characteristic artefact assemblage of the Early Mesolithic is dominated by axes for cutting timber, burins for working bone and antler and non-geometric microliths, made on broad blades, from which composite projectiles were constructed. Material of this kind is found widely over the Wessex countryside from a variety of environments though comparatively few well-excavated assemblages are available and organic material and associated environmental evidence is rare.

A group of sites clustering in the valley of the river Kennet, between Newbury and Thatcham, suggests intensive exploitation of this favoured location. Systematic excavation of one location at Thatcham between 1958 and 1961 has thrown considerable light on camp sites of the Earliest Mesolithic (Wymer 1962; Churchill 1962). The settlement was established on a gravel terrace overlooking a reed swamp with an extensive forest dominated by birch and pine rising up behind. Faunal remains, recovered from the swamp, show that red deer, roe deer, pig, aurochs and elk were hunted in the forest, while birds including crane, teal and mallard were trapped or shot in the marsh. Evidence of fish was sparse but such an important food resource, abundant in the fast flowing river nearby, would hardly have been over-looked. The considerable quantity of hazel-nuts found around the site is a reminder of the importance of vegetable foods to the diet which tends always to be understated in archaeological excavation. It is possible that Thatcham represents a camp site occupied from time to time by groups of hunters during the winter and early spring. The balanced tool kit recovered, including microliths, scrapers, burins, saws, axe/adzes and awls, reflects a wide range of activities such as the working of bone and antler, the preparation of skins and the repair of wooden equipment, all appropriate pursuits for the quiet months before the group broke up for the spring and summer hunt.

The environmental study of the Thatcham settlement, together with a series of radiocarbon dates, allowed the period of occupation to be placed precisely within the sequence of pollen zones. The transition from zone IV to zone V produced three dates – 9840, 9780 and 9670 bp – while the commencement of zone VIa produced a single date of 9480 bp. The earliest occupation, from hearth sites on site III, has produced dates of 10,367 bp and 10,030 bp. Taken together the evidence suggests that occupation began about 9400 BC and lasted until the second half of the eighth millennium (Churchill 1962). It should, however, be stressed that since this date series is based on 'baulked samples' they are of dubious accuracy.

A rather different range of environments was available in the western part of Somerset during the Early Mesolithic period (Fig. 1.8). Within comparatively short distances there was considerable variation, from the wide gravel flood valleys (of the precursors of the rivers Parrett, Brue, Sheppey and Axe) choked with woodland and teaming with fish and wild fowl, to the uplands of Mendip and the Quantocks with areas of open woodland and scrub providing rich grazing for large game such as deer.

Archaeological evidence for the period consists largely of surface finds and collections from small-scale excavations but sufficient survives to show that Early Mesolithic settlers were well established in the region (Wainwright 1960; Norman 1982). Greylake Sand Quarry at Middlezoy on the edge of the Burtle Sands overlooking a shallow valley, and Shapwick, in a similar location on the north side of the Polden Hills, have both produced assemblages generally similar to material from Thatcham. Another large collection of Early Mesolithic material was recovered in 1973 at North Petherton on the eastern edge of the Quantocks. The assemblage consisted of scrapers, burins, awls and serrated blades suggesting a base camp where skins were worked and hunting equipment was made and repaired. The camp was ideally sited to allow for the seasonal exploitation of the Quantock uplands and the Parrett valley (Norman 1975).

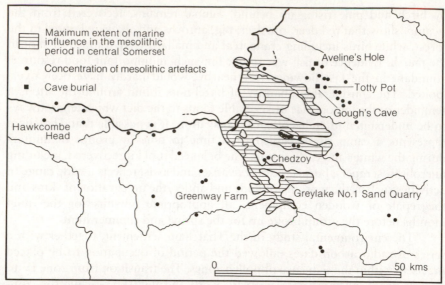

Figure 1.8 Mesolithic settlement in Somerset. (After Norman 1982: Fig. 3.2)

A somewhat different, but equally specialist, assemblage was found on Hengistbury Head which at this time was at least 20 km from the sea (Barton 1992). The narrow range of tools, including microliths, end scrapers and small denticulates but without burins, axes or adzes suggests a community involved in the hunting of small game.

The greensand of the western Weald presents another extensively studied environment. Though geomorphologically part of the south east a substantial tract of Wealden greensand extends into Hampshire, overlooked by the high scarp of the chalk downs. The best known of the many Mesolithic sites in the region is the complex at Oakhanger, the subject of intensive excavation (Rankine 1952, 1956, 1958, 1960, 1961; Rankine and Dimbleby 1960). Sites V and VII together covered an area of some 420 sq m and produced almost a ton of worked flint typical of the Early Mesolithic making it one of the richest sites of this period so far excavated in Europe. A series of six radiocarbon dates ranging between two extremes of *c.* 9300 and 8800 bp are entirely consistent with the Early Mesolithic phasing demanded by the typology of the artefacts. Several radiocarbon assessments taken early in the excavation giving later dates are now thought to be unreliable (Jacobi 1981: 11).

Oakhanger is not the only Early Mesolithic site on the Hampshire greensand. Others have been identified, largely from surface collections from Kingsley Common, Petersfield Heath, Bentley and Trottsford Farm, and just over the county boundary, at Iping Common (W. Sussex), an important site

24

of this period has been excavated (Keef, Wymer and Dimbleby 1965). Evidently the greensand environment was much favoured by the Earliest Mesolithic hunters.

It is unfortunate that the settlements on these well-drained sandy soils seldom produce evidence of the organic component of the material culture since even bone and antler are dissolved away in the predominantly acid conditions. But several sites have yielded contemporary pollen sequences. At Oakhanger site VII the earliest level was characterized by a scrub woodland vegetation of alder, lime, oak and some elm dominated by hazel. The presence of heather and grasses suggests the existence of local glades. In the next level the pollen of ivy suddenly becomes dominant though hazel remained much in evidence. A massive influx of ivy is hardly likely to have happened naturally and has been explained in terms of the hunting band deliberately collecting ivy from other environments and bringing it to the camp. One possible reason for this behaviour might be that ivy was deliberately used as a lure to encourage deer who, in the winter months when feed was short, would tend to congregate around fodder heaps and thus present themselves more easily for the kill (Simmons and Dimbleby 1974). The possibility, however, remains that the ivy pollen may have been caused by a downward migration of modern pollen. The doubt nicely points to the fragility of the available data. The upper levels of the sequence showed that after further disturbance scrub forest once more re-established itself.

The dominance of hazel in the pollen sequences from Oakhanger and Iping strongly suggests some kind of manipulation by man in favour of the plant, possibly the clearance of other trees from the immediate vicinity to encourage the hazel to flower more freely and thus to produce a greater abundance of nuts. That considerable quantities of broken hazel-nut shells were found at Oakhanger is a further indication of the use of the fruit as an essential part of the diet (Jacobi 1978: 82–4).

The pollen evidence, then, provides some hints of the food-gathering strategy but it would be wrong to think of the communities relying entirely upon the resources of the greensand. Oakhanger, like many of the greensand sites, is sited close to the Wealden fringe where a variety of rocks outcrop in quick succession. Walking westwards from the site for four kilometres one would cross the heavy Gault clay, the lighter calcareous Upper Greensand and the scarp slope and crest of the chalk downs. Each environment would have offered a distinct range of resources and there can be little doubt that all came within the compass of the groups who camped for part of the year beside streams in the hazel woods of the greensand. The dominance of processing tools at Oakhanger is an indication of autumn and winter occupation allowing the possibility that at other times of the year the communities lived in other environments.

Recent work on the Wealden Mesolithic assemblages has allowed a distinctive regional group to be distinguished which lies typologically between the Early and Later assemblages. It has been called the *Horsham* phase and is distinguished by a combination of obliquely blunted points, mainly isosceles triangles, bitruncated rhombic microliths and concave basally retouched points (Jacobi 1981: 11–12). Two characteristic assemblages have been found in Hampshire at Sleaford and at Longmoor Inclosure. Typological arguments would suggest a date *c.* 8000–7500 BC which is supported by radiocarbon dates from Longmoor.

The Later Mesolithic

Later Mesolithic assemblages are characterized by the use of narrow blades for the manufacture of flint tool components among which small scalene triangles, rod-like forms and rhomboidal and trapezoidal shapes dominate. The microliths were usually manufactured from the blades by a notching and/ or snapping technique and in all probability these tiny components were fitted into wooden shafts to make a variety of missiles ranging from arrows to multiple-barbed harpoons (Fig. 1.9). The narrow blade technique is comparable to that used over much of adjacent Europe and must, in its opening stages, reflect direct contact possibly involving the movement of hunting groups over wide territories but by the last quarter of the seventh millennium the British groups take on a more regional appearance as Britain becomes separated from the Continent.

Over much of the British Isles the Later Mesolithic appears to have been a time of population expansion: a greatly increased number of sites have been recognized and a far greater variety of environments seem to have been colonized. As a broad generalization this is undoubtedly so but certain regional differences can be detected. In the western Weald, for example, on the greensand, fewer sites in the Later Mesolithic have been identified (Jacobi 1981: 13). It is not immediately clear how this should be interpreted but when viewed in a broader context the Wealden sites should be seen in the context of the dense occupation of the neighbouring chalk downs, for example in the region between Froxfield and Alton (Shennan 1981: Fig. 29), at East Meon and Butser Hill (Draper 1968) and at Windmill Hill, Chalton (Cunliffe 1973a) all on or close to patches of clay-with-flints (Fig. 1.10). From the regional perspective therefore there was clearly no diminution in the population exploiting the variable resources of the Wealden fringe. While the dating evidence for these downland sites is sparse many produce tools characteristic of the later period though earlier material is known. One interpretation, therefore, is that by the Later Mesolithic a greater use was being made of the wooded upland environment. This does not, however, mean that the

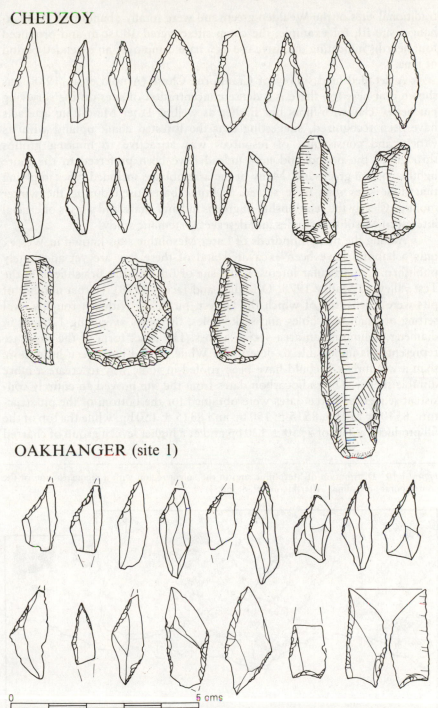

CHEDZOY

OAKHANGER (site 1)

0   5 cms

Figure 1.9   Later Mesolithic implements. (Scale 1/1.) (Chedzoy, after Norman 1982: Fig. 3.4; Oakhanger, after Jacobi 1981: Fig. 3)

traditional sites of the Wealden greensand were totally abandoned. At Oakhanger site III, for example, the camp site covered 100 sq m and produced four hearths indicating intensive use as a base camp over an extended period of time.

A detailed field survey of Cranborne Chase (Arnold et al. 1988) has shown that here too there is a dense concentration of sites on the surviving patches of clay-with-flints but Earlier as well as Later Mesolithic artefacts have been recognized, suggesting that the forested chalk upland with its variety and consistency of resources was attractive to hunting groups throughout the period and may indeed have been preferred to the more lightly wooded greensand. Many of the assemblages included types implying that these sites may have served as home bases used during the winter months. Clearly the relationship of greensand and chalkland sites is of crucial interest to Mesolithic studies and deserves systematic study.

Among the many hundreds of Later Mesolithic sites known in Wessex only a handful have been excavated and of these few are yet adequately published. Of particular interest is the site of Broom Hill, Braishfield, in the Test valley (O'Malley 1978; O'Malley and Jacobi 1978). Here a number of pits were discovered of which the largest, pit 3, lay within a roughly oval setting of small post-holes and stake-holes, the posts averaging 170 mm in diameter, delimiting an area 4–5 m across. The exact form of the structure represented is impossible to determine. While it need have been little more than a windbreak it could have been roofed in some way to create a more durable shelter. The radiocarbon dates from the site proved an entirely consistent sequence. Three dates were obtained for the bottom of the pit structure, 8540 ± 150 bp, 8515 ± 150 bp and 8315 ± 150 bp, while the top of the fill produced a date of 7750 ± 120 bp and at a higher level a group of charred

Figure 1.10 Distribution of Mesolithic sites in the Solent region with a reconstruction of the contemporary coastline. (After Jacobi 1978: Fig. 4)

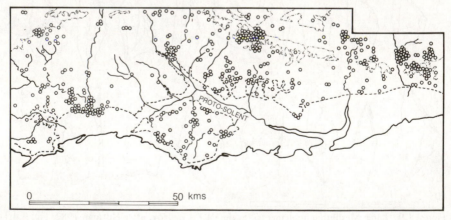

hazel-nuts were dated to 7220 ± 120 bp. A hearth found in a nearby pit provided a date of 6535 ± 125 bp. Thus, taking these assessments on their face value, Broom Hill could have been occupied, if intermittently, over a period of 2000 years from about 7500 to 5500 BC. Its location, on a south-ward-facing slope of Eocene sand overlooking a spring within easy reach of the chalk to the north and the densely forested clays of the Hampshire basin to the south, was a highly favourable one providing a congenial base from which a variety of resource potentials could be exploited: herein lay its attraction.

The flint assemblage from Broom Hill is considerable, nearly 90,000 worked fragments. It includes gravers, scrapers, over 100 core axes and 2,600 geometric microliths characteristic of the Later Mesolithic. The large number of axes and axe sharpening flakes is unusual and may reflect some element of specialist production, using the high quality local flint to make items for exchange. A similar assemblage was found at Wallington on the chalk hill of Portsdown (Jacobi 1981: 17; Hughes and ApSimon 1978: 34).

Evidence of settlement structures like those found at Broom Hill is rare in Wessex but not unknown. At Wakefords Copse, Havant, Hampshire, a series of shallow depressions were discovered together in an activity area and around some of these were found stake-holes, probably representing wind-breaks (Bradley and Lewis 1974). A single date of 5680 ± 120 bp was obtained. At Downton, in the valley of the Wiltshire Avon, a scatter of stake-holes, associated with an assemblage of Later Mesolithic flints has also been interpreted as a possible shelter (Higgs 1959).

Finally in the Kennet valley, at Wawcott, Berks., a number of Late Mesolithic sites have been identified and some of them sampled by excavation (Froom 1972, 1976). The range of artefact material includes microliths, scrapers, burins and tranchet axes found together with bones of wild cattle, pigs and red deer and carbonized hazel-nut shells. Taken together the evidence could allow that the sites were intensively occupied home bases but they could equally well be seasonally occupied short-stay camps: the only structures recovered were a series of shallow pits. A single radiocarbon date of 6120 ± 134 bp confirms the Late Mesolithic phasing indicated by the typology of the artefacts.

Most of the sites mentioned so far, and the many hundreds of others known largely as flint scatters collected from across the face of Wessex, represent the temporary camps of hunting bands utilizing woodland and riverine resources. A rather different series of resource potentials would have been available to the communities living in the coastal regions. However, sea-level changes over the years have obscured much of the evidence. Along most of the southern coast of Wessex, eastwards from Purbeck, the Mesolithic shore line would have been well to the south of the present coast, approximately to the 10 fathom mark (Fig. 1.10) and the shore-edge camps, which must have been prolific, have long since been eroded away or obscured by marine sediment. But many of the settlements of the present coastal plain were well within range of the contemporary shore and could have been the inland bases of communities working the varied resources of the sands and brickearths of the coastal plain as well as those of the rivers and estuaries and the shore line itself (Bradley and Hooper 1975). The groups, living for part of the year on the brickearths in the shelter of the chalk ridge of Portsdown, were only 12 km from the estuary of the Solent river and no more than 30 km from the shore itself. These distances could well have been encompassed by a migratory band so long as the inducements to travel were sufficient.

Although many sites are known on the coastal plain only one, Mother Siller's Channel, in Christchurch Harbour, has been sampled by excavation (S. Palmer 1972). Hearths incorporating slabs of Portland limestone were uncovered and since the nearest outcrop was 24 km to the south west one can only assume that these coastal groups migrated over considerable territories carrying such materials with them. The community camping here would have been barely 10 km from the sea shore.

To the west of Purbeck the present coast of Wessex takes on a generally more precipitous aspect and the contemporary Mesolithic sea shore cannot have been very far to the south. Thus the known settlements must have been within easy reach of the shore. One site where clear evidence of coastal exploitation has been discovered is Culver Well on the Isle of Portland (S. Palmer 1970, 1976). Here a large shell midden composed largely of limpets and winkles was uncovered beneath a surface of deliberately laid limestone slabs. Charcoal samples for levels within the midden gave radiocarbon dates of around 7100 bp, consistent with the Later Mesolithic character of the artefacts which here were made largely of Portland chert. Culver Well provides us with a rare insight into the economy of a coastal base.

Another site within easy reach of the contemporary shore line was discovered at Blashenwell on Purbeck barely 4 km from the sea (Clark 1938; Preece 1980). Evidence of Mesolithic activity was stratified in a tufa deposit, the non-marine mollusca from which allowed the changing environment to be reconstructed. It showed a transition from open marshy ground to a more shaded landscape but at a late stage there was a partial opening up of the vegetation cover which may tentatively be ascribed to human activity. Radiocarbon dates of 5750 ± 140 bp and 5425 ± 150 bp have been obtained for animal bones from this late horizon. It is not possible to assign with certainty the remains of hazel-nuts and the bones of red deer, roe deer, bos and pig found stratified within the tufa to the collecting activities of the Mesolithic community but the shellfish from the midden deposit, including limpet, winkle and peppery furrow shell, must have been collected on the nearby shore and brought to the camp site, probably from the vicinity of Chapmans Pool less than two hours' walk away. The varied soils of Purbeck with its accessible rocky coastline would have provided a rich range of food resources.

The other area of Wessex with a coastal interface is western Somerset which opens onto what is now the Bristol Channel. Originally a series of rivers flowing in gravel-floored valleys drained into the major inlet which occupied the channel, but as the sea-level rose throughout the seventh millennium the valleys became flooded creating large areas of reed fen giving way to expanses of salt marsh and mud flats exposed at low tide (Kidson and Heyworth 1976). The maximum effects of the marine transgression were felt in the late fifth millennium (Fig. 1.8). This range of environments together with dry lowlands and the upland massif of the Mendips provided varied resource potentials.

Surface collecting has identified a number of camp sites on the Polden Hills and the Godney ridge. At Chedzoy a comparatively large late assemblage has been collected (Fig. 1.9) including burins, scrapers, awls and other tool forms appropriate to a base camp where tools and weapons were made and repaired (Norman 1982: 18–19). The Mendip ridge supported a number of camp sites during the Later Mesolithic but detailed analysis is lacking. At Totty Pot, however, situated on the exposed crest of the ridge overlooking Cheddar Gorge, a small assemblage produced only bladelets and microliths without the cores and debris characteristic of microlith production. The implication is surely that the microliths were manufactured elsewhere and brought to the site, presumably by a group of hunters using the location either as a temporary shelter or as a kill site (Norman 1982: 21). Chedzoy and Totty Pot represent two different aspects of the complex and highly mobile life of Mesolithic hunting communities. No doubt other specialized sites remain to be discovered reflecting the different hunting and gathering strategies which together made up the food-producing system.

Only in the extreme west of the region, at Exmoor and the Brendon Hills, is there any stretch of land which can reasonably be regarded as a highland zone. Few sites are known on the extreme upland but a large scatter of Later Mesolithic flints have been collected over an area of about 1.6 hectares around the head of a spring at Hawkcombe Head on Porlock Common at an altitude of 410 m. The coomb falls steeply to the Vale of Porlock whence there is easy access to the sea. The assemblage was made from flint beach pebbles collected from Barnstable Bay and was heavily biased towards microliths of the rod and subtriangular form: tools of fabrication are rare. The implication would seem to be that the head of the coomb was used over an extended period of time by hunting groups exploiting the resources of the upland zone whose home bases were probably sited in the coastal zone (Norman 1982: 20).

The Nature of the Man–Landscape Relationship

In the pages above we have explored a selection of the evidence available for settlement in Wessex during the first 5000 or so years of the Post Glacial period. It was a time of dramatic environmental change during which the open tundra of the last phases of the Devensian gave way to dense mixed oak forest forcing the herds of large mammals, previously so important as a food source, to migrate northwards. It was also a period of sea-level change when Britain became an island and vast tracts of lakes, marshes and estuaries occupying the area of the North Sea and the Channel were inundated.

The traditional view of Mesolithic economic strategies was that human groups remained small and hunted within discrete territories causing no significant disruption to the ecosystem save possibly for hunting elk to extinction. Recent work has however suggested that some modification to this simple model is required. There is now increasing evidence that Mesolithic hunting groups deliberately modified their environments to facilitate hunting and collecting procedures and may even have been deliberately manipulating herds of deer. The evidence for these views derives largely from the pollen recovered and has already been mentioned in passing above but deserves a more general consideration.

Among the tools available for modifying the environment was fire. Large areas of woodland could be cleared rapidly creating open glades in the forest canopy. Grasses and other herbs would soon grow and woodland would begin to regenerate producing tender shoots and stems close to ground level. Environments of this kind would have been particularly attractive to the herds of deer, wild cattle and pig, encouraging them to congregate thus presenting themselves as easy prey to hunters.

Another advantage of clearing the wild forest was that certain trees – those with rapid regenerative capabilities – could be favoured by expending comparatively little effort cutting down the new growth of unwanted competitors. Indeed, it is a distinct possibility that the sharp rise in hazel pollen during the Boreal period was caused in this way. Hazel coppices freely and its root stock would not normally be destroyed by forest fire. The rapid re-emergence of hazel after a fire would soon have been noted and would have attracted communities engaged in collecting forays. It is a short step from this to the deliberate use of fire and the axe to maintain the hazel groves for annual collection.

Clearances, whatever the initial motive for their creation, if maintained could lead to soil degeneration. The evidence from Oakhanger shows that the ground was bare enough to allow sand to blow about and accumulate to a depth of 15 cm, while at Iping Common the pollen sequence shows that after a period of use dominated by hazel pollen the locality became heath land. In both cases the interference of man caused an ecological impact which, in the case of Iping, was irreversible.

The degree to which Mesolithic groups actively herded deer or other animals is debatable. The fact that dogs (domesticated wolves) are known as early as the Earlier Mesolithic period is an indication that some form of herd manipulation may have been practised while the exceptional concentrations of ivy pollen found in association with occupation debris at Oakhanger and Winfrith Heath (in Dorset) raises the distinct possibility that ivy was being deliberately collected and used as fodder either to encourage wild deer to congregate at specific clearings where they could more easily be killed, or to provide winter feed for semi-domesticated herds (Simmons and Dimbleby 1974; S. Palmer and Dimbleby 1979). It has been estimated that a herd of 180 red deer would be sufficient to feed five people if no other source of energy was available. A herd of that size would have required a forest territory of 7200–13,000 hectares. Figures of this kind are only very approximate, and there are too many variables to allow cohesive economic models to be built, but at best they indicate something of the sparseness of the population which these survival strategies could have supported.

In summary, sufficient evidence now exists to show that sophisticated techniques of crop and herd control were being practised in the Mesolithic period. The change to a food-producing economy in the Neolithic period was therefore not such a violent revolution, even for Britain, as it was once thought to be.

Territories and Mobility

It is not possible, from the archaeological evidence, to offer any objective assessment of how the Mesolithic hunting bands moved around their territories during the course of an annual cycle or how big those territories might have been. In spite of various attempts to do so critical examination of the evidence shows that the database is still far from adequate (Whittle 1990b). We can, however, be certain that some degree of mobility was maintained, individual bands working their own territories for part of the year and coalescing as larger groups for more communal activities at other times. Base camps, like those at Oakhanger, Thatcham and Broom Hill, were used over considerable periods of time, probably in the winter months when a more sedentary existence would have allowed time for making new equipment and repairing old.

The study of more recent hunting communities shows that the territories worked by individual bands were usually circumscribed and the pattern of

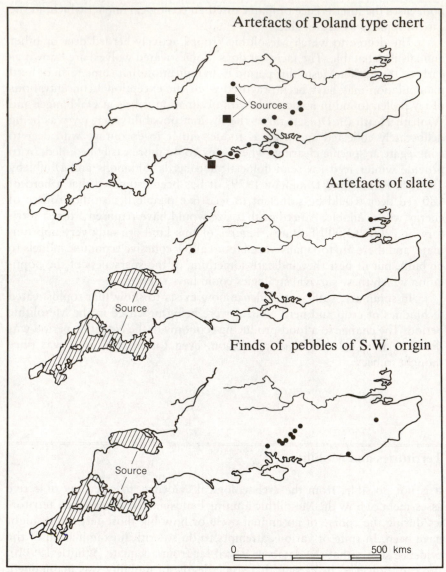

Figure 1.11 Stone imported throughout Wessex in the Mesolithic period. (After Jacobi 1981: Fig. 7)

hunting and collecting within them was ordered and cyclic. So it probably was in forests and estuaries of Mesolithic Wessex.

Within this loose-knit system of territorial hunting and gathering, people from one zone would, from time to time, have come into contact with those from another whether by arrangement or by accident and at these times exchanges may well have taken place. Some hint of this is provided by the distribution of distinctive 'rare' materials such as Portland chert, slate blades and pebbles of Palaeozoic rocks from Devon and Cornwall (Fig. 1.11). These distributions offer a very pale reflection of the complex patterns of social interaction which must have existed. They are sufficient, however, to serve as a reminder that regional systems of social intercourse had already developed by the Later Mesolithic perhaps as a response to the rapidly increasing population density suggested by the archaeological record.

Chapter 2

The Inception of Food-Producing Economies: 4500–3000 BC

The fifth and fourth millennia BC saw a major transformation in the landscape of Britain. At the beginning of the period much of the countryside, but for the highlands, was covered with forest dominated by oak, elm, ash, lime, hazel and alder, interrupted only in very local patches by the cutting and burning activities of Mesolithic hunting groups: by the end of the fourth millennium substantial clearances had been created, particularly on the Wessex chalklands, supporting arable plots or areas of established pasture, and over most of the country food-producing strategies based on the cultivation of wheat and barley and the husbanding of cattle, sheep, goats and pigs had largely replaced the mobile hunting bands of the Early Post Glacial period. These dramatic changes were enacted against gradually changing climatic conditions. Throughout the Atlantic period (zone VIIa) north-western Europe was experiencing a warmer and somewhat damper climate than before but just before *c.* 4000 BC there is some slight evidence of a colder spell followed by a generally drier sub-Boreal phase (zone VIIb). The changes were not sufficiently dramatic to have affected human communities, but the disappearance of the large herds of elk and an apparent decline in the density of red deer caused by the changing climate necessitated some modification of regime among the earlier hunting groups.

Changes in the habitat are at present best reflected in the pollen record. The evidence is varied, complex and open to differing interpretations (A. G. Smith et al. 1981) but simply stated two phases of forest clearance can be recognized in the British Isles at this time. The first, beginning about 4500 BC involved the creation of limited clearances, usually of short duration, of the kind which might be expected to have resulted from the activities of small groups of pioneer farmers (A. G. Smith 1970; I. F. Smith 1974), though much the same effect could have been caused by hunting bands making openings in the woodland to maintain browse for deer herds. The evidence from the Sweet Track in Somerset, dated by dendrochronology to 3807–3806 BC, shows that some limited clearances had already appeared about 150 years before the track was constructed (J. M. Coles and B. J. Coles 1990). This phase was followed about 3900 BC by more sustained and extensive clearances coinciding with a dramatic decline in elm pollen.

The causes of the elm decline have been much discussed. While the cutting of elm branches to provide leaf fodder for cattle during a period of winter stalling has frequently been argued to be the cause, the almost synchronous appearance of the phenomenon over much of the British Isles, in a period of two or three centuries around 3900 BC, has suggested to some that non-human factors may have been the prime mover. Indeed had the demand for leaf fodder been the *sole* cause then an enormous cattle population would have to be envisaged. The rapid spread of elm disease in recent years has offered one possible explanation but this is not entirely satisfactory for coincident with the decline in elm it is possible to recognize a general decline in tree pollen and a corresponding increase in herb pollen. It is safer therefore, on present evidence, to see this second phase of clearance as simply an intensification of a process which had begun, on a smaller scale, many centuries earlier exacerbated perhaps by climatic changes. As we shall see, there is ample evidence from Wessex that clearance was underway by the time that the first monuments of earth and stone were being built in the fourth millennium.

The change from a hunter-gatherer economy to one involving food production brought with it a series of technological changes. The microlithic industries of the Mesolithic came to an end and in their place more massive implements of stone became the norm. The tool kit, though generally similar, was now dominated by large axes of flint or igneous stone carefully ground to produce the smooth surface and sharp cutting edge needed for ring-barking large trees as a prelude to land clearance. Arrows were now tipped with leaf-shaped arrow heads and skins were cleaned with large scrapers. Stone saddle querns for grinding grain became an essential part of the equipment while the appearance of pottery is a reflection of a more sedentary mode of existence. Although the technological change was significant it would be wrong to see it as a sudden occurrence. Indeed there is now some evidence to suggest that there was a considerable continuity over the procurement of flint.

Alongside these changes in material culture is found evidence of new plant cultivates and animal domesticates, adopted to augment the hunting and foraging strategies. The principal cereal crops were emmer wheat (*Triticum dicoccum*), einkorn (*Triticum monococcum*) and barley (*Hordeum vulgare*), while the domesticated beasts of the farmyard included cattle, pigs and sheep/goats, the cattle and pigs differing from the indigenous wild type in that they were considerably smaller. There can be little doubt that the seed corn and the sheep and goats were brought to Britain in boats from the Continent and although it is conceivable that local domestication of indigenous cattle and pigs, involving a rapid diminution in size, could have taken place in Britain throughout the fifth millennium, it seems more likely that these domesticates also arrived by boat from mainland Europe. By what processes the stock was transported to the Island and how the economic strategies of which they formed an essential part were introduced into the forests of Britain are impossible questions to answer. On one extreme it is possible to envisage a significant folk movement from the Continent, introducing the raw materials and technology necessary to support their life style in an alien and potentially hostile environment. On the other we may imagine a period of acculturation by the coastal communities of Britain who, by making periodic trips across the Channel, acquired the desire, the knowledge and the basic stock to modify their own food-generating system to one putting increasing weight on cultivation and husbandry. The differences between the two 'explanations' are more apparent than real since they are the two extremes of a continuum, and it is highly unlikely that archaeological method will ever allow a sharp distinction to be made (Case 1969; Whittle 1977; Bender 1978; J. Thomas 1988).

The fifth millennium was therefore a period of gradual adaptation from a mobile hunting/gathering strategy in a largely forested wildscape to a more sedentary food-producing economy in an increasingly organized and open landscape. The 'Neolithic' economy can be shown to have been in operation at Shippea Hill, Cambs., by *c.* 4300 BC, at Broome Heath in Norfolk a few decades later, and at Ballynagilly in Ireland by 4100 BC. Clearances were underway at Cross Mere in Shropshire by 4100 BC while Neolithic settlement is attested at Thirlings, Northumberland, a little later and in Grampian and Shetland before 3900 BC. The construction of the Sweet Track across the Somerset marshes in 3807–3806 BC was a major act of landscape organization. Thus the adoption of the new mode of production spread rapidly throughout the British Isles. But the spread was not even, nor was it universal. Pockets of 'Mesolithic economies' persisted in many places. At Wawcott in the Kennet valley, for example, a typical hunting camp has been excavated dated to 4100 BC. Perhaps the most appropriate image to have of this phase is of a patchwork of clearances and still much physical mobility.

Man and Landscape in Wessex

Although much of the land mass of Wessex was composed of chalk and limestone characterized today by a thin soil cover, in the fifth millennium it was covered with a mantle of loess-rich detritus derived from periglacial activity. The calcareous zone with its thin redsinas and perhaps some thicker rich brown earths created by several thousand years of forest growth, and the not inconsiderable areas of clay land, supported a dense and largely continuous forest dominated by alder, hazel and oak. On the more fragile soils of the sandy areas, in the Weald and the Hampshire basin, Mesolithic activity, as we have seen, had created clearings which in places had already degenerated into heath. At this time the Somerset Levels presented a more varied landscape. The few wooded ridges stood above a vast area of marsh dominated in the summer by reeds (*phragmites*) scattered with a few squat trees of birch, willow and alder, and with tufts of cotton grass here and there. In the winter the entire landscape was flooded.

The effects of Early Neolithic economies on the landscape of Wessex have been extensively studied in recent years most particularly on the Wiltshire chalkland where buried soils beneath Neolithic long barrows have yielded a range of environmental data derived, in particular, from a study of the mollusca and to a limited extent pollen (Evans 1971; Dimbleby and Evans 1974). So comprehensive is the evidence that it is possible to offer in outline a synthesis for the Avebury region (R. W. Smith 1984) relying essentially on the soils preserved by the barrows at Horslip, South Street and Beckhampton Road where early clearances have been recorded. Perhaps the most intriguing point to emerge from the study is that Mesolithic debris has been recovered from within 200 m of all the sites producing evidence of early farming. While direct continuity cannot be demonstrated it is tempting to suggest that the earliest farmers began their food-producing activities in clearings which had already been created by earlier hunting groups. The evidence beneath the Horslip barrow shows that a clearing was being recolonized by hazel scrub when the monument was built. The soil from beneath the South Street barrow has also produced a few 'Mesolithic' flints together with pottery and bones of domesticated sheep and ox deposited after the site had been used for agricultural activities (R. W. Smith 1984: 113). These tantalizing scraps of evidence hint at the potential complexity of the cultural interactions at the time when the food-producing mode was being developed.

Taking a somewhat broader view of the north Wiltshire chalkland and the upper and middle Kennet valley, where some Mesolithic data are available, Alasdair Whittle has shown that the best explanation of the current evidence is to suppose that the early farming groups in the Avebury area had moved into a region that was marginal to that exploited by Mesolithic hunters. This allows the possibility of the co-existence of the two food-generating strategies at least for a few centuries (Whittle 1990b).

The Early Neolithic (*c.* 4400–3500 BC) exploitation of the region was typified by a variety of land use strategies. At Beckhampton Road the barrow had been constructed in a pastoral clearing of some several centuries duration, while at Horslip the pre-barrow soil demonstrated a transitional phase of cereal growing. Only at South Street was there clear evidence of intensive cultivation involving the use of the rip-ard to break the ground and the clearance of stones to the edge of the field plots (Fig. 2.1). The pollen evidence suggests that the neighbouring woodland was being managed for pannage and browse: it also showed that the fields were suffering from

SOUTH STREET, LONG BARROW

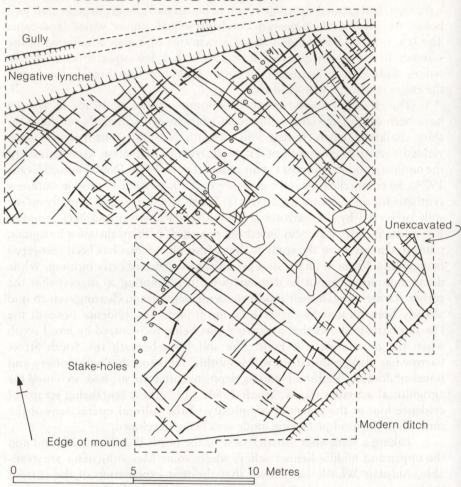

Figure 2.1 Neolithic ard marks found beneath the South Street long barrow, Wilts. (After Fowler and Evans 1967: Fig. 1)

infestations of bracken and other weeds. Too much should not be based on the evidence from only three sites but its variety provides a salutary reminder of the potential complexity of these early agricultural systems.

By the Middle Neolithic (*c.* 3500–3100 BC) the situation had become even more complicated. Some of the early farmed sites like Horslip and South Street show signs of woodland regeneration and may have been abandoned altogether. This has led to the suggestion that the phase of early exploitation was followed by one of economic regression (Whittle 1977) possibly exacerbated by climatic deterioration (A. G. Smith et al. 1981: 206). However, such a view must be balanced against an array of evidence which suggests the continued opening up of the region. At Windmill Hill and Beckhampton Road, for example, there is clear evidence of land being broken for arable production for the first time while elsewhere pastoral clearings were developing. The data available at present are too sparse to support elaborate models of change. At best they suggest a continuous development of agricultural exploitation on a shifting basis with new land being brought under cultivation as older weed-infested plots were abandoned.

Another area which has been subject to detailed assessment is the South Dorset Ridgeway south of Dorchester. Here, using a variety of evidence it is possible to chart the progressive opening up of the chalkland landscape from the beginning of the fourth millennium BC when the virgin forest was already broken by a number of small clearings to the third millennium by which time the clearances had grown and begun to coalesce. By the early second millennium the entire area had taken on the appearance of open downland broken only by small patches of woods (Woodward 1991: 129–40).

The intensity of archaeological activity in the Kennet valley/Avebury area, along the Dorset Ridgeway and in the Stonehenge region, provides an invaluable insight into the development of early agricultural regimes. Elsewhere in Wessex the evidence is more scattered but several pollen sequences are now available (Waton 1982). In the Itchen valley, near Winchester, pollen samples from peat accumulations show clear evidence of elm decline dated to 4400 BC associated with an increase of herbs, grasses and cereal, suggesting intensive woodland clearance accompanied by the development of arable and pastoral farming. The beginning of the clearance episode seems to lie several centuries earlier allowing for the possibility of Mesolithic interference. At Rimsmoor in Dorset, a bog situated on Reading Beds clay just off the edge of the chalk, elm decline is associated with the very small quantities of cereal pollen but with evidence for pastoral activity dated to between 4000 and 3400 BC, while further north at Snelsmore on the edge of the Berkshire Downs there appears to have been little disturbance of the forest cover until the Iron Age.

A rather different array of data comes from the Somerset Levels where the discovery of timber trackways crossing the marsh provides vivid evidence of woodland management. The earliest of the tracks, the Sweet Track dating to 3807–3806 BC, was made of poles or rails of ash, oak and hazel brought from the nearby hills fixed to the ground with pegs of hazel, holly, alder, ash and elm. Upon this base were laid heavy planks of mainly oak and ash and lime between pairs of oblique pegs. The entire track, more than 2 km of it, was built as a single project over a comparatively short period of time. The sheer volume of the timber needed, the skill with which it was selected and prepared and the fact that the hazel pegs strongly suggest that coppicing was practised, give a vivid insight into the degree of woodland management and exploitation at this time (J. M. Coles, Hibbert and Orme 1973; J. M. Coles and Orme 1976, 1984; Rackham 1977; J. M. Coles 1989; J. M. Coles and B. J. Coles 1990). It also provides an example of the way in which the products of deforestation, possibly associated with the development of arable, could be put to ancillary uses.

Food Resources

Apart from the dog, which existed in domesticated form in the Mesolithic period, the earliest domesticated animals known from Wessex are cattle and sheep or goat, both of which have been identified at the long barrows of Lambourn (*c.* 4200 BC) and Fussell's Lodge (*c.* 4000 BC). Domesticated pigs are first recorded in the pre-enclosure level at Windmill Hill in a context dated to *c.* 3800 BC.

The quantities of animal bones from Early and Middle Neolithic sites in Wessex are not large and comparatively few site reports have published precise quantifications but the following have been extracted by Grigson (1981: Table 4.1).

	Total	Cattle	Sheep/goat	Pig
Windmill Hill (pre camp)	182	66%	16%	18%
Windmill Hill (camp)	961+	60%	24%	16%
Robin Hood's Ball	81	76%	16%	8%
Knap Hill	73	78%	7%	5%

The sample size for each site is far too small to permit a detailed analysis of the flocks and herds, nor can we be sure that the recorded bones reflect normal domestic activity, as opposed to specialized ritual behaviour, but taken on their face value they indicate the dominance of cattle followed by sheep/goat and pig in approximately equal proportions.

Cattle were well suited to the heavily wooded environment since they are both browsers and grazers. Pigs were also a woodland creature being content with the pannage which the mixed oak forest would provide. Sheep, on the other hand, were essentially grazing beasts requiring open pasture. A landscape comprised of plots of arable and pasture scattered in a predominantly woodland environment would therefore be consistent with what little we know of herd composition.

It is difficult to say to what extent game was hunted. With the exception of red deer antler, which was extensively used for tools but could be collected as shed antler at certain times during the year, bones of non-domesticated animals are rare from those sites which have been excavated and analysed.

The largest assemblage comes from the Causewayed Camp of Windmill Hill where in addition to dog and horse the list includes red deer, roe deer, aurochs, fox, badger, cat, horse and probably wild pig. Even so the wild component was less than 7 per cent of the total bone assemblage. Whilst it is possible to argue that the causewayed camps from which the bulk of the evidence comes do not contain a 'normal' domestic assemblage, taken on its face value the available evidence seems to suggest that hunting did not form a significant element in the Early and Middle Neolithic economy. But that the situation may be complicated is indicated by the contents of a pit, dating to *c.* 3800 BC found near the later henge monument at Coneybury near Stonehenge. In addition to a surprisingly large quantity of pottery the pit produced bones from a major butchery episode representing the slaughter of at least ten cattle, several roe deer, two red deer and a pig as well as beaver and fish. The deposit may be the result of a special ceremony involving feasting, but the presence of wild animals and resources derived from the nearby river valley is a reminder that, at this early stage in the Neolithic, hunting regimes developed in the Mesolithic period may well still have been in operation (J. Richards 1990: 40–61).

When larger samples of animal bones become available for study it should be possible to approach such questions as herd management. Some hints of future advances come from a preliminary assessment of the faunal assemblage from Hambledon Hill where it has been possible to demonstrate high proportions of old females among the cattle suggesting that the maintenance of herds for milk was a prime concern (Mercer 1980: 61).

Direct evidence for cereal cultivation, while persistent, is too scattered to allow for any significant quantification. On the Wessex chalkland, emmer wheat with lesser quantities of einkorn comprised the staple crop, eked out with much smaller quantities of barley: grain impressions in pottery from Windmill Hill were found in the ratio of 91.6 per cent wheat to only 8.4 per cent barley. When, however, systematically collected samples of carbonized plant material are studied the comparative sparsity of cereals as compared to wild fruits and nuts is noticeable on many sites in Britain (Moffett, Robinson and Straker 1989). Little satisfactory evidence is available from Wessex but the presence of hazel-nuts, crab apple pips and the stone of what may be a sloe from Windmill Hill hints at the significance of collecting to the economy but does not allow any direct comparison to be made between the relative importance of cultivation and collecting. The point that we should not lose sight of, however, is that arable farming may have been of comparatively little importance to the economy, possibly until as late as the middle of the second millennium.

What emerges from this brief discussion of Neolithic food-producing strategies is that during the period *c.* 4500–3000 BC the Wessex communities relied on a varied range of resource potentials. Small plots of arable land produced wheat and a little barley, areas of pasture carved from the forest or

43

created from disused arable provided pasture for sheep and at times for cattle, while the all-important forest, never far away, yielded ample browse for cattle, pigs and goats. It was also a place where fruits and nuts could be collected and where a wide range of basic materials – timber, furs, resin, tinder – were readily to hand. The strength of the economic system lay in its diversity – the temporary failure of one facet was not sufficient to jeopardize the entire system.

Craft, Production and Exchange

The production of a range of stone tools was crucial to the well-being of the community and flint, abundant in the Wessex chalk, provided an ideal material for the manufacture of a varied assemblage of axes, adzes, sickles, knives, scrapers and arrow heads. For the most part suitable flint nodules could be acquired in the ploughed fields or in the bolls of uprooted trees: they could also be dug out of the superficial patches of clay-with-flints which blanket areas of chalk uplands. One such area is known at Hackpen Hill, near Avebury, and another at Windmill Hill, Chalton, in Hampshire where an extensive scatter of waste from the production of axes and scrapers litters the hilltop (Cunliffe 1973a). Mining for flint does not appear to have been extensively practised in Wessex in the Early and Middle Neolithic period but shafts are known on Easton Down with a radiocarbon date suggesting activity *c.* 3100 BC and others, of Late Neolithic date, have been found at Durrington: some possible shafts have been identified at Hambledon Hill in Dorset.

The possibility should not be overlooked that many of the fine polished flint axes of Wessex may have come from outside the region, from Sussex or Norfolk, where flint mining was well-established at this time. The exchange of axes over considerable distances is attested by the widespread distribution of polished stone varieties made of igneous rocks, the sources of which can be identified. The commonest of these imports found in Wessex were produced in Cornwall with smaller quantities coming from Great Langdale in Cumbria and Craig Llwyd in north Wales (Fig. 2.2). The social processes by means of which these items were transported will be considered below.

The other materials widely used for tools and weapons were bone, antler and wood. A variety of bone pins, points and scoops are recorded; antler was used to make picks for breaking out chalk and limestone when digging ditches or making earthworks, and also for making combs thought to have been used in the preparation of skins. Wood was of universal value but seldom survives in the archaeological record except in the peats of the Somerset Levels which have produced a remarkable array of implements including a long bow, arrow shafts, a mallet, paddles, bowls and pins, providing a tantalizing glimpse of the extremely rich material culture of the period.

While the woodworking techniques, including the use of bark and basketry, were long established and were no doubt brought to a high degree of sophistication in the Mesolithic period, the manufacture of pottery was a skill developed first by the Early Neolithic farmers. The earliest pottery consists of plain round-bottomed vessels usually with an out-turned rim and often a slight shoulder angle (Fig. 2.3) though regional variants are evident

Figure 2.2 Distribution of stone axes from four sources, groups I, VI, VII and XX. Stippling shows relative frequency (%). (After Cummins 1979)

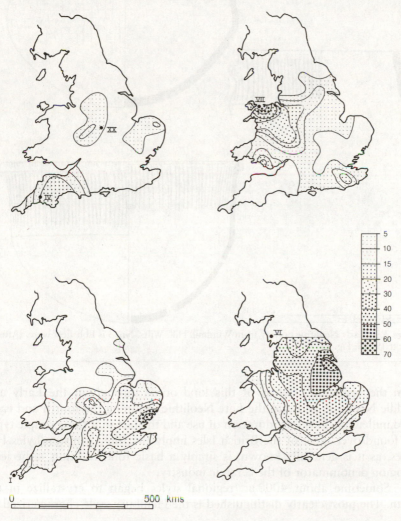

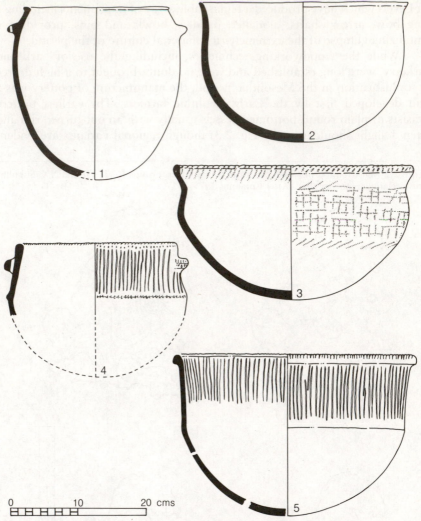

Figure 2.3 Early Neolithic pottery from Windmill Hill, Wilts. No. 3 is Ebbsfleet ware. (After S. Piggott 1973b: Fig. 11)

from the beginning. Forms of this kind occur throughout the Early and Middle Neolithic and into the Late Neolithic spanning the fourth and early third millennia. This long duration of use and the fact that these simple types are found over most of the British Isles imply that the Grimston/Lyles Hill series, as it is generally known, is simply a basic folk tradition – the least common denominator of the ceramic industry.

Sometime about 4000 BC regional styles began to crystallize in the south. The most clearly distinguished is the Hembury style characterized by fine, plain, round-bottomed bowls sometimes with low girth angles and horizontally perforated 'trumpet lugs'. Classic Hembury style pottery has been shown to have been made of a gabbroic clay found only in the south-west peninsula (Peacock 1969). Imported vessels have been found on a number of Wessex sites, in comparatively large numbers on sites near the coast, like Maiden Castle and Corfe Mullen and in much smaller quantities further inland, e.g. at Robin Hood's Ball and Windmill Hill (Fig. 2.4). The implication is that they were imported by sea along the south coast. The date range spans the period from *c.* 4000 BC at the type site to *c.* 3100 BC at Windmill Hill.

The influence of these imports is soon seen on ceramic production in Wessex and there evolves a style made in local fabrics which has been called the Hembury-Maiden Castle group but is probably better referred to as the Wessex-Hembury style. Pottery of this type was no doubt made in a number of centres in Wessex and Sussex. One production focus can be located to the Bath–Frome region, the vessels being easily identified by inclusions of fossil shell and oolites in the clay. These products seem to have been widely exchanged. Nearly one-third of the pottery from Windmill Hill is of this type and it occurs on several of the Wessex chalkland sites.

About 4000 BC decorated pottery begins to appear in the Wessex region. The earliest is at present an assemblage from the Fussell's Lodge long barrow for which there is a single radiocarbon date of about this time. These

Figure 2.4 Distribution of pottery made in gabbroic clay from Lizard Point, Cornwall, showing percentages compared with other fabrics. (After Peacock 1969: Fig. 1)

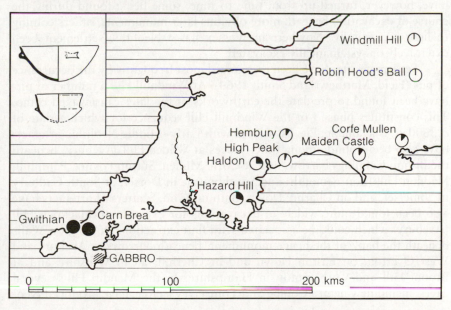

vessels belong to the broadly defined Abingdon style which at its Oxfordshire type site is dated to *c.* 3900–3100 BC. At Windmill Hill Abingdon style wares and other decorated pottery are found with pottery of Wessex-Hembury type but below another distinctive decorated style known as the Ebbsfleet style characterized by cord impressions. Ebbsfleet ware seems to have developed in the Lower Thames region by 3400 BC and its appearance at Windmill Hill may be a century or two later. It is this style that lies at the beginning of a long tradition of decorated wares collectively known as the Peterborough style which runs throughout the Late Neolithic. The fact that at Windmill Hill pottery of Abingdon and Ebbsfleet style are made in both local and oolitic fabrics is a reminder that we are not dealing with imports from the Thames valley but with generalized styles adopted widely by disparate communities.

Settlements

Leaving aside for the moment the question of causewayed camps, comparatively little is known of settlements of the Early and Middle Neolithic in Wessex. The absence of recognizable upstanding features and the erosion caused by subsequent agricultural activities have obscured, and in many places destroyed, all trace of settlement activity. Fragments of settlements have, however, turned up from time to time, some being found during the course of excavation beneath more obvious later monuments, others coming to light accidentally. Nowhere in Wessex has a Neolithic settlement been extensively or systematically excavated.

Settlement sites have been recognized most frequently by the occurrence of pits (Field, Matthews and Smith 1964). At Windmill Hill a number of pits have been found to pre-date the earthworks of the later causewayed camp. This constitutes phase I of the Windmill Hill sequence for which a date of *c.* 3600 BC is available. Pits associated with Early–Middle Neolithic artefacts have also been found among other places at Waden Hill, Avebury, beneath the Bishop Cannings barrow, and at Corfe Mullen, Sutton Poyntz, Pamphill, Haddon Hill (Bournemouth) and Southbourne in Dorset, at South Cadbury in Somerset, and on Charmy Down, Bath in Avon. Scatters of artefacts have also been found quite widely in excavations for example on Hackpen Hill (Avebury) which could be associated with flint extraction, Durrington Walls beneath the bank of the henge monument, beneath barrows at Avebury and West Overton, on Easton Down and at Cherhill, all in Wiltshire and at Broom Hill and Corhampton in Hampshire. In the Mendip Hills several caves, including Chelm's Combe and Tom Tivey's Hole, have produced Neolithic occupation layers. This brief listing of the more important sites shows that settlement of the period 4500–3000 was surprisingly widespread.

That settlement was, in many areas, even denser is strongly suggested by flint scatters recorded in various parts of the region. At the confluence of the Avon and Stour in the vicinity of Hengistbury Head and Christchurch Harbour, casual finds made over the years, when brought together, imply intensive settlement and exploitation of the gravel terraces of the lower river valleys. This dense pattern appears to contrast to the nearby chalk uplands of Cranborne Chase where, in spite of a systematic search very few comparable sites have been located (Gardiner 1985, 1987; J. Barrett, Bradley and Green 1991). The implication would seem to be that the Christchurch Harbour region was particularly favoured. One reason for this may be its accessibility to sea-borne 'traders' (a question to which we shall return) but the comparatively light gravel soils and the wide range of different resource zones readily available must have been among the prime attractions, particularly in the early stages of the opening up of the landscape.

Intensive and systematic survey in east Hampshire, on the edge of the Weald, has shown that here too there is a surprising density of flint scatters (Shennan 1981). Much the same can be said of the Stonehenge region where a detailed survey has suggested not only denser and lighter zones of activity but also a distinction between domestic and industrial assemblages (J. Richards 1990). In both cases, while it is difficult to subdivide the material into its different chronological groups, the overall impression is of extensive activity throughout the period 4500–1500 BC. Another example pointing to the same conclusion comes from the Basingstoke region of the Hampshire Downs, where random field walking by a single individual produced over 100 flint axes.

Rather different evidence for the intensity of settlement is provided by the Somerset tracks built to provide ways across the marsh between the Polden Hills and the islands of Westhay and Meare, a distance of some 3 kilometres. The effort involved in the construction of Sweet Track dating to *c.* 3800 BC shows that ample surplus labour was available. If the function of the track was simply to link the communities of the two adjacent dry-land areas then the implication must be of a degree of social organization involving intensive exploitation. We should not however overlook the possibility that the trackway had a ritual function, leading perhaps to a sanctuary. The quantity of artefacts found alongside it, including unused axes of flint and jadeite, may be thought to reflect deliberate acts of propitiation through deposition.

Standing back from the mass of disparate evidence for settlement, most of it acquired in a totally non-systematic way, it is difficult to resist the conclusion that the thousand years from 4000 to 3000 BC saw a significant increase in population leading to the more organized exploitation of large tracts of the Wessex countryside. While the density of settlement will have varied considerably with differing resource potentials, and every area is likely to have shown fluctuations in exploitation strategies over time, the overall picture is one of expanding settlement leading to a permanent opening up of the landscape. This impression is enhanced when the contemporary ritual monuments – the causewayed enclosures and long barrows – are taken into account.

Causewayed Enclosures

The causewayed enclosures of Wessex are among the best known Neolithic monuments of the country and yet their function (or functions) is still very much in doubt. Since the first systematic excavations of Windmill Hill by Alexander Keiller between 1925 and 1929 (I. F. Smith 1965, 1966) most of the known Wessex examples have been examined, some of them on more than one occasion, and several general surveys have been published (in particular I. F. Smith 1971; Mercer 1980).

Causewayed enclosures are characterized as areas of differing sizes enclosed or partially enclosed by one or more lines of earthwork. These earthworks consist of a discontinuous ditch made up of a series of elongated pits separated by narrow causeways, the spoil often being piled up on the inside of the ditch to form a bank continuous except for the main entrance ways. They vary in size and plan, as will be apparent from Fig. 2.5, two distinct size groups being distinguishable: the larger, including Windmill Hill (Plate 2.1), Hambledon Hill and Maiden Castle (Wheeler 1943) are between 7.5 and 8.8 ha in overall extent, the smaller including Whitesheet Hill (S. Piggott 1952), Robin Hood's Ball (N. Thomas 1964), Rybury (Bonney 1964) and Knap Hill (Cunnington 1912; Connah 1969) are between 1 and 3 ha.

Any consideration of function must be prefaced by the reminder that there is no reason why all causewayed enclosures need have been used in the same way. The adoption of the causewayed ditch to define an enclosed area is no more than a technique for enclosure: it does not necessarily take with it an implied range of functions. In the discussion to follow we shall, of course, deal only with sites from Wessex.

Evidence for internal activity is not extensive, due largely to the destructive activity of weathering and ploughing, which would have removed all superficial stratigraphy and the majority of the shallower features such as stake-holes and post-holes. Even so the sparsity of internal features at Windmill Hill strongly suggests that the site was not 'occupied' in the sense of being a domestic settlement.

The causewayed enclosure on Hambledon Hill has been more exten-

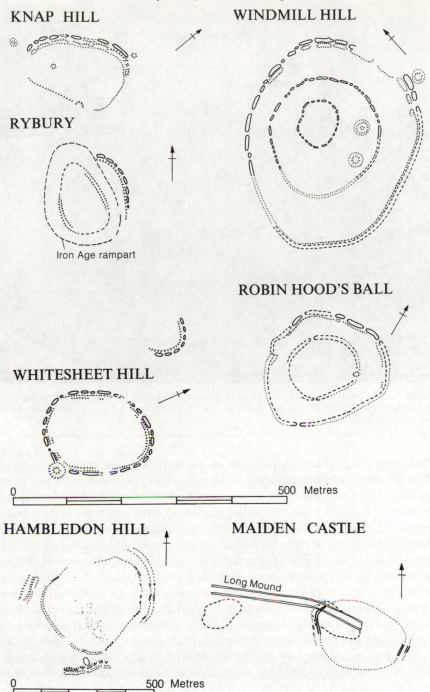

KNAP HILL

WINDMILL HILL

RYBURY

Iron Age rampart

ROBIN HOOD'S BALL

WHITESHEET HILL

0   500 Metres

HAMBLEDON HILL

MAIDEN CASTLE

Long Mound

0   500 Metres

Figure 2.5 Comparative plans of causewayed camps from Wessex. (Various sources)

Plate 2.1 The Neolithic causewayed camp of Windmill Hill from the air. The three concentric and widely spaced ditch circuits are apparent. The circular barrows are of second millennium date. (Photo: Mick Aston)

sively examined, about 20 per cent of the interior being totally excavated (Mercer 1980). Although erosion had been intense, the bases of 97 pits have been located. These were irregularly cut and would originally have been quite shallow, between 0.5 and 1 m in depth. Many of the pits seem to have been left open for a brief period before a series of deliberate deposits were placed in them and they were then backfilled: some were subsequently recut. The deposits found in the pits appear to be of non-domestic character as if they were carefully selected in response to some system of beliefs. When flints were buried there was usually a marked bias towards one type of artefact. Pottery seems to have been selected for its rarity, sandstone rubbers from the West Country were frequently chosen and so were fossils and naturally perforated pebbles and in fourteen examples substantial quantities of red deer antler were deposited. These very deliberate patterns of deposition, together with the total absence of anything suggestive of a purely domestic function, strongly implies ritual use. But before examining the question further we must consider the evidence from the causewayed camp ditches.

Again it is Hambledon that is the most revealing, not least because over 250 m of the ditch (20 per cent of the total) has been excavated. Taken together the evidence suggests a series of well-defined phases in the slow filling of the main inner ditch. After initial silting the ditch segments were almost completely cleaned out and a deposit of organic-rich debris was carefully placed along the centre of the ditch bottom. The deposit included bone, pottery, flint-working debris and a variety of disarticulated human bone including several skulls which had been placed on the ditch floor. Three careful burials, two of children and one of the articulated remains of the trunk of a young man, were also found. The deliberate deposits of phase II were then left to become buried by natural silting derived from the erosion of the ditch sides and the bank (phase III). Then followed the digging of a series of pits into the fill (phase IV). These were filled with dark ashy material containing a range of debris including frequent fragments of human skeletons. After this there was another long period of natural erosion (phase V) during which time the ditch silted almost to the top. Another phase of redigging followed (phase VI) resulting in a shallow trench barely 0.5 m deep and of the same width cut into the upper levels of the silt. In some places the trench was backfilled, the filling containing quantities of cattle bones and some human remains. Finally in phase VII, dated to *c*. 2000–1700 BC, a mass of flint nodules was deposited in the ditch top.

The remarkable sequence at Hambledon leaves little doubt that the ditch served as the focus for a series of ritual acts involving the periodic redefinition of the enclosed area, each time associated with the deliberate deposition of a range of selected debris. Reviewing the evidence the excavator has suggested that the primary purpose of the main inner enclosure was for excarnation – the exposure of dead bodies (Mercer 1980: 37–9). If so then the redefinition of the ditch with its attendant rituals presumably marked significant events in the use of the site.

Turning now to the other extensively excavated causewayed enclosure, Windmill Hill, we can hardly expect to find the same detailed evidence from an excavation undertaken in the 1920s but even so the surviving information is revealing. Extensive dumps of occupation material were found in the ditches, particularly the inner ditch. In one sector a series of separate dumps of animal bone were found on the primary silt each surrounded by decayed organic matter and charcoal. In another sector an antler tine, ox skull and sarsen rubber were found together. Two burials of children were also discovered, both in the outer ditch, but human bone was found in all three ditch circuits. One was found on the bottom in the same level as skeletons of a young pig and young goat. While the evidence from Windmill Hill may be less focused than that from Hambledon it is clear that both shared the same pattern of ritual depositions. The much slighter excavations at Robin Hood's Ball, Whitesheet and Maiden Castle have produced comparable evidence. In a general review of causewayed camps, published before the recent programme of excavations at Hambledon, Dr Isobel Smith was able to show that the deposition of organic remains at different times in ditches, recutting, and the use of the bank material to cover ditch deposits, were recurring but variable characteristics of causewayed enclosures (I. F. Smith 1971).

If, then, the ditches of causewayed enclosures were the focus for complex ritual activity, taking place at intervals over a considerable period of time, is it reasonable to apply Roger Mercer's explanation of Hambledon as a centre for the exposure of corpses to all similar enclosures? The answer must be that there is insufficient evidence to be sure largely because of the inadequacy of the excavated samples. At Hambledon human remains were found at all levels in the ditch including not only the careful burials from primary positions but also isolated bones and groups of bones occurring in sufficient quantity to suggest that there must have been much skeletal material lying about the site. At Windmill Hill the sample of human remains recovered is by no means negligible and indeed bodies were being buried on the site before the causewayed enclosure was constructed (Whittle 1990c). In addition to the two careful burials of infants from primary levels in the outer ditch, 27 scattered human bones of children, adolescents and adults were recovered. Although the density of human remains is not as great as at Hambledon it requires explanation in terms of some form of cult practice involving the disposal of the dead. The suggestion has been made that the bones were brought to the site from neighbouring chambered tombs (I. F. Smith 1965: 137) but in view of the evidence from Hambledon the possibility of excarnation on the site should be seriously entertained. The other causewayed enclosures of Wessex have not been sampled on a large enough scale to be meaningful but Maiden Castle has produced a small assemblage of human remains (Sharples 1986).

The 'ceremonial' aspects of causewayed enclosures are further emphasized by a study of the artefact assemblage from Windmill Hill (I. F. Smith 1965, 1971). The presence of polished stone axes from the Lake District and Cornwall, of Portland chert probably from the Dorset coast and of imported pottery (0.2 per cent gabbroic from Cornwall and 30 per cent oolitic from the Bath–Frome region) shows that significant quantities of non-local material were being brought to the site (see also Howard 1981). The presence here of an unusually eclectic body of decorative styles of pottery is a further indication of the wide-ranging contacts enjoyed. Much the same can be said of Hambledon Hill, Maiden Castle and, to a lesser extent, Robin Hood's Ball. Together the evidence is consistent with the view that causewayed enclosures were regional centres of ceremonial and social significance, where the larger community could gather, perhaps annually in ditch-defined woodland clearings, to maintain and reproduce their social systems. Such a view is by no means inconsistent with one of the functions of the enclosures being to define an area where the dead could be excarnated. A sacred location dedicated to ancestors would be an entirely appropriate place for such a gathering.

The distribution of causewayed enclosures (Fig. 2.6) gives the impression that, with the exception of the two small enclosures of Knap Hill and Rybury, there is a regularity of spacing of the kind that might be expected if each served as the focus for a territory. These spatial questions will be returned to below (pp. 72–4) but here it is relevant to ask if the pattern as we know it fairly reflects the original distribution. Given the fragility of the evidence and the fact that several sites have been obscured by later hillforts, it seems highly likely that there are more enclosures to be found in Wessex. One possibility which stands out is Ham Hill, Somerset, from which an extensive collection of Neolithic material has been gathered including forty leaf-shaped arrow heads, at least thirty-two flint and stone axes, five of which came from Cornwall, and a quantity of pottery of gabbroic type from the Lizard peninsula. Other sites have been suggested from time to time (e.g. Beacon Hill and Butser Hill in Hampshire) but are less convincing. However, that more causewayed enclosures remain to be discovered in Wessex seems highly likely.

The date range of causewayed enclosures has been firmly established by a number of radiocarbon assessments. Hembury in Devon has so far produced the earliest evidence with dates from *c.* 4000–3800 BC and a comparable early date of *c.* 3800 BC was obtained for Abingdon, Oxon. Within Wessex a date of *c.* 3600 BC for the pre-enclosure occupation at Windmill Hill suggests a slightly later start. Occupation continued with a date of *c.* 3100 BC for the lower fill of the ditches and one of *c.* 1800 BC for Late Neolithic and Beaker occupation. A similar range came from Knap Hill with a less reliable date of *c.* 3400 BC for primary levels and *c.* 2100 BC for the Beaker phase. From Hambledon Hill one of the internal pits yielded a date of *c.* 2700 BC. The main causewayed enclosure ditch produced dates in the range of *c.* 3600–3300 BC for phase II and 3400–3100 BC for the redigging of phase III. The phase VII deposition was associated with Beaker pottery traditionally dated to 2100–1700 BC. Finally from Maiden Castle a series of radiocarbon dates have been obtained. From the primary filling of the inner ditch they span the period 3900–3300 BC, while material from the secondary filling lies within the range 3600–3000 BC. The primary fill of the outer ditch produced a similar range from 3800–3300 BC. Taken together the Wessex evidence offers a remarkably consistent picture suggesting that the enclosures originated soon after 4000 BC and were intensively used until about 3000, though given the imprecision of radiocarbon dates the span could have been much shorter. Thereafter occupation seems to have been more sporadic until *c.* 1700 BC.

So far we have considered only the causewayed enclosure itself but the recent work at Hambledon Hill has stressed that the main enclosure here may be only one element in a complex organized landscape (Fig. 2.7) which included two long barrows, a separate causewayed enclosure on the Stepleton spur and a series of outworks. On both the east and south sides of the main causewayed enclosure a double cross dyke had been dug and recut. There

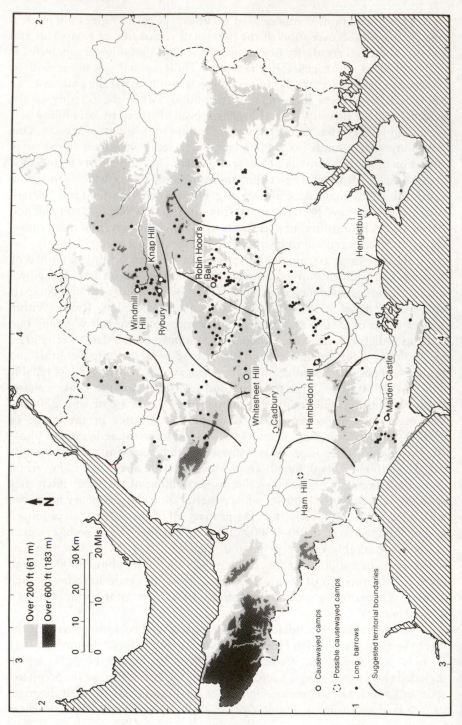

were no deliberate deposits in these ditches and it seems not unreasonable then to see them as boundaries between the activities in the main enclosure and those on the adjacent spurs.

Both spurs were protected by outworks. That on the eastern (Shroton) spur comprised a ditch, significantly larger than the enclosure ditch, which had been allowed to silt naturally. Behind it, although the bank had been destroyed, were a number of post-holes suggesting that the earthwork was intended to provide a defensive barrier. The ditch produced four charcoal samples dated within the range 3400–2900 BC. The outworks defending the Stepleton spur were more extensive – in excess of a kilometre in length. Set within was a small causewayed enclosure about one hectare in area. Excavation has demonstrated that the ditch was more massive than the main enclosure and was probably backed by a continuous ramp topped by a wattle breastwork. At some stage the timberwork seems to have caught fire leaving an extensive deposit of charcoal in the ditch associated with which was the skeleton of a young man lying prone on the ditch fill. A leaf-shaped arrow head, found within his thoracic cavity, points to the likely cause of death. Following the burning there is evidence to indicate that the rampart collapsed. Radiocarbon determinations for charcoal found within the ditch produced dates of between 3700 and 3300 BC suggesting that the Stepleton enclosure was of the same date range as the main causewayed enclosure. Area excavation within the defences points to intensive domestic activity.

The extensive programme of excavation at Hambledon Hill provides a rare insight into a major structural complex of Middle Neolithic date. The contrast between the two enclosures, one ritual the other domestic, the extensive outworks and the suggestion of attack and destruction at the smaller enclosure, are a reminder of the potential complexity of these Neolithic ceremonial/settlement agglomerations and a warning against over-simple generalizations.

The possibility that other such complexes may exist deserves brief consideration. A prime candidate is Whitesheet Hill where the causewayed camp lies at one end of a plateau upon which two other enclosures (one thought to be an Iron Age hillfort) and several cross dykes are known to exist. Another possibility is Butser Hill in Hampshire (S. Piggott 1930), an extensive upland plateau defined by cross dykes. No trace of a causewayed enclosure has been found here but Neolithic flints occur in a number of concentrations. The cross dykes of Butser are generally similar to those found at a number of locations in Wessex. These have been referred to as *plateau enclosures* (Cunliffe 1971a: 57) but in the absence of adequate excavation there can be no assurance that they constitute a distinct class of monument: nor is there any firm evidence of

Figure 2.6 Distribution of long barrows and causewayed camps. The hard lines indicate the hypothetical boundaries between the principal territorial groups

HAMBLEDON HILL

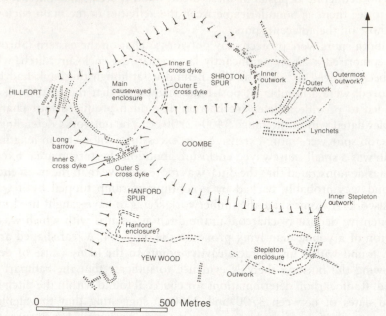

- Inner E cross dyke
- SHROTON SPUR
- Inner outwork
- Outer outwork
- Outermost outwork?
- Main causewayed enclosure
- Outer E cross dyke
- HILLFORT
- Lynchets
- Long barrow
- COOMBE
- Inner S. cross dyke
- Outer S cross dyke
- HANFORD SPUR
- Inner Stepleton outwork
- Hanford enclosure?
- Stepleton enclosure
- YEW WOOD
- Outwork
- 0   500 Metres

Figure 2.7   The Neolithic earthworks on Hambledon Hill, Dorset. (After Mercer 1980: Fig. 9)

their age. The whole question of the nature and distribution of Middle Neolithic ceremonial/settlement sites is one deserving of a detailed study.

Death and Burial

The Early and Middle Neolithic rituals associated with death and the subsequent treatment of the body are so complex as to defy adequate description (Kinnes 1975; Shanks and Tilley 1982; Thorpe 1984). At best we can distinguish only those acts or episodes which happen to survive in recognizable form in the archaeological record and from them attempt to piece together something of the patterns of beliefs which they may reflect.

Discussion must begin with the burial monuments of Wessex – the long barrows and chambered tombs. Earthen long barrows have been studied in detail as a class by Paul Ashbee (1970) (see also RCHM(E) 1979a; C. T. Barker 1985). In all between 250 and 300 are known in England of which the majority have been found in Wessex (Fig. 2.6). Ashbee has distinguished six major concentrations: the Dorset Ridgeway and coast group (20 examples); Cranborne Chase group (35); Salisbury Plain West group (25); North Wiltshire (Avebury) group (20); Salisbury Plain East (Stonehenge) group (29); Hampshire Uplands group (16). Although many of them have been dug into, only about ten have been adequately examined according to modern standards. Discussion must be based on these, with occasional reference to results from older excavations.

As their name implies earthen long barrows consist of a long mound composed of earth and rubble usually derived from two flanking ditches. Size varies considerably but the majority lie between 30 and 60 m in length with the full range spanning 22 to 135 m. The mounds may be parallel sided or slightly trapezoidal. About 80 per cent are orientated approximately east–west. Most of the mounds covered a variety of structures associated with burials but a few were without burials.

The internal structures of those long barrows which have been adequately excavated display a bewildering variety best appreciated by looking at individual examples.

Any discussion of the burial rituals involved in the construction of long barrows must begin with the Hampshire barrow at Nutbane (Figs 2.8 and 2.9) excavated in 1957 (Morgan 1959). The structural sequence here was complicated reflecting an extended series of burial rituals. In the first place a small timber structure (a 'forecourt') 4.8 by 4.3 m was built consisting of four large upright timbers placed in individual post-holes (Fig. 2.8). It was probably at this time that a small earthwork enclosure was created adjacent to the timber structure immediately to the west of it consisting of a shallow bank of soil thrown up on the outside of two irregular quarry ditches with two large post-holes at both the east and west ends and two large posts on the axis inside. It seems likely that these two axial posts were the supports of a mortuary chamber possibly of the kind found at Fussell's Lodge and Wayland's Smithy 1 to be considered below. Three burials were placed on the ground surface between the posts.

In the second phase the timber structure of the forecourt was rebuilt on several occasions, the ultimate plan being best appreciated from Fig. 2.8. It comprised two elements, a rectangular structure of four posts with a further three along a central north–south axis, and a surrounding fence composed of massive timbers set in foundation trenches, continuous except for two gaps in the western side. The structure is complex and may well have evolved over time. A possible three-stage interpretation is offered in Fig. 2.10. It was probably during this period that the mortuary enclosure was rebuilt. The banks were filled back into the ditches and rammed down and in its place a new rectangular enclosure of vertical timbers supporting horizontal boards was constructed. The old mortuary enclosure was demolished and a new burial added after which the four bodies were covered with a cairn of chalk.

In the third and final stage the long barrow mound was constructed.

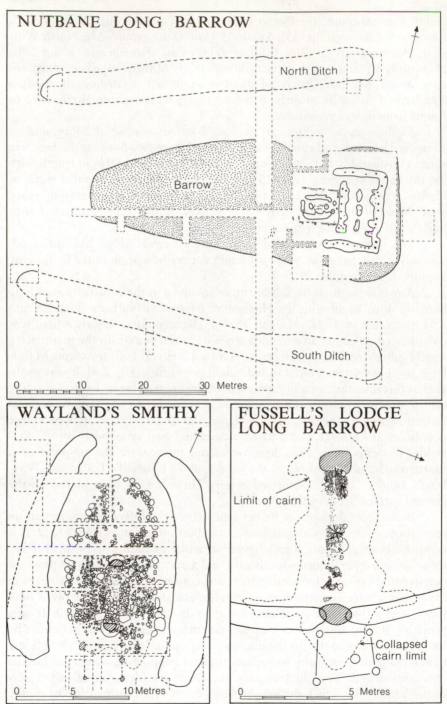

Figure 2.8 Long barrows with mortuary enclosures. (Nutbane, after Morgan 1959: Plan 1; Wayland's Smithy, after Atkinson 1965: Fig. 1; Fussell's Lodge, after Ashbee 1966: Fig. 4)

NUTBANE LONG BARROW

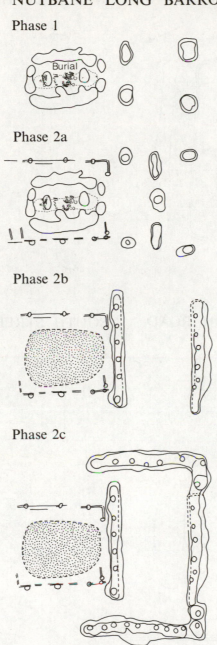

Phase 1

Phase 2a

Phase 2b

Phase 2c

0   5   10 Metres

Figure 2.9   Suggested development of the Nutbane long barrow mortuary chamber.

FUSSELL'S LODGE

WINDMILL HILL (HORSLIP)

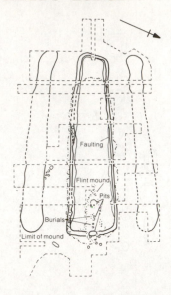
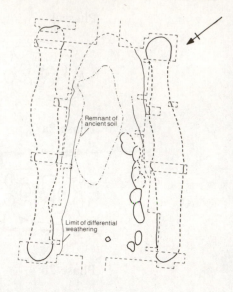

BECKHAMPTON ROAD

SOUTH STREET

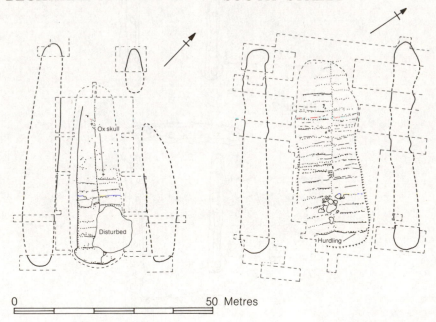

0   50 Metres

Figure 2.10 Wessex long barrows showing various internal structures. (After S. Piggott 1973b: Fig. 4)

First the mortuary enclosure was filled with soil from the flanking ditches and a primary mound was built around both enclosure and forecourt. The timbers of the forecourt were then burnt after which the mound was completed.

The excavation at Nutbane provides a most valuable insight into the complexities of burial ritual. It shows that a long period existed when the bodies were being exposed in a specially constructed mortuary complex which was rebuilt and extended on more than one occasion. When the process of burial was finally considered to be complete the long mound was built above them.

The type of mortuary chamber used at Nutbane also appears to be represented at Wayland's Smithy in barrow 1 which precedes the construction of the chambered tomb to be described later (Atkinson 1965). Here two massive posts had been set up at either end of a pavement of sarsen boulders upon which the remains of at least fourteen individuals had been placed between two lateral mounds of sarsens (Fig. 2.8). Close to the southern post were two flanking flat-sectioned sarsen slabs set at an angle so that they leaned inwards. This arrangement was reflected by two timbers at the north end. The excavator's suggestion is that the two massive uprights took a horizontal ridge beam at a height of about 1.5 m against which the timbers and sarsens leaned with smaller timbers in between though subsequent reconsideration of the evidence has suggested that the chamber is best interpreted as an embanked box-like structure (information from Alasdair Whittle). In front of the mortuary house was a roughly rectangular setting of five posts smaller than, but otherwise not dissimilar to, the early 'forecourt' structure at Nutbane. The entire structure forming the mortuary house remained in the open until the process of accumulating bodies was complete. It was then buried in an elongated mound of chalk, derived from two flanking ditches, contained within a sarsen kerb.

The third barrow to throw light on mortuary practices was excavated at Fussell's Lodge in Wiltshire in 1957 (Figs 2.8 and 2.10). Interpretation of the sequence is not entirely without problems (Simpson 1968; Ashbee and Simpson 1969). On the evidence presented (Ashbee 1966) the first structure consisted of a rectangular enclosure, roughly trapezoidal in shape, some 45 m long and up to 12 m wide composed of upright timbers set side by side in a foundation trench continuous except for a gap in the centre of the wide end. The excavator suggests that in a second stage a pitched mortuary house was erected composed of three vertical posts, one of which filled the entrance gap. If this were so it is difficult to see how access could have been obtained and why the burials lay across the filling of the central hole. These problems can, however, be overcome by supposing that the central pit was not structural and that the mortuary house together with a four-post setting in front of it preceded the construction of the trapezoidal enclosure. The most economic explanation would then be to suppose that a period of time elapsed before the timbers of the enclosure (or at least those in the centre of the front facade) were removed or had rotted, allowing a flint cairn to be piled up over the burial deposit. In the final stage the long mound was heaped up using material derived from the two flanking ditches. If this interpretation is accepted then the mortuary chamber with its fronting four-post structure would be closely comparable to the structures found at Nutbane and Wayland's Smithy 1.

Another barrow which deserves consideration is Wor Barrow in Dorset excavated by General Pitt Rivers almost a century ago and reinterpreted by Stuart Piggott (1954: 54–6). Here the ritual deposits were enclosed within a rectangular fenced enclosure. Contemporary photographs suggest that a mound of chalk rubble had been piled up against the outside, the material presumably being derived from shallow flanking ditches. In a final stage, after a layer of turf had developed over the low bank, the barrow mound was constructed, the material being quarried from massive flanking ditches.

Standing back from the evidence reviewed so far, two distinct phases can be recognized in the burial ritual: the first when the bodies are exposed usually in some kind of timber structure; and the second when a long mound is piled over them. Since these represent two separate acts it is, in theory, conceivable that either one may have been carried out without the other. This would appear to have been the case.

An example of a mortuary enclosure was excavated on Normanton Down, near Stonehenge in 1959 (Vatcher 1961). All that survived the extensive ploughing to which the area had been subjected was a discontinuous ditch enclosing an area of 22 by 40 m but traces of the bank piled inside still remained (Fig. 2.11). The only internal structures to survive were two settings of three posts forming either some kind of entrance feature or, more likely, an excarnation platform. Whether burials had ever been left within the enclosure it is impossible to say.

A small group of long barrows are also known with no burials or mortuary structures beneath. The Beckhampton Road barrow, re-excavated in 1964 consisted of a mound 46 m long and 12 m wide flanked by quarry ditches (Fig. 2.10). The mound had been constructed within a grid of hurdles but apart from this no internal structure was found although three ox skulls had been placed on the ground surface. A similar barrow was excavated nearby at South Street in 1966–7 (Fig. 2.10). It too was hurdle-framed and contained no mortuary structures or deposits (Ashbee, Smith and Evans 1979). Hurdle framing is also suggested at Thickthorn (Bradley and Entwistle 1985). At Horslip close to Windmill Hill the barrow was discovered to be apparently without burials (Fig. 2.10) though considerable damage by ploughing might have led to their destruction. Finally at Holdenhurst, Hants., large-scale excavation revealed no trace of human burials even though animal bones survived (S. Piggott 1937).

So far we have considered only earthen long barrows but the Wessex

NORMANTON DOWN

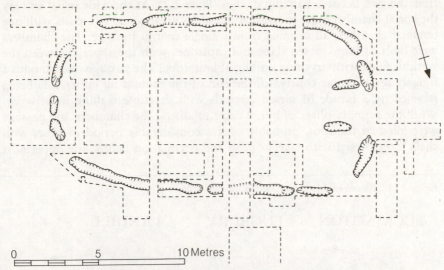

Figure 2.11   The mortuary enclosure on Normanton Down, Wilts. (After Vatcher 1961: Fig. 2)

region also includes a few long barrows containing stone-built chambers of the kind so widespread in the west and north of Britain. Two distinct groups of these chambered tombs occur: one group in south Dorset is small, not well known and most of the examples have been extensively damaged. The other group, extending from Somerset into northern Wiltshire, comprises outliers of the extensive Severn–Cotswold group (Darvill 1982). To understand the variety a selection of the better studied examples may be described.

The earthen long barrow which constitutes the first phase of Wayland's Smithy has already been mentioned. After it had served its primary purpose the barrow was entirely absorbed in a new long mound of chambered type (Fig. 2.12) measuring some 60 m long and 16 m wide at its broadest (south) end. The sides and back of the barrow were delimited with a continuous wall of upright sarsen stones. The wide south end terminated on an elaborate facade originally built of six sarsens 3 m high. Behind this, within the mound, was a chamber of cruciform plan built of large sarsen uprights capped with sarsen slabs, the spaces between the uprights being filled with neat drystone walling. Although the burial deposit had been largely removed in the last century it is clear from contemporary descriptions that human remains had been present. In the final stage the entrance had been blocked with a single slab (Atkinson 1965).

Wayland's Smithy 2 is similar in plan though not in size to the famous West Kennet tomb near Silbury Hill excavated in 1955–6 (S. Piggott 1962; Thomas and Whittle 1986). The mound, some 113 m in length, was com-

posed of an axial core of sarsen boulders covered by chalk rubble derived
from the two massive flanking ditches (Plate 2.2). At the wide (east) end lay
the burial chambers, five individual chambers arranged in two pairs with one
terminal chamber, all opening from a single central passage. The chambers
were built of large sarsen slabs and capstones with the spaces between the
verticals filled with drystone walling of limestone. The passage opened onto a
roughly semicircular courtyard, the end of the mound on either side being
retained by a facade of sarsen verticals with drystone walling in between.
When the primary phase of burial came to an end the chambers and passage
were filled to the roof, probably over a considerable period of time, with
chalk interspersed with layers of ash and occupation debris, the uppermost

Figure 2.12 Chambered long barrows. (Various sources)

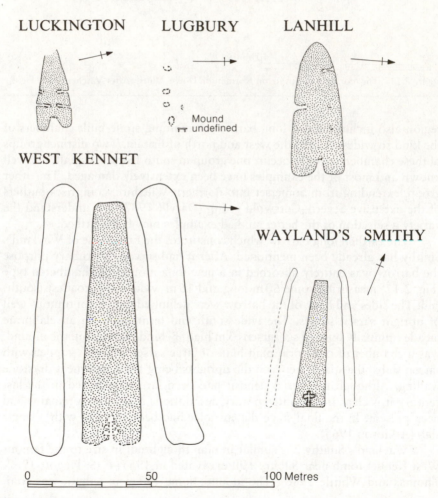

LUCKINGTON   LUGBURY   LANHILL

Mound
undefined

WEST KENNET

WAYLAND'S SMITHY

0   50   100 Metres

Plate 2.2 The West Kennet long barrow from the air. The chamber is at the east end (right-hand side). (Photo: Mick Aston)

filling incorporating material of Beaker date. The end came when the tomb was finally sealed by filling the courtyard with sarsen boulders and building a new facade of massive sarsen uprights across the front.

The barrow at Manton, Wilts., now destroyed, shared some of the characteristics of West Kennet, though on a far smaller scale. Its burial chamber was a single rectangular cell built of sarsen slabs. The main facade, represented only by its stone holes, was recessed to form a shallow courtyard to which the chamber opened. It too had been finally blocked with a new facade of sarsen uprights. Millbarrow was also chambered in some form.

One further monument of this class, Stoney Littleton in Somerset, deserves mention if only for its state of preservation. The tomb has three pairs of side chambers and one terminal chamber opening onto an axial passage, the whole set within a trapezoidal mound. The entrance had been blocked by a single massive slab.

The chambered tombs so far described all had functional chambers communicating to a central gallery which opened in the centre of the principal end facade. The second main type of chambered tomb found in the

Severn–Cotswold group had one or more isolated chambers set within the body of the mound communicating directly to the exterior through short passages. In the principal facade a blind portal had usually been set up with no chamber behind. Excavated examples include Lugbury, Luckington and Lanhill, all in northern Wiltshire (Fig. 2.12). In all probability this type is a later variant of those with axial chambers.

Of the west Dorset group of chambered tombs there is little to be said. The Grey Mare and Her Colts at Gorwell has a rectangular chamber opening straight from the orthostatic facade at the main end. The Hell Stone at Portisham is the remains of a chamber set in a barrow but over-restoration has made interpretation uncertain. About eight other possible megalithic chambers are known.

Before considering the nature of the burial rite practised at these monuments something must be said of chronology. The radiocarbon assessments for earthen long barrows and mortuary enclosures suggest the following approximate dates:

Lambourn, Berks.	4200 BC
Horslip, Wilts.	4000 BC
Fussell's Lodge, Wilts.	4000 BC
South Street, Wilts.	3500–3300 BC
Wor Barrow, Dorset	3400 BC
Nutbane, Hants.	3400 BC
Normanton, Wilts.	3300 BC
Beckhampton Road, Wilts.	3200 BC

The dates are sufficiently cohesive to suggest that earthen longbarrows were being built throughout the fourth millennium but probably began a little earlier. The date range is exactly coincident with that of the causewayed enclosures. The only date relevant to the construction of chambered tombs comes from Wayland Smithy where a sample from the turf-line above the earthen barrow but underlying the chambered tomb suggested a date of *c.* 3500 BC. However, the latest material from the chambers of West Kennet shows that some at least of the chambered tombs were being used as late as the earlier part of the second millennium.

The majority of the burial monuments excavated have produced human remains but only at sites excavated in recent years has the record been adequate enough to allow the nature of the burials to be assessed. Considerable variation exists between sites both in number of bodies represented and mode of disposal (most conveniently assessed by Thorpe 1984). At Nutbane the deposit consisted of the contracted skeletons of three adult males and one adolescent. At Fussell's Lodge on the other hand the stacked remains of between 53 and 57 individuals were recovered but some were represented by only a few bones. The burial deposit from Wayland's Smithy 1 was more complex. The central deposit contained representative parts of at least fourteen individuals and skull fragments of a further three or four. The state of the corpses differed. A preliminary study by the excavator suggested that some had been in almost complete articulation when deposited, several were sufficiently decomposed to have come apart at the waist while other corpses had rotted to such a degree that the limbs had separated. Some bones showed signs of having been gnawed by rodents while many of the smaller bones were missing. The inevitable conclusion must be that the bodies had been exposed for differing periods of time before being assembled in their final burial position. The absence of gnawing by carnivores suggests that exposure may have taken place on an elevated platform (Atkinson 1965: 127–30) or that these bodies were placed directly in the mortuary chamber.

A similar picture is provided by the chambered tombs. At West Kennet, bones representing some 40 individuals were found on the floors of the chambers variously disarticulated but sorted by age and sex: a single articulated body was found in the north-east chamber. At Lanhill one articulated and eight disarticulated skeletons were found in one chamber with eleven or twelve, all disarticulated, in another. Finally, in a number of investigations, excavators have recorded the careful stacking of bones of like kind. It was noted at Fussell's Lodge that skulls and long bones were separated in the stack, at Chute the excavator remarked upon the circular arrangement of skulls with long bones, possibly tied in bundles, in the centre, while at Wor Barrow, Pitt Rivers recorded how the limb bones had been laid out by the side of the skull.

We have dwelt long, perhaps overlong, on these details of death: it remains now to attempt to see how the disparate fragments can be built into some semblance of a belief system.

Let us begin with some figures. Of the 34 earthen long barrows in Wessex for which some data survive the total number of bodies recorded is in the order of 160+ (Ashbee 1970: 138–40). That is an average of say five bodies per barrow. Given that there are about 150 known barrows in the area then the total number of bodies buried in them is likely to have been 750 and allowing for a number of barrows having been destroyed we might increase the number to *c.* 1000. Even if the date range of the barrows is as little as 500 years the number of burials would average only two per year. Clearly this number is far too small if all the Neolithic dead were afforded burial in earthen long barrows (Atkinson 1968). In other words this mode of burial is likely to have been enjoyed by only a minority segment of the population.

Given this basic realization, then the suggestion that at least some of the causewayed enclosures were mortuary sites where the dead were exposed takes on a new significance. Indeed it seems likely that the majority of the population may well have been disposed of in this way. Colin Renfrew's demonstration (1973) that there is a close correspondence between the groups of long barrows, as defined by Ashbee, and the siting of the major causewayed enclosures, can more easily be understood if both are seen as complementary elements in a single system of death and deposition.

At its very simplest therefore we might suggest that the dead were divided into two groups, a division presumably based on status. The majority group were taken to the major causewayed enclosures for exposure, their bones eventually being used in the rituals which led to the periodic deposition of organic material in the ditches of the enclosures, either in the ditches as originally dug or in trenches or pits dug into the earlier filling. The minority group on the other hand were removed to special locations in the countryside where they were exposed, very probably on platforms raised above ground represented now by settings of four or more posts. The bodies, in varying states of decomposition, were removed to the adjacent mortuary house when the next member of the group died and needed to be exposed. This process continued until the set was considered to be complete at which time the construction of the barrow began.

An explanation in these terms would also fit well with the evidence from the chambered long barrows. It would require there to be an excarnation platform somewhere nearby, perhaps in the forecourt area, from which the disintegrating bodies were removed from time to time for deposition in the chambers. At the end of the process the tomb was sealed.

But even if we are correct in this general scenario it is evident that the rituals were more complex. The incomplete nature of the human remains must mean either that bones were removed during the process of exposure and deposition or that additional bones were brought in from elsewhere, possibilities which are not necessarily exclusive of each other.

The minority rite, involving exposure, collective deposition and burial beneath an earth mound is one most likely afforded to the higher rank members of society and implies a veneration of ancestors. Alternatively the differences could reflect the status of different lineages. The creation of the barrow was an act of monumentalization. The earthen long barrows completed the ritual but, if we are correct, the chambered long barrows began it. This may be nothing more than a chronological or regional variation within the same broad belief system.

The long barrows with no burials (if they are indeed a real category and not just an artefact of modern destructive agriculture) are a particularly interesting phenomenon since they appear to separate the desire for monument construction from the act of burial. The fact that a high percentage of these 'cenotaph' barrows are found close to causewayed enclosures (e.g. Windmill Hill and Hambledon) may be significant but defies simple explanation.

It has been suggested that long barrows were indicators of territory and demonstrations of the prowess of the community (Renfrew 1973). This may well be so but how the system worked in time is more difficult to understand. If each barrow represents a set of ancestors covering a span of say 10–50 years, what happened to succeeding generations? In other words it is possible that a single lineage was responsible for the construction of a number of barrows. Taking one extreme view it could be argued that the 20–30 barrows in each of the main distribution groups represent the successive monuments of a single dominant aristocracy over the 700–800 years covered by the Early and Middle Neolithic. The question is worth raising in that it shows the potential complexity of the subject, but is unlikely ever to be answered.

What changes over time, if any, can be detected in the burial record depend on the reliance one is prepared to place on the comparatively few radiocarbon dates at present available. It has been suggested that there may have been a move from barrows containing a large number of disarticulated bodies to those containing a smaller number of articulated bodies or no burials at all and that a greater diversity of barrow form, including oval or oblong barrows with ditches continuous around one end, appeared first in the later period (Thorpe 1984: 54–8). While this is a plausible sequence the available dating evidence does not appear to require it.

One further aspect of burial rite must be mentioned – the occurrence of a small number of complete bodies buried carefully and singly. The tradition appears to be a long established one. One body was discovered in a grave at Windmill Hill in a context pre-dating the enclosure and as we have seen burials of children were found in the bottoms of the ditches at Windmill Hill and Hambledon Hill. A few other graves have come to light from time to time. One found at Handley Hill, Dorset, was marked by a post. There is also some evidence to suggest that burials beneath round barrows may have begun as early as the Middle Neolithic (Kinnes 1979). One of the clearest, found at Mere in Wiltshire, was a cremation covered by an Early Neolithic bowl set beneath a low round barrow. These indications, that the single burial tradition so common in the Late Neolithic, may have begun earlier has interesting implications to which we shall return again below (pp. 112–15).

Towards the end of the Earlier Neolithic period the concept of the long mound seems to change and there emerge two distinct kinds of 'long monuments', bank barrows and the cursuses. Bank barrows may be defined as long parallel-sided mounds of spoil between flanking parallel ditches while cursus numents are long parallel-sided enclosures defined by ditches with slight internal banks. Bank barrows have sometimes been found in relation to cursus monuments usually close to the ends, as in the case of the Dorset cursus and the Long Bredy cursus (also in Dorset), a relationship which hints at a degree of contemporaneity and there is some evidence to suggest that some of them at least may have developed as extensions of existing long barrows (Bradley 1983: 16–17). At Maiden Castle the famous bank barrow, nearly 600 m in length, lay over the ditches of the silted up causewayed enclosure. Radiocarbon dates from the ditch of the barrow centre on 3000 BC. Without detailed excavation it is difficult to be more precise as to their date or function but one possible explanation would be to see these exceptionally long mounds as the ultimate manifestation of the long barrow phenomenon, quite possibly devoid of burial connotations, being little more than a symbolic statement of the community's prowess or its territorial claims.

Finally we must consider the cursus monuments. These enormously long ditched enclosures are found in three locations in Dorset, at Long Bredy to the west of Maiden Castle, on Cranborne Chase not far from Hambledon Hill, and on Salisbury Plain just north of Stonehenge. Radiocarbon dates for the Dorset cursus on Cranborne Chase suggest construction as early as 3300 BC (Bradley 1986) for the first phase. Here, the initial cursus was over 5 km long: at a subsequent date a further 4½ km was added to its north-eastern end. There is no firm evidence as to function: all that can safely be said is that they were ceremonial monuments of some kind probably dating to the end of the Earlier Neolithic cycle. The siting of the three groups each within 5–10 km of a causewayed enclosure strongly suggests that they were created under the same authority as was responsible for the enclosures. Though the dating evidence is as yet too imprecise it seems possible that the cursus monuments began to be constructed later than the causewayed enclosures and may in a sense have 'replaced' them. The association of cursus monuments with long barrows, especially in the case of the Dorset and Stonehenge cursuses, implies a degree of 'ritual' continuity and the fact that several display phases of extensions shows that the phenomenon was not of short-lived significance.

Space and Society

The distinct clusterings of long barrows on the chalkland of Wessex and the fact that each major cluster contains one large causewayed enclosure strongly suggest the existence of six major social agglomerations on this geomorphological zone. But the chalk-biased distribution of the major monuments should not be allowed to distort the picture too much. Concentrations of material exist elsewhere. On the Mendips, for example, a group of long barrows (without evidence of chambering) occurs together with ample evidence of the use of cave sites. The Jurassic ridge is similarly well endowed. The barrow cluster around Stoney Littleton forms one focus, another is most likely represented by a prolific settlement area on Ham Hill, while it is possible that South Cadbury formed a third. Nor should we forget the remarkable concentration of occupation centred on Christchurch Harbour on the Solent coast. Altogether, then, there are at least eleven clusters of artefacts and structures which might reasonably be considered to be the foci of socio-economic territories.

How society was organized at this stage is a matter of speculation. The most likely model would be to see the basic unit as the small-scale autonomous group supporting itself by exploiting a range of environments within its social territory and indulging in gift exchange with its neighbours – in anthropological terms this would be called a segmentary society. In such a model the monumental tomb would be seen as a symbol legitimizing the right to territory by demonstrating communal power and the prowess of ancestors. In simple societies of this kind survival depended on the ability of the group to act together in the common interest. Massive constructions like tombs and causewayed enclosures would have served to remind society of this fact and also to reduce the desire of the individual to engage in disruptive competition for personal gain (Hodder 1984).

One system, essential to the maintenance of order in society, was gift exchange – the offering of gifts not in anticipation of immediate repayment but in the expectation of eventual reciprocity. In this way social groups became enmeshed in a web of obligation. The distribution of polished stone axes is one visible manifestation of such a process. Axes made in Great Langdale in Cumbria seem to have been transported in some number, by some totally unknown social mechanism, to the Humber region whence they were distributed through exchange processes getting rarer and rarer towards the south and west. Axes produced in north Wales show a similar fall off as distance from source increases. That both types were found in Wessex indicates that the region was acquiring prestige goods from the north. More impressive, however, are contacts with the South West, which have already been mentioned in passing, especially the distribution of polished stone axes from the west of Cornwall. The pattern (Fig. 2.2; Cummins 1979: Fig. 4; I. F. Smith 1979) is particularly interesting in that it suggests bulk distribution by sea to a point on the Dorset coast, quite probably Poole or Christchurch Harbour, and to the Essex coast, from where secondary distribution took place. From the Dorset coast the axes were distributed, presumably along the Stour and Avon, into the heartland of Wessex. Other commodities brought from the South West along similar routes include whetstones and the gabbro-tempered pottery. The distribution pattern of the pottery, however, differs from that of the axes in that there seems to be a progressive fall off inland away from the South West and the south coast. This suggestion, that two totally different distribution mechanisms were in operation, is a reminder of the potential complexity of the situation.

In addition to these interregional contacts a wide range of more local products changed hands through systems of social exchange the most clearly exemplified being the appearance of oolitic-tempered pottery, probably deriving from the Stoney Littleton area, at the causewayed enclosures of the Avebury and Salisbury Plain West zones. Patterns of this kind are a reminder that societies needed to interact in order to redistribute surpluses and to acquire the rare raw materials necessary not only to maintain subsistence but also to enable them to reproduce their social systems (G. Barker and Webley 1978).

Against this background we must remember that warfare was endemic in prehistoric society: the need for individual and group defence was ever present the more so as population increased and with it pressure on accessible land. In the defensive earthworks on Hambledon Hill, with the phase of burning at the Stepleton enclosure and the body in the ditch with an arrow embedded in its chest, we can glimpse the pressures which were beginning to develop.

Chapter 3

The Rise of the Individual: 3000–1500 BC

The Later Neolithic and Early Bronze Age, covering the period from 3000 to 1500 BC, was a time of dramatic change. It is most simply characterized as a period of social transition between the comparatively egalitarian society of the earliest food-producing communities and a far more rigorously structured hierarchic society based on the control of resources. The contrast between the two extremes is most clearly demonstrated by burial rite. In the Earlier Neolithic the kin-group was all important. As we have seen a segment of the population was chosen for collective burial in impressive long mounds to symbolize the power and legitimacy of the community through a reverence for its ancestors. By the end of the period burial rite had completely changed: burials were now invariably individual though often the individuals were grouped in barrows or cemeteries. The dead person, either cremated or inhumed, was frequently provided with personal equipment appropriate to status and the burial was usually marked by a round barrow. This change from communal to individual burial symbolizes the deep-seated transformations that were taking place in society.

Behind this simple scenario lie highly complex patterns of evidence which only now, after a century and a half of intensive study, are beginning to come into focus. This is not the place to offer a detailed review of changing concepts of archaeological interpretation, entertaining though such a diversion would be. Suffice it to say that in two seminal works, one on the Neolithic and the other on the 'Beaker Culture', Stuart Piggott provided an elegant survey of the data presenting a series of cohesive models to contain the then current state of knowledge (Piggott 1954, 1963). From about 1960 the pace of study has increased dramatically. New large-scale excavations have greatly extended the database, aspects of material culture have undergone intensive analysis, while radiocarbon dating has begun to provide a broad chronological framework. Out of all this two new overviews have emerged. In 1977 Humphrey Case offered a considered account of the period when beakers were in use, while a few years later Alasdair Whittle reviewed the entire period of the Later Neolithic in two important papers (Whittle

1980; 1981). Whittle's new terminology has been adopted in this chapter. Subsequently a number of more theoretical studies have attempted to offer explanations for the perceived changes (e.g. Bradley and Gardiner 1984) and three major landscape studies have begun to show how complex the interrelation of the various settlement and burial elements really are (J. Richards 1990; Woodward 1991; J. Barrett, Bradley and Green 1991).

Before we begin to examine the rich variety of evidence presented by the Wessex landscape, something must be said of terminology. The period of the Later Neolithic can most simply be divided into three: the pre-Beaker phase (3100–2800/2700 BC), the Early Beaker phase (2800/2700–2100/2000 BC) and the Late Beaker-urn phase (2100/2000–1500 BC or later) (Whittle 1980; 1981).

This scheme is somewhat at variance with traditional terminologies which would see the appearance of implements and weapons of copper alloy *c.* 2700 BC (i.e. at the beginning of the Early Beaker phase of the Later Neolithic) as marking the beginning of the Early Bronze Age, which was followed some time about 1900 BC by the Middle Bronze Age. All observer-imposed terminologies have their disadvantages. Here we will accept the convention that by 'Later Neolithic' we encompass the traditional Late Neolithic–Early/Mid Bronze Age and will recognize three phases: pre-Beaker, Early Beaker and Late Beaker/urn.

Each phase has very distinctive characteristics. The pre-Beaker phase seems to have been a period of conservatism or even regression following the initial agricultural expansion of the Early and Middle Neolithic. Causewayed enclosures, cursuses and long barrows ceased to be constructed, though some continued to be used and there was a pause in the creation of communal works. All this changes some time about 2800–2700 BC when the Early Beaker period begins. This is the time when the Wessex landscape becomes monumentalized. Huge henge enclosures like Avebury, Durrington Walls and Stonehenge I are built together with the remarkable mound of Silbury Hill. The investment of communal labour in these undertakings was colossal. The period seems to end somewhere around 2000 BC with another phase of activity which can best be characterized as a time of *lithicization* when many of the existing monuments were further enhanced by rows, circles or horseshoe settings of standing stones.

The final phase, the Late Beaker/urn phase, was a period when no further modifications seem to have been made to the communal monuments but instead the process of individual burial, already established perhaps as early as the Earlier Neolithic period, came into its own, many of the burials now being provided with a range of grave goods demonstrating status. It was also a time when networks of long-distance exchange brought a range of exotic goods to Wessex to adorn the graves of the emerging aristocracy.

To divide the period into three in this way greatly over simplifies the complexity of the changes taking place while at the same time obscuring the strong thread of continuity throughout. No simple treatment can do justice to the intricate mesh of fast-changing systems so characteristic of this millennium and a half, the more so since there are still substantial gaps in our knowledge; nonetheless an attempt must be made to tease out the main threads.

The Changing Landscape

The Later Neolithic period coincides with the Sub Boreal or Zone VIIb of the pollen assemblage zones which, in broad terms, can be regarded as a warm episode with phases of changing wetness. Summer temperatures are thought to have been 2–3 °C higher than at present thus allowing crops to be grown at significantly higher altitudes. Recurring cycles of wetter weather occurred throughout, the first at about 3400 BC (Aaby 1976). The effects of these variations on Later Neolithic economic strategies are difficult to assess: such differences that can be detected are more likely to result from social and technological factors but the intensifying effects of climatic variation cannot be entirely ruled out. In more fragile environments, like the Somerset Levels, quite substantial changes to the natural environment can be seen. During the fourth millennium considerable tracts of the reed swamp had been transformed into fenwood with clumps of birch, alder and willow. By 2500 BC, however, the fenwood had almost disappeared as increased rainfall transformed the area into raised bog dominated by sphagnum moss; by the end of the second millennium flooding had become widespread. The growing hostility of the Levels environment had an effect on human exploitation. While the islands of Burtle and Westhay were joined by a substantial trackway, the Abbots Way, and there is evidence of clearance of regenerated woodland, links with the Polden Hills seem to have been only sporadically maintained.

Whilst the evidence from the Somerset Levels, suggesting a diminution in settlement activity, could be explained in terms of the effects of climatic change on a fragile local environment, it is possible that in many areas of the British Isles forest regeneration, following a phase of agricultural clearances, had begun by *c.* 3300 BC (Whittle 1978). In Wessex the picture is more complicated. Few pollen sequences have been obtained outside the Somerset Levels but at Rismore, Dorset, and Snelsmore, Berks., on the fringes of the chalk, and at Winnall Moors in the Itchen valley, well within the Hampshire chalk uplands, evidence of forest regeneration has been recorded (Waton 1982). On the chalk uplands, however, beneath the monuments of Durrington Walls, Marden, Avebury and Silbury Hill, built *c.* 2800/2700 BC, soil structure and molluscan evidence point to extensive areas of well-established grassland which must have existed for a long period (Evans 1971: 67) though the ditches of some long barrows suggest a woodland episode in certain locations (Evans 1990). The maintenance of such a landscape would have been impossible without regular grazing.

These changes, taken together, have been seen to imply, if not a period of regression at least a standstill in the exploitation of the land at the end of the Earlier Neolithic period (Whittle 1978: 37–40). They could well be explained, as Whittle suggests, in terms of the Earlier Neolithic population putting such stress on the available resources that the soil became depleted, production dropped and a decline in population ensued. In this scenario the fragile soils would have been abandoned to woodland while settlement retracted to areas of more durable soil, leaving the marginal tracts to regenerate to woodland or, in some instances, to be used as permanent pasture. Though the prime cause, in this model, is over exploitation, coupled with limited technological competence, the regression, once in motion, could well have been accelerated by the onset of a cycle of wetter weather (A. G. Smith et al. 1981, 206).

The pre-Beaker phase is, then, best characterized as a time of standstill in agricultural colonization but it must also have been a time of readjustment when the economic strategies of the Earlier Neolithic period were being drastically modified. The success of this process, which lasted for only 500 years (*c.* 3300–2800 BC), is vividly demonstrated by the ability of the Wessex communities to engage in a new round of monument building creating Silbury Hill, Stonehenge I, Avebury, Durrington Walls and others, each one of which required an enormous input of manpower. We shall return to this question again below.

The evidence for maintained grassland, found beneath the monuments of Silbury, Durrington Walls and Marden, demonstrates that by *c.* 2800 BC areas of open landscape had been created on the chalk uplands. That this kind of environment was, or at least became, more widespread is suggested by the very large numbers of round barrows which spread over the downs during the course of the second millennium. Beneath a number of excavated examples fossil turf-lines have been identified containing mollusca indicative of open grassland. The geographical spread, which includes Earl's Farm Down, Amesbury, Hemp Knoll near Avebury and Roughridge Hill near Bishops Canning, all in Wiltshire, Arreton Down on the Isle of Wight, and Farncombe Down, Berks., (Evans 1972), gives some hint of just how extensive these tracts of pasture had become. Whilst it could be argued that monuments and barrows would tend to be built in open areas, and therefore the sample is biased, the sheer number of the funerary and ritual monuments in existence by the middle of the second millennium BC is sufficient to demonstrate the extent of the open grassland.

On other soils, too, there is clear evidence for deforestation by the third millennium. This is particularly true of the sandy soils of the New Forest where from beneath barrows and other earthworks pollen analysis has shown that there was much open land in the process of succeeding to heath or to hazel scrub (Dimbleby 1962; Tubbs and Dimbleby 1965). The evidence at present available, therefore, suggests that the environment of Wessex during the Later Neolithic was considerably varied. While large areas of the chalk uplands were becoming open grassland and heaths had already developed on some of the lighter sandy soils of the Hampshire basin, on the denser soils fringing the chalk, and even in some of the valleys, there are signs of forest regeneration. The massive timbers used in the West Kennet Farm monument (below, p. 108) show that tracts of mature woodland must have been at hand. These varied patterns were largely the result of human activity: they were created and maintained by economic strategies. Only in the Somerset Levels is it possible to recognize environmental change due wholly to natural phenomena.

The Food-Producing Economy

Our understanding of Later Neolithic farming regimes has changed quite radically in the last few years but such is the paucity of reliable data that further changes are only to be expected.

The debate has centred around the relative importance of stock rearing and grain production. Until comparatively recently the only evidence for cereal cultivation in the Later Neolithic came from grain impressions on beakers and because most of these were barley it became conventional to regard the period as one dominated by barley cultivation. Since, however, the beaker is a very specialized form of pot, which could have been made away from the normal domestic site, too much reliance should not be put on the limited database even though barley is particularly well suited to the light downland soils (Dennell 1976: 17). The absence of cereal impressions on Grooved Ware pottery, together with evidence for large expanses of upland pasture, for a while encouraged the general belief that the Later Neolithic economy was predominantly pastoral, the limited barley crop being used largely for the production of beer (Fleming 1971).

However, the advent of flotation techniques has added a new tier of data, though samples are still few (Jones 1980; Moffett, Robinson and Straker 1989). Grains have been recovered from three Later Neolithic sites in Wessex. Spelt wheat was identified at Kings Barrow Ridge, Wilts., and wheat of uncertain species at Down Farm, Dorset, but both were represented by only one grain. At Coneybury, Wilts., on the other hand, the considerable quantity of identifiable grains was entirely of barley of both the hulled and

Table 3.1   Percentages of domesticated animals from selected sites

		Pig	Ox	Sheep/goat	Horse	No. identified
c. 2700–*c.* 2000 BC						
Durrington Walls	Grooved Ware, pre henge	61	35	3.5	0.3	603
	Grooved Ware, henge	68	29	2	1	8500
	Grooved Ware, pits	67	33	1	0	309
Marden	Grooved Ware, henge	42	42	11	5	320
Mount Pleasant	Grooved Ware, henge	55	26	16	3	630
c. 2000–*c.* 1800 BC						
Windmill Hill	Causewayed enclosure, late occupation	21	68	11	0	87
Mount Pleasant	Henge, late occupation	39	36	25	0	1946
Snail Down	Round barrows	10	47	38	5	480

Source: Data after Grigson 1981

naked varieties. At Down Farm barley grains greatly outnumbered wheat. The evidence then, while slight, tends to support the long-held view that barley was the dominant crop in the Later Neolithic.

Traces of ploughing associated with beaker pottery have been identified at Cherhill and South Street in north Wiltshire (Evans and Smith 1983: 108–9), and beneath the barrow on Earl's Farm Down near Amesbury (Christie 1967: 347) but the extent of arable land at this time is impossible to estimate.

Our knowledge of animal husbandry is based on a few reasonably sized assemblages of bone. The simple statistics may be briefly given (Table 3.1).

Taken at their face value the figures from the Early Beaker phase sites imply the numerical dominance of pig though in terms of meat yield the cattle would have provided a greater bulk. By comparison the assemblages from the Late Beaker phase indicate that, at least in some areas, cattle had regained their dominant role. There are, however, problems in dealing with this data set not least that the sites are too few and are unrepresentative of settlements as a whole. In the Early Beaker phase all are large ceremonial monuments and it could therefore be argued that the assemblages were the result of ritual activity, possibly feasting, and the percentages are thus unrepresentative of normal domestic consumption. This may be so but it is worth pointing out that the pre-henge occupation at Durrington Walls, associated with Grooved Ware, which could have been of a secular nature, showed similar high percentages of pig (Grigson 1982: 306–7). If, then, we are prepared to accept the limited data so far available as fairly representative of the husbandry regimes, the inescapable conclusion is that one result of the economic re-organization which took place in the pre-Beaker phase was that swine herding became far more central to the food-producing strategy and remained so through the Early Beaker phase. By the Late Beaker phase a more mixed herding regime had been introduced with cattle once more the principal domesticate but with sheep/goats gaining in importance.

This interpretation is not at all unreasonable when seen against the evidence for forest regeneration after the Earlier Neolithic. Pig and cattle are woodland animals: moreover the pig would have been of particular value in clearing abandoned fields of scrub and bracken (Grigson 1982: 308–9). Thus a pig-dominated husbandry could be seen as one of the strategic readjustments developed in the pre-Beaker phase to combat the effects of earlier over-exploitation. As the new system asserted itself, and more land was again opened up, so a more balanced pattern of husbandry could be gradually introduced.

The importance of the woodland environment to the Later Neolithic economy is indicated in other ways. The collection of hazel-nuts is evidenced at several sites, especially Kings Barrow Ridge. Crab apple, sloe and haw-thorn also occur in domestic debris on other Wessex sites of the period (Moffett, Robinson and Straker 1989: Table 1). Sparse though it is, the available evidence is a reminder that such a valuable food resource would have been fully exploited. It has also been suggested that the characteristic transverse arrow head of the Later Neolithic period, with its sharp chisel-like cutting edge, was specifically developed for the hunt, the wide blade being designed to cut the muscle bands of the prey thus weakening them for the kill. The universal adoption of this type of arrow could be taken as another indication of the significance of the forest resource. Actual evidence for wild game is not prolific but aurochs (wild cattle), brown bear, red deer, roe deer are all attested together with fur-bearing animals, such as fox, badger, pine marten and beaver. Among the birds identified duck and woodcock would have made acceptable eating.

The totality of the evidence is therefore consistent with the view that following the pioneering opening up of the landscape in the Earlier Neolithic there was a period of regression or standstill during which the food-producing strategy changed from one of intensive production to one of extensive exploitation. The forest resource was fully used, the pig became the dominant domesticate and arable production on the thin downland soils was focused upon barley. By c. 2000 BC the regression to forest had been reversed. Large areas of pasture had been created allowing higher percentages of cattle and sheep to be reared. Some measure of the success of the food-producing systems introduced in the pre-Beaker phase can be seen in society's ability to create huge monumental earthworks. An alternative view would be to suggest some causative link between clearance and the social desire to create monuments but here we are already beyond the reasonable limit of archaeological inference.

Craft and Production

The most outstanding characteristic of the material culture of the Later
Neolithic period is its diversity. At the beginning the range of materials
available was restricted and types of artefact were limited in their variety, but
by the end many new materials were to be had including gold, amber, jet,
faience and copper alloys, and craft skills had developed to a high pitch of
competence to serve the growing demands of society. The change is a reflection of many processes but most important is the way in which items were
consumed in increasingly complex social patterns. To put it at its simplest, at
the beginning of the period comparatively few exotic materials were available: those that were, in particular the polished stone axes, were used in
social exchanges at community level. By the end of the period an enormous
range of materials had been introduced to enhance and demonstrate the
prestige of individuals. While it could be argued that the trajectory of change
in society created the demand for a greater variety of prestige goods, system
changes are seldom as simple as that. External demands for raw materials
may well have created conditions which influenced change. These matters
will be returned to later.

Pottery

Throughout most of the Later Neolithic period a complex series of decorated
pottery styles, collectively known as Peterborough ware (Fig. 3.1), were
widely used in Wessex (I. F. Smith 1974: 111–12). The tradition, still very
poorly understood, began in the Earlier Neolithic with cord-impressed vessels
of the Ebbsfleet tradition (dating as early as *c*. 3400 BC). Slightly later, and
certainly by the end of the fourth millennium, a more elaborately decorated
style had emerged, the decoration involving complex impressions made by
bird bones and finger nails, often arranged in zones. This style is known as
Mortlake ware. Later, soon after the middle of the third millennium BC, two
developments can be recognized. The first is the appearance of Fengate ware,
essentially a continuation of the highly decorated Neolithic tradition of
domestic pottery but with narrow flat bases. In parallel with this there emerge
collared urns of the first series which are thought to have developed from the
indigenous Mortlake/Fengate tradition influenced by beakers. This complex
of changing styles represents a ceramic folk-tradition deeply rooted in the
Earlier Neolithic period and with a widespread distribution over much of
England.

82

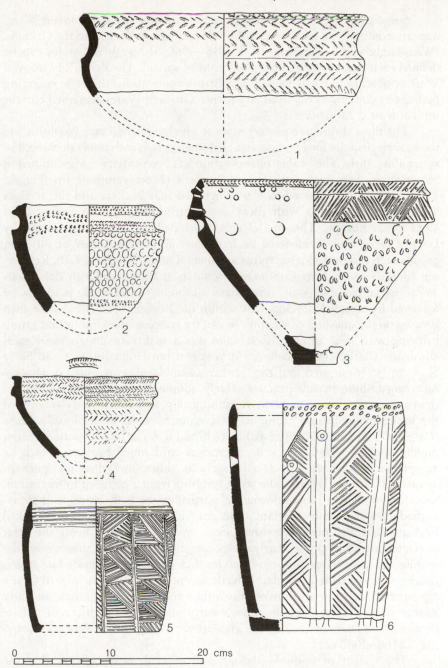

Figure 3.1 Later Neolithic pottery. 1 Ebbsfleet ware, 2 Mortlake ware, 3 and 4 Fengate ware, 5 and 6 Grooved ware. 1–4 from West Kennet, 5 from Durrington Walls and 6 from Wilsford. (After S. Piggott 1973b: Fig. 12)

Some time *c.* 2900 BC a new pottery style, known as Grooved Ware, appears eventually to become distributed widely from Wessex to the Orkneys (Wainwright and Longworth 1971: 235–306). Although sub-styles can be defined each has a considerable geographical spread. The origin of Grooved Ware is obscure but it is evidently a British innovation, the style emerging perhaps by copying in clay basketry forms. Grooved Wares remained current until at least *c.* 2100 BC.

The most distinctive pottery style to emerge in the Later Neolithic are the beakers, usually finely made, flat bottomed vessels intricately decorated in zones and panels. The beaker phenomenon has been extensively examined in recent years, beginning with Stuart Piggott's classic summing up (Piggott 1963) written at a time when it was believed that beakers and the artefact assemblages associated with them were introduced by immigrants from Continental Europe. This model was developed in considerable detail by David Clarke who divided the beaker material into a number of different groups each assigned to a separate Continental origin (Clarke 1970). Reviewing Clarke's work, two Continental scholars (Lanting and van der Waals 1972) suggested that only one phase of immigration took place to be followed by regional development within the British Isles. The debate then focused on the question of whether or not the concept of an immigrant group bringing with it a cultural assemblage was a reality or an archaeological construct. Clarke (1976) believed it was real but Colin Burgess and Steve Shennan (1976) argued that the 'beaker assemblage' represented a package reflecting fashion in cult practice widely adopted for social reasons rather than a manifestation of an intrusive ethnic group. In a considered overview of the beaker phenomenon Humphrey Case put forward a simplified scheme (Case 1977) in which he suggested three broad *styles* of beaker pottery, early, middle and late. The early style comprises cord-zoned beakers, which he accepts may have been introduced largely by 'diffusion by fashion', perhaps as early as 2700 BC. The middle style, resulting from a phase of immigration, includes a range of beaker forms, in particular the bell, barrel and short-necked beakers, while the late style contains the distinctive long-necked beakers. Case also proposed three *phases* each of the *styles* being the most characteristic of its phase. Early styles can, however, occur throughout the middle and late phases and middle styles may be found alongside late styles. In a more recent review Alasdair Whittle accepts the main principles of Case's scheme but finds it more convenient to refer to two beaker phases, an Early Beaker phase, which includes Case's early and middle styles, and a Late Beaker phase characterized by the appearance of the Late Beaker style starting *c.* 2100–2000 BC.

The weight of opinion, though still divided, now believes that the beaker phenomenon in Britain is essentially the result of the adoption by an indigenous population of exotic cultural practices which spread as exchange systems with the Continent developed. In other words it was a social phenomenon and not the result of large-scale immigration. Yet there must remain the possibility that some movement of population did take place. After all ideas cannot move without people to carry them. The question, then, is one of scale. Were the contacts with the Continent few and transient or did they involve the actual settlement of individuals? It is not within the competence of the archaeological record to decide.

Flint and stone industries

The production and exchange of polished stone axes continued throughout the Later Neolithic period until the end of the Early Beaker phase (I.F. Smith 1979), the main production centres being, as before, located in Cornwall, the Lake District and north Wales. But from *c.* 2600 BC a new range of polished stone implements with shaft-holes came into existence. These are variously classified according to shape as battle axes, axe hammers, mace heads, shaft-hole adzes and pebble hammers (F. Roe 1979). Insofar as dating evidence is available the mace heads tend to be earliest, beginning around 2600 BC thus overlapping the use of simple stone axes. Battle axes, shaft-hole adzes and axe hammers concentrate in the Late Beaker phase (I. F. Smith 1979: 15–16). The Wessex shaft-hole implements derive from a number of sources. In addition to Cornwall, north Wales and the Lake District, items have been identified from quarries in south-west Wales, the Welsh Marches and the Midlands.

Flint continued to be widely used not only for the transverse arrow heads mentioned above but also for elegant barbed and tanged arrow heads characterizing the Beaker phases and thin convex scrapers which were frequently struck from prepared cores. To what extent the flint was locally derived is difficult to say but flint mines dating to the end of the Earlier or beginning of the Later Neolithic are known on Easton Down, Wilts., where at least 90 shafts have been identified covering an area of 17 ha. The excavated shafts show that the miners were intent on reaching a seam of high quality flint nodules about 3 m below the surface. Debris found nearby derived largely from the production of chipped and polished axes (Stone 1933). Another, apparently abortive, attempt to mine flint was located at Durrington.

Other materials for everyday use

A wide range of organic materials such as wood, leather, wool and bone would also have been in use. Red deer antler was commonly employed as wedges and rakes for digging ditches and splinters of bone were adapted to make a variety of pins and toggles for dress as well as punches and awls for more functional purposes. Little is known of the use of other organic materials but it must have been extensive. Leather no doubt provided most clothing needs but woollen fabrics have been recognized in the rich late burials at Bush Barrow and Manton. There is, however, no reason to assume that wool was the sole preserve of the aristocracy.

Artefacts of copper and bronze became widespread in Wessex in the Late Beaker phase. The earliest group comprised tanged and rivet-tanged knives, double-pointed awls, thick butted flat axes and, more rarely, dress pins made in forms and from alloys distributed from Ireland to north-western Europe. In addition to items of copper, an impressive range of other artefacts, making up the array of personal goods accompanying the dead, have been recovered from burials, manufactured from a variety of materials including jet, amber, faience and gold. The Beaker burial from Chilbolton Down, Hants. (Russel 1990) provides an interesting indication of the luxury that could accrue around an individual some time about 2100 BC. Here the body, buried in a mortuary chamber set beneath a round barrow, was provided with a beaker, an antler spatula, two pairs of gold earrings, a gold tubular bead, 55 stone beads and a copper dagger. Later, as the millennium progresses, even richer burials begin to appear but these will more appropriately be discussed in a later section (pp. 120–7).

Settlement

If we exclude for a moment the monumental structures, direct evidence of settlement is sparse and no site has been excavated on even a barely adequate scale, yet a surprisingly large number of settlement remains have been located by chance. At both Durrington Walls and Mount Pleasant phases of settlement, dating respectively to c. 3100 and c. 2700 BC, were found beneath the banks of the later henge enclosures while at Avebury, Grooved Ware was found in a similar position. In the whole of Wessex about 25 discoveries of Grooved Ware have been made in contexts other than those associated with the use of large ritual monuments. Some were sherds incorporated in later barrow mounds, therefore presumably deriving from pre-barrow occupation in the vicinity, others came from isolated pits or groups of pits. Two sites have produced additional evidence. At Cherhill in north Wiltshire a sequence of occupation was uncovered. An Earlier Neolithic phase, dating to c. 3300 BC, was followed by a dense Later Neolithic occupation producing sherds of Peterborough ware and traces of flint flaking. This was followed by a period of ploughing within ditched boundaries associated with material of the Late Beaker phase. Although only a small area was explored it is clear that occupation, while not necessarily continuous, was long lived (Evans and Smith 1983). At Poundbury in Dorset some thirteen pits were excavated, many of them containing occupation material including Grooved Ware and debris from flint-working. It seems probable that some of the larger and more irregular pits were quarries designed to reach a layer of tabular flints (C. S. Green 1987, 22).

Two settlements of the Beaker phase have been excavated on a reasonable scale. At Easton Down, Wilts. (Fig. 3.2), close to the flint mines, a settlement area was exposed comprising ten irregular scoops in the chalk, averaging 2 by 3 m, each surrounded by stake-holes. All of the hollows contained a layer of occupation debris and one also had a small pit filled with ash dug through its floor (Stone 1933). The evidence is sufficient to suggest that the features recovered were probably walled and roofed and may well have served as houses. Another occupation site was partly excavated at Downton in Wiltshire. Here the structural evidence consisted of a series of shallow depressions, smaller than those at Easton Down, interspersed with a scatter of post-holes. Occupation debris produced pottery in the Peterborough tradition as well as beaker sherds (Rahtz 1962). The Downton settlement is in a valley location reminding us that situations of this kind, seldom explored archaeologically, may well have been favoured for early settlements.

Beaker occupation has also been discovered in a well-stratified sequence of sands and other deposits on the side of Brean Down in Somerset (Bell 1990). The lowest level, a buried soil, produced sherds and flints which were buried by blown sand in about the nineteenth century BC. Continued cultivation, upslope, led to deposition of a further layer of soil above the sand around an oval stone-built structure producing sherds of biconical urns. This level was in turn sealed by more blown sand. It would seem, therefore, that Brean Down, probably at this time an island at high tide, was continuously occupied during the second millennium BC by a small farming community.

The slightness of the features found at Easton Down and Downton hints at the reason why Later Neolithic sites are not better known: there is little to show up as earthworks or as crop marks on aerial photographs and ploughing in the later prehistoric or more recent period could have destroyed all trace. The fugitive nature of these sites is well demonstrated by a recent programme of field-work on the Marlborough Downs where two out of three of the Middle to Late Bronze Age settlements chosen for excavation have produced beaker assemblages, in one case associated with a pit (Gingell 1980). The implication would seem to be that here (and why not elsewhere in Wessex?) the settlements of Bronze Age date often chose sites which had already been inhabited. Similar evidence from beneath a Bronze Age en-

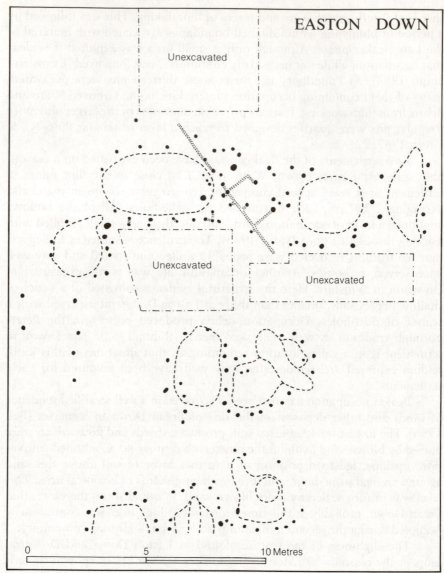

EASTON DOWN

Unexcavated

Unexcavated

Unexcavated

0   5   10 Metres

Figure 3.2   Late Neolithic settlement on Easton Down, Wilts. (After Stone 1933: Plate IX)

closure south of Badbury Rings in Dorset (Gingell 1987) shows that the phenomenon was geographically widespread. Elsewhere, for example at Preshute Down and Rockley Down in north Wilts., extensive field-work has located a number of scatters of beaker pottery presumably representing ploughed out settlements (Meyrick 1973). In summary, the Later Neolithic period can no longer be characterized as one of transient nomadism. The evidence now available for both settlement and agriculture hints not only at settled communities but also at a substantial population.

Ceremonial Monuments

The Later Neolithic was the time when the landscape of Wessex was transformed by ceremonial monuments created in a new tradition. The variety is considerable but it is at present customary to divide them into three categories:

1 henges, henge enclosures and hengiform monuments
2 stone circles and alignments
3 large circular mounds (of which Silbury Hill is the prime example).

The classification, though convenient, should not be allowed to obscure the wide variation within each of these observer-imposed categories (Clare 1986, 1987).

The ceremonial monuments of Wessex are, without exaggeration, the most remarkable manifestation of human belief and endeavour to be seen in prehistoric Europe. Each one represents a high degree of organizational skill commanding community enterprise, whether voluntary or coerced. Their meaning is beyond recovery: at best we can but describe certain aspects of their form, recognize regularities in their relationships and development sequences and offer tentative explanations conditioned by our limited awareness of human behaviour. How close our interpretations come to the truth we will never know.

Ceremonial monuments cluster together at comparatively few well-defined locations (Fig. 3.3) which, for convenience, we can name after one or more of the principal monuments in each:

1 the Mount Pleasant group, Dorset
2 the Knowlton group, Dorset
3 the Durrington/Stonehenge group, Wilts.
4 the Marden group, Wilts.
5 the Avebury/Silbury group, Wilts.
6 the Mendip group, Somerset.

Recent work, particularly in the vicinity of Mount Pleasant and Avebury, has emphasized that the picture is far more complex than the standing monuments alone imply, offering a timely warning that our vision of the ritual

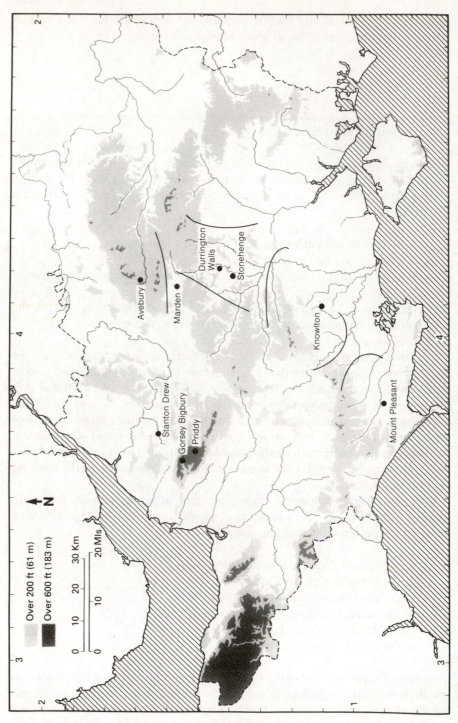

landscape may be distorted by the few upstanding sites. While this proviso must always be borne in mind, the clustering of ritual sites within circum- scribed landscapes is a most striking feature of the archaeological record as it is at present known. To give some idea of the complexity of the situation we must consider each of the main clusters in turn before standing back to see what general patterns can be discerned.

The Mount Pleasant group

The ridge of chalkland between the river Frome and South Winterbourne is densely packed with Neolithic monuments (Fig. 3.4). There are two distinct foci: in the Earlier Neolithic period the causewayed camp of Maiden Castle and the long mound which developed slightly later appears to have been the centre of activity but already on the north side of the ridge pits with Hembury ware at Flagstones House (Woodward 1988: 269) and a possible long barrow at Arlington dated to *c*. 3100 BC demonstrate earlier activity over- looking the river Frome.

Later Neolithic ritual activity at this northern focus seems to begin just before 2700 BC with the construction of a massive timber monument dis- covered at Greyhound Yard, Dorchester (Woodward, Davies and Graham 1984). It was composed of posts roughly a metre in diameter set in individual post pits a metre apart. The exact form of the monument is obscure and it is not yet clear whether it is an enclosure or a sinuous linear structure. A series of radiocarbon assessments centring on 2700 BC indicates the likely date of construction and the internal stratigraphy suggests abandonment in the Early Bronze Age after which the area became arable land.

Several contemporary monuments are known in the immediate vicinity. At Flagstones House a circular setting of discontinuous quarry ditches about 100 m in diameter enclosed a centrally placed ring ditch which in turn sur- rounded a central grave pit. The enclosure ditch produced dates centring around *c*. 3000 BC while the central burial of a crouched adult, which was covered by a large sarsen boulder, was a millennium later. The outer ditch, which was rapidly refilled with chalk rubble, bore a remarkable array of engravings on the walls. Infant burials were found on the ditch bottom and within the fill (Woodward 1988).

The Flagstones monument was sited on the crest of the ridge not far from the Conquer Barrow at Mount Pleasant, a substantial mound sur-

Figure 3.3 Distribution of the principal henge monuments with their hypothetical territories indicated

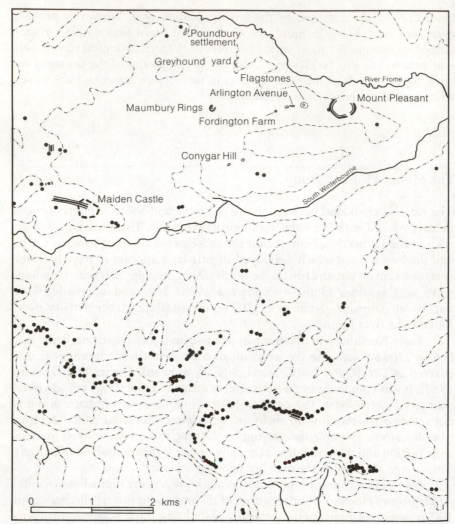

Figure 3.4 Neolithic monuments (named) and the barrow cemetery of the South Dorset Ridge Way

rounded by a discontinuous quarry ditch approximately 85 m in diameter (Wainwright 1979b: 65–8). The ditch produced a single radiocarbon assessment of *c*. 2700 BC which suggests that both the Flagstones barrow (if indeed the burial was once covered by a mound) and the Conquer Barrow were broadly contemporary.

The hill of Mount Pleasant supports a second structure which deserves to be considered in this context. About 80 m to the north east of the Conquer Barrow a massive circular timber building enclosed by a penannular ditch (known as site IV) was excavated (Wainwright 1979b: 9–34). It comprised five concentric circles of posts, the maximum diameter being 39 m (Fig. 3.5). Structures of this kind are, as we shall see, a recurring feature of Later Neolithic ritual monuments though their interpretation as roofed buildings, rather than simply as rings of posts, is a matter of debate. The exact date of the Mount Pleasant building is uncertain, but the primary filling of the surrounding ditch (which could be contemporary or slightly later) has produced radiocarbon assessments focusing on 2500 BC.

The fourth monument which must here be mentioned is Maumbury

Figure 3.5 Comparative plans of the large timber buildings of the Late Neolithic. (After Wainwright 1979b: Fig 90)

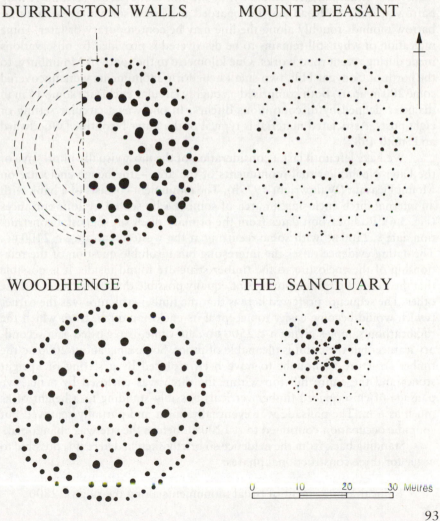

DURRINGTON WALLS

MOUNT PLEASANT

WOODHENGE

THE SANCTUARY

Rings, later incorporated in the Roman amphitheatre of Dorchester (Bradley 1976). The limited excavation carried out at the beginning of the century disclosed a roughly circular setting of deep shafts, probably about 45 in all, each about 10–11 m deep set in the base of a continuous ditch, describing a circle of 52 m diameter. Around the outside was a bank surviving to a height of 3 m. The shafts contained deposits of artefacts and bone which seem to have been deliberately covered with backfilled chalk. Two radiocarbon assessments suggest a date of around 2500 BC for construction and primary use.

These four monuments, stretching along the ridge from Mount Pleasant to Maumbury, together with the huge Greyhound Yard monument, all dating to *c.* 2700–2500 BC, give some idea of the variety of structures which can make up a ritual landscape. That they are not alone seems certain. A long barrow at Alington Road may be regarded as a precursor while several other barrow mounds roughly along the line may be contemporary or later. Some indication of what still remains to be discovered is provided by observations made during recent road works. One kilometre to the south of Maumbury, to the north of Conygar Hill, two small hengiform monuments were uncovered some 200 m apart. Both comprised a roughly circular enclosure some 15 m in diameter defined by discontinuous ditches. In one was a circular setting of eight posts. Associated material is typical of the Later Neolithic (Woodward and Smith 1987).

We have left until last a consideration of the most visually impressive of the Later Neolithic ritual monuments of the area – the henge enclosure on Mount Pleasant (Wainwright 1979b). The monument consists of a bank with an internal ditch enclosing an area of some 4.6 ha served by four entrances (Fig. 3.6). Radiocarbon dates from the primary ditch silt suggest a construction date *c.* 2500 BC with some recutting at the western entrance *c.* 2100 BC. The dating evidence raises the interesting but insoluble question of the relationship of the enclosure to the timber structure found inside. It is possible that the two were contemporary but equally possible that either preceded the other. The sequence preferred here is that the timber structure was the earlier (which would become easier to accept if its enclosing ditch, from which the radiocarbon samples giving a *c.* 2500 BC date came, is regarded as a secondary feature) but the point is incapable of proof. Some time about 2000 BC the timber structure is thought to have been replaced by a setting of upright stones and the entire hill top within the ditch was enclosed by a massive palisade of close-spaced timber verticals possibly standing to a height of as much as 6 m. The palisade was eventually burnt and partially removed but sporadic occupation continued to *c.* 1200 BC before the site was abandoned.

Standing back from the evidence so briefly sketched here it is possible to argue for three constructional phases:

1 linear arrangement of ritual monuments along the ridge *c.* 2700

DURRINGTON WALLS, WILTSHIRE

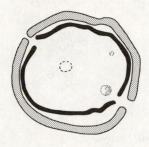

AVEBURY, WILTSHIRE

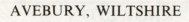

MOUNT PLEASANT, DORSET

MARDEN, WILTSHIRE

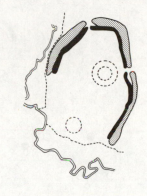

KNOWLTON, SOUTH CIRCLE

0   500 Metres

Figure 3.6 The large henges of Wessex. (After Wainwright 1979b: Fig. 95, with additions)

2 construction of the henge enclosure around one of the existing timber structures *c.* 2500

3 replacement of the timber structure with a stone setting *c.* 2000 and the enclosure of the hill top with a massive palisade.

It must, however, be admitted that the separation of phases 1 and 2 though possible is not based on strong evidence. We shall see to what extent this pattern is repeated elsewhere.

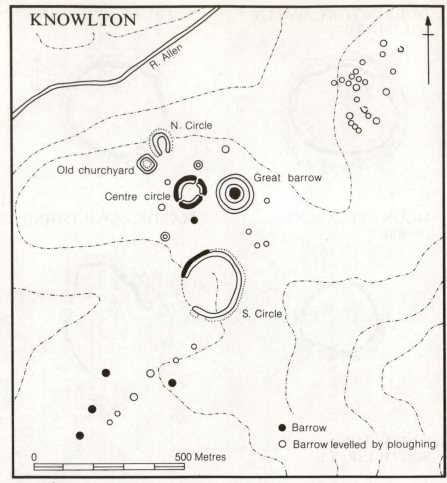

KNOWLTON

R. Allen

N. Circle

Old churchyard

Centre circle

Great barrow

S. Circle

● Barrow
○ Barrow levelled by ploughing

0   500 Metres

Figure 3.7 The Late Neolithic monuments and Bronze Age barrows in the vicinity of Knowlton, Dorset. (After *RCHM(E)* Dorset V, 114)

The Knowlton group

In contrast to the ritual monuments of the Mount Pleasant group those of Knowlton are little known apart from their physical appearance and evidence derived from aerial photographs (Fig. 3.7 and Plate 3.1). The group consists of four 'henge monuments' and a massive barrow sited close together on a spur overlooking the river Allen. The largest of the 'henges' is an enclosure some 250 m across defined by a bank with an internal ditch. To the north is a

Plate 3.1 The Knowlton Circles, Dorset. (Photo: RCHM(E))

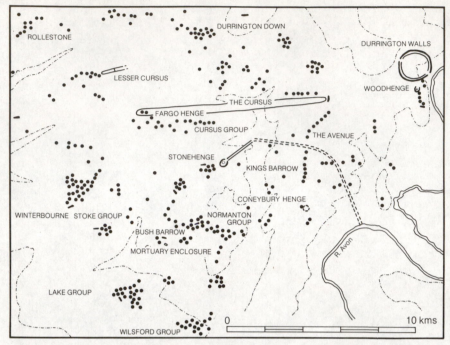

Figure 3.8   Late Neolithic and Bronze Age monuments of the Stonehenge region

smaller 'henge' – the central circle – roughly 115 m across. North west of this are two monuments known only from air photographs, one in the form of a horseshoe-shaped bank with an internal ditch, the other smaller and squarer in plan. Close to the central circle is a massive barrow, the largest in Dorset, some 7 m high and 45 m in diameter surrounded by two concentric ditches the outer measuring 12 m wide and nearly 2 m deep. The whole complex lies in the centre of a linear group of more than forty barrows (S. Piggott and C. M. Piggott 1939: 152–5).

Brief description does scant justice to a remarkable group of monuments but without excavation it is unlikely that much more can be learnt of them.

The Durrington/Stonehenge group

The complex of monuments which makes up this group comprises three separate groups of structures, the Stonehenge Cursus which we have already considered (p. 72), the Durrington Walls and Woodhenge group and Stonehenge itself together with its avenue (Figs 3.8–3.10).

The monuments associated with Durrington Walls are comparatively well known as the result of a series of excavations (Cunnington 1929; Stone, Piggott and Booth 1954; Wainwright and Longworth 1971) from which it is evident that Later Neolithic activity in the area was intense (Fig. 3.9). Three substantial timber buildings have been uncovered. The first to be found, that of Woodhenge (Figs. 3.10 and 3.5), consists of six roughly concentric settings of posts the outer circle measuring *c.* 43 by 40 m comparable in size to the timber buildings found inside the enclosure at Mount Pleasant. The Woodhenge structure was enclosed by a ditch with an external bank leaving only

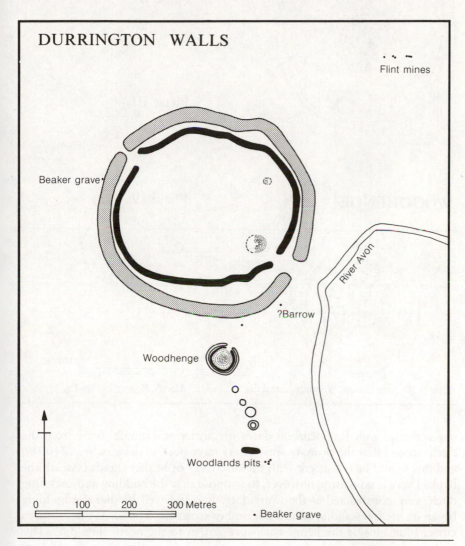

Figure 3.9 The Late Neolithic monuments of the Durrington Walls group. (After Wainwright and Longworth 1971: Fig. 2)

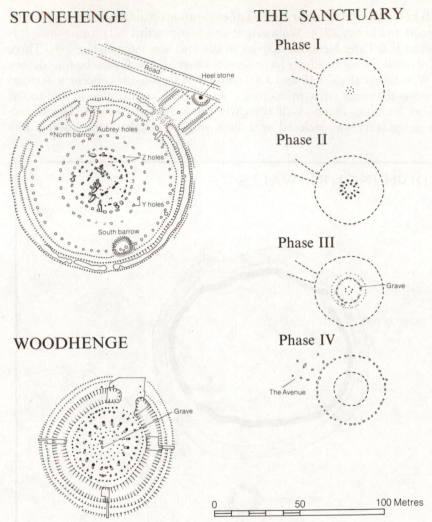

Figure 3.10 Stonehenge, Woodhenge and the Sanctuary. (After S. Piggott 1973b: Fig. 8)

one entrance gap. Radiocarbon dates for antler and animal bone from the ditch suggest that the primary silting may have been underway by *c.* 2100 BC and this would be consistent with the discovery of beaker sherds beneath the bank. There is no reason, however, to suppose that the building and enclosing ditch were constructed at the same date. It could well be that the building began its life freestanding as did the timber structure, known as the southern circle, found inside the henge enclosure 250 m to the north (Fig. 3.5). This building, measuring 38 m in diameter, was slightly smaller than Woodhenge but also comprised six concentric circles of timber. It had been preceded by a simpler structure based on four circles. Radiocarbon dates for the construction of the second phase centre on *c.* 2400 BC.

Further to the north was another timber structure, the northern circle, consisting of four massive posts within a circular setting 14.6 m in diameter, with an external fence well outside it, reached by an avenue of paired timbers. There is also some possibility here of an earlier phase.

These three timber buildings were clearly part of a single complex of structures and activities which extended along the ridge of Woodhenge (Fig. 3.9). Pits and post settings have been found in several places to the south pre-dating a series of ring ditches once surrounding barrows (Cunnington 1929). Beneath Circle 2 was a setting of features including four pits or large post-holes apparently enclosed within a roughly circular setting of small post-holes in plan not unlike the north circle within the henge enclosure. Further south again, at Woodlands, four pits were found producing a quantity of occupation material including Grooved Ware, flint and bone implements and part of a polished stone axe from Graig Lwyd (Stone and Young 1948; Stone 1949). One final point needs to be mentioned: in 1951–2 a rescue excavation on the south bank of the henge enclosure demonstrated the existence of a double row of posts marking roughly the southern extremity of the bank which could be shown to have been standing at the time when the bank was being built (Stone, Piggott and Booth 1954).

In summary, wherever excavations have taken place along the ridge flanking the Avon, in the Durrington area, structural activity, much of it of a ritual nature, has been discovered associated with Grooved Ware: the known spread of this built environment is 800 m. That so much has been found by 'accident' suggests that we are dealing with a ritual landscape of considerable complexity and extent (C. Richards and J. Thomas 1984).

The most impressive of the Durrington monuments is undoubtedly the henge enclosure – a massive structure covering an area roughly 520 by 500 m with an external bank and internal ditch provided with two entrances, comparable in size to Avebury, Marden, Knowlton and Mount Pleasant. Radiocarbon dates for material from the base of the ditch cluster around 2500 BC and are thus indistinguishable from dates for the southern timber circle found inside. It is impossible to say whether both were constructed at the same period. While evidence would allow this it would also be consistent with the view that the timber structures, including the Woodhenge building, pre-dated, if only slightly, the enclosure of Woodhenge and the construction of the great henge enclosure.

Just over 5 km south west of the Durrington complex lies Stonehenge (Plate 3.2), so well known that it requires little description, but from the point of view of the present discussion a few salient points deserve to be emphasized. Three major phases can be recognized (Fig. 3.10) (Atkinson 1956). Phase I consists of a bank with an external ditch enclosing an area *c.* 98 m across with a single entrance to the north east. Just within the bank is a

Plate 3.2 The stones of Stonehenge set within the circular ditched enclosure of Neolithic date approached by the avenue. (Photo: Mick Aston)

circular setting of 56 pits known as the Aubrey Holes 0.8 to 2.0 m in diameter and up to a metre deep. After the holes had silted up a cremation cemetery had developed over the east and south-eastern perimeter. Probably of the same phase is the Heel Stone and its now-missing partner, two other stone holes and four post-holes lying just outside the entrance (Pitts 1982). The intriguing possibility remains that a circular timber building may have existed within the centre of the monument (A. Burl 1987: 52–4) though whether it is earlier than, or contemporary with, the ditched enclosure, remains uncertain. A series of radiocarbon dates centring on *c.* 3000 BC for the construction of the bank and ditch are consistent with the associated Grooved Ware from the primary ditch silt with beaker sherds in the secondary silt. More recent work has shown that after the ditch had been dug and allowed to silt up the site was abandoned and scrub or woodland began to develop. This was followed by a phase of clearance after which there was some deliberate back filling of the upper part of the ditch before phase II began (Evans 1984). In other words there is now clear evidence of a long phase of abandonment, say *c.* 2800–2100 BC which coincides with the period when the major structural work was going on at Durrington Walls nearby.

In phase II blue stones from the Prescelly Mountains in south-west Wales were brought to the site and it is argued that an attempt to set these up in a double circle of holes in the centre of the enclosure was aborted. At this time the Heel Stone seems to have been enclosed by a ditch and an avenue of parallel banks was laid out eventually leading to the Avon. A single radio-carbon date obtained for one of the unfinished stone holes and another for a beaker grave containing fragments of blue stones focus between 2100 and 1900 BC.

Phase III began with the demolition of that part of the blue stone monument that had been erected followed by the setting up of the dressed sarsen monument consisting of a 'cove' of trilithons enclosed by a circle of uprights surmounted by a continuous lintel. It may be to this stage that the four 'station stones' on the periphery of the enclosure belong. A single date of *c.* 2100 BC was obtained for an antler pick associated with the construction phase of the great trilithon. Later stages involved the rearrangement of the blue stones within the outer sarsen circle.

In the sheer sophistication of its architecture Stonehenge is a unique monument, yet it conforms to the general development of Later Neolithic ritual monuments in Wessex in that two distinct stages can be recognized in its evolution, the first dating to *c.* 3000–2800 BC, when it appears to have been essentially an earthwork though possibly with internal timber buildings, and the second, dating to *c.* 2100–1900 BC, at which time it was monumenta-lized in stone.

Taking a broader look at the landscape of Stonehenge and Durrington in the light of the programme of intensive field survey undertaken between 1980 and 1986 and the radiocarbon dates now available it is possible to chart, albeit in broad terms, the development of this remarkable assembly of ritual monuments (J. Richards 1990: 263–75). The two cursus monuments – the Stonehenge Cursus and the Lesser Cursus – provide a link with the Earlier Neolithic tradition represented here by the causewayed camp of Robin Hood's Ball. Both may still have been functioning when earth and timber Stonehenge (Stonehenge I) was constructed around 3000 BC and it was about this time that the small ditched enclosure – the Coneybury Henge – was built on a neighbouring hill just over a kilometre to the south east (J. Richards 1990, 123–57). The later third millennium saw a shift in focus: both Stonehenge I and Coneybury were abandoned as new ritual structures were built and maintained on the Durrington ridge overlooking the Avon. But by the end of the millennium Stonehenge once more had become the prime monument with the erection of the standing stones, first the blue stones and later the sarsens, and the construction of the ceremonial avenue leading to it. In its monumentalized form Stonehenge served as the symbolic focus for the great barrow cemeteries of the second millennium which hug the ridges all round it. That so much can be said is a credit to those who have researched the landscape so thoroughly but the recent 'accidental' discovery of the Coneybury Henge is a reminder of how much may still lie beneath the soil totally unrecorded.

The Marden group

Further up the river Avon a complex of ritual monuments has been identified at Hatfield Farm, Marden (Wainwright and Longworth 1971). The principal components are: a circular enclosure 60 m in diameter situated close to the river; a massive mound, known as the Hatfield barrow, which once measured 7 m in height and 147 m in diameter but was levelled in the early nineteenth century; a circular timber building 10.5 m in diameter with uprights 2.5 m apart, excavated 1966–7; and a huge henge enclosure, covering some 14.6 acres, composed of a wide ditch with an external bank (Fig. 3.6). Radiocarbon dates for material from the ditch bottom span the period 2500–1800 BC with an emphasis on the later end of the range. Pre-enclosure occupation has produced a single date of around 3300 BC. No clear chronological relationship has been established between any of the constituent structures.

The Avebury group

The upstanding monuments of Avebury are well known – the great henge enclosure itself, the avenue of standing stones, the Sanctuary and Silbury Hill

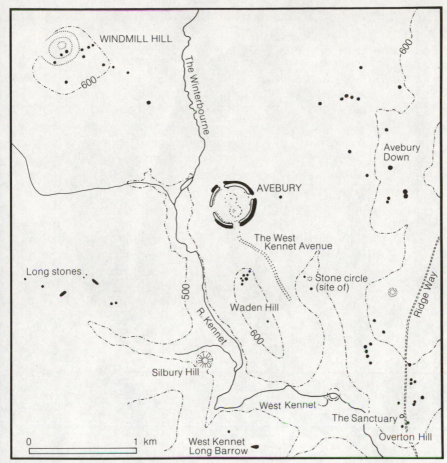

Figure 3.11   The Neolithic and Bronze Age monuments of the Avebury region

— but these are only the most evident part of a ritual landscape the extent of which is only now beginning to become apparent (Figs. 3.11 and 3.6).

The great henge enclosure of Avebury is surprisingly ill-understood in spite of a series of investigations and excavations beginning in 1908 and lasting until 1939 (I. F. Smith 1965; A. Burl 1979; Malone 1989). In essence it consists of a roughly circular enclosure defined by a massive inner ditch and external rampart nearly 400 m across provided with four entrances (Plate 3.3). Just inside the lip of the ditch was an outer circle originally of about 100 standing stones. Within, two smaller stone circles, but large by any normal standards, have been identified. The northern inner circle appears to have enclosed a 'cove-like' setting of standing stones while the southern inner circle enclosed a more complex setting of stones and posts including one large central stone 7 m high. Dating evidence is sparse but Grooved Ware pottery

105

beneath the bank and beaker sherds high in the ditch silt suggest a main phase of use focusing in the Early Beaker phase. Little can be said of the sequence of events leading to the emergence of the monument as we now know it. Whilst it could be all of one period of construction, a more extended sequence involving pre-enclosure structures (the north and south circles or timber precursors) is possible (Ucko et al. 1990). In addition the construction of the enclosure may have preceeded by some time the erection of the stones around the inner lip of the ditch.

The great circle was joined by one or perhaps two avenues of standing stones. The West Kennet Avenue is best preserved. In its original form it ran for a distance of 2.4 km from the south entrance of the circle to the site of the Sanctuary and comprised about 100 pairs of standing stones. The Beckhampton Avenue has been largely destroyed but originally is thought to have run for a considerable distance from the western entrance (I. F. Smith 1965: 216). The avenues are not closely datable but a Later Neolithic site along the line of the West Kennet Avenue is thought to be earlier. Three burials laid in pits dug against stones, two with early beakers and one with a Grooved Ware vessel, are sufficient to indicate a date towards the earlier part of the Later Neolithic period.

The Sanctuary, to which the West Kennet Avenue runs, is a complex of post-holes and standing stones set on Overton Hill (Figs 3.10 and 3.5). It was largely excavated in 1930 (Cunnington 1931) and has subsequently been reinterpreted. The reinterpretation offered by Stuart Piggott (1940) suggests four phases. Phase I consisted of a simple circular setting of posts which in phase II was surrounded by two concentric rings of more massive posts. In phase III the complex was totally reconstructed and comprised a circular setting of stones alternating with timbers, enclosing a smaller central ring of posts and in turn enclosed by an outer circle of smaller posts. In phase IV, it is suggested, an outer ring of standing stones was added. Other interpretations are possible (A. Burl 1979). A simpler scheme would be to suppose a succession of timber structures (roughly as in phases I–III) followed by a single phase when the timbers were removed and the two stone circles erected perhaps contemporary with the construction of the avenue. A Beaker burial against one of the stones would be consistent with a *c.* 2000 BC date. The view of Joshua Pollard (at present awaiting publication) is that the timber monument was of a single phase associated with Grooved Ware and that the stone element could be contemporary or later with the Beaker activity later still.

Several other major monuments existed in the area between the Sanctuary and Avebury. A stone circle was recorded in the valley bottom a kilometre south east of the great circle but little is known of it. More recently

Plate 3.3 The great henge monument of Avebury from the air looking north. The standing sarsen stones can be seen on the ditch edge in the western part of the enclosure. (Photo: Mick Aston)

Plate 3.4 Silbury Hill, Wilts. The largest man-made mound in Europe. The quarry ditch providing material for its third and final stage can be seen filled with water. (Photo: Mick Aston)

a group of major monuments has been discovered in the valley bottom on either side of the river Kennet at West Kennet Farm (Whittle and Smith 1989; Whittle 1990a, 1991) halfway between Avebury and Silbury Hill. Trial excavations and air photography have disclosed two adjacent enclosures. Enclosure 1, over 200 m in diameter, was defined by two concentric trenches, the outer reaching 2.7 m in depth, the function of which was to take a palisade of timbers 25–40 cm in diameter, placed vertically and packed tightly in place with earth and sarsen boulders. The second enclosure, 180 m across, was defined by a single palisade of similar construction. Aerial photography shows that these structures are only one element in a highly complex pattern of features the extent and interrelationships of which remain to be defined but both are associated with Grooved Ware. Radiocarbon assessments for enclosure 1 suggest a construction date *c.* 2200–2000 BC – broadly contemporary with the palisade added to Mount Pleasant in its last phase.

Finally we must note the existence of Silbury Hill – the largest prehistoric mound in Britain (Plate 3.4). Excavations have shown it to consist of four major stages of construction very probably part of a continuous process

(Atkinson 1978). Silbury I was a comparatively small structure of turf, soil and gravel 5.5 m high and 36.5 m in diameter. In period II the mound was increased in height with chalk dug from a surrounding ditch with an inner diameter of 116 m but before this was completed the ditch was filled and the mound was increased again in size (period III) to cover the earlier ditch. The material for the period III mound was derived from the ditch which can still be seen. The enlarged mound seems to have been built as a stepped cone with the steps later infilled to give a smooth profile. In period IV additional chalk for the upper levels of the mound was obtained from an extension to the ditch. The dating of the sequence relies on a small group of radiocarbon dates. Vegetation incorporated in the primary cone suggests a date of about 2700 BC. Material from near the bottom of the contemporary ditch spanned 2400–2100 BC. Perhaps the most significant thing about Silbury Hill is not that it began as a large mound comparable in size to the great mound at Knowlton and the Hatfield barrow at Marden but the colossal size of its final form, which makes it truly unique. It is tempting to suggest that the surge of communal energy which gave rise to Avebury was turned to even more monumental enterprises at Silbury in a single cycle of massive creativity.

Taken together the few tantalizing glimpses we have of the remarkable ritual landscape of the Avebury region strongly suggests that it was far more extensive and complex than we might at first perceive. It is not yet possible to place the different elements in their correct chronological contexts but we might tentatively suggest an early phase starting *c.* 2800–2700 BC with timber structures like that found at the Sanctuary and the early mound of Silbury I, to be followed perhaps with the construction of the large henge enclosure at Avebury, allowing the stone circles at Avebury and the Sanctuary and elsewhere together with the avenues to come a little later at a time roughly contemporary with the monumentalizing of Silbury from period II onwards. Some such sequence would be broadly consistent with the other Later Neolithic complexes we have been considering.

The Mendip group

Outside of the chalkland of Wessex, ritual monuments of henge type are rare. The only cluster known is at Priddy, on the Mendips, where there are four large circles arranged roughly in a line, one of which appears to be unfinished: each consists of a bank with an external ditch, diameters ranging from 150 to 170 m. What little excavation there has been demonstrates that the bank was revetted front and back with vertical timbers but no trace of occupation debris of any kind was recovered and the monuments are there-

fore undated (Tratman 1967). A single 'henge' was found 6 km to the east at
Gorsey Bigbury. Unlike the Priddy circles, the ditch lay inside the bank and it
was substantially smaller at *c.* 60 m diameter. Excavation revealed little in the
centre but beaker material was recovered from the ditch (ApSimon 1950).

Stone circles and alignments

We have already seen that standing stones in the form of 'coves', circles and
alignments form an integral part of the grammar of the ritual complexes of
Wessex. A small number of other stone circles are known in Wessex, the most
impressive of which is the complex at Stanton Drew, 10 km south of Bristol,
consisting of three circles, two of which have attached avenues leading from
them, and a 'cove' of three standing stones. The largest of the circles is an
impressive structure 113 m in diameter second in size, in Britain, only to
Avebury. There has been no adequate excavation and therefore the monument is strictly undated though by analogy is likely to belong to the Early
Beaker phase.

Summary

Our discussion of the ritual monuments of the Later Neolithic has, of necessity, been somewhat brief but sufficient will have been said to give some idea
of the variety of structures represented and of their density and clustering in
the landscape. Adherence to the classificatory term 'henge monument' and an
understandable emphasis on large 'henge enclosures' has, I think, tended to
obscure the order inherent in the evidence. Our understanding is rapidly
advancing, not least as the result of recent excavations in the Dorchester and
Avebury regions, and in advance of final excavation reports it may be pre-
mature to draw firm conclusions, but a certain patterning in the data is now
discernible.

Three broad phases may tentatively be suggested. In the first, dating
from *c.* 2800 BC in Wessex (though 400–500 years earlier in the Midlands),
the ritual monuments take many forms and are widely scattered within their
landscapes. The principal types that can be defined are

1 complex circular timber structures (Mount Pleasant, Marden,
   Durrington Walls, Woodhenge and the Sanctuary)
2 very large settings of vertical timbers (Greyhound Yard, Dorchester)

3 circular settings of pits or shafts enclosed within banks and ditches (Stonehenge I and Maumbury Ring)
4 large circular ditched monuments (Flagstones House)
5 large circular mounds (Great barrow, Knowlton; Hatfield barrow, Marden; Silbury I; the Conquer Barrow, Mount Pleasant; and, possibly, the Marlborough mound).

As we have seen, these elements may be scattered over extensive but circum-scribed landscapes within which there may be other individual burials. This kind of pattern is found in other parts of the British Isles from as early as *c.* 3100 BC.

In the second phase large henge enclosures were erected at Mount Pleasant, Knowlton, Durrington Walls and Avebury enclosing those first phase structures which continued in use. It is possible that the enclosure of the Woodhenge timber building took place at this time. That the available radiocarbon chronology is not sufficient to distinguish between the proposed first and second phases implies that if they do indeed exist as separate acts the time gap between must be comparatively slight.

In the third phase, dating roughly to between 2100–2000 BC, we see the lithicization of certain sites, most notably Stonehenge and Avebury but also evident at Mount Pleasant. It is not unlikely that the more scattered stone circles and alignments belong to the same general period and are clearly part of a process which affected much of the western part of the British Isles. In the 'collapse' which follows, the large palisaded enclosures of West Kennet Farm and Mount Pleasant were constructed.

Thus taking a country-wide perspective it is only in the scale of the huge henge enclosures of our second phase and the labour input and degree of sophistication in the succeeding monumentalizing phase (which includes Stonehenge and the later phases of Silbury Hill) that the chalkland of Wessex differs significantly from developments in the rest of the country.

Finally we must turn to even more speculative matters. A very great deal has been written in recent years about the potential astronomical significance of Later Neolithic monuments (most conveniently summarized and assessed in Ruggles and Whittle 1981 and A. Burl 1987). While it is evident that those who laid out some of the stone circles possessed a notable degree of practical skill there is no convincing evidence to support claims that the circles were observatories, computers or that they involved sophisticated planning of the kind requiring long-term observation or a knowledge of complicated geometry. Having said this it is abundantly clear that many of the circles were set out to align on significant astronomical events like the Midsummer sun rise to which Stonehenge so clearly faces. In a simple agrarian society of the type with which we are dealing it is no surprise to find that the community was concerned to chart the course of the seasons. That there does seem to have been a change from a lunar to a solar focus between the Early and Late

Neolithic has interesting, if unfathomable, implications for society's sense of time and identity.

Death and Burial

Rituals associated with death and the disposal of the body display a bewildering variety in the Later Neolithic period but to simplify we may say that while the old established rites of excarnation and collective burial continued two new traditions become more evident: cremation cemeteries make a brief appearance while the practice of single inhumation, usually under a round barrow, becomes a dominant rite at least for the disposal of a segment of the population. It is this change from the collective burial of ancestors beneath long barrows to the burial of the individual accompanied by grave goods, that heralds a major change in social structure from a situation in which common lineage is celebrated to one displaying the status of the individual.

Several of the old causewayed camps continued to be visited and used if only sporadically to the beginning of the second millennium BC and at Hambledon Hill trenches were cut along the line of the ditch long after it had silted almost to the top. Human remains found in the trenches, while possibly reflecting the continuation of old traditions, could have derived from earlier deposition. In any event the process was at an end by *c*. 2000–1800 BC when piles of flints were deposited possibly as a last act of sealing. Reuse, associated with beaker material, has also been recorded at Knap Hill and at Windmill Hill, which in addition has a barrow cemetery laid out across it.

Isolated human bones and occasional skeletons have been found in the ditches of the henge enclosures at Avebury, Mount Pleasant, Durrington Walls and Marden as well as at the Sanctuary and Woodhenge. Bearing in mind the comparatively small samples of the ditches that have been excavated the amount of human bone recovered is considerable. The possibility remains therefore that the practice of excarnation, which is believed to have been a major function of the causewayed enclosures, was also carried out at the later henge enclosures. Indeed it will be argued later that excarnation remained the principal means of disposing of the bulk of the Wessex dead until the end of the first millennium BC. The continued use of at least some of the earlier chambered tombs is clearly demonstrated by the excavation of the West Kennet long barrow where, after the last of the burials had been laid on the floors, the chambers and passage had been filled gradually with ashy rubble containing quantities of occupation debris (J. Thomas and Whittle 1986). In the north-eastern chamber the cremated remains of two individuals had been placed above the primary burials. The pottery from these latest fills included a

112

full range of Later Neolithic wares with beakers of both early and late types. How widespread the Later Neolithic use of chambered tombs was in Wessex it is difficult to say because so little of the original deposits have survived the attentions of unscientific excavations.

Cremation seems to have been extensively, if sporadically, adopted in Britain in the Later Neolithic period. In Wessex it is evident at Stonehenge where about 55 individual parcels of cremated human remains were buried over the south-eastern sector of the monument, some dug into the fillings of the Aubrey Holes, some in the bank, others in the ditch, the majority being in positions which suggest that deposition took place after, but not long after, the original henge monument was constructed. One interesting observation is that the individual cremations seem to have been only small samples rather than entire cremations suggesting that here at Stonehenge we are dealing with symbolic deposition rather than regular burial.

The most evident mode of burial to develop in the Later Neolithic was single burial usually beneath a round barrow. The rite appears to have begun in Wessex in the Earlier Neolithic but examples are few and ill-known (Kinnes 1979) largely because the excavations, such as they were, were conducted many years ago. However, the careful excavation of a large barrow on Earl's Farm Down, known as Amesbury 71, provides a valuable insight into the development of single burial tradition (Christie 1967). Four distinct structural phases were recognized (Fig. 3.12). In phase I an inhumation (later totally disturbed) was set within a roughly C-shaped setting of stakes enclosed by a slight ring ditch. It is not immediately clear whether the body was buried or was simply exposed. Some time later, phase II, an unaccompanied inhumation was buried in a deep central pit and was covered by a bell barrow comprising a barrow mound incorporating a concentric circular setting of stakes surrounded by a ring ditch. Charcoal from the grave provided a radiocarbon assessment suggesting a date about 2500 BC. In phase III the mound seems to have been truncated to provide a surface upon which a range of rituals were practised, resulting in the burial of four inhumations and at least two cremations following which the mound was made good and heightened with a stack of turves. Accompanying the burials were a series of food vessels and a collared urn. A single date of about 1900 BC was obtained for this phase. After the mound had been completed a number of cremations of the Middle–Late Bronze Age were inserted into the ditch fill (phase IV).

Amesbury 71 is somewhat unusual in showing multiple period use but other Wessex examples are known at, for example, Long Bredy and Frampton, both in Dorset. The significance of these sites lies in suggesting a date for the initial burial at the very beginning of the Later Neolithic period or even earlier.

By the Early Beaker phase the single grave tradition had become widespread, the principal burial rite being inhumation. While there is considerable variation in detail certain characteristics frequently recur. In the Earlier

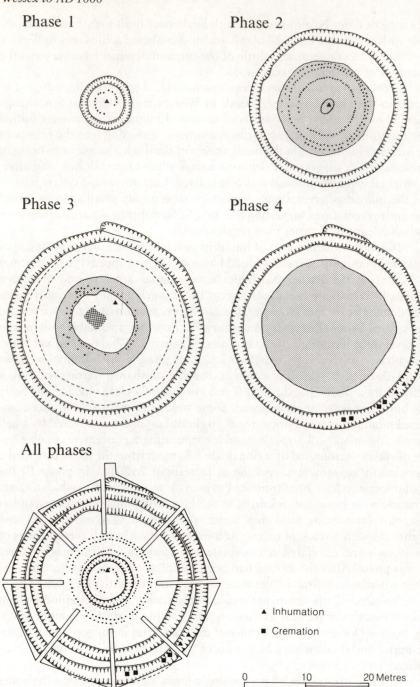

Figure 3.12   The Earl's Farm Down barrow, Amesbury 71, showing its development. (Based on Christie 1967: Fig. 2)

Beaker period burials normally take the form of crouched inhumations in oval pits. Some may be isolated or in small groups with no trace of there having been a mound. Others may be marked by bowl barrows averaging 15 m in diameter. There are, of course, exceptions like that at Fargo Plantation just north of Stonehenge. Here an incomplete inhumation was found in a large grave pit together with a Late phase beaker, a food vessel and three cremations, set within two arcs of ditch of massive proportions. Another exceptional burial was found beneath a small barrow known as Winterslow 20, where, in a large pit, a human skull was found with a vertical flint blade beside it. A number of the Wessex burials were also interred in coffins (Ashbee 1960, Fig. 26), an innovation begun in the Beaker period.

We have already seen at Amesbury 71 that barrow construction can be quite complicated, in this case incorporating three concentric settings of vertical posts. A number of other Wessex examples are known at, for example, Amesbury 61, Snail Down, Basingstoke, Bishops Canning and elsewhere (Ashbee 1960: 60–5).

By the Later Beaker phase certain changes of emphasis can be detected in burial rite. In the first place cremation becomes more common while at the same time the covering barrows tend to become bigger and more elaborate. Several distinct forms can be recognized: bell barrows, disc barrows, saucer barrows and pond barrows. There is also a tendency over time for barrows to be built together in large cemeteries like those that straggle along the south Dorset ridge way (Fig. 3.4) or cluster around Stonehenge (Fig. 3.8 and Plate 3.5).

Several cemetery clusters have been examined in recent years: among the most notable are those at Amesbury (Ashbee 1984; Christie 1967) and Milton Lilbourne (Ashbee 1986). The barrows excavated at Amesbury provide an insight into the variety of barrow form and ritual current in the third and second millennia. In brief, barrow 71 as we have seen, ostensibly a bowl barrow, proved to be a complex multiphase structure begun in the mid third millennium and used for 600 years. Another bowl barrow (no. 61) covered a stake circle within which were an inhumation and cremation dating to *c.* 1900 BC. Bowl barrow 72, containing an urned cremation, was overlapped by the ditch of a saucer barrow surrounding two cremations accompanied by a bronze awl and shale bead. Grave goods were also found in the disc barrow, no. 61a. Here the rectangular grave pit contained a cremation accompanied by a globular miniature vessel, faience and amber beads and a bronze awl: three inhumation barrows were found nearby. The latest of the group, a bell barrow, no. 58, produced a central cremation with a fabric- and moss-wrapped bronze knife dagger for which a radiocarbon date of *c.* 1700–1600 BC was obtained.

The small cluster of barrows at Milton Lilbourne was extensively examined. The main group comprised a disc barrow with a cremation accompanied by an awl dating to *c.* 1700 BC. Next to it were two large bell barrows

Plate 3.5 The barrow cemetery at Winterbourne Stoke cross roads just south west of Stonehenge. The Neolithic long barrow can be seen (top left) close to the cross roads. The second millennium round barrows are of bowl, bell and disc type. (Photo: Mick Aston)

with a small bowl barrow between, the bells yielding a variety of dates between 2200 and 1700 BC. The cremation burial in the southern bell was placed in a small timber coffin. The fifth barrow was a bowl barrow covering a cremation in an inverted collared urn for which a date of *c.* 1700 BC was obtained.

The two cemetery groups, both excavated to high standards in recent years, are reasonably representative of the variety which can be expected in second millennium burials.

Single burial itself implies that significance was attached to the individual. This focus was further enhanced in the sight of the community by the construction of barrows above the graves but the arrangement of these barrows, often in linear cemeteries, may well reflect the need of the social group to express its cohesion and common ancestry in a defined grouping of grave monuments. If so it could be argued that a row of round barrows retained the same social meaning as that expressed in communal burial of ancestors within single long barrows. However, this is not to underestimate

116

the growing importance of the individual in society. The existence of grave goods and the increasing diversity and elaboration of grave sets with time is sufficient to demonstrate the point (J. Barrett 1990).

One final question which needs to be considered here is to what extent the single burials of Wessex represent the normal burial rite of the population. That the barrows are numerous there can be no doubt. It is estimated that in Wessex there are over 6000 recognizable barrows (Grinsell 1958: 93). A survey of all the published barrow excavations from the country suggests that on average there are two burials to each barrow (Atkinson 1972: 113). Thus if we accept a total of say 8000 barrows, to allow for a percentage that have been destroyed, we arrive at a buried population of 16,000 for Wessex covering a period of 1000 years (i.e. 2500–1500 BC) – sixteen burials per year. This estimate, albeit an extremely approximate one, is far too low to represent the *total* deaths in any one year for the size of population which it is reasonable to suppose was supported in Wessex at this time. Taking 40 deaths per 1000 as a reasonable rate for the period this would imply a total population of no more than 500! Although figures of this kind are at best guestimates they at least indicate an order of magnitude. The conclusion must surely be that the barrows represent the burial of only a small segment of the population presumably selected by rank or status, the rest being disposed of by some method of which little recognizable trace remains. The simplest suggestion would be that excarnation, so evident in the Earlier Neolithic period, continued throughout the third and second millennia as the normative rite.

Territoriality

We have already seen that the distribution of long barrows of the Earlier Neolithic period is far from even and that on the Wessex chalkland six broadly defined clusters can be recognized (Ashbee 1970). Five of these clusters correspond roughly to what may tentatively be regarded as the 'territory' of a causewayed enclosure (the apparent exception being the Hampshire Downs group). Much the same division is suggested when the monuments of the Later Neolithic are considered. Not only do the henge monument complexes of Mount Pleasant, Knowlton, Durrington/Stonehenge and Avebury roughly correspond with the supposed territories of Maiden Castle, Hambledon, Robin Hood's Ball and Windmill Hill, but also each of the complexes lies within or close to exceptionally dense distributions of round barrows (Fig. 3.13). The coincidence is remarkable and strongly suggests a high degree of continuity in territorial organization (Renfrew 1973; Fleming 1971).

The exceptions deserve some note. There is no known 'henge' successor to the causewayed enclosure of Whitesheet Hill and round barrow densities in the area are comparatively slight, suggesting perhaps a decline in importance of this focus. The henge complex at Marden presents another interesting anomaly. It is quite possible that it succeeds the causewayed enclosures of Rybury and Knap Hill which lie on the opposite side of the Vale of Pewsey but there is no concentration of round barrows in the Vale nor is it easy to draw a line between the long barrows which might 'belong' to the Windmill Hill focus and those of the Rybury/Knap Hill focus. Clearly we are dealing with an evolving situation which the archaeological evidence is too crude at present to fully reflect. The Hampshire Downs present another anomaly. Long barrows cluster between the rivers Bourne and Itchen but no causewayed enclosures or henge complexes are known and the round barrows though quite numerous are fairly evenly scattered (Fasham and Schadla-Hall 1981: Fig. 12). The evidence, such as it is, implies a less centralized form of social organization in this eastern region. The Mendips offer a somewhat different picture with a dense cluster of round barrows around the 'henges' of Gorsey Bigbury and Priddy sufficient to suggest that a focus had developed here during the Later Neolithic. A smaller cluster of barrows occurs on the Quantock Hills in the west of the region.

Thus, if the recorded archaeological evidence fairly represents the actual prehistoric situation, it would appear that the centres of power in the Later Neolithic lay on an arc stretching along the chalk from southern Dorset to northern Wiltshire focused on five major ceremonial complexes. A similar focus occurred on the Mendips. Elsewhere a more dispersed form of social organization seems likely.

Society, Social Change and the Wider World

Any attempt to reconstruct social structure and change in the Later Neolithic is thwart with problems. Renfrew (1973) has seen, in the great ceremonial complexes, the emergence of chiefdoms dominating the Wessex landscape. In a series of more recent studies the nature and display of traditional or ritual authority, the development of prestige goods economies and the possible meanings of different patterns of deposition, have all been considered (Brad-

Figure 3.13 Barrow densities in Wessex related to major Late Neolithic centres. Contours reflect more than two barrows per sq km and more than five barrows per sq km. (After Renfrew 1973: Fig. 5; Ellison 1982: Fig. 6.3; Fasham and Schadla-Hall 1981: Fig. 12)

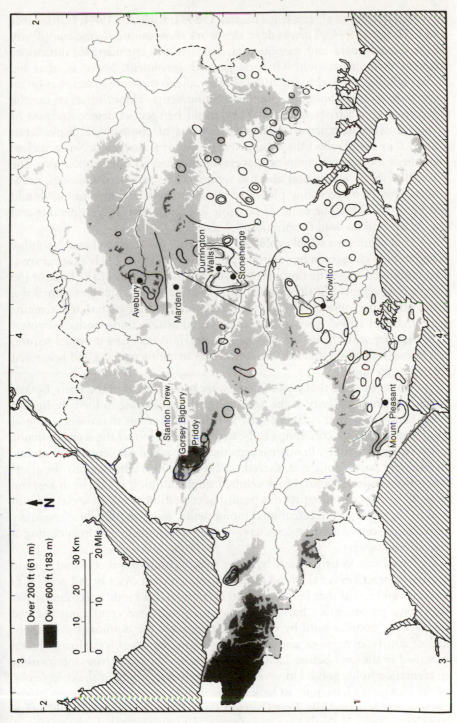

Over 200 ft (61 m)
Over 600 ft (183 m)

N

30 Km
20 Mls

Avebury
Marden
Durrington Walls
Stonehenge
Knowlton
Stanton Drew
Gorsey Bigbury
Priddy
Mount Pleasant

ley 1982; Bradley et al. 1984; J. Thomas 1984; J. Richards 1984; C. Richards and J. Thomas 1984). The result of this work shows not only the complexity of the existing data and its potential, but also the considerable difficulties inherent in interpretation. There is general agreement, however, that the ritual complexes reflect a structured society able to mobilize manpower on an impressive scale to construct communal monuments. These, however, may be interpreted in a variety of ways. They could be seen as demonstrations of group prowess designed to feature in systems of competitive display, but equally they could reflect the compulsive power of a theocracy. Nor is it clear that these monument complexes were maintained in continuous use. The possibility that construction and use represented short-lived episodes, occasioned perhaps by recurring phases of stress or political competition, should not be overlooked. The range of possible interpretations is considerable and the debate will no doubt continue.

That significant social evolution was taking place in the Later Neolithic is apparent in changes in burial practice. While it is highly likely that excarnation continued to be the normal rite used for the disposal of the bulk of the people, one segment of the population, presumably an elite, was afforded a more structured mode of disposal. Communal burial of curated remains beneath long barrows gave way to single burial usually under round barrows. This together with the inclusion of grave goods, usually of a personal nature, is a strong indication that the individual was being recognized and honoured according to rank.

While it is true that grave goods were being buried in the Early Beaker period the great majority of the accompanied burials date to the Late Beaker period and after (after *c.* 2000 BC) by which time it seems that the ceremonial monuments, though continuing to be used, were no longer the scene of major constructional activity. In other words the phase when the ceremonial monuments were being built and altered, *c.* 2800–2000 BC, belongs to the transition from collective burial to developed single burial. It would be in keeping with the evidence to interpret this period of transition as one of social turmoil and to suggest that the ceremonial monuments, requiring for their construction the concerted effort of society, were a mechanism for maintaining a precarious stability.

Burial rite in or beneath barrows was a complex process and a wide variety of practices is evidenced in the excavated data. As a broad generalization it can be said that before *c.* 2000 BC the normal mode was inhumation in a grave pit beneath a barrow but as time progressed cremations became increasingly popular until by *c.* 1400 BC they were the dominant rite. There are, of course, exceptions and as we have seen cremation was already being practised in the area before 2500 BC: nonetheless the trend from inhumation to cremation holds good. However, to illustrate something of the complexity of the picture we have only to look at one well-excavated example – a round barrow on Overton Hill (West Overton G6b) excavated in 1962 (I. F. Smith

WEST OVERTON

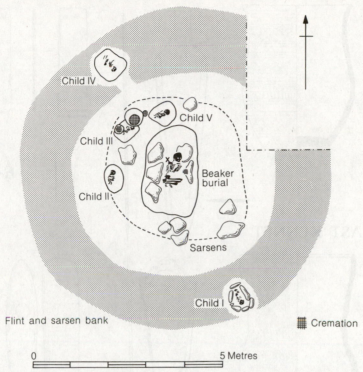

Figure 3.14   The West Overton G6b barrow. (After I. F. Smith and Simpson 1966: Fig. 2)

and Simpson 1966) (Fig. 3.14). The first phase involved the construction of an annular bank of flints and sarsens covering two separate inhumations of children and enclosing a central grave pit containing a flexed inhumation accompanied by a beaker. After this and spanning an unknown period of time three inhumations of children and three cremations were inserted just to the north west of the central grave. The area was then sealed with a layer of grey clay with sarsen boulders around the periphery and this was followed by the creation of a turf stack and mound. The use of a single burial location over a period of time is not unusual. Evidently the belief patterns involved in a structure like the Overton barrow were highly complex but throughout the emphasis was on the interment of single individuals.

Not all of the single burials were provided with grave goods but when they are present they reflect the sex and social status of the individual interred (S. Piggott 1973b: 340–7). Males were usually accompanied by weapons: arrow heads and archer's wrist guards, tanged copper daggers or daggers of flint or copper and flint and stone axes and battle axes (Fig. 3.15). Other male

121

ROUNDWAY

EAST KENNET

MERE

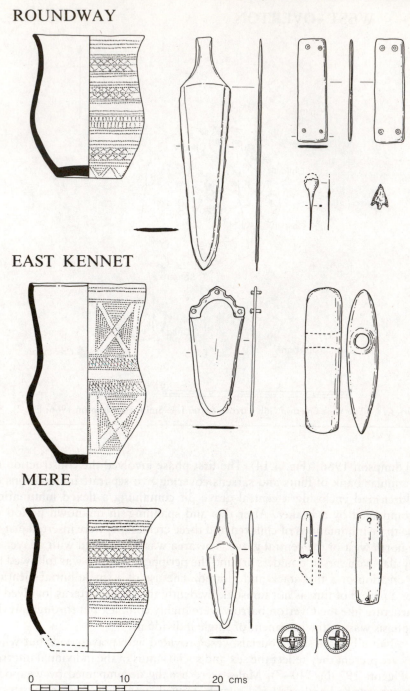

0   10   20 cms

Figure 3.15   Beaker burial assemblages from Wiltshire. (After S. Piggott 1973b: Figs 13 and 14)

equipment includes belt rings, gold button caps and amber buttons. These individuals may reasonably be regarded as warriors. The only items exclusive to females were beads of shale or jet. Other grave goods found with both male and female burials include scrapers, blades and knives of flint, bone and bronze awls, earrings of gold or bronze, jet buttons and single riveted bronze knife-daggers.

The barrow at West Overton has produced an interesting specialist assemblage of grave goods (I. F. Smith and Simpson 1966). Here the central inhumation was accompanied by a late-phase beaker, a bronze awl, two elongated shale plaques (known as 'sponge fingers'), an antler spatula, a flint knife, a flint strike-a-light and a ball of marcasite (a naturally occurring iron ore). This has been interpreted as the tool set of a leather worker. That similar assemblages, though not always as complete as the West Overton set, have been found beneath other barrows implies a degree of standardization and the existence of an artisan class. It has also been suggested that small cushion-shaped stone tools, like those found at Upton Lovell, burial 2a, and Winterbourne Stoke, burial 8, may be part of a specialist metalworker's kit (S. Piggott 1973b: 344).

Some time about 2000 BC rich graves began to appear and the tradition continued until as late as 1400 BC. In all about a hundred 'rich graves' have been identified, the majority of them being in Wessex (Figs 3.16 and 3.17). Within this general category, however, there is a considerable variety in indicators of wealth, no doubt representing a gradation in status of those afforded such burials. When the rich Wessex burials were first discussed over half a century ago, it was suggested that they represented a distinct 'culture' which was probably introduced from Brittany and maintained links with the Mycenaean world of the Aegean (S. Piggott 1938). It is now generally agreed that the 'Wessex Culture' phenomenon simply resulted from the desire among the upper echelons of the indigenous population to display the status of their lineage through exotic grave goods which now they had the means of acquiring.

The chronology of Wessex burials is still in some doubt not least because few radiocarbon dates are available but two broad phases can be recognized on the basis of dagger type: an 'early' group, usually known as Wessex I or the Bush Barrow phase, and a 'late' group, or Wessex II, now called after the type sites of Aldbourne-Edmondsham (ApSimon 1954; Gerloff 1975; Burgess 1980b: 98–111). Radiocarbon dates are few but a single determination for a Bush Barrow phase burial at Amesbury 39 would allow for a beginning perhaps as early as *c.* 2000 BC while dates for Edmondsham in Dorset and for Aldbourne-Edmondsham burials at Earl's Barton, Northants., and Hove, Sussex, suggest that 'late' Wessex burials were still being made by as late as 1400 BC. We may tentatively therefore date the early Wessex burials to *c.* 2000–1700 BC and the later phase burials to 1700–1400 BC. If rich burials were interred at regular intervals throughout this

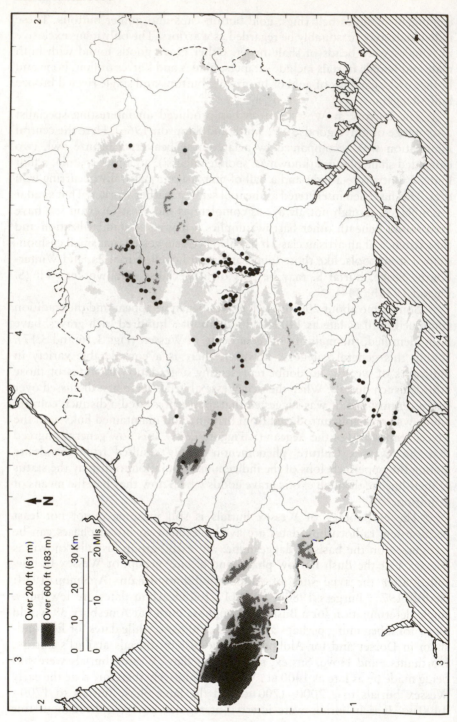

period the rate of deposition would have been in the order of one every five years or so.

Two examples must suffice to indicate the style of these rich burials. One of the richest was found in Bush Barrow, near Stonehenge (Fig. 3.17). Here the body of a male was laid out directly on the old ground surface accompanied by three daggers (of which two survive): the hilt of one had been inlaid with gold wire. Nearby were copper and bronze rivets from something organic since rotted, two gold decorated lozenges, a gold belt hook, a stone mace head, bone decorative fittings from a wooden staff and a bronze axe originally wrapped in cloth. A somewhat later burial, this time the cremation of probably a female, was found in a barrow at Upton Lovell in the Wylye valley (Fig. 3.17). She had been buried with a decorated gold plaque, a five-strand amber necklace with spacer plates, a gold-plated shale cone, two gold studs, eleven gold beads, a bronze knife, a bronze awl and two pottery vessels. Together the two assemblages give an idea of the opulence of these aristocratic burials. Other items found in graves of this kind include bronze dress pins of various types, small pendants in the form of miniature torcs and halberds, beads of faience (a blue glass-like composition), bone tweezers, perforated whetstones, cups of shale and a musical pipe made from a bone of a swan. Taken together they show not only the wide range of raw materials available to the elite but also the craft skills which they could now command. That luxury products were deposited in this quantity implies two things – that the social system required this form of conspicuous consumption to be practised and that goods were available in sufficient quantity to allow it.

Some of the materials consumed in the burial rituals of the elite segment of the population were local products – flint, bone, shale and no doubt leather and woollen fabrics – but many of them, the gold, amber, jet, copper and bronze and possibly the faience, could be acquired only through wide-flung trade networks. Already in the Earlier Neolithic, as we have seen, long-distance exchange was in operation allowing polished stone axes to be passed from community to community over considerable distances and the appearance of jadeite axes at this time shows that contacts had been established with the Continent. Early in the Later Neolithic period the beaker phenomenon, and its associated tradition of metalworking, developed roughly in parallel in Britain and on the Continent, implying that continuous interchange was maintained – a fact further demonstrated by the discovery in the Avebury area of pieces of Niedermendig Lava imported from the Rhineland, possibly as grindstones.

Wessex was conveniently placed to enjoy the fruits of these early exchange networks. Via the Thames valley it was directly linked to the Low

Figure 3.16 Distribution of rich Wessex burials of the second millennium. (After S. Piggott 1938: Fig. 24 with some additions)

BUSH BARROW

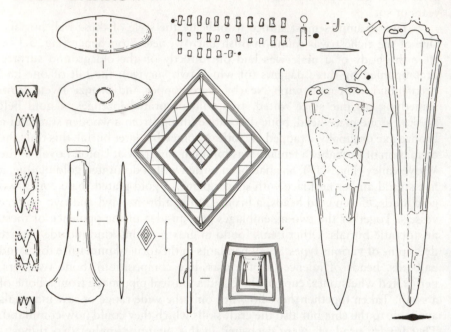

UPTON LOVELL

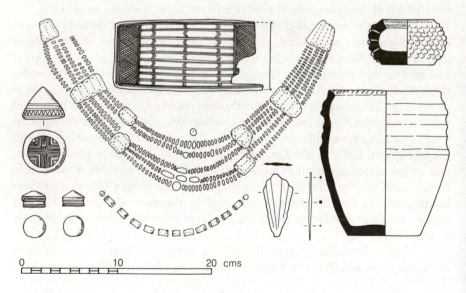

0   10   20 cms

Figure 3.17 Elite burial assemblages from Wessex. (After S. Piggott 1973b: Fig. 21)

Country: the Solent harbours gave easy access to the Atlantic routes to Brittany and the south or to the south-western peninsula of Britain and to Ireland beyond. The Somerset Avon linked conveniently to the Severn estuary and to Wales, while the Jurassic ridge provided direct access to the north of Britain. There can be little doubt that commodities passed along all these routes and the emerging elite of Wessex benefited. From about 2000 BC contacts with the European mainland intensified. To begin with, in the Bush Barrow phase, links with Brittany were particularly well developed and there were strong similarities between the elite buried on the two sides of the Channel. Their daggers were so alike that some of them could have been produced in the same workshop (Burgess 1980b: 110). There are similarities too in the gold work both in the decoration of plaques and the use of gold studs inset into dagger butts. Presumably we are seeing here items passing between the two elites in cycles of gift exchange. It was in this way a jet spacer bead from Britain, found in a burial at Kerguvarec, would have reached Brittany. In any such exchanges the harbours of Poole and Christchurch and the river systems serving them would have provided the principal lines of communication.

After about 1700 BC there seems to have been a change in the orientation of contact, emphasis being now more to the east, to Normandy, Picardy and even up to the Rhine. From this interface the Wessex elite received a range of dress pins and whetstones and the inspiration for the later Camerton-Snowshill type of dagger. Amber, too, may have come this way from the Baltic. More distant links with the Mycenaean world have been claimed but apart from a handful of segmented faience beads some of which might conceivably have been made in Egypt, the evidence is tenuous and unconvincing and other faience beads were probably locally made. However, the development of Mycenaean culture around the Aegean created the demand for raw materials and this demand, satisfied in part by the peripheral communities of barbarian Europe, may well have caused an intensification of exchange systems in more distant parts, the elite of Wessex feeling the benefit though through many removes.

Intensification of production and distribution leading to a variety of exotic commodities becoming available for the emerging elite characterize the period 2000–1400 BC in Wessex. Whilst it is possible that internal social evolution provided the motive force it is far more in keeping with the full range of evidence to see the elite burials of Wessex as part of a European-wide phenomenon, caused ultimately by the emergence of complex consumer societies in the east Mediterranean. This Minoan-Mycenaean core required a constant inflow of commodities to fuel its systems of display and conspicuous consumption. Peripheral communities, no matter how distant, so long as they could command a throughput of raw materials, could engage, albeit unwittingly, in these systems: throughout barbarian Europe elites emerged, the Wessex group was simply one of these. Why Wessex became a focus is difficult to say. It was located at a convenient route node which would have helped but it is difficult to resist the suggestion that it may have been the concentration and size of its great ceremonial monuments that drew people in. In their shadow people from distant areas could meet in safety to take part in ceremonies and to indulge in the processes of gift giving and exchange that usually accompanied gatherings of this kind. In such circumstances the local elites would have been the ultimate beneficiaries.

The span of the rich Wessex burials is, on present showing, 2000–1400 BC. This would imply that the early elites of Wessex were benefiting from patterns of exchange developing in the period which saw the emergence of Mycenaean power, while the later elites of 1600–1400 BC were contemporary with Mycenaean society at the height of its power and at the most expansive phase of its trade networks (Barfield 1991). Thereafter internal social changes in the Mediterranean world brought contacts with the distant peripheries to an end and the communities of Wessex were left to develop in a greater degree of isolation than they had experienced for eight hundred years.

Chapter 4

Across the Threshold: 1500–600 BC

The period 1500–600 BC saw a major transformation in British prehistory.
At the beginning came the systems of land division, production and the
maintenance of elites, characterized by the Wessex 'culture' burials, which
can be seen as the culmination of a cycle of development that began with the
inception of an agricultural economy. Social cohesion was created first
around the celebration of ancestors, then by the construction and maintenance of ceremonial monuments and finally by the aggrandizement of elites
whose status was defined by their ability to command a range of prestige
goods. Throughout this time agricultural regimes and the accompanying
settlements left little permanent mark on the landscape. By the end of the
transition phases considered in these chapters much had changed. Land was
now rigorously divided, settlements had become permanently established
with systems of fields and trackways, and over much of the area of Wessex
strongly defended hillforts were beginning to be established. Individual
burial, by inhumation or cremation, was virtually unknown. The overall
impression is that land holding had become the focus of attention and that
power and prestige were now based on the control of territory and the
exploitation of its productive capacity.

   The division of this millennium of transition into recognizable chronological phases depends largely upon an assessment of pottery styles and
bronze technology aided by a scattering of radiocarbon dates.

   The ceramic sequence is not in doubt. It begins with a well recognized
assemblage of urns, found in both settlement sites and cremation cemeteries,
and named Deverel-Rimbury after two Dorset type sites. Then follows a
phase when plain vessels were in regular use. Assemblages of this kind have
been called 'post-Deverel-Rimbury' (J. Barrett 1976, 1980). Finally this tradition gives way to an assemblage of highly decorated wares known after the
Wiltshire type site of All Cannings Cross. Details of the different assemblages
will be considered below but here we are concerned with the use of the
pottery sequence as a chronological indicator.

   There are, it must be admitted, problems. These are essentially

129

problems of overlap. To what extent did the different traditions coexist in any one area? And did different parts of the region adopt different styles at different times? The problems are particularly acute in this period because of the lack of well-stratified sequences and the vagaries of radiocarbon dating. Recent discussions have tended to rely rather too heavily on the few radiocarbon dates that are available, interpreting them with a greater accuracy than they deserve with the result that the picture presented has become unnecessarily over-complicated

However, it is now tolerably certain that the Deverel-Rimbury assemblage had begun to develop while the rich Wessex burials were still being interred. Indeed it has been argued that the barrel urns which characterize the Deverel-Rimbury assemblage developed from the Grooved Ware tradition and must therefore date back to the early second millennium BC (Burgess 1980b: 136). Some support for this comes from an early radiocarbon date of around 2100 BC for a bucket urn at Worgret, Arne in Dorset and dates of between 1900 and 1750 BC for barrel urn cremations at Kimpton, Hants. These early dates taken together with the late dates for some of the classic Wessex burials leave little doubt that there was an overlap in tradition in the later part of the second millennium. The classic Deverel-Rimbury assemblage, of barrel, bucket and globular urns, occurs from the sixteenth–fifteenth centuries BC, if the two, from the Wilsford shaft and from a phase F burial at Kimpton, can be accepted as reliable. Thereafter dates become comparatively plentiful continuing well into the ninth century BC at the Dorset cemeteries of South Lodge, Hadley and Simon's Ground. Thus on the evidence of the Wessex radiocarbon dates alone the Deverel-Rimbury assemblage would appear to date to the period approximately 1500–800 BC, allowing for a formative period to precede the developed phenomenon. This is somewhat at odds with the evidence from the Thames valley where a range of radiocarbon dates suggests that the 'post-Deverel-Rimbury' tradition of plain wares was widespread by *c.* 1250 BC (J. Barrett 1980). There is no difficulty in reconciling the evidence if we assume that the 'post-Deverel Rimbury' tradition developed in the Thames valley in the thirteenth or twelfth century BC, possibly as the result of intensified overseas contacts, and that elements of this new tradition were only gradually adopted in the Wessex region. That the two traditions do indeed occur alongside is suggested by evidence from the settlement of Burderop on the Marlborough Downs and Eldon's Seat in Dorset (Cunliffe and Phillipson 1968) where bucket urns were found stratified with plain shouldered jars. In addition to the above sites, plain wares have been found at Westbury, Hants. (Lewis and Walker 1976), South Cadbury (Alcock 1972: 114–20) and possibly the Angle Ditch on Cranborne Chase (Pitt Rivers 1898) but the tradition does not appear to have been widespread.

On the evidence at present available for Wessex it would seem reasonable to divide the ceramic sequence into two broad phases: *Classic Deverel-*

Rimbury dating to approximately 1500–1200 BC typified by barrel, bucket and globular urns, and *Late Deverel-Rimbury* lasting from *c.* 1200 BC until 800 BC, by which time the decorated globular urns were declining but a range of bowls and jars in finer fabrics ('plain wares') were beginning to be introduced alongside the traditional bucket and barrel urns.

Following the Late Deverel-Rimbury there develops an elaborate assemblage of highly decorated wares displaying considerable technical skills in potting. Those vessels will be discussed in more detail later. They are well represented at the classic site of All Cannings Cross (Cunnington 1923) after which the assemblage is most conveniently named, prefixed 'Early' to distinguish it from later developments on the site, but the recent excavations at Potterne (Gingell and Lawson 1985) will ensure that Potterne will soon become the type site. From Longbridge Deverill, Cow Down, which produced a similar assemblage of wares, comes a single radiocarbon date of the eighth century BC. It is reasonable to see the All Cannings Cross assemblage following the Late Deverel-Rimbury from about 800 BC and lasting, with certain internal developments, until about 600 BC.

In parallel with the development of pottery there were distinctive changes in the bronze assemblage. The most widely used terminology (conveniently summarized in Burgess 1969 and 1974 but modified later in Burgess 1980a; Gerloff 1981) sees the development passing through five stages, Acton Park, Taunton, Pennard, Wilberton and Ewart Park, all named after well-known hoards. The significance of these changes in terms of technological and social development are of considerable interest and will be considered below – here our concern is with chronology.

The usual way to date the various bronze assemblages is by reference to Continental development. This carries with it some uncertainties, not least the possibility that in Wessex at this time development did not always keep pace with that on the Continent. A further problem is that bronzes only rarely occur in settlement or burial contexts where they can be cross-related to ceramic sequence of radiocarbon assessments. A potential confusion exists in that the technological phases are usually given dates in calendar years (BC) while settlements and pottery are conventionally referred to in radiocarbon years (bc). Conversion of one to the other is not a straightforward matter. However this being said a broad correlation can be offered:

	BC (calendar years)	bc (radiocarbon years)
Acton Park	1500–1300	1250–1100
Taunton	1300–1200	1100–1000
Pennard	1200–1000	1000–900
Wilberton	1000–900/800	900–700
Ewart Park	900/800–600	700–550

131

Thus our Classic Deverel-Rimbury phase equates to the Acton Park and Taunton phases, the Late Deverel-Rimbury to the Pennard and Wilberton and the Early All Cannings Cross to the Ewart Park. The correlation must be regarded as approximate. The rare associations of metalwork with settlement material clearly demonstrate the problem: a few examples will suffice. At Chalton a Taunton-style low-flanged palstave was found in a context producing a radiocarbon date more appropriate to the earlier Acton Park phase while at Hadley Downs a twisted torc of Taunton phase was found with radiocarbon dates suggesting Pennard or Wilberton. At the Angle Ditch a transitional palstave of Pennard type was associated with Deverel-Rimbury pottery of roughly comparable date but at Burderop Downs a south-western socketed axe of Ewart Park type was apparently found with material of the earlier Late Deverel-Rimbury type. While these examples do not invalidate the broad correlations and datings suggested above, they do warn that precision is not possible. There has been a tendency recently to argue too closely from data that cannot, by their very nature, provide the accuracy demanded of them: even less can they support complex models of social development.

Settlements of the Deverel-Rimbury Phase

Viewed at a general level the Deverel-Rimbury period was a time when distinct settlements of family or extended family size were being constructed and maintained in a landscape which had begun to take on a distinctive structure, with well-defined fields served by deeply worn trackways. In other words, while in the preceding period settlements existed within a patchwork of arable land, it was not until the fifteenth–fourteenth centuries BC that settlement began to take on a degree of permanence sufficient to impose itself as earthworks on the landscape.

Several settlements of this period have been excavated in Wessex. Some appear to have been unenclosed. At Chalton, Hants., two circular buildings were found terraced into the hill slope (Fig. 4.1). The larger, some 7 m in diameter, produced a number of items of domestic equipment including a knife, a whetstone, an awl, a low-flanged palstave, a decorated bronze disc and a loomweight. The smaller hut nearby, measuring 5–6 m across, was dominated by a large central hearth. Other settlement elements included two small working floors and several pits large enough to have served a storage function (Cunlife 1970). No trace of ditches, banks or palisades were found

Figure 4.1   Later Bronze Age homestead at Chalton, Hants. (After Cunliffe 1970: Fig. 3)

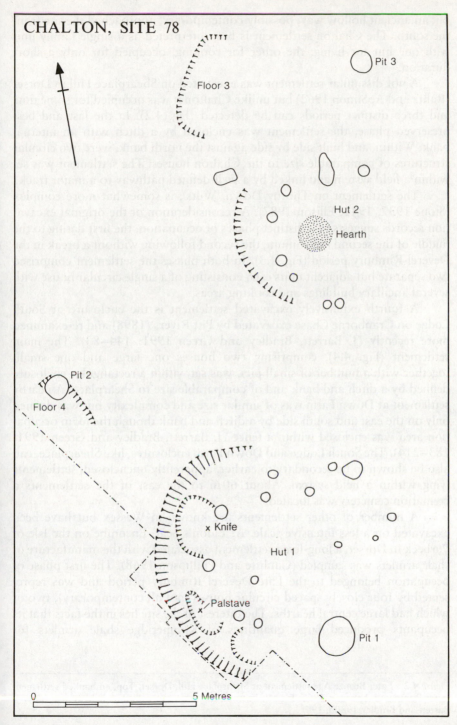

CHALTON, SITE 78

Pit 3

Floor 3

Hut 2

Hearth

Pit 2

Floor 4

x Knife

Hut 1

x Palstave

Pit 1

0   5 Metres

but an ancient hollow way, possibly contemporary, approached the site from the south. The Chalton settlement is best interpreted as a single family unit with one hut for living, the other for cooking, occupied for only a short duration.

A not dissimilar settlement was excavated on Shearplace Hill in Dorset (Rahtz and ApSimon 1962) but unlike Chalton it was occupied for some time and three distinct periods can be detected (Fig. 4.2). In the last and best preserved phase, the settlement was enclosed by a ditch with an internal bank. Within, and built side by side against the north bank, were two circular structures of comparable size to the Chalton houses. The settlement was set within a field system and linked by a well-defined pathway to a major track.

The settlement on Thorny Down, Wilts., is somewhat more complex (Stone 1937, 1941; Ellison 1987). A reconsideration of the original excavation records suggests two distinct phases of occupation, the first dating to the middle of the second millennium, the second following without a break in the Deverel-Rimbury period (Fig. 4.3). In both phases the settlement comprised two separate but adjacent units each consisting of a single circular house with several ancillary buildings and cooking areas.

A fourth extensively excavated settlement is the enclosure at South Lodge on Cranborne Chase excavated by Pitt Rivers (1898) and re-examined more recently (J. Barrett, Bradley and Green 1991: 144–83). The main settlement (Fig. 4.4), comprising two houses one large and one small, together with a number of small pits, was set within a rectangular enclosure defined by a ditch and bank and of comparable size to Shearplace. A nearby settlement at Down Farm was of similar size and complexity but was defined only on the east and south side by a ditch and bank though the main occupation area was enclosed within a fence (J. Barrett, Bradley and Green 1991: 183–214). The South Lodge and Down Farm enclosures, like Shearplace, can also be shown to be secondary to earlier, apparently unenclosed, settlements lying within a field system. About 60 m to the east of the settlements a cremation cemetery was located.

A number of other settlements are known in Wessex but have been excavated on a less intensive scale. At Eldon's Seat, Encombe on the Isle of Purbeck in Dorset, a long-lived settlement associated with the manufacture of shale armlets was sampled (Cunliffe and Phillipson 1968). The first phase of occupation belonged to the Late Deverel Rimbury period and was represented by four closely spaced circular houses (not all contemporary), two of which had large central hearths. The interest of the site lies in the facts that its occupants produced large quantities of Kimmeridge shale armlets for

Figure 4.2 Later Bronze Age settlement at Shearplace Hill, Dorset. Top, embanked settlement (after Rahtz and ApSimon 1962: Fig. 4). Bottom, the enclosure within its field system (after J. Barrett and Bradley 1980b, 190)

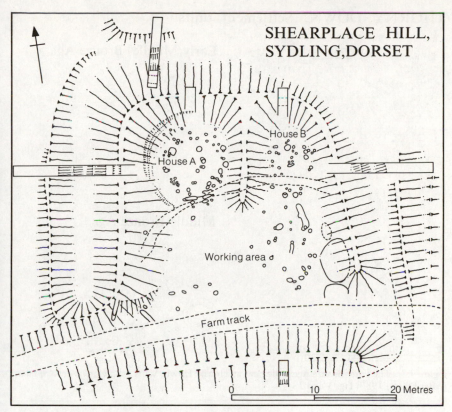

SHEARPLACE HILL,
SYDLING, DORSET

House A

House B

Working area

Farm track

0   10   20 Metres

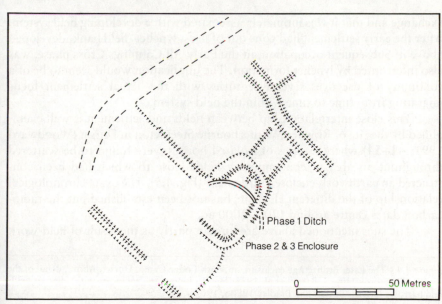

Phase 1 Ditch

Phase 2 & 3 Enclosure

0   50 Metres

THORNY DOWN, Settlement units

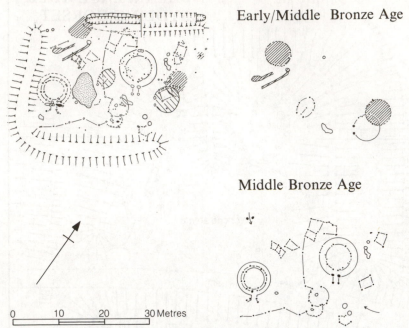

Early/Middle Bronze Age

Middle Bronze Age

0   10   20   30 Metres

Figure 4.3   The Later Bronze Age settlement at Thorny Down, Wilts., showing its development. (After Ellison 1987: Figs 1 and 2)

exchange and that it was intimately associated with a developing field system. After the early settlement had gone out of use a lynchet (field bank) developed above it. Subsequent occupation, in the Early All Cannings Cross phase, was also interrupted by lynchet formation. The implication would seem to be of a continuity of use over several centuries with the actual settlement focus migrating from time to time within the field system.

This close interrelationship between fields and settlement is well exemplified by the site of Rowden, Winterbourne Steepleton in Dorset (Woodward 1991: 41–54) where a series of isolated houses were found to be scattered throughout an area of contemporary fields close to which had been constructed an earthwork-enclosed settlement (Fig. 4.5). The exact chronological relationship of the different elements has not been established but the radiocarbon dates centre around 1200–1000 BC.

The sites mentioned above are known partly as the result of field-work

Figure 4.4   The Later Bronze Age enclosure at South Lodge Camp, Dorset. Above, detail of the settlement features (after J. Barrett et al. 1983: Fig. 2); below, the enclosure with adjacent fields and barrows (after J. Barrett and Bradley 1980b, 190)

136

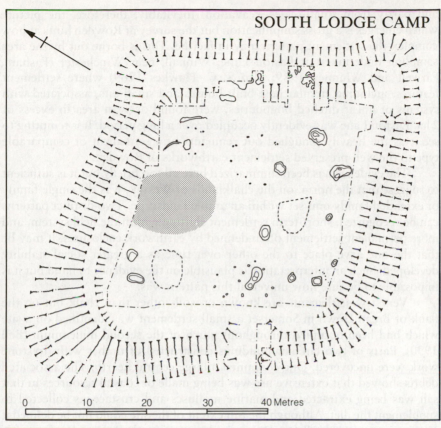

SOUTH LODGE CAMP

0   10   20   30   40 Metres

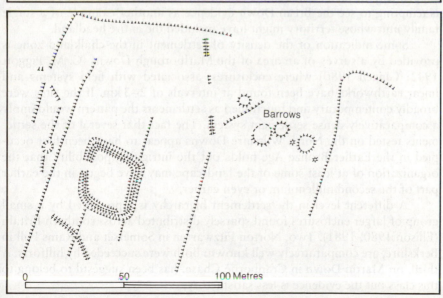

Barrows

0   50   100 Metres

and partly from small-scale excavation. Inevitably, therefore, the picture which emerges is a gross simplification but the survey at Rowden hints at how complex the settlement pattern may in fact be. This is borne out by the area sampling undertaken at Easton Lane, Winnall, near Winchester (Fasham, Farwell and Whinney 1989; also S. C. Hawkes 1969) where settlement features, including circular post-built houses and small pits, associated with systems of linear ditched boundaries, were found over an area in excess of 2 ha. Easton Lane was evidently occupied over a long period. It is tempting to see it as the heavily ploughed out remnants of a settlement of comparable type to the well-preserved settlement earthworks of Rowden.

The evidence has been summarized here all too briefly but it is sufficient to suggest that the norm, on the chalklands of Wessex, was the single family or extended family unit set within an arable landscape. Two distinct patterns can be recognized, short-term settlement shifting within the field system, and more permanent settlement often defined by earthwork enclosures. It may be that the one gave place to the other over time as a greater social stability developed. Such an interpretation is plausible on the evidence to hand but it is impossible to be sure how universal this pattern was.

Very few settlements are known on soils other than chalk but on the flank of Brean Down in Somerset a small settlement was identified on a site which had been occupied throughout much of the second millennium (Bell 1990). Parts of two circular buildings constructed of timber with drystone work were uncovered. One contained a large central hearth. The associated debris showed that extensive use was being made of coastal resources in that salt was being extracted and marine molluscs and crustaceans collected to supplement the diet. Although the full extent of the site could not be defined it is tempting to see the Brean Down evidence as another example of a single family unit whose territory might have included the entire headland.

Some indication of the density of settlement in the chalkland zone is provided by a survey of an area of the Marlborough Downs (C. M. Piggott 1942; Gingell 1980) where enclosures, associated with field systems and linear earthworks have been found at intervals of 2–3 km. If the sites were broadly contemporary and functioned as settlements the pattern would imply a comparatively dense settlement system. The fact that several of the settlements tested on the North Wiltshire Downs appear to have been first occupied in the Earlier Bronze Age holds out the intriguing possibility that the organization of at least some of the landscape may have begun in the earlier part of the second millennium or even earlier.

A different level in the settlement hierarchy is represented by a small group of larger enclosures found sparsely distributed across southern Britain (Ellison 1980, 1981). Two, Norton Fitzwarren in Somerset and Rams Hill in Berkshire, are comparatively well known: both were succeeded by hillforts. A third, on Martin Down in Cranborne Chase, has been suggestd to belong to this class but the evidence is less satisfactory.

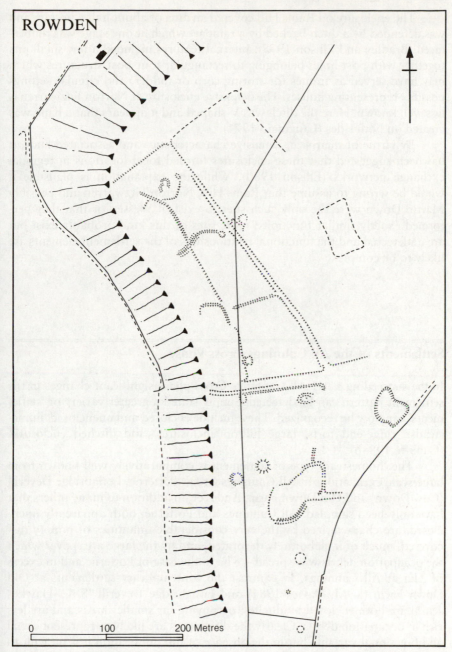

Figure 4.5 The Later Bronze Age landscape at Rowden, Dorset. (After Woodward 1991: Fig. 21)

The enclosure on Rams Hill covered an area of about half a hectare and was defended by a ditch backed by a rampart which at one stage was timber-faced (Bradley and Ellison 1975). Internal features included a few small pits together with post-holes belonging to rectangular four-post structures which may have served as frames for storing corn or fodder, and circular settings possibly representing houses. The defensive enclosure at Norton Fitzwarren is less well known. Here the ditch was V-shaped and it appears that a bank was created on both sides (Langmaid 1971).

By virtue of their size, defensive characteristics and associated finds, it has been suggested that these enclosures formed focal locations in regional exchange networks (Ellison 1980). While the explanation is plausible it would be wrong to assume that Rams Hill, Norton Fitzwarren and possibly Martin Down were the only such sites to exist in Wessex or that they per-formed exactly similar functions: more sites of this kind probably exist but are undetected and the functional relationships of the settlement elements are likely to be complex.

Settlements of the All Cannings Cross Phase

In the succeeding Early All Cannings Cross phase significant changes in the settlement pattern can be detected. Simply stated a greater variety of 'settle-ments' can now be recognized. These include enclosed and unenclosed 'home-steads', ridge-end forts, large hilltop enclosures, and ditched enclosures (Cunliffe 1984b).

The 'homestead' type of settlement is comparatively well known from large-scale excavations at All Cannings Cross, Potterne, Longbridge Deverill (Cow Down) and Old Down Farm, Andover, in addition to many others that have only been sampled. All Cannings and Potterne, both apparently unen-closed, are characterized by the very considerable quantities of pottery dis-covered, much of it elaborately decorated, and by the large areas over which the occupation debris was spread – 5 ha in the case of Potterne and in excess of 2 ha at All Cannings. In contrast the contemporary settlements at Old Down Farm (S. M. Davies 1981) and Longbridge Deverill (S. C. Hawkes 1961) are both enclosed by ditches, occupying far smaller areas and are less rich in occupation debris. Clearly the differences are likely to represent social and functional variants but in the absence of full publication it is difficult to speculate further except to suggest that All Cannings and Potterne may have served as focal points in regional exchange networks. The discovery of a gold bracelet at Potterne (J. J. Taylor 1984) might imply that the site was of high status. Old Down Farm and Longbridge Deverill are both ditched enclosures

140

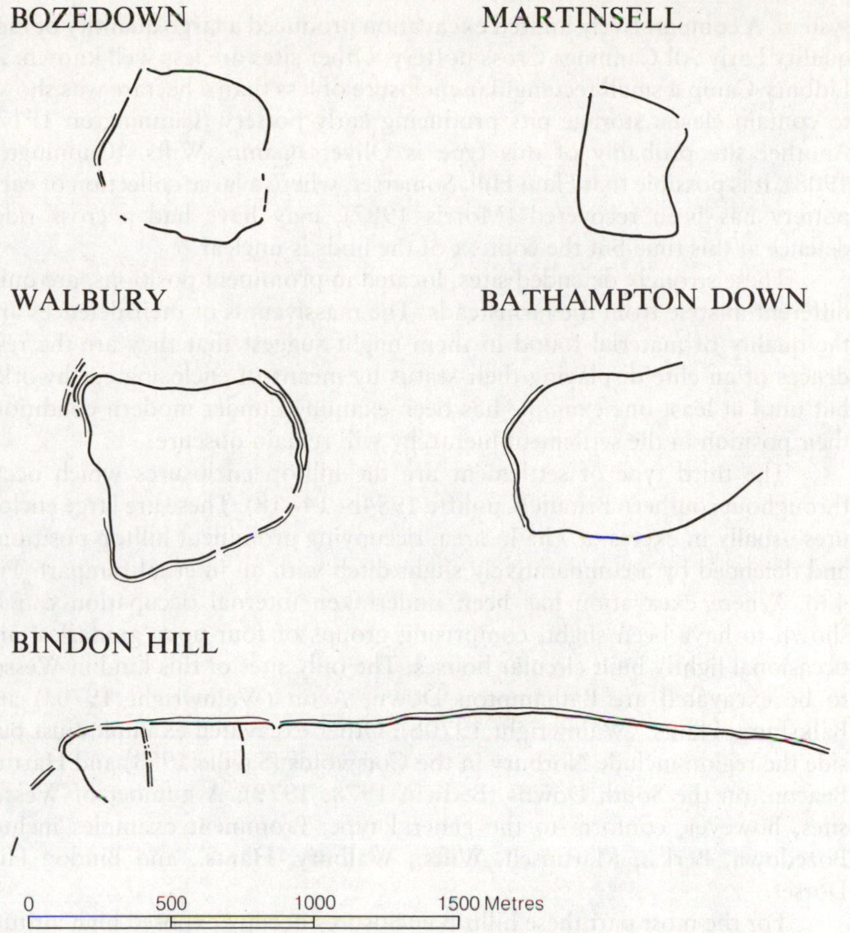

BOZEDOWN   MARTINSELL

WALBURY   BATHAMPTON DOWN

BINDON HILL

0	500	1000	1500 Metres

Figure 4.6   Large hilltop enclosures of the eighth–sixth centuries. (After Cunliffe 1984b: Fig. 2.6)

containing circular houses and storage pits, typical of the settlements which were to become widespread over the Wessex chalkland in the second half of the first millennium BC. Compared with the farmsteads of the immediately preceding period they are significantly larger, with a considerably increased storage capacity (if pits are assumed to have been used for corn storage). Possible reasons for this change will be considered below (pp. 163–4).

The second type of settlement to be recognized is the small fortified enclosure often occupying a ridge-end position. While the type has not been well explored several are known in Wessex. At Budbury, Avon, a roughly rectangular enclosure of about 3 ha was examined (Wainwright 1970a). It occupied the end of a steep promontory and was defended by a double ditch system. A comparatively limited excavation produced a large quantity of high quality Early All Cannings Cross pottery. Other sites are less well known. At Lidbury Camp a small rectangular enclosure of less than a hectare was shown to contain eleven storage pits producing early pottery (Cunnington 1917). Another site probably of this type is Olivers Camp, Wilts. (Cunnington 1908). It is possible that Ham Hill, Somerset, where a large collection of early pottery has been recovered (Morris 1987), may have had a cross ridge defence at this time but the context of the finds is unclear.

These strongly defended sites, located in prominent positions, are quite different in style from the farmsteads. The massiveness of their defences and the quality of material found in them might suggest that they are the residences of an elite displaying their status by means of enclosing earthworks, but until at least one example has been examined under modern conditions their position in the settlement hierarchy will remain obscure.

The third type of settlement are the hilltop enclosures which occur throughout southern Britain (Cunliffe 1984b: 14–18). These are large enclosures usually in excess of 7 ha in area, occupying prominent hilltop positions, and defended by a comparatively slight ditch with an internal rampart (Fig. 4.6). Where excavation has been undertaken internal occupation can be shown to have been slight, comprising groups of four-post 'granaries' and occasional lightly built circular houses. The only sites of this kind in Wessex to be excavated are Bathampton Down, Avon (Wainwright 1970a) and Balksbury, Hants. (Wainwright 1970b). Other excavated examples just outside the region include Norbury in the Cotswolds (Saville 1983) and Harting Beacon, on the South Downs (Bedwin 1978, 1979). A number of Wessex sites, however, conform to the general type. Prominent examples include Bozedown, Berks., Martinsell, Wilts., Walbury, Hants., and Bindon Hill, Dorset.

For the most part these hilltop enclosures occupy exposed high altitude positions. This fact together with the paucity of associated occupation evidence suggests that they might have functioned on a seasonal basis perhaps to facilitate the rounding up of animals for culling, castration and redistribution or even for corralling over winter. If so then the four-post structures could best be interpreted as fodder ricks.

The final category of 'settlement' to be considered are the ditched enclosures. These can be defined as enclosures of 4–18 ha in extent enclosed by a single comparatively small ditch with the spoil disposed of on either or both lips. The positions chosen for these enclosures vary but there is no particular emphasis on dominant or naturally defended locations. Two examples suffice to illustrate the general range of characteristics involved. At Danebury, Hants., the hillfort was preceded by an 'outer earthwork' defining an area of 16.2 ha. Originally there were at least three entrances one of which, wider than the rest, was approached by a linear earthwork of double ditched form which linked with the enclosure ditch. It is difficult to distinguish from the dense occupation of the later period, features belonging to this early phase but a number of four-post structures can be shown to precede the hillfort (Cunliffe and Poole 1991).

The second example lies on Hog Cliff Hill near Dorchester in Dorset. Here the dominant feature was a somewhat irregular ditched enclosure occupying 10.5 ha. Excavation has shown it to have had a long history (Ellison and Rahtz 1987) beginning with an early second millennium field system within which, at a later date, a series of timber houses were erected (phase 2). At this time or a little later the settlement was enclosed within a lightly constructed ditched enclosure some 5–6 ha in area (phase 3). In the final phase (phase 4) the enclosure was enlarged to 10.5 ha. Contemporary structures included crescentic dumps of flints enclosing hearths and pits associated with debris indicating the conspicuous consumption of food suggesting that these structures may have been used sporadically for feasting. Dating is based largely on the evidence of pottery. Phases 2 and 3 belong to the period of currency of Early All Cannings Cross types, going perhaps a little later, while the pottery of phase 4 is best matched by forms current in the sixth century. The emphasis on the ditch alone as the enclosing feature in both phases of Hog Cliff is closely comparable to the early Danebury enclosure: the dating too is broadly similar.

The existence of other ditched enclosures of this type in Wessex is highly likely: Buzbury in Dorset and Suddern Farm and Ladle Hill in Hampshire share many of the characteristics, though evidence from excavation is at present wanting (Cunliffe 1990), and others may well exist ploughed out or obscured by later hillfort earthworks.

One final feature must be considered here – the so-called 'ranch boundaries' or linear ditch systems which divide up large areas of the Wessex chalkland into distinct territorial blocks. Excavations at Quarley Hill, Hants., showed that here the ditch system pre-dated the construction of a palisaded enclosure which preceded the hillfort (C. F. C. Hawkes 1939). This observation led to the conclusion that the ditch system as a whole should be dated to the Later Bronze Age, a view confirmed by a recent programme of survey and excavation in the region north of Salisbury (Bradley et al. forthcoming). The best preserved part of the system, on either side of the river Bourne, gives the impression that the ditches were laid out as part of a single programme to divide the land into a series of territories a number of which included a variety of resource potentials spanning the high downs to the river flood plain. Elsewhere linear earthworks were laid out in relation to ditched enclosures as, for example, at Danebury, Ladle Hill, Suddern Farm and Buzbury Rings (Cunliffe 1990). The Danebury linear runs from the enclosure for several kilometres across the downs, past rectangular enclosures integrated with it to end up on the fringes of the Test valley. Some of the linears are associated with field systems but it is often difficult to define the exact relationships. On Stockbridge Down, however, a linear earthwork running along the crest of the Down, was joined by two parallel linears at right angles between which an extensive field system was laid out which could be shown to pre-date the construction of the hillfort of Woolbury (Fig. 4.7). In this instance at least the linears were used to divide pasture and arable land into well-defined blocks.

Standing back from the detail so briefly summarized above the dominant impression is of the increasing complexity of settlement structures as time proceeds. While accepting that precise dating is difficult it would appear, as a broad generalization, that in the Classic and Late Deverel-Rimbury periods (i.e. *c.* 1500–900/800 BC) settlements tended to be small single family units scattered between the contemporary field systems with a few larger defended settlements, like Rams Hill, occupying prominent positions and possibly serving as regional centres for exchange.

In the All Cannings Cross phase (*c.* 900/800–600 BC) there was a sudden and dramatic change: large tracts of the chalk uplands were divided into a series of territories by systems of linear ditches associated with ditched enclosures, while in more open areas extensive hilltop enclosures were con-

Figure 4.7   Woolbury, Hants. The hillfort of the fifth century was built on the edge of a block of fields bounded by ditches laid out in the Late Bronze Age. (After Cunliffe 1990: Fig. 5)

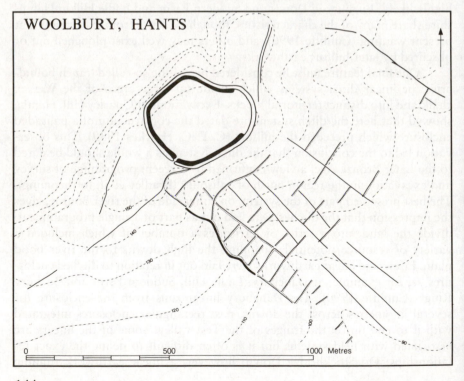

WOOLBURY, HANTS

structed. A programme of works on this scale must have involved a huge labour force working under some form of coercive leadership. In addition to all this, the emergence of defended settlements of high status and the growth in the number and variety of farmsteads, some of which, once established, continued in use for centuries, point to a new stability. The pit storage capacity found at most of the settlements from this time forwards suggests that the stability of the system was firmly based on agricultural production. One final point of difference with the earlier Deverel-Rimbury phase is that the settlement units were now larger.

Taken together these changes demonstrate that a major social and economic reorganization was taking place in the early centuries of the first millennium BC. The simplest way to explain it is in terms of changing attitudes to land holding. We may well be witnessing the transition from a system in which land was communally held to one in which ownership was vested in individual family groups. The implications of this suggestion will be considered in more detail below.

The Food-Producing Economy

While our knowledge of settlements is comparatively full, evidence for the economy is still rather sparse. Well-studied assemblages of animal bone are very few but the excavations of Pitt Rivers on Cranborne Chase long ago showed that cattle predominated in this period. This has been borne out on other sites on Cranborne Chase, e.g. Down Farm, and elsewhere. At Eldon's Seat for example, where a comparatively large sample of bones was recovered, the first period (Late Deverel-Rimbury) showed cattle to be represented by 50.6 per cent of the bones with sheep/goat at 40.7 per cent. In the second period, roughly dating to the sixth century, cattle had fallen to 28.3 per cent compared to 61.7 per cent sheep/goat. At Rams Hill where the sample is too small to justify detailed analysis cattle bones were one and a half times more common than sheep. A similar dominance of cattle was noted at Shearplace Hill and Easton Lane. Taken together, then, faunal remains point to the consistent domination of cattle in terms of numbers of animals represented and, even more so, in terms of meat consumed.

The Eldon's Seat figures, which show a decline in cattle at the expense of sheep by the sixth century, reflect the changes taking place across the whole of the Wessex chalkland: by the second half of the first millennium sheep greatly outnumber cattle on almost every site. Thus the animal bone data, sparse though it is, suggests that the period began with a husbandry pattern similar to that of the earlier second millennium but that some time

145

after 900/800 BC there was a comparatively rapid transformation to the sheep-dominated system characteristic of the subsequent Iron Age.

Evidence for crop growing in Wessex at this time is very limited but viewing the data from southern Britain as a whole Martin Jones (1981) has seen the Late Bronze Age as a time of diversification and of regional specialization. By the sixth century BC crops like the celtic bean (*Vicia faba*), cultivated oats (*Avena sativa*), bread wheat (*T. aestivum/compactum*) and spelt (*T. spelta*) had joined the traditional staples of emmer wheat (*T. dicoccum*) and barley (*Hordeum* sp.). On present evidence this change in cropping regimes took place during the period 1500–700 BC probably towards the latter part of this span.

Sufficient has been said to show that the period covered by this chapter saw a dramatic change in the agricultural systems practised in Wessex from an extensive system designed to produce a sufficiency to an intensive system geared to maximizing production. To this end land was carefully apportioned and reallocated, husbandry practices changed from cattle dominated to sheep dominated – the sheep being far easier to run in large numbers on the poorly watered downland, and a wider range of crops was introduced to make better use of soil variability. The appearance of storage pits as a regular feature of settlements by the end of the period could be taken to suggest that surpluses yielded by these improved regimes were stored for social manipulation. Why such a revolution in production should have taken place is a question to which we shall return.

Settlement along the Solent Coast and around the Somerset Levels

So far the discussion has been concerned largely with settlements on the chalk or upper greensand for the simple reason that comparatively little is known in detail of settlements on other soils but rescue excavation along the Solent coastal zone has indicated a surprising density of activity. This is particularly clear in the area around Christchurch Harbour and along the lower reaches of the Stour and Avon valleys where considerable spreads of settlement material of Classic and Late Deverel-Rimbury type have been distinguished usually with contemporary Urnfield cemeteries in close proximity (Fig. 4.8) (Calkin 1964; Cunliffe 1978a: Fig. 10). Isolated discoveries in the Hampshire basin east of Southampton Water, e.g. at Hook, near Warsash (Ashbee 1987), leave open the possibility that much of the coastal plain was intensively occupied at this time.

In the Early All Cannings Cross period a similar, though apparently less intense picture is presented with the emergence of an extensive occupation

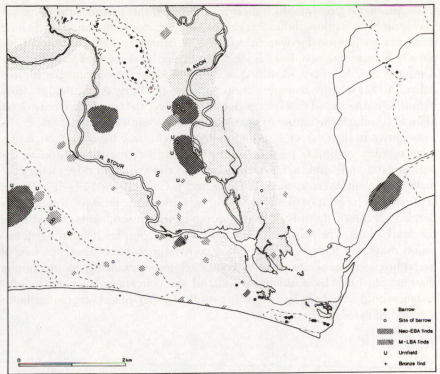

Figure 4.8   Distribution of Neolithic and Bronze Age settlement in the Hengistbury region. The stipple shows extent of alluvial deposits. Neo–EBA, Neolithic to Early Bronze Age; M–LBA, Middle to Late Bronze Age. (After Cunliffe 1978a: Fig. 10)

site on the flank of Hengistbury Head overlooking Christchurch Harbour (Cunliffe 1987: 336–8) and the appearance of a number of settlements on the limestone uplands of the Isle of Purbeck associated with the extraction of salt from sea water and the working of Kimmeridge shale, from nearby coastal outcrops, for the manufacture of bracelets, beads and pendents (Calkin 1948). These early extractive industries mark the beginning of a process which was to turn Purbeck into a veritable industrial landscape by the Roman period.

In sum the coastal region of the Solent was fast being developed. Access to raw materials, a range of soil types allowing for a variety of food-producing strategies, and easy routes of communication by sea to the Continent and other coastal areas and by river within the Wessex hinterland, together combined to give the zone an enhanced importance. By the end of the period the Solent interface, and in particular the harbours of Christchurch and Poole, provided Wessex with a contact zone, through which the region became closely linked with European systems.

147

Another region for which there is evidence at this period is the Somerset Levels and the flanking hills. Settlement sites are not common. The ditched enclosure at Norton Fitzwarren and the settlement on Brean Down have already been mentioned. In addition a large open settlement of Late Deverel-Rimbury date has been identified at South Cadbury preceding the hillfort (Alcock1972) where occupation continues into the Early All Cannings Cross period. Occupation of this later phase also appears to have been intensive on Ham Hill though the nature of the settlement is completely unknown.

Down in the Levels the second millennium BC saw the construction of a large number of timber trackways, crossing the wet moorland, joining the pasture land and arable fields of the islands to the mainland ridges where the main settlements were located (B. Coles and J. Coles 1986: 114–36). Tracks continued to be built until about 800 BC by which time renewed inundations flooded several of the ways bringing down base-rich sediments eroded from the nearby hills. The reasons for this flooding are complex. Climatic deterioration may well have been one, but a contributory factor, perhaps one of overriding significance, was the clearance regimes now being adopted along the flanking hills: by removing woodland the delicate balance of the eco-system would have been upset and as a result the marshland was plunged into a period of extensive flooding.

The Social Significance of Pottery

The pottery of the period (Fig. 4.10) is a useful indicator not only of the technological changes taking place but also of the broader social and regional groupings which had emerged. The assemblage of the Classic Deverel-Rimbury period (1500–1200 BC) comprises three basic types traditionally known as Barrel, Bucket and Globular urns. Collared urns of the earlier second millennium continued in use until about 1500/1400 BC and occur in primary contexts in several Deverel-Rimbury cremation cemeteries providing a thread of continuity with indigenous ceramic technologies. Barrel urns, so much a feature of the Deverel-Rimbury period, can also be traced back to earlier second millennium origins and appear before the Bucket and Globular types, for example at Kimpton (Dacre and Ellison 1981: 191–2). These observations, together with the suggestion that the Bucket and Globular urns may have their origins in the Grooved Ware tradition (Burgess 1980b: 136) enhance the widely held view that the Classic Deverel-Rimbury assemblage is an entirely indigenous development.

The vessels can also be considered in functional terms by categorizing them as fine wares (decorated Globular urns), everyday wares (medium-sized

Bucket urns) and heavy duty wares (thick-walled storage vessels and burial urns strengthened with raised cordons). Considered distributionally these three categories behave in different ways. The heavy duty wares appear to have been made locally as one might expect. The everyday wares, on the other hand, can be divided into a number of regional groups (Fig. 4.9) which points to numerous production centres each serving a limited territory, while the fine wares can be distinguished into fewer groups each with a wide distribution – a pattern suggestive of a degree of specialist, and possibly centralized, production (Ellison 1980: 129–30).

It is the fine wares – the decorated Globular urns – which provide the clearest indication of regional grouping. If it is accepted that distinctive

Figure 4.9 Later Bronze Age pottery distributions in central Wessex. (After Ellison 1981: Fig. 15.4)

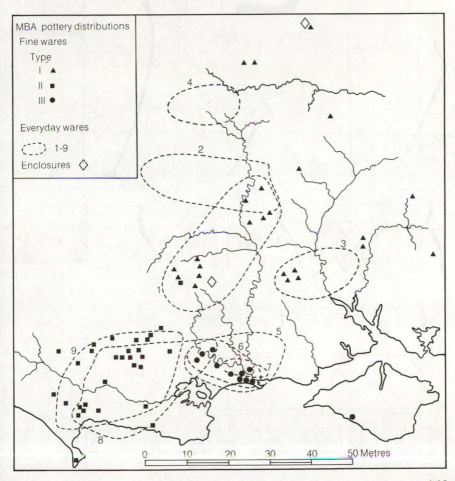

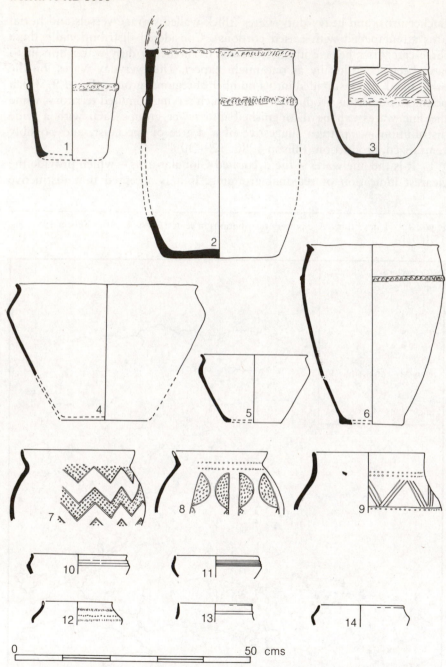

Figure 4.10 Later Bronze Age-Early Iron Age pottery. 1–3 Classic Deverel-Rimbury from Kimpton, Hants.; 4–6 Late Deverel-Rimbury from Eldon's Seat, Dorset; 7–11 Early All Cannings Cross from All Cannings Cross, Wilts.; 12–14 Kimmeridge-Caburn from Kimmeridge, Dorset. (Various sources)

decorative techniques may reflect ethnic entities then the distribution patterns of the decorated Globulars may provide some idea of the social territories into which Wessex was divided at the time. In all some four groups can be distinguished (Fig. 4.9): Group I in central Wessex, Group II (divisible into two sub-groups) in Dorset and Group III in the region of the Avon–Stour valley. A further group of vessels, known after the Cornish site of Trevisker, covers the south-western peninsula extending eastwards into Somerset. The groupings are broad and are clearly influenced by natural geographical division but the divide between Groups I and II in Cranborne Chase reflects a boundary which we have recognized as early as the fourth millennium (above, Fig. 3.13). Such a coincidence may indicate an ancient and persistent tribal divide.

By the Late Deverel-Rimbury phase (c. 1200–900/800 BC) the classic ceramic forms, especially the decorated Globular urns, had largely disappeared although the plain Buckets and those with finger-impressed cordons continued. Alongside these a new range of finer plain wares appeared, the principal forms being large shouldered jars and smaller shouldered bowls usually with outcurved lips. Well-stratified assemblages of this kind are rare in Wessex but the group from Eldon's Seat I in Dorset (Cunliffe and Phillipson 1968) and from the nearby site of Sheepslights (Calkin 1948: 30–2) are typical of the period. Similar groups have been noted from the Marlborough Downs particularly at Burderop Down (Gingell 1980). The appearance of the new plain ware component is not easy to explain but a comparable assemblage, without forms derived from the Deverel-Rimbury tradition, has been found on several sites in the Thames valley where it has been called 'Post Deverel-Rimbury' (J. Barrett 1980; J. Barrett and Bradley 1980b). One possible explanation is that the development arose in the Thames valley, possibly influenced by imported metal types, and that the ceramic styles were gradually adopted by the Wessex communities who still continued to make a range of coarse wares derived from traditional forms. It is for this reason that the term Late Deverel-Rimbury is preferred for these mixed assemblages of Wessex.

The final stage in the ceramic development of this transitional period is one of innovation and rapid technical advance. Strictly speaking two distinct but overlapping assemblages can be recognized: the Early All Cannings Cross assemblage which is distributed across Wessex from Somerset to the Berkshire Downs and the Kimmeridge-Caburn assemblage which concentrates in the coastal zone of Dorset and is closely similar to developments extending along the coastal plain of Sussex (Cunliffe 1978b: 35–6).

The Early All Cannings Cross assemblage is characterized by a range of well-made jar forms with evenly outcurved rims and rounded shoulders and bodies. Many of the vessels are highly decorated with stamped, stabbed or incised motifs often contained within chevron- or triangular-shaped panels. In addition to the jars there is a bowl component typified by bipartite bowls with beaded rims and sharp shoulders between which there is often decoration in the form of stamping or furrowing: some of these bowls are coated with a haematite slip. Other types include 'coarse ware' jars of bipartite or tripartite form. Some of the better-made vessels are finely produced with cordons at the junction of rim and shoulder but others are roughly finished with finger impressions along the shoulder angles. Vessels of this Early All Cannings Cross assemblage are best known from the type site and from Potterne (Gingell and Lawson 1985) but are found widely scattered across Wessex (Fig. 4.11). At present it is impossible to relate the assemblage to earlier and later material in stratigraphical sequences but the publication of the important excavations at Potterne and at Longbridge Deverill will greatly enhance our knowledge.

The Kimmeridge-Caburn assemblage, typified by the comparatively large group of material from Kimmeridge (Cunliffe and Phillipson 1968: 231–3), shares many of the characteristics of the Early All Cannings Cross group the principal difference being that the bowls and coarse ware jars are far more common and the large decorated jars occur much more rarely. It is simplest therefore to accept that the two assemblages are regional variants of the same broad tradition. At the type site of Kimmeridge the assemblage can be shown to have been stratified above a layer containing plain wares typical of the Late Deverel-Rimbury group, thus establishing the relationship between the two.

The elaborately decorated pottery of the All Cannings phase raises a number of extremely interesting questions not least the reason for the dramatic change to high-quality decorated ware and the source of inspiration for the motifs adopted. One possible answer to the first question is that the Wessex communities may at this time, 900/800 BC, have found it necessary to express their identity in some overt manner to distinguish themselves from those around the borders: distinctive decorative motifs displayed in a variety of media is one way in which this might have been done. A possible cause is the large-scale social and economic upheaval which was being experienced at the time. The further implications of this intriguing question will be returned to below (pp. 199–200).

That there are distinct similarities in decorative style between the All Cannings Cross vessels and the late Urnfield pottery of France and western Germany is not in dispute but that the similarities were caused by a migration from the Continent is a view no longer widely held. It is not to deny that links with the Continent intensified during the period: indeed the concentration of settlements around the main harbours of the Solent may be a reflection of this. Exchange of bronze, as implements or scrap, was widely practised and it is quite likely that metal vessels introduced into Britain became prototypes for

---

Figure 4.11 Distribution of Early All Cannings Cross pottery. (After Cunliffe 1984b: Fig. 2.2)

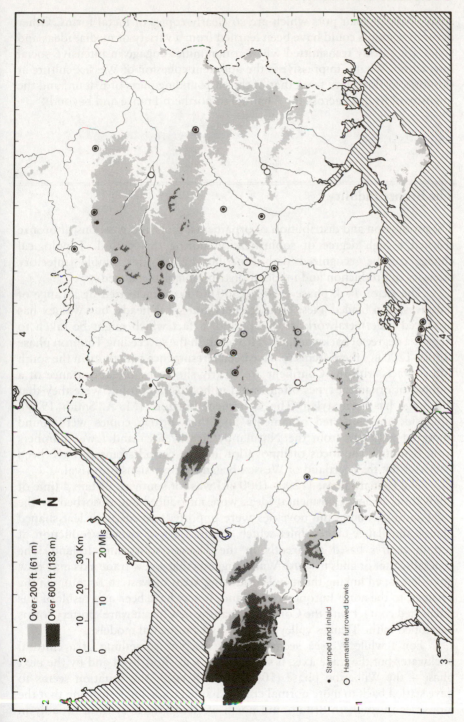

some of the angular pots which are so clearly copies of metal forms. Other decorative motifs could have been learned from a variety of media: ideas and styles are quickly transmitted when communities engage in intensive social interaction. What is impressive is the apparent cohesion of Wessex culture at this time, its difference from that of the surrounding parts of Britain, and the intensity of its links across the Channel to northern France and beyond.

The Bronze Industry

The production and distribution of ornaments, tools and weapons of bronze reached a high degree of sophistication during this period. Typological change can be recognized with time but against this simple trajectory intensity of production and mode of distribution also changed.

The Acton Park phase (1500–1300 BC) is characterized by a range of palstaves, thin bladed axes, dirks, rapiers and spear heads, but Wessex has produced little metalwork of this period, a fact which might be taken to suggest a degree of backwardness. However, in the succeeding Taunton phase (1300–1200 BC) there seems to have been a resurgence of activity in the south and contacts with the Continent are clearly shown by the appearance of a number of ornament types often found in hoards. So prolific were they that this stage has been styled 'The Ornament horizon' (M. A. Smith 1959). Alongside the imported ornaments and their British copies were found imported palstaves from the Normandy/Picardy area and fewer numbers from Brittany. The focus of innovation in this period seems to have been Somerset but the heartland of Wessex began to show signs of revival.

The Pennard phase (1200–1000 BC) was for southern Britain a time of innovation as new Continental ideas were introduced and absorbed by the local smiths. Among the novelties were imported swords with leaf-shaped blades and flange-tanged hilts which inspired active sword production at certain centres based apparently in the Thames valley and Ireland. The general scatter of finds in south Wales suggests that a new trade axis may now have developed linking the metal-producing areas of western Britain, via the Thames, to the north European mainland. It may have been as a result of this intensified contact with the Continent that the new 'plain ware' pottery forms developed in the Thames valley inspired by Continental models.

For a while Wessex seems to have become something of a cultural backwater but the trade axis, if such it was, was short lived and by the next phase – the Wilberton phase (1000–900/800 BC) – the situation seems to have settled back to more normal cross-Channel trade links ensuring that the industries in southern Britain and north-western France evolved broadly in parallel. In Britain leaf-shaped swords, pegged spear heads and socketed axes cast in a high lead bronze accounted for the bulk of the production.

The final phase of the period under consideration in this chapter – the Ewart Park phase (900/800–600 BC) – saw a sudden increase of exotic elements deriving not only from north Europe but also from the Atlantic seaways and the Mediterranean beyond. The carp's tongue sword, a specifically British product of the south-east was quite widely distributed in north-western France and along the Atlantic coast to Iberia. But within the wider distribution area regional industries can be distinguished characterized by local axe types. It was towards the end of this period that Breton axes, made in considerable quantity in the Armorican peninsula, began to reach Britain.

Viewing the overall development it would seem that after a period of stagnation the bronze industry of the Wessex region began to pick up in the Taunton phase (1300–1200 BC) but for the next two centuries or so the main focus of Continental contact lay with the Thames valley communities, leaving Wessex in some degree of isolation. But from about 1000 BC contact southwards through the Solent ports to Brittany and beyond began to develop, gradually increasing in intensity.

Such a scenario is entirely compatible with the ceramic development of the region. The main development of the Deverel-Rimbury pottery coincides with the Taunton phase, during which Wessex was open to a variety of Continental influences. Thereafter the focus of innovation in both ceramics and bronze technology passed to the Thames valley, leaving the Wessex communities to continue to manufacture their pottery in traditional style. But by the Ewart Park phase (900/800–600 BC), when contact between Wessex and the Atlantic sea routes was at its height, the Wessex ceramic industry entered a period of innovation and technological change, out of which emerged the varied range of vessels constituting the Early All Cannings Cross assemblage. While it must be admitted that direct correlation between metal technology and ceramic development is difficult to demonstrate with precision the generalized picture to emerge is, at least, consistent.

The implication of what has been said is that developments external to Wessex had a significant effect on the cultural development of the region. It is certainly true that throughout the period under discussion communities on both sides of the Channel were intimately bound up in systems of exchange. In the case of Wessex the links were naturally with north-western France and in particular with the Armorican peninsula. But this system was only part of a much more extensive Atlantic regional economy (Rowlands 1980) which in turn was intimately related to the economic systems of central Europe and the Mediterranean.

The eighth to sixth centuries BC saw the Atlantic regional system at its most expansive both in terms of the great increase in bronze production and in the wide range of products now available. This intensification may have been in part due to a decline in availability of central European copper and in consequence a greater dependence upon Iberian sources (Rowlands 1980: 42–3). The distribution of material of the carp's tongue sword complex along the Atlantic sea-ways is a clear reflection of this regional system at work. It can plausibly be argued that the intensity of the system was, in part at least, due to trading activities of the Phoenicians who were able to tap into the Atlantic system at the southern Iberian interface in the Huelva-Cadiz region, the latter site being their major port-of-trade in the west (Frankenstein 1979). By the early sixth century, the Phoenician involvement in the western Mediterranean had largely ceased and had been replaced by a new system based on the Greek domination of south-eastern Iberia. The reorientation which followed deprived the Atlantic system of its main sources of rare metals from southern Iberia, this being one of the factors which undermined the vitality of the Atlantic system.

This brief excursus into the wider fields of European prehistory has been necessary to remind ourselves that the social and technological changes in the Wessex region that we have been considering in this chapter were not entirely internally generated: rather they were the result of a complex interaction between large-scale external and small-scale internal developments. To understand the patterns reflected in the archaeological record it is necessary to view them from different perspectives.

Finally, to return to the Wessex patterns themselves. A detailed survey of the Middle Bronze Age metalwork, i.e. the Acton Park to Pennard phases (Rowlands 1976), has demonstrated three distinct levels of organization reflected in the distributions of tools, ornaments and weapons. Distributions of tool types, mainly palstaves, are characterized by a number of small regional groups suggesting that production and distribution were on a local level. Ornaments, on the other hand, relate to larger groupings implying fewer production centres. In Wessex two have been recognized, one based on the Somerset/Wiltshire/Dorset border, the other in Hampshire/Sussex. Weapon distributions reveal an entirely different pattern. No local groupings can be defined and typological differences show no spatial patterning. This is best explained in terms of specialist production, very probably based in the Thames valley, whence these elite products passed into the local distribution networks. Much the same divide appears to hold for the Late Bronze Age (Wilberton and Ewart Park phases) (Burgess 1969). Weapon production remains focused in the Thames valley while tools and ornaments show more local patterns of distribution.

Other Crafts and Industries

Apart from pottery and bronze there is surprisingly little evidence of other technological skills at this time. However, the trackways of the Somerset

Levels and the occasional wooden artefact associated with them provide a reminder that woodworking craft was well advanced, nor should we forget in this context the quite sophisticated tool kit available to the carpenters – axes, gouges and chisels of bronze are widely distributed in the region.

Some insight into specialist production is offered by sites on the Isle of Purbeck where Kimmeridge shale was being worked to make armlets, beads and pendants on a scale which would have provided a considerable surplus for redistribution. The workshops at Kimmeridge (H. Davies 1936) and Eldon's Seat (Cunliffe and Phillipson 1968) have yielded quantities of waste derived from different stages in the manufacturing process. The principal tools used for cutting the shale were flint blades but the bronze chisel from Eldon's Seat could have been a shale worker's tool.

Eldon's Seat also produced a number of bone awls and rib knives suggesting that leather preparation may have played an important part in the local economy. Leather production needed salts for curing the skins. The burning of Kimmeridge shale, much in evidence at Eldon's Seat, would have provided a potash-rich ash suitable for such a process and not far away at Kimmeridge there is evidence that salt was being extracted from sea water by evaporation (Calkin 1948: 56–7). While salt had an economic value in its own right it was also useful in the curing process not only for skins but also for meat.

Thus the evidence from the Purbeck sites, which were quite prolific in number, points to the production of shale ornaments, hides, salt and perhaps salted meat in surplus. The specialized products of this comparatively small area will have had an important part to play in the regional exchange networks (p. 163).

Death and Burial

Throughout the period cremation was the ritual of death most widely represented in the archaeological record, the cremated remains being frequently placed in urns set either upright or inverted in a pit. It is estimated that in Wiltshire, Hampshire and Dorset about 1800 such urn burials have been recorded (Ellison 1980: 115).

Cremations were often grouped together in cemeteries but the detailed form of the arrangement varies considerably. One of the most common traditions was burial within round barrows, either as secondaries in existing round barrows or as primary burials, singly or in groups under specially built mounds. In this case the mounds were usually much smaller than barrows of the Early Bronze Age. Burials beneath or within barrows account for more than 75 per cent of the known burial sites of this period. The remaining burials occurred in flat 'urnfields' comprising any number of burials up to several hundred.

One significant difference between these late cremations and those of the Earlier Bronze Age is that the later group were almost invariably buried without grave goods of any kind, implying a very significant change in attitudes to displaying status. There were, however, differences in style of deposition. Some cremations were buried without being placed in urns, some were in fine ware vessels, others in heavy duty wares. Urns could be placed upright or inverted and some were marked by stone slabs or upright timbers. These variations in practice, whatever they might mean in terms of status, lineage or sex, are of quite a different kind to the burial of rich grave sets with the deceased.

A detailed reconsideration of all the relevant burial evidence (Ellison 1980) shows there to be a distinct patterning in burial groupings. More than three-quarters of the cemeteries with multiple burials contained under forty burials and about half of these fewer than twelve burials. Moreover in the larger cemeteries it is often possible to recognize discrete clusters of between ten and thirty burials. In the few cases where anatomical detail is available burials of adults and children of both sexes are found intermixed. It seems, therefore, that the individual burial clusters are best interpreted as kin groups.

To demonstrate something of the range represented by the burials of this period a selection of well-published sites will be briefly considered.

Barrow G1 at Broad Chalk, Wilts., provides an example of the burial beneath a single barrow (Rahtz 1970). The primary burial was placed in an inverted barrel urn associated with three post-holes, possibly belonging to a mortuary house, and token deposits of pot sherds and food bones. The whole was then covered by the mound of a small barrow. A similar burial was excavated at Worgret Hill, Arne in Dorset (Wainwright 1965). The primary pit, beneath the barrow of turf and gravel, was empty but two burials in large bucket urns appear to have been inserted as secondaries.

A more complex situation was recorded during the excavation of the Knighton Heath barrow in Dorset (Petersen 1981). Here the main sequence began with the burning off of the vegetation cover (providing a radiocarbon date in the fifteenth century BC). Then followed a phase of activity during which at least four urn burials were deposited, and light timber structures were put up. The four burials produced dates in the fourteenth century BC. The primary mound was then built and more activity followed involving urn burial, unaccompanied cremations, the digging of small pits, and the setting of upright stone slabs and stakes. The mound was then capped and the ditch completed after which a further series of burials were inserted. Clearly the burial site had been in intensive use over a long period.

A more extensive cemetery was examined at Simon's Ground, a few

SIMON'S GROUND

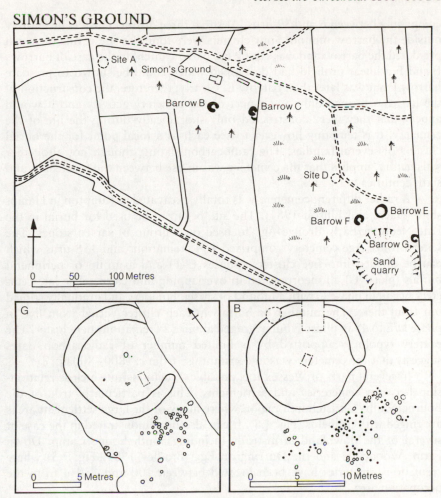

Figure 4.12   The Urnfield at Simon's Ground, Dorset. (After White 1982: Figs 1, 2 and 13)

kilometres to the north (White 1982). Here at least seven barrows are known to have been spread out along the crest of an escarpment over a distance of about half a kilometre (Fig. 4.12). Of these five were examined by excavation. The barrows were about 10 m in diameter and, with one exception, were surrounded by penannular ditches, presumably to allow easy access to the mound for ritual purposes. Several of the mounds were built over the remains of mortuary houses or exposure platforms, the former usually consisting of simple four-post settings. In two cases there were primary cremation burials in the centre. For the most part the 300 or so burials lay in dense scatters to the south of the barrows but detailed analysis showed that the situation was quite complex. In all some 15 distinct clusters of burials have been identified comprising between 6 and 52 urns. At site B three distinct clusters lie entirely outside the barrow mound. Four clusters were found at site C one of which pre-dated the barrow and was cut by the barrow ditch. In the case of barrows E and F a linear urnfield had developed which could be shown to pre-date barrow F but was later than barrow E. Clearly, therefore, the construction of the barrows formed only one aspect of the cemetery activity and it would appear that they were constructed only sporadically during the life of the cemetery. It is tempting however to see each as a focal point for the burial clusters of several families. The radiocarbon dating, though not altogether satisfactory, implies that the cemetery was in use between the fourteenth and sixth centuries BC.

A rather different cemetery was totally excavated at Kimpton in Hampshire (Dacre and Ellison 1981). The site began to be used for burial in the Late Neolithic/Early Bronze Age focused on a group of sarsen stones. The Later Bronze Age cemetery comprised 164 cremations and 158 urns which can be divided into five clusters (phases C–F) and a group of peripheral burials (phase G) all incorporated in overlapping flint cairns. The late cemetery began in phase C with a mound of sarsen boulders and gradually spread out from there. The number of burials in each cluster varied from five in phase D/E to 48 in phase E but averaged about 32 cremations per cluster. The pottery typology supported by a limited number of radiocarbon dates suggests that the cemetery was in constant use from *c.* 1800–800 BC.

In several parts of Wessex it is possible to demonstrate a close relationship between cemeteries and settlements. This is particularly true of the Bournemouth–Christchurch region where many of the large settlement areas are ringed with urnfields (Fig. 4.8). It can also be demonstrated in the case of several of the downland farmsteads including South Lodge Camp, Down Farm (Woodcuts) and the Durrington Egg (Bradley 1981: Fig. 7.5) where cremation cemeteries have been located between 100 and 150 m from the occupation area.

The Later Bronze Age cemeteries of Wessex present a dramatic contrast to those of the Earlier Bronze Age. The emphasis is no longer on defining the status of individuals with large burial mounds and elaborate grave goods but more on individual cemetery foci used by discrete family groups over a long period of time. That a number of family 'clusters' are sometimes found together making up much larger cemeteries suggests a degree of social cohesion. A further sign of a break with earlier tradition is that the large early barrow cemeteries around Stonehenge and along the Dorset ridgeway no longer form significant foci for Later Bronze Age burial.

On the basis of the few radiocarbon dates it could be argued that the development of these Later Bronze Age cremation clusters had begun before the demise of rich Wessex-style burials and that there was something of a regional divide, the late Wessex burials continuing on the chalk uplands while the cremation clusters developed on the tertiary soils of the Hampshire basin

(Bradley 1980, 1981). Such a picture is consistent with the available dates though more dates would be required to test its validity. It does, however, remind us that the chalkland may no longer have been the innovatory centre of the region and that with renewed emphasis on overseas trade social change may have proceeded most rapidly among the communities along the Solent interface. However, sites like Kimpton, in the heart of the chalk uplands, where cremation clusters began early, show that in the present state of knowledge generalizations may be misleading. At any event by about 1000 BC, the rite involving cremation clusters had become widespread throughout Wessex.

One final question which deserves to be raised here is whether cremation was the rite used for the disposal of all the dead or whether it was used for only a segment of the population. That some inhumation may have been practised is suggested by three inhumations, tentatively dated to this period on the Easton Lane site (Fasham, Farwell and Whinney 1989: 49–50). The possibility of widespread excarnation, though possible, remains unproven. There are, however, hints that the urn cemetery may not have catered for the entire population throughout the period. At Kimpton the 320 or so burials represented covered a period of about 700 years, that is about one burial every two years. If the cemetery represents the burial place of a single family or extended family then it could be argued that the entire population was cremated and buried here. There is, however, the suggestion that the number of burials decreased in the later period, in which case it would be necessary to suppose that either a new cemetery was being developed in parallel or that a different mode of disposing of the dead was being adopted alongside cremation – always assuming that is that the population remained approximately the same size. The Kimpton example shows how difficult it is to approach the question even with a large sample of well excavated material.

Ritual and Religion

Apart from burial practices evidence for ritual and religion in the Later Bronze Age is sparse. In general there seems to have been very little interest shown in the large ceremonial monuments of Wessex except possibly for Stonehenge where the ring of Aubrey Holes dug around the periphery are reported to have contained sherds of Deverel-Rimbury pottery.

However, two unusual 'monuments' may have religious connotations. The most dramatic is the Wilsford shaft, not far from Stonehenge. It comprises a circular pit dug to a depth of 30 m, several metres below contemporary water-level. Radiocarbon dates from the bottom of the shaft centre on 1400 BC and were associated with wooden objects, amber beads, bone pins and a shale ring. Deverel-Rimbury sherds came from higher up the fill (Ashbee, Bell and Proudfoot 1989). The digging of the shaft was a feat involving engineering skill and organized communal effort but there is nothing about the filling which requires it to be interpreted solely as a ritual structure. The presence of a wooden bucket and rope might indeed point to a more mundane explanation. Even so water sources and wells were often associated with deities among Iron Age and later societies and it is possible that the Wilsford shaft, whatever its prime function, may have been endowed with religious significance in the minds of those who constructed and used it.

Another shaft of a rather different kind was discovered at Swanwick in southern Hampshire (Fox 1928, 1930). It had been cut into the clay bedrock to a depth of nearly 8 m below the present surface (Fig. 4.13). The lower two metres suddenly narrowed from 2 m to a metre in diameter and in the centre, set upright in the bottom, was an oak trunk with bark intact surviving to a height of 1.7 m. The lower part of the pit was coated with a brown deposit which, on analysis, was claimed to have derived from blood. The sole dating evidence is a group of cylindrical loom weights of Late Bronze Age type from the filling part way up the shaft. Whether or not the suggestion of blood is accepted the upright timber in the shaft has close analogies with Continental examples of Iron Age date which clearly have religious associations.

Figure 4.13   A 'ritual shaft' found at Swanwick, Hants. (After Fox 1930: 31)

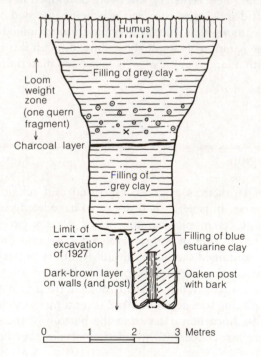

Two shafts are hardly sufficient evidence upon which to reconstruct the belief system but it is tempting to see them as representing increased reliance on chthonic forces. As we shall see in the next chapter the digging of pits, possibly for storage in the first instance, was heavily bound up with a complex of propitiatory rites and it is clear that by this time a new belief system was in place. The Later Bronze Age with its change of emphasis to land holding and the exploitation of the productive capacity of the land may well have been accompanied by a shift in religious belief away from one focused upon the sky and the movement of the sun, moon and stars to a system concerned with the productivity of the land and of the earth and water deities who controlled it. It may be, in this general context, that we can best understand the increasingly large number of bronze hoards buried in the ground and items, especially weapons, thrown into rivers. Both could be interpreted as propitiatory offerings to the deities of earth and water.

Society and Social Change

Sufficient will have been said in this chapter to show that the period of the Later Bronze Age (i.e. the Middle and Late Bronze Age in traditional nomenclature), dating roughly from 1500 to 600 BC, was a time of dramatic change during which long-established systems of acquiring prestige and demonstrating elite status through the acquisition of prestige goods disappeared and new systems based upon the ownership of land and the production of agricultural surpluses came into force. The most obvious manifestations of this transformation were the emergence of a settlement pattern and a system of land division redolent of a new and much more rigorous control of territory, and a burial pattern which eschewed conspicuous consumption in death and instituted what appear to be family-based cemeteries. In parallel with this major changes were taking place in agriculture and animal husbandry, and in particular there is evidence of a greater diversification in crop production.

There are also hints of an intensification in non-agricultural production and the suggestion that distinct regional systems may have been emerging. The downland economy was based on cereal growing while the communities living on the Isle of Purbeck were producing a range of commodities including shale, salt, and possibly hides and salted meat. The large populations now developing on the river terraces and coastal plain of Hampshire were well placed to raise cattle and also to engage in the exchange of their surpluses with the Purbeck and downland communities. Similar complex regional systems no doubt linked the communities of the Somerset Levels, those living

163

on the Jurassic ridge and the populations exploiting the clay vales to the east. The evidence is not yet sufficient to begin to explore these complexities.

Emphasis on land and productivity as a means of acquiring and maintaining status is likely to have increased social tension and aggression, especially if climatic deterioration and population increase were also significant factors at this time. The building of strongly defended ridge-end settlements reflects both the need to display status and a requirement for defence, while the appearance of swords in some number, brought into Wessex from the Thames valley, offered the elite an item of display consistent with the increasingly aggressive mood of the times.

Superimposed on these essentially local changes were the demands and opportunities created by overseas markets. For a while Wessex occupied a marginal position on the fringe of the Thames valley, which was closely bound to the Continent by an active network of exchanges, but with the flowering of the Atlantic exchange system throughout the eighth and seventh centuries BC the coastal communities of Britain, from Cornwall to Sussex, could benefit, and for a while they shared a markedly similar culture. In these developments may lie the reasons for the rapid increase in population and productivity apparent in the region around the harbours of Poole and Christchurch.

The inland communities occupying the downland, especially the fringes of the chalk massif, where a greater variety of soils were available for exploitation, also seem to have benefited. The elaborately decorated pottery displayed a new technical competence and the sheer quantity of artefacts created at this time are sufficient to indicate a greatly increased level of production. These Wessex groups would have benefited by being able to command the trade routes bringing bronze from the west to the southern ports, and local products principally corn, wool and hides may well have contributed to the list of acceptable commodities carried south from Britain. While the Atlantic trading system was at its height Wessex benefited but by the sixth century it was in a state of rapid decline. As we shall see in the next chapter this had a profound effect on the subsequent development of Wessex society.

Chapter 5

Tribal Society: 600–100 BC

The second half of the first millennium BC saw the emergence of what appears to have been a stable settlement pattern in Wessex dominated, over much of the area, by hillforts. But while it is true that many of the hillforts and a high percentage of the settlements, once established, remained in use throughout much of the period, the nature and intensity of the occupation at each location often varied considerably with time. Variations such as these can be recognized only as the result of quite extensive excavations. Thus, while in comparison with the preceding period, the late first millennium can be regarded as a time of settlement stability, in that a certain structural continuity had been imposed on the landscape which remained little changed, at a more detailed level the settlement pattern was undergoing constant modification.

The period can be divided into two phases of roughly equal length: the Early Iron Age dating from c. 600 to c. 350 BC and the Middle Iron Age which lasts from c. 350 to c. 100 BC. The division is based largely upon an assessment of pottery styles controlled within stratified sequences and dated by a now-considerable number of radiocarbon assessments. Fluctuations in the calibration curve make it difficult to convert radiocarbon dates to real dates in this period with any degree of precision but the broad division into two phases, with the transition coming with the fourth century BC, seems to hold good (Cunliffe and Orton 1984).

The Rise of Hillforts

The most visual manifestations of Early and Middle Iron Age society are the hillforts which dominate the landscape (Cunliffe 1984b) (Fig. 5.1). Already in the preceding period large earthwork enclosures, the hilltop enclosures and

165

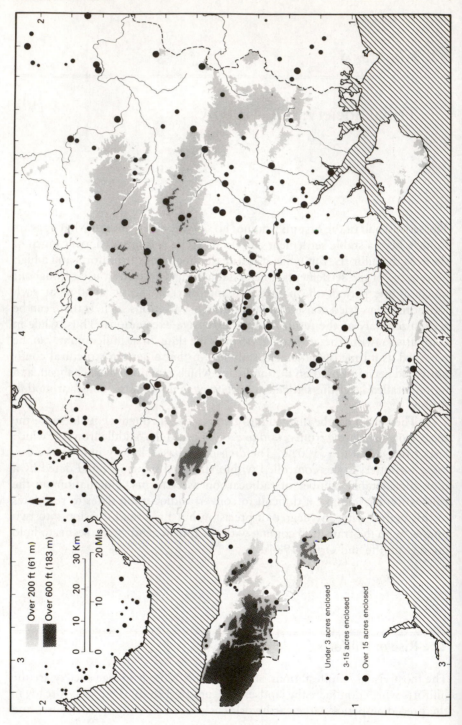

the ridge-end fortified homesteads had come into existence but these were comparatively few and are unevenly scattered. From the sixth century BC the hillfort proper spread across the landscape. These *early hillforts* were usually univallate contour works averaging 5–6 ha in extent and appear to have been comparatively numerous. By the fourth century a number had been abandoned as fortifications (though sporadic occupation may have continued inside): a few, however, continued in use and these were usually increased in defensive strength and sometimes in size. These Middle Iron Age hillforts, showing defensive elaboration and dense interior occupation, can be styled *developed hillforts*. This simple model fairly reflects the general situation but as the result of several major excavations it is now possible to examine the process of hillfort development in finer detail.

The origin of the early hillforts raises a number of difficult problems but there is now sufficient evidence to suggest that some of them at least may have developed out of the earlier ditched enclosures attached to linear boundary earthworks or at focal points along the network of linears constructed earlier in the millennium. A good example of the latter is Quarley Hill in Hampshire (C. F. C. Hawkes 1939; Cunliffe 1990). Here, at a nexus in a system of linear boundaries a palisaded enclosure was constructed, obscuring certain lengths of ditches but clearly integrated within the system as a whole (Fig. 5.2). There is no direct evidence of date but some time later, probably in the fifth century BC (on the basis of the associated pottery), the rampart and ditch of an early hillfort were constructed. At Danebury a broadly similar sequence can be detected. Here, within a ditched enclosure at the end of a Late Bronze Age linear, there is evidence to suggest that a palisaded enclosure may have been constructed within which were set up a number of four-post storage structures. A little later, in the middle of the sixth century, the palisade was replaced by a rampart and ditch (Cunliffe 1990). The third site of relevance is Ladle Hill, also in Hampshire (S. Piggott 1931; Cunliffe 1990), where the construction of a hillfort began within an early enclosure attached to a linear earthwork but was never completed.

The sequence at Quarley and at Danebury suggests, therefore, that palisaded enclosures, built in the seventh or early sixth centuries BC, were being constructed on sites some of which were to develop into hillforts. How many hillforts began life in this way it is impossible to say since palisade lines could easily be destroyed by later ditches (as in the case of both Quarley and Danebury) but at Hod Hill in Dorset a palisade trench outside the main ditch and buried beneath the 'counterscarp' bank could be interpreted as the earliest enclosure preceding the early rampart and ditch (Richmond 1968: Fig. 64). Although little systematic work has been done on the question it

---

Figure 5.1 Distribution of hillforts of the first millennium BC. (After Ordnance Survey map of *Southern Britain in the Iron Age*)

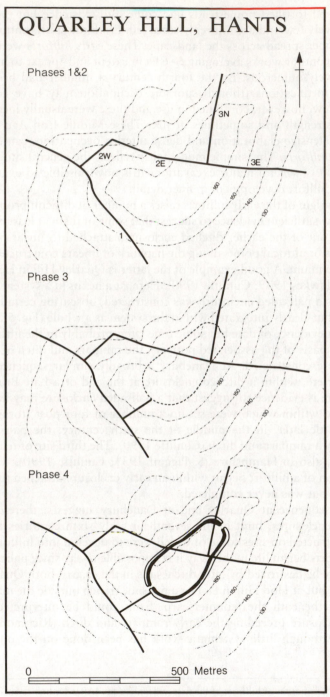

QUARLEY HILL, HANTS

Phases 1&2

3N

2W
2E
3E

160
150
140
130

1

Phase 3

160
150
140
130

Phase 4

160
150
140
130

0   500 Metres

Figure 5.2   The linear ditches and hillfort at Quarley Hill, Hants. (After Cunliffe 1990: Fig. 3)

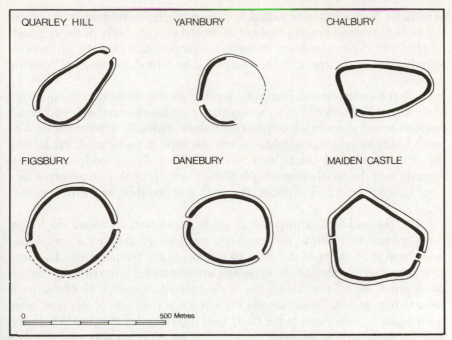

QUARLEY HILL   YARNBURY   CHALBURY

FIGSBURY   DANEBURY   MAIDEN CASTLE

0   500 Metres

Figure 5.3   Comparative plans of early hillforts. (After Cunliffe 1984b: Fig. 2.9)

remains a distinct possibility that many hillforts may have begun as palisaded enclosures.

Early hillforts, comprising a rampart and ditch, usually with two entrances on opposing sides of the enclosure, were constructed in some number across the face of Wessex in the sixth and fifth centuries BC (Fig. 5.3). The earliest forts were defended with a faced rampart – that is one in which the outer face was kept vertical or nearly so with the aid of timber fencing, stone walling or a combination of the two. A variety of styles can be found. In the earliest phases at Maiden Castle (Wheeler 1943), South Cadbury (Alcock 1972), Winklebury (Robertson-MacKay 1977) and Danebury (Cunliffe 1984a) a box-like construction, composed of two parallel lines of vertical timbers, suitably cross braced, was created, infilled and backed by rubble derived largely from the ditch. At Chalbury (Whitley 1943) the inner and outer vertical faces were built of drystone walling. When, at South Cadbury, the rampart came to be rebuilt the front face was constructed of vertical timbers set at intervals with drystone walling in between.

A rather simpler kind of construction was recognized in the first ramparts at Yarnbury (Cunnington 1933), Hod Hill (Richmond 1968) and Poundbury (Richardson 1940). In all three the rampart was fronted by vertical timbers, no doubt with close set boarding between, but with no inner set

169

of verticals. Such a structure would have been inherently unstable unless there had been horizontal bracing timbers anchored into the body of the rampart. At Hod Hill, when the defences were reconstructed, a new set of verticals were bedded in the front of the rampart 2 m behind the original fronting timbers.

That a variety of constructional techniques was used raises the question of dating and sequence. It is tempting to argue that the ramparts with inner verticals as well as outer were earlier than those with only outer verticals. The South Cadbury sequence would support this view but we cannot yet be sure that it was universal throughout Wessex. What dating evidence there is suggests that the faced-ramparts of Wessex were probably constructed in a comparatively brief period during the sixth and possibly early fifth centuries BC.

By the mid-fifth century BC it seems faced-ramparts were no longer being constructed. Instead the emphasis was now on creating a continuous slope from the bottom of the ditch to the top of the rampart. This has been called the 'glacis' style and the ramparts are sometimes referred to as 'dump-constructed'. In all probability the style evolved as earlier faced-ramparts came to be repaired. Two examples are known of ramparts of this type being constructed on virgin sites in the Early Iron Age, Quarley Hill and Woolbury, both in Hampshire, and in both cases there is some evidence to suggest a date in the fifth century.

The early hillforts tend to conform to a standardized type most, being contour works of 5–6 ha in extent with two entrances on opposed sides of the enclosure. Entrances, for the most part, were simply gaps in the defensive circuit protected by timber-built gateways but in the case of Danebury (south-western entrance) and Maiden Castle (eastern entrance) forward projecting hornworks were constructed to create elongated passages in front of the actual gate. This style of hornwork is known elsewhere in Wessex but only at Danebury and Maiden Castle can it be shown to belong to the Early Iron Age.

These enclosures with their massively constructed banks and ditches, some with complex foreworks, are redolent of defensive capability: they were meant to impress and to provide protection (Plate 5.1). To what extent they may be taken to imply a state of endemic warfare is a question to which we shall return later. Suffice it to say that at Danebury there was ample evidence of defence in the form of large quantities of sling stones immediately behind the rampart, and traces of burning at both gates may reflect an attack.

The Middle Iron Age, which began in the fourth century, saw a dramatic change. A large number of the early hillforts were abandoned while others were extended, in defensive strength, in area or in both. A few examples will suffice. At Maiden Castle and at Yarnbury the extent of the

---

Plate 5.1   The hillfort of Battlesbury, Wilts. (Photo: Institute of Archaeology, Oxford)

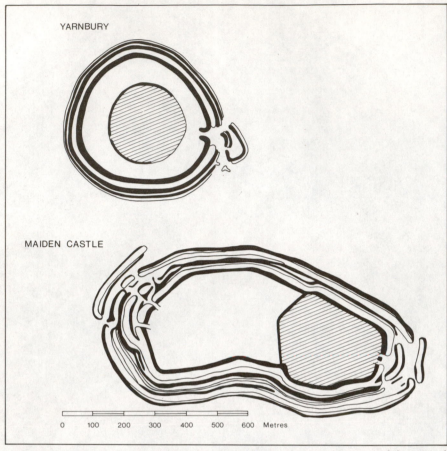

Figure 5.4 Yarnbury, Wilts., and Maiden Castle, Dorset, showing the extent of the original early hillforts (shaded) and their subsequent growth to become developed hillforts. (After Cunliffe 1984b: Fig. 2.16)

original early hillfort was more than doubled, the first by an extension of the original defensive circuit, the second by abandoning the original circuit altogether and creating a new, larger enclosure around (Fig. 5.4 and Plate 5.2). At other forts like South Cadbury, Poundbury, Winklebury and Danebury the original defences were simply enlarged by digging quarries behind the early ramparts and piling the fresh material onto the original rampart. At Danebury, as part of this process, the south-western entrance was blocked and the

Plate 5.2   The hillfort of Maiden Castle, Dorset, showing the massive multivallate defence and complex western entrance (front). The original early fort occupied only the eastern (far) summit. (Photo: Major Allen)

172

eastern entrance subsequently enlarged with complex foreworks. Surface features at Beacon Hill, Hants, and Uffington Castle, Oxon, suggest one of the entrances had been blocked at both of these forts.

The result of these refurbishings was to create more massive defensive circuits. At Danebury the distance from the bottom of the ditch to the crest of the rampart was 17 m, at Maiden Castle it was about 25 m. Some forts like Maiden Castle and South Cadbury increased their defensive capabilities still further by creating additional circuits of earthworks. Another characteristic of these *developed hillforts* was the care lavished on their entrances which were invariably provided with complex outworks requiring anyone who approached to have to wind their way between a maze of overlapping banks overlooked by platforms upon which defenders, armed with slings, could position themselves (Plate 5.3). At both Maiden Castle and Danebury large quantities of sling stones were scattered in the entrance ways and stored in pits just inside the gates. The gates themselves, substantial timber structures, may well have been provided with towers or raised platforms from which this last barrier could be vigorously defended.

The development of hillforts throughout the Early and Middle Iron Ages (*c.* 600–100 BC) saw increasing emphasis on their defensive capabilities. No doubt they were, in addition, symbols of authority and of dominance, but that they were also required to serve as defensive structures, and were from time to time attacked, is strongly suggested by the available evidence.

Although a not inconsiderable number of Wessex hillforts have been sampled by excavation only a few have been examined on a large enough scale to provide a reliable indication of their chronological development and patterns of use. But sufficient is now known to suggest that throughout the period the picture was constantly changing. At its simplest level it would appear that the sixth and early fifth centuries was a time when a very large number of early hillforts were constructed over most of Wessex. By the fourth century many had been abandoned but the few which continued had greatly increased in strength. While it is impossible to give much geographical precision to this generalization it does seem that the developed hillforts which emerged to be dominant centres were fairly evenly spaced across the landscape in a pattern which suggests that power was becoming concentrated at central points in a densely occupied landscape. Taking those forts, which on a variety of grounds may be supposed to be developed hillforts, their spacing over much of Wessex is remarkably even (Cunliffe 1976b). A microcosm of what may have been happening quite widely is provided by the area between the rivers Test and Bourne where all the forts have been examined. By the fifth century forts had been established at Quarley, Bury Hill, Figsbury, Danebury and Woolbury (just east of the Test), though Danebury had already passed through several stages of development by this time. By the fourth century only Danebury remained in occupation and was refortified on a large scale, being now intensively used. The simplest explanation for all this

Plate 5.3 The hillfort of Danebury, Hants. The ring of trees grow on the main rampart. The main entrance is largely clear of trees and shows overlapping earthworks protecting the gate with the road snaking between. The excavation of 1987 is in progress. (Photo: Danebury Trust)

would be to see the Early Iron Age as a time when the region was divided between many competing social groups: by the end of the fourth century, these had coalesced into a single polity. To what extent the primacy of Danebury remained unchallenged through the Middle Iron Age is difficult to say but by the end of this period Bury Hill was being redefended on a substantial scale suggesting, perhaps, that the power responsible may have begun to challenge the traditional leadership of Danebury.

While the general picture provided by the Test/Bourne region is likely to be broadly true for the Wessex region there will have been a great deal of local variation and the relationships of the developed hillforts to each other must have been constantly evolving.

So far we have considered hillforts largely in terms of their defensive capabilities but a sufficient number of sites have now been excavated on a large enough scale to enable something of their internal arrangements to be distinguished. Chalbury is an early fort which appears to have been occupied only in the Early Iron Age (Whitley 1943). Although excavation was limited, surface indications suggest the existence of thirty or more large circular structures, three of which, on excavation, have proved to be houses. A number of smaller depressions probably represent pits. There does seem to be some kind of internal patterning, the houses concentrating in the peripheral zone with the pits restricted to the northern part of the central area.

In the early phase at Danebury (Cunliffe and Poole 1990) a similar zonation can be recognized. A road across the site between the two gates divided the enclosed area into two. In the southern half several paths ran roughly parallel with the rampart, and along them were aligned a series of circular houses together with a scattering of pits, of which a number were rectangular. Thick deposits of rubbish were dumped against the rampart in this sector. The central and northern part of the site seems to have been set aside largely for storage pits but houses became dense again in the peripheral zone just behind the rampart.

While it is impossible to prove that a site was in continuous occupation rather than was being used seasonally or even more sporadically, the density of structures at Danebury and Chalbury and the quantity of occupation debris deposited is suggestive of intensive use over a considerable period of time. A rather similar pattern occurs at Winklebury in the early period (K. Smith 1977). It is also probably true for Maiden Castle, where excavation of the relevant areas has been on a much more limited scale, and South Cadbury, the full report on which is not yet published. However, the sparsity of occupation evidence within the defences of Woolbury is a reminder that not all early hillforts were heavily used.

Those hillforts which continued in use into the Middle Iron Age, and were massively redefended, also continued to be occupied on an increasingly intensive scale. This is certainly true of Maiden Castle, South Cadbury and Danebury. In all three occupation was particularly dense in the quarry

Plate 5.4 One of the houses excavated within the hillfort of Danebury, Hants. The house was circular and built of wattlework. The measuring rod lies parallel to the doorsill. In front the chalk spread provided a firm approach. (Photo: Danebury Trust)

hollows behind the ramparts where successions of superimposed buildings have been discovered. The evidence from Danebury is particularly striking. The entire periphery immediately behind the rampart was occupied by houses, post-built storage structures, open working areas and groups of storage pits, served by track ways (Plates 5.4 and 5.5). Some of the houses had central hearths and ovens, others were without. Elsewhere hearths and ovens occurred in open working areas. Inside this peripheral zone the large central area was divided into two by the main road running across the site from which a series of subsidiary roads branched. The southern half of the area was occupied by rows of four- and six-post storage buildings laid out along

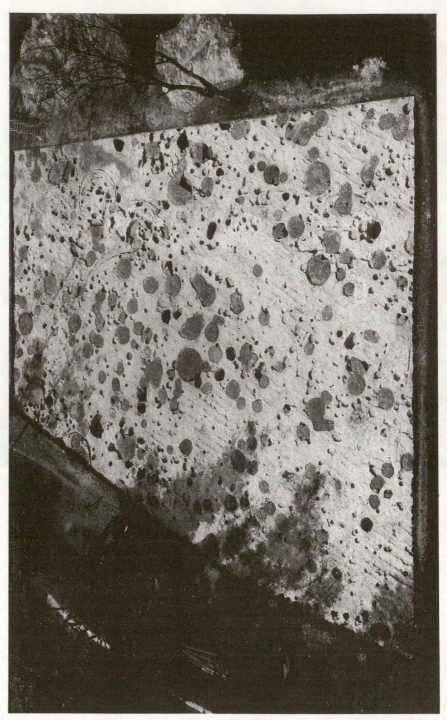

the roads and rebuilt many times on the same plots. In the northern half a small group of buildings interpreted as shrines occupied a central position. There were also numerous storage pits in the area. The general impression given by the excavation is that the interior of the fort had been divided into different functional zones and that these were maintained over a long period during which buildings were constantly being repaired and replaced. There is nothing about the surviving evidence to suggest that the settlement within the fort was other than an agglomeration of family groups living together under some form of coercive authority. There are, however, certain features, especially the enormous potential storage capacity, which distinguish these developed hillfort settlements and will need to be further considered below (p. 199).

Most of our evidence for the internal arrangements of developed hillforts in Wessex comes from Danebury, where about 55 per cent of the enclosed area has been excavated. While it would be wrong to generalize too far from a single excavated example, excavations at Maiden Castle and South Cadbury show that both conform to the same general pattern of ordered layout and intensive occupation and what little is known of the interior of Yarnbury (Cunnington 1933) implies an equally dense scatter of pits. Middle Iron Age occupation within the defences of Winklebury is somewhat different. Settlement structures are far less dense and appear to be localized. This could, however, be explained by suggesting that what we are seeing is a farmstead occupying an abandoned hillfort enclosure in much the same way as a small Middle Iron Age farm developed within the long-abandoned hilltop enclosure at Balksbury. That the late use of Balksbury and Winklebury can be interpreted in this way is entirely due to the fact that both had been examined on a large scale – a more limited excavation would have led to confusing interpretations.

The Farming Settlements of the Chalkland

A number of Iron Age farmsteads have been examined in Wessex, mostly on the chalk uplands, and hundreds more are known from air photography and from field survey. What emerges is a complex picture showing both variety and recurring patterns.

Plate 5.5 Excavation within the interior of the hillfort of Danebury showing pits, roads and circular houses. (Photo: Danebury Trust)

Three broad types of settlement can be distinguished: large open settlements apparently without well-defined boundaries; large ditched enclosures of Little Woodbury type; and smaller 'banjo' enclosures approached by a narrow road flanked by ditches continuous with the enclosure ditches. These three 'types' may merge one into another and some settlement locations may be occupied by more than one type in successive periods.

Perhaps the least known are the open settlements typified by Boscombe Down West (Richardson 1951) and Easton Lane, Winnall (Fasham, Farwell and Whinney 1989). At Boscombe Down West occupation features of the Early and Middle Iron Age were traced over an area more than a kilometre in length, though there appear to have been unoccupied zones within this. The data were recovered under rescue conditions and comparatively little detail is available. At Easton Lane, Winnall, on the other hand, while the work was again rescue, the examination was more extended and the results accordingly fuller. The site had already been subject to increasingly intensive and extensive occupation throughout the Middle and Later Bronze Ages. In the Early Iron Age (phase 6) the main occupied area was contained within a sub-rectangular ditched enclosure of Little Woodbury type but in the succeeding period (phase 7) assignable to the early part of the Middle Iron Age, the settlement had spread to the north-west and was now unenclosed. A little later (phase 8) the original enclosure area once more became the focus of settlement but the phase 6 enclosure ditch had long since silted up. At its most expansive the settlement extended for about 200 m but not all of the structural elements need have been in use at any one time.

The Easton Lane excavation provides an object lesson. The original excavation took place because the ditched enclosure was recognized on an aerial photograph. That the full extent of the Bronze and Iron Age settlements became apparent only after systematic exploration, prior to the construction of a major road intersection, is a timely reminder that ditched enclosures, which in the past have so often formed the focus of excavations, may be only one quite short-lived element of far more complex and extensive settlement systems. Much the same point is made by the scatter of pits and post-holes found to extend, apparently unenclosed, for at least 300 m along the ridge to the north of Battlesbury hillfort (Chadwick and Thompson 1956). These observations suggest that straggling unenclosed settlements may have been a far more widespread phenomenon than previously has been appreciated. It is impossible to gauge the size of the social group represented by such sites at any one time, but in phase 7 at Winnall, where the evidence is well preserved, the seven or eight circular buildings *could* have been contemporary – if so then the settlement may have comprised two or three families.

Ditched enclosures of circular or sub-rectangular form up to a hectare in area occur widely in Wessex in the Early and Middle Iron Age (Fig. 5.5). The best known is Little Woodbury in Wiltshire excavated just before the Second World War (Bersu 1940). Centrally placed within the enclosure was a

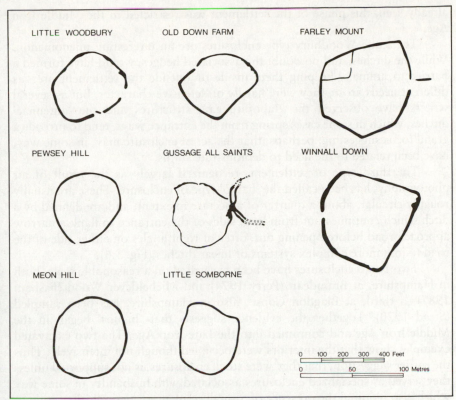

Figure 5.5 Comparative plans of settlements of Little Woodbury type. (From Cunliffe 1984b: Fig. 2.12)

substantial post-built house with a small house, probably of later date nearby. Associated features included storage pits, four-post 'granaries', two-post 'drying racks' and large 'working hollows' possibly associated with cooking or corn drying. Together these features comprise what has come to be known as the typical Little Woodbury economic unit which in social terms may have housed an extended family.

Two other enclosures of this kind have been excavated on a large scale: Gussage All Saints in Dorset (Wainwright 1979a) and Winnall Down, Hants. (i.e. phase 7 of the Easton Lane site) (Fasham 1985). At Gussage the phasing of the individual features was difficult and deep ploughing has removed most of the evidence of shallow post-structures but many of the elements of the classic Little Woodbury assemblage were present on a site occupied through-out the Early and Middle Iron Age. The Winnall Down enclosure contained several circular houses together with the usual pits and storage structures. How many were in contemporary use it is impossible to say but, as we have

181

already seen, this phase of the settlement was restricted to the Middle Iron Age.

The Little Woodbury type enclosures are an interesting phenomenon. While the ditches, and no doubt the associated hedges, would have formed a barrier to animals, keeping them inside or outside the settlement area as different needs arose, they were hardly of defensive character. But as several writers have observed the elaborate gate structures and the 'antennae' ditches, which in some cases spring from the entrance ways, tend to provide a grand focus suggesting, perhaps, that the act of enclosure may, in some way, have been related to the need to demonstrate status.

The third type of settlement, recognized largely as the result of air photography, has been called the 'banjo' type of enclosure. These are usually roughly circular, about a quarter of a hectare in extent, and are defined by a ditch which continues out from both sides of the entrance to flank a narrow approach road before opening out, often at right angles on either side of the road to join more complex systems of linear ditches (Fig. 5.6).

Two banjo enclosures have been excavated on a reasonable scale, both in Hampshire, at Bramdean (Perry 1974) and Micheldever Wood (Fasham 1987); a third, at Blagdon Copse, also in Hampshire, has been sampled (Stead 1970). Together the evidence suggests that 'banjos' began in the Middle Iron Age and continued into the Late Iron Age. The two excavated examples show that the interiors were occupied though not intensively. Thus the earlier suggestion, that they were stock enclosures, is not supported unless they served as specialized enclosures associated with husbandry in some way which also required the presence of a small resident, or periodically resident, population. The sample is too small to be sure and the excavation of a superficially similar site at Groundwell Farm in Wiltshire (Gingell 1981) produced an entirely different settlement pattern involving well-built houses reconstructed over a considerable time span, thus warning against over-simple generalizations.

The number of Early to Middle Iron Age sites known in Wessex greatly exceeds those of the Mid to Late Bronze Age and while there may be a variety of factors which mitigate against the survival of the earlier sites there can be little doubt that by the third and second centuries BC much of the more accessible Wessex chalkland was densely packed with settlement. Detailed field-work in the vicinity of Chalton in eastern Hampshire has produced evidence of thirteen settlements within an area of 9 square kilometres (Cunliffe 1973a: Fig. 4), while to the south of Danebury, in the valleys of the Wallop Brook and the Test, settlements were established at one kilometre intervals on gently sloping land between the flood plains of the rivers and the higher downland (Cunliffe 1984a: Fig. 10.2). Although these sites have not been excavated, and therefore exact contemporaneity cannot be demonstrated, the regularity of the spacing suggests that we are looking at a mature settlement pattern that had reached a state of equilibrium. The results of these

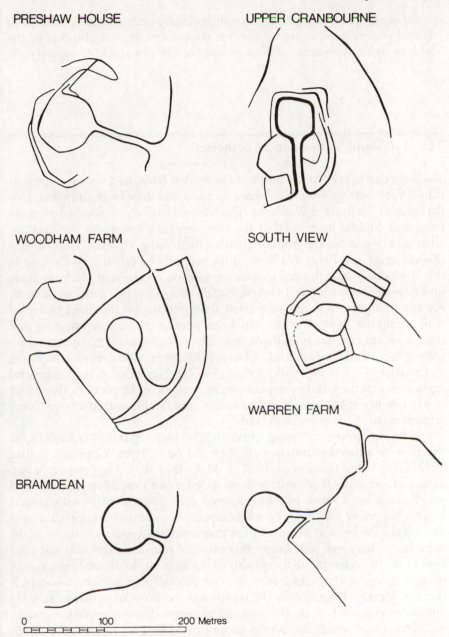

Figure 5.6   Comparative plans of Banjo enclosures. (From Cunliffe 1991: Fig. 12.5)

PRESHAW HOUSE

UPPER CRANBOURNE

WOODHAM FARM

SOUTH VIEW

WARREN FARM

BRAMDEAN

0   100   200 Metres

two detailed surveys imply that, not only had there been a notable increase in population during the course of the first millennium BC, but also that by the Mid Iron Age certain areas of Wessex had become populated to capacity.

The Marshland Settlements of Somerset

The Somerset Levels, to the north of the Polden Hills, had been the scene of considerable activity from Neolithic times and it is clear from stray finds that the Polden Hills and the Wedmoor ridge were intensively exploited during the Early and Middle Iron Age but the two sites best known in the area are Glastonbury and Meare, both originally called 'Lake Villages'. Glastonbury (Bulleid and Gray 1911, 1917) can quite properly be called a lake village in that it was built on a flooded morass founded on an artificial platform made up of brushwood, timber, bracken, rubble and clay. The artificial 'island', roughly triangular in shape, supported about 80 circular buildings protected with a palisade. Not all of the buildings were in use at any one time and though an attempt has been made to isolate discrete social groupings representing individual families (D. L. Clarke 1972), the results are not convincing (J. Barrett 1987; B. and J. Coles 1986: 164–71). Nevertheless there is general agreement that the Glastonbury community was never larger than about four or five families at the most – a size broadly comparable with the large 'open' settlements of the Wessex chalkland.

The settlement, or more correctly the two separate settlements, at Meare were altogether different (Bulleid and Gray 1948; Gray and Bulleid 1953; Gray 1966; Orme et al. 1981; J. M. Coles 1987). They consist of two groups of mounds, 60 m apart, built on the edge of a raised bog. Each mound was created by a series of superimposed clay floors usually with central hearths but unlike Glastonbury, where ample traces of timber superstructures survive, the evidence at Meare implies that superstructures were flimsy in the extreme and may well have been temporary and transient. This is at first sight curious when seen against the wealth of occupation debris and evidence of manufacturing activity which survives. One possible explanation, however, is that the Meare 'villages' were the traditional locations of periodic, possibly annual, meetings where people coming from some distance could congregate for purposes of social interaction accompanied by exchanges and perhaps religious observances (J. M. Coles 1987). The explanation has much to commend it, not least because Meare seems to be on a major tribal boundary where meetings of this kind might be expected to have taken place (below, Fig. 6.4). The site is a reminder of the difficulties of interpreting settlement evidence.

The Agrarian Economy

By the beginning of the Early Iron Age the agricultural economy of Wessex seems to have reached a stage of equilibrium. Naked barley, so popular in the earlier prehistoric period, had been largely replaced by the hulled variety (*Hordeum hexasticum*) and spelt wheat (*Tricticum spelta*) was beginning to compete with the more traditional emmer wheat (Jones 1984: 121–2). While barley can grow on most soils, emmer wheat favours lighter soils of the kinds found on chalk and limestone bedrocks. It is, however, susceptible to frost. Spelt has the great advantage that it will grow on most soils, particularly heavy clayey soils, and is hardy enough to withstand cold and frost. Thus it was a particularly valuable crop to have available at a time of agricultural expansion and diversification. It could be sown in the winter and would be available for harvest significantly before the spring-sown varieties – a considerable advantage not only in spreading the period of harvest but also in providing grain earlier in the year at the time when stored supplies might have been running low. Another advantage is that spelt would allow the areas of clay, capping the chalk, to be efficiently exploited. That they were is shown by the occurrence of the acid-loving weed of cultivation, *Chrysanthemum segetum*, among the grain deposits recovered from the chalkland settlements of Danebury and Micheldever Wood. Other weeds from Danebury suggest that areas of the nearby flood plains were now also being cropped.

There is ample evidence of widespread agriculture blanketing the downs. Celtic field systems, composed of patchworks of small rectangular fields, cover hundreds of hectares. Exact dating is difficult, since fields of this kind were in use from the second millennium BC well into the Roman period but a sufficient number of instances occur where Iron Age use can be inferred leaving little doubt that very substantial areas were cropped at this time. One of the most spectacular examples lies on Farley Mount, Hampshire where a settlement of Little Woodbury type formed the focus for a system of regularly laid out fields (Cunliffe 1978b: Plate 8). Field systems immediately adjacent to the hillforts of Danebury and Woolbury were also in production during the life of the forts.

The intensity of arable farming is amply demonstrated by the potential storage capacity available at settlement sites of all kinds. Two different modes of storage were used: above ground 'granaries' and pit silos. The 'granaries', represented by settings of four, six and less frequently five and nine post-holes, were probably wooden buildings raised well above the damp ground surface to allow air to circulate beneath the floors, in the manner of eighteenth- and nineteenth-century granaries which still survive in the region. They occur consistently on settlement sites and in some considerable numbers in hillforts like Danebury. Storage pits were usually circular and were dug to

185

a maximum depth of two and a half metres either with vertical sides or with steeply undercut sides giving rise to a bell-shaped profile. Experiments have shown that if properly sealed at the top, grain would survive well in such conditions. No lining was required but occasionally, in or near limestone areas, pits lined with drystone work have been encountered. Storage pits are common on Early and Middle Iron Age settlements particularly in the developed hillforts.

Both pits and 'granaries' have in the past been interpreted as grain storage structures, the conventional view being that the consumption grain was stored above ground, where it was readily available on a daily basis, while the seed corn was stored in pits. Such an interpretation is not at all unreasonable. It should, however, be remembered that there were many other commodities which may have required storage. The slighter four-post structures very probably served as the basis for fodder ricks while the more robust buildings may well have been multifunctional. The pits too could have been used to store a variety of foodstuffs benefiting from the constant cool temperature maintained in them. These provisos offer a warning against attempting to calculate the grain storage capacity of any single site, an aim made even more hazardous when it is remembered that it is impossible to say which structures were in use at any one time. One observation, however, is valid and that is that the developed hillforts have a much higher proportion of pits and 'granaries' per unit area than do the settlement sites – a fact which suggests that they may have served a centralized storage function.

While wheat and barley formed the staple crops, other cereals were grown on a less intensive scale. Rye, a particularly hardy crop suitable for both autumn and winter sowing, was introduced in the first millennium. Oats is also recorded but is less tolerant of the drier soils and of frosts. Another first millennium introduction was the celtic bean (*Vica faba*) which became quite widespread in southern Britain during the Iron Age. Its capacity for nitrogen-fixing made it particularly valuable as a break crop used to improve soil fertility.

Animal husbandry also appears to have reached a level of stability by the Early Iron Age. As we have seen the principal change – the increase in the number of sheep compared with cattle – took place during the early years of the first millennium. At the late second millennium sites on Cranborne Chase cattle amounted to between 50 and 70 per cent of the animal population. At the early phase of Eldon's Seat, dating to the eighth or seventh century cattle still amounted to 50 per cent in number but by the later phase, belonging to the Early Iron Age, the percentage had dropped to less than 30 per cent. At Danebury in the Middle Iron Age it was as low as 10 per cent. In contrast the percentage of sheep rises sharply to about 70 per cent of the total animal population at Danebury by the end of the Middle Iron Age. At some sites the percentage is even higher: at Glastonbury for example sheep outnumbered cattle by seventeen to one. This does not, however, mean that the diet had become one dominated by mutton: the average meat yield of a cattle carcass at this time is estimated at more than seven times that of a sheep (Cunliffe 1978b: 183–4).

The widespread and really quite dramatic increase in the number of sheep in relation to cattle raises interesting questions. The explanation probably lies in the different characteristics of the two animals. Cattle were undoubtedly valuable. They provided a more or less constant supply of food in the form of fresh milk and cheese which could be stored and eaten when the cattle were not lactating but the disadvantage of cattle is that they need to drink large quantities of water twice a day. For this reason they could never be kept far from a permanent water supply. Sheep on the other hand, while having a comparatively low food value, can fend for themselves for long periods without open water, being content to gather the moisture they need from damp vegetation. Both animals produce a valuable byproduct – manure. Now, with the spread of agriculture to the higher downland, well away from running water, the only way to maintain the fertility of the thin and often friable soils would have been to run large flocks of sheep. Thus it could be argued that the ratios outlined above reflect not the decline in importance of cattle as a source of wealth and protein but simply an increase in the number of sheep kept to maintain the fertility of the upland fields.

Sheep were of course eaten and ewe's milk would have been available from time to time. Their contribution to the diet could, in some cases, have matched that of cattle. They also produced wool and there is ample evidence in the form of spindle whorls, loom weights and combs, which could have been used for plucking and weaving, that the production of woollen fabrics intensified dramatically during the Iron Age. If, however, the system we have outlined is correct then the production of surplus wool in Wessex (for surplus it must be) was a byproduct of the need to maintain and expand the agricultural system.

Pigs were also vital to the economy. On most chalkland sites they varied from 10 to 20 per cent of the animal population but at some sites like Groundwell Farm close to a large tract of heavily wooded clay land, they were far more numerous (Gingell 1981). The value of the pig lay in its ability to convert substances, inedible to man and other animals, into protein. They could root deeply, eat acorns and other forest products, sup excess milk and gobble up offal and all the time grow fatter. Moreover pork once cured could be stored for long periods. Another great advantage was that turned loose on a cropped field their rooting activity would break and turn the soil as they manured it.

Horses occurred in varying numbers but were seldom more than 5 per cent of the total. For the most part they are found in settlement deposits as mature animals, a fact which might suggest that they were left to breed in the wild and the young were rounded up once a year for breaking and training. The discovery of bones of young horses at Gussage All Saints (Wainwright

1979a: 189) could suggest that the farm specialized in horse training. It is conveniently close to the New Forest where even today ponies roam wild to breed.

Finally, most communities kept dogs to help with rounding up flocks and herds and with hunting. Numbers were never large except at Highfield in Wilts. (F. Stevens 1934) where 22 per cent of the bones recovered were of dogs ranging in size from types like fox hounds to those like fox terriers. Taken at face value it might appear that the community at Highfield specialized in dog breeding, but the excavation was an old one and the sample may be unreliable.

It is impossible from archaeological evidence to estimate the relative importance of animal husbandry and cereal growing to the basic economy since the two data sets cannot be compared, but in all probability the diet at this period was cereal- and milk-based supplemented by meat. It cannot be over stressed that the two means of production must have been closely bound up in a single interdependent system. With increasing population and the possibility that the fragile downland soils were beginning to show signs of exhaustion, meeting the community's basic needs may have become increasingly difficult. In such a situation surpluses produced in one region would have been carefully husbanded and stored to exchange for a different range of surplus products generated in other areas. In the emphasis on horse training at Gussage All Saints, pig rearing at Groundwell Farm and possibly dog breeding at Highfield we may be seeing the dim reflection of the true complexity of agrarian specialization.

Industrial Production

The term 'industrial production', carrying with it the implication of systems organized on a large scale, is by no means inappropriate to the processes behind the extraction and distribution of certain sparsely distributed raw materials in the Iron Age. Although it is difficult to provide quantified data, compared with the preceding period there can be little doubt that production had increased markedly. This may have been partly because of an increase in population but it may also have been a result of an intensification in systems of exchange caused by the production of surpluses in certain regions. In other words once agricultural surpluses began to be produced there would have been a social need to exchange them thus creating a demand for other goods which could be used in systems of reciprocity.

Commodities like iron were, for the most part, extracted beyond the fringes of Wessex, especially in the Forest of Dean, Northamptonshire and the Weald but there were supplies to be had near Abbotsbury in Dorset and

Westbury in Wiltshire and there is the strong possibility that marcasite, an iron sulphide occurring naturally in the chalk, was collected from the fields for roasting and smelting. The transport of raw iron took place in the form of ingots usually of sword or bar shape (Allen 1968). A number have been found in hoards on settlement sites as for example at Worthy Down (Dunning et al. 1929) and Danebury (Cunliffe 1984a: 357–61) where they were presumably stored as raw material or deposited in a ritual act, but fragments of bars from a number of sites show that they were being cut up for manufacture. Caesar, writing of Britain in the first century BC, talks of bars of iron used as currency, implying that by this time they had a recognized value. Most of the iron used in Wessex must have come from southern Britain but a pair of double pyramidal ingots from Portland are of Continental type and were probably imported via one of the Breton ports.

Another commodity produced in quantity was salt. Most of that used in Wessex would have come from the south coast where there is ample evidence of the evaporation of sea water stretching from the Fleet behind the Chesil bank to Langston Harbour east of Portsmouth. At sites like Kimmeridge (H. Davies 1936) salt extraction began in the eighth or seventh century BC but by the Middle Iron Age production had intensified and a number of production sites were in operation. Salt cake, packed in briquetage containers, was exported inland and occurs in quantity on settlement sites. There is some possibility that at certain locations, such as hillforts like Danebury where large quantities of briquetage are found, the salt was redistributed into the local system. In the west Midlands at Droitwich and in Cheshire salt was also being extracted from salt-rich springs and packed into distinctive containers for distribution, some of it reaching the northern parts of Wessex (Morris 1985).

Another specialist product was Kimmeridge shale extracted from a very limited region on the Purbeck coast and used to make armlets, rings and beads. Extraction had begun earlier but in the Early and Middle Iron Age production seems to have increased and shale jewellery was finding its way to many of the Wessex homesteads. Production took place at a number of settlement sites in Purbeck, like Eldon's Seat, but there is evidence from Glastonbury, Danebury, Hengistbury and elsewhere that rough discs of shale were also being exported, later to be turned into artefacts. Thus some at least of the shale was passing into the exchange system in its raw form in much the same way as the iron ingots.

Quernstones for grinding corn were essential to the well-being of the community and since suitable stone was not everywhere available querns had to be transported, often over considerable distances from production sites at the quarries. The study of querns is still in its infancy but already it is clear that a high percentage of the Wessex querns were derived from greensand deposits. Only one quarry has so far been identified, at Lodsworth near Midhurst in Sussex (Peacock 1987) and it was from here that a high percentage of the querns used on Hampshire farms derived. Further west a wider range of gritstones was available and these tend to dominate nearby sites. Whetstones too were an important part of the tool kit. An analysis of those found at Danebury shows that a variety of West Country sources were being exploited.

Intensification is also apparent among what could be regarded as the cottage industries – that is the activities carried out at the farmsteads. At its simplest level this manifests itself in the greatly increased number of artefacts recovered especially from Middle Iron Age settlements. Among the commonest tool kits are those associated with the spinning and weaving of wool – loom weights, spindle whorls, combs, bobbins and needles – reflecting the importance of wool production on the chalk and limestone hills.

Metalworking activities, especially the forging of iron and the casting of bronze, are attested on a number of sites by the presence of crucibles, forging slag and, more occasionally, by the tongs, hammers, chisels, punches and field anvils which make up the blacksmith's equipment. The general impression gained is that metalsmithing was widely practised and it may well be that the majority of settlements had their own resident craftsmen capable of supplying the daily needs of the community.

An exceptional discovery was made at Gussage All Saints (Wainwright 1979a). Here, in a single pit, the debris from a complex programme of bronze casting was found including broken clay moulds discarded after the casting of a range of bronze horse harness fittings. The items represented included pairs bridle bits, terret rings, linch pin heads, strap unions and button and loop fasteners. It is estimated that in the order of 50 sets were produced in this single workshop (Spratling 1979: 140; Foster 1980). The process used to manufacture the majority of the items was *ciré perdu*. The desired shape was created in beeswax using bone spatulas to arrive at a finely finished surface and the model invested with a carefully prepared refractory clay. The whole was then baked to harden the clay and melt the wax so that it could be poured away. Finally molten bronze was introduced into the void: when it had cooled the clay mould was broken away and discarded. Although the process involved considerable skill, the materials required – bronze, beeswax and refractory clay – and the tools – spatulas and crucibles – were comparatively simple to acquire and to manufacture.

The Gussage discovery raises a number of fascinating questions about the status of the craftsman and his relationship to the community. Was he resident or itinerant? What was his social status and was he an individual worker or part of a team? There can be no firm answers.

The production of 50 or so sets of harness and chariot gear in a comparatively short time can perhaps be best understood against the background of surplus production for exchange which characterizes the Middle Iron Age. It is tempting to believe that alongside the Gussage bronze smith, blacksmiths, carpenters and leather workers were at work producing chariots and harness, nor is it irrelevant that there is some evidence for horse breeding on the site. Could it be that the community was producing complete chariots and pony teams for exchange? The question is at least worth raising.

Among the other forms of specialist production there is also convincing evidence that glass beads were being produced at Meare (Henderson 1981) but the volume of manufacture is difficult to judge.

The relationship of the different systems of production – agricultural and industrial – to questions of social structure and dominance will be considered later: here it is sufficient to stress that by the Middle Iron Age the production of goods, foodstuffs and raw materials had reached an intensity never before witnessed in Britain.

Ceramic Production

Part of the productive energy of the community was channelled into the manufacture of high-quality pottery, from the study of which it is possible to recognize the emergence of a distinct pattern of territoriality (Cunliffe 1978b: 31–55). In Wessex three broad phases of ceramic development can be defined: these can be categorized as early, intermediate and late. The early stage is typified by assemblages composed of distinct types of vessels: large coarse ware jars and smaller, more finely finished bowls, both classes being fired in oxidizing atmospheres giving rise to reddish or brownish wares. The fine ware bowls were often coated with an iron-rich slip to give a bright red finish to the vessel and many of the bowls were highly decorated. In broad terms the early stage can be dated to the sixth and fifth centuries BC. By the intermediate stage the differences between the two categories were beginning to blur and there was a change from predominantly oxidized firings to reduced firings producing grey and black wares. Decoration had almost disappeared. The late stage, which begins in the late fourth century BC, was dominated by reduced wares, the principal finish of both bowl and jar forms being a black often highly burnished surface. Although a range of forms was being produced, the dichotomy between fine and coarse wares had all but disappeared. Decoration in the form of shallow tooling and sometimes stamping on the leather-hard vessels before firing was widely practised.

Against this general pattern of development it is possible to recognize distinct regional groupings or style-zones. In the early stage two well-defined groups can be distinguished, one based on Dorset, concentrating south and west of the Stour valley, the other focusing on the upper valley of the Wiltshire Avon and its tributaries (Fig. 5.7). The Dorset group is characterized by finely made bowls, with vertical sides above the shoulder angle, covered in an iron-rich slip. The Wiltshire group is distinguished by distinctive 'scratched-

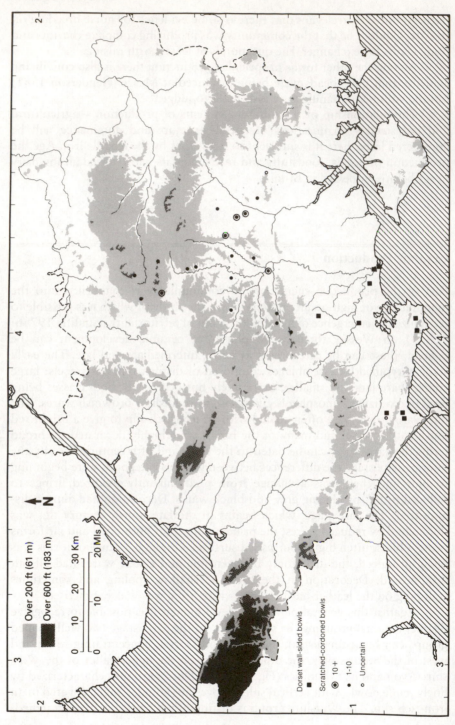

Over 200 ft (61 m)

Over 600 ft (183 m)

N

20 Mls

30 Km

Dorset wall-sided bowls

Scratched-cordoned bowls

10+

1–10

Uncertain

cordoned' bowls – sharp-angled vessels coated with iron-rich slip and with a geometric decoration scratched in zones on the body. Fabric analysis has suggested that most of these bowls may have been made from brickearth occurring to the north of Salisbury. Their close similarity and the skill with which they were formed suggests a degree of professionalism and centralization. Material from Somerset is much sparser but there is the suggestion that here too a regional style can be defined.

The vessels of the intermediate stage show little regional differentiation but by the late stage a variety of distinctive regional styles had once more emerged. Three basic groups can be recognized: a Dorset group (called the Maiden Castle-Marnhull style), a Somerset group characterized by highly decorated jars of a type which used to be known as 'Glastonbury ware', and a Hampshire-Wiltshire-Berkshire group typified by decorated tub-shaped vessels called saucepan pots (Fig. 5.8). Within this broad saucepan pot continuum the occurrence of distinctive decorative techniques allows further subdivisions to be made. There is a well-defined Wiltshire Avon group made from a local clay containing the mineral glauconite. Much of the rest of Hampshire shares a common range of decorative motifs, while a rather different decorative repertoire is to be found in the Kennet valley and on the Berkshire Downs.

Standing back from the detail, what emerges is the appearance of a distinct pattern of territoriality. The style-zones once established in the sixth century seem to have been maintained (with possibly a brief interlude in the early fourth century) throughout the Middle Iron Age and, as we shall see in the next chapter, considerably after that. If, as seems probable, these style-zones represent social groupings, perhaps of a tribal nature, then we can tentatively suggest that the social transformation which led to their genesis lay some time between the seventh and the sixth centuries, for this was the time which saw a rapid change from the almost universal use of a distinctive pottery assemblage distributed across the whole of Wessex to the discrete style-zones which appeared at the beginning of the Early Iron Age. As we have seen it was also a time of far reaching readjustment in settlement pattern and hierarchy.

Ritual and Religion

Evidence for religious belief and ritual activity, though scattered, is surprisingly plentiful in the Early and Middle Iron Age. There are, however, a

Figure 5.7 Distribution of two different styles of pottery of the fifth century BC. (After Cunliffe 1984b: Fig. 2.8)

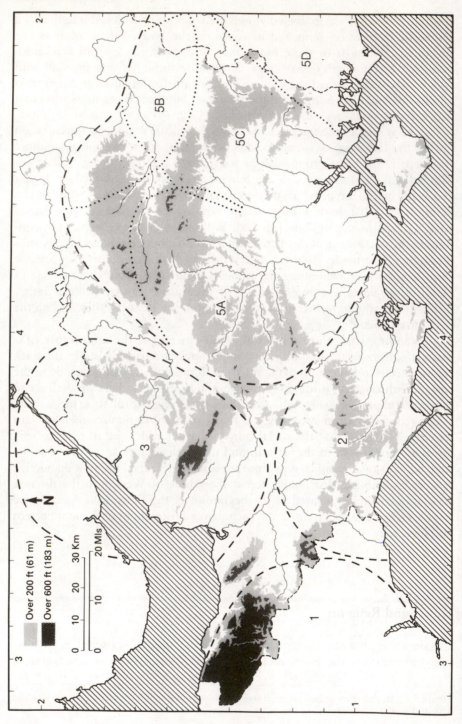

number of striking contrasts with the traditions of the second millennium suggesting that a rapid change in the belief patterns had taken place in the period of transition. This is particularly evident in rituals associated with the disposal of the dead. For centuries careful burial in defined and long-lived cemeteries had been widely practised, the rite of cremation becoming the norm by the last centuries of the second millennium. Many of the cemeteries established by this time continued to be used down to the seventh century BC but there is little evidence of any significant continuation after that: instead the burial record just fades out. Evidently some new means of disposing of the dead was being practised which has left little or no archaeological trace.

This is not to say that human remains are not found. Indeed a surprising quantity of human bones are found but always on settlement sites and usually associated with occupation debris. Most settlements have produced some human remains, the quantity depending upon the extent of the excavation. Reviewing the material as a whole certain distinct categories can be recognized. Most dramatic are complete skeletons usually found in tightly flexed positions on the bottoms of abandoned storage pits. Less frequently bodies were placed in specially dug pits beneath ramparts where they have been interpreted as foundation deposits. A high percentage of the burials in pits were covered with large flints or blocks of chalk in a way which suggests that the souls of the dead were being prevented from escaping.

A second category is the burial of parts of the human carcass hacked or sliced from a body while the sinews were still binding the bones together. At Danebury for example one pit contained an arm severed at the elbow, together with part of a torso, while another produced the pelvis of a young man with the heads of the femurs still in position, the body having been sliced in two across the stomach and the legs hacked off at the top of the thighs. One part of the body commonly found is the head – a reminder of the widespread practice of head hunting among the Continental Celts.

The third category is infant burials. These are rarely found but at Danebury neonatal infants who had died at or soon after childbirth were buried in small purpose-dug holes scattered about the settlement – a practice which continued in southern Britain well into the Roman period.

Finally, isolated human bones are frequently found amid the general occupation debris accumulating in settlements. There is no evidence to suggest that they were treated in any way differently from normal debris like animal bones or pot sherds. The quantity of these isolated fragments is often quite considerable.

Now what can be made of all this? Perhaps the most important point to

---

Figure 5.8 The distribution of the main styles of Middle Iron Age pottery. 1 South Western decorated; 2 Maiden Castle Marnhull; 3 Mendip decorated; 5 Saucepan pot styles with variants indicated. (After Cunliffe 1984b: Fig. 2.13)

stress is that what survives in the excavation record can represent only minority rites – the prime means of disposal has not been directly identified. The simplest explanation of both this positive and negative evidence is that the normal rite was excarnation – that is the exposure of the dead usually on raised platforms in a sacred area well clear of the settlement. Excarnation rituals can be quite complex. One widespread belief was that there existed a liminal period between physical death and the time when the soul finally departed. In such a system the bodies were usually left during this time but afterwards bones were cleared away and some brought back to the settlement. An explanation in those terms could account for both the absence of a recognizable normative disposal procedure and the presence of so many isolated bones in settlement deposits. There are further implications which might be worth considering. Excarnation does seem to have played a significant role in the Neolithic period (above, p. 53) and there is a good case to be made out for it continuing throughout the second millennium to explain what happened to the bulk of the population who were not afforded special burial beneath barrows or in the later urnfields. In other words, excarnation may have been a common practice throughout prehistory, the surviving burial record representing only a small sector of the population selected, for social or religious reasons, for a more conspicuous form of disposal.

Any system would have had its exceptions – infants, the unclean, enemies, etc. who were disposed of in different ways. The neonatal burials at Danebury reflect a minority rite and it could be that the cut up bodies and heads were of enemies dispensed with in a way designed to insult them. Indeed insult cannibalism – eating a token part of the enemy – cannot be ruled out. The same physical evidence could also result from human sacrifice said by the classical writers to have been prevalent among the Celts. The few complete bodies in the bottoms of disused storage pits are open to a variety of interpretations. On the one hand they could be the 'unclean' – those not fit to enjoy the normative rite – but they could equally well be sacrificial victims. There is no archaeological way of distinguishing between the two, though comparison with other forms of depositions in pits would tend to support the latter suggestion.

A detailed survey of the Iron Age pits found in Danebury and Bury Hill shows that a high percentage contained some form of special deposition usually placed on the pit bottom. In addition to the human bodies, there were whole animal carcasses (sometimes more than one), cow and horse skulls usually placed against the side of the pit, complete horse legs, groups of pots, quernstones, tools and cart fittings (Plate 5.6). The depositions are sufficiently repetitive to imply that they represent a recurring pattern of behaviour. Similar depositions occur widely on settlement sites of all kinds in Wessex.

Thus it seems that after the pits had served their primary use, presumably for the storage of seed corn, an offering was placed in the bottom before

Plate 5.6 Ritual burial in a pit at Danebury. A dog with the leg of a horse. (Photo: Danebury Trust)

they were allowed to fill up. Sometimes subsequent offerings were made at later stages during the process of the silting. That such a high percentage of the Danebury pits produced recognizable depositions raises the interesting possibility that *all* pits may have been so furnished. Woollen fabrics, hides, cheese, skins of milk, wooden barrels of mead, etc. are among possible deposits which would have left no archaeological trace. The question is intriguing but at present insoluble.

Depositions in pits are best explained by supposing that they were designed to propitiate the gods. It is tempting to go further to suggest that the act of propitiation was linked to the storage of seed corn, the 'gift' being in recognition of the fertility of the stored grain, as a thank offering for the harvests, or in anticipation that the harvest would be good. This raises the possibility that the practice of pit storage was part of the belief system. After all why go to the trouble to dig a pit for the seed corn when perfectly serviceable above-ground granaries were in common use for the consumption cereals? The suggestion that it provided added security in times of raid is not particularly convincing: a more plausible explanation would be that by placing the vital seeds in the ground they were consigned to the protection of the deities of the earth, who, having completed their task, had then to be propitiated. It is tempting to go one step further and argue that the appearance of widespread pit storage for the first time in the seventh–sixth centuries BC was a reflection of the change, which we have already considered (pp. 163–4), to there being a far greater emphasis on land ownership and its productive capacity. Like all matters of this kind we can only speculate.

Another pattern of ritual behaviour, widespread in Britain at the time though only sparsely represented in Wessex, was the deposition of prestige metalwork in watery contexts – in rivers, springs and bogs. This is a pattern which had developed towards the end of the second millennium and continued throughout the first millennium though with a decreasing intensity. Not all rivers were so treated: some were evidently more revered than others. The Thames for example has yielded a considerable amount of prestige metalwork whereas the rivers of Wessex have produced virtually nothing nor are there convincing examples of bog or spring deposits in Wessex at this time. The absence might be more apparent than real but it could reflect regional differences in beliefs (Cunliffe 1991: 514–18).

While it is apparent that the religious life of the community was rich and complex, direct evidence of ritual structures – temples and sanctuaries – is not prolific and for some while it was argued that since the classical writers believed that the Celts built no sanctuaries, but rather chose to meet in sacred groves and inaccessible woods, temple buildings would not be found in Britain. In recent years, however, several buildings have come to light which can, quite reasonably, be considered to be shrines. At Maiden Castle a well-built circular structure of timber, dating to the Iron Age, preceded a stone-built circular structure of Roman date which accompanied a Romano-Celtic temple: the implication is of religious continuity. Two other Wessex hillforts, South Cadbury and Danebury, have also produced evidence of religious buildings. In both cases the buildings were rectangular and occupied prominent positions within the fort. Those at Danebury span most of the Early and Middle Iron Age. In neither case, however, is there direct evidence of ritual activity: the interpretation is based entirely on a plan which tends to reflect that later adopted for rural temples of Roman date – the so-called Romano-Celtic temple. Evidence from France and elsewhere in Britain suggests that many of the Romano-Celtic temples were built on sites already sanctified in the pre-Roman period: so it may be for Wessex.

The Tribal System

The amount of data available for the period 600–100 BC is sufficient to allow a cohesive outline of social development to be sketched. Perhaps the most significant point is the emergence of hillforts as densely occupied locations spread throughout the landscape. In the sixth and fifth centuries many forts were being built: the fourth century saw a pause followed by a rapid decline in the number maintained, those that survived becoming more strongly defended. It can be argued that these 'developed hillforts' performed a range of central place functions. Storage facilities far outstripped what would have been necessary to support the resident community, there is evidence in the form of stone weights that careful measurement was being practised, and the sheer quantity of artefactual material recovered implies production and consumption on a large scale. Actual evidence of redistributive systems is more difficult to find but at Danebury it is clear that salt cake, contained in briquetage moulds, was being brought to the site from the coast. Briquetage was plentiful hinting that the salt may have been 'imported' directly to the fort for redistribution to the neighbouring communities. It is quite possible that other commodities such as quernstones, whetstones, iron ingots, etc. were treated in the same way. If so then we could argue that the social power based on developed hillforts may have maintained their pre-eminence by controlling the supply of rare commodities.

The surplus products directly available to the majority of hillfort communities were limited to the agricultural produce they could generate in excess – corn, wool, cheese, etc. These would have been used to acquire rarer commodities like salt, querns, shale, whetstones and iron which were now being intensively produced in specially favoured locations. While it is difficult to argue that these specialists were wholly separated from their agrarian base it is clear that production was now on a considerable scale, in other words society was moving towards a divide between agrarian and industrial producers. This being said we must not underestimate the overriding importance of agriculture to the economic base.

Compared with the preceding period there are stark contrasts but also some similarities. Perhaps the simplest way to view the situation is to see the Iron Age system as the culmination of processes already underway in the Late Bronze Age. It was possible to discern an increasing emphasis on land ownership. This would lead to the use of agrarian products as a means of establishing and displaying status. Surplus would then be used in cycles of exchange which would, of themselves, generate the need for more specialist products to maintain the cycle. The result would be a rapid increase in production and social consumption and would necessitate the crystallizing out of a system of redistribution like that manifest in the developed hillforts. The model sketched so far is at least consistent with the observed facts.

The question then arises as to the form of social control vested in the hillforts. Are we seeing here the seats of local leaders and their entourages maintaining their authority by controlling regional surplus and the dissemination of rare commodities or are the forts serving as communal structures created for the benefit of a group of equals equivalent perhaps to an aristocracy dispersed in the surrounding countryside. The options are not mutually exclusive and archaeology provides little evidence on which to make a judgement. We can, however, suggest that the developed hillforts may be the focal points of individual polities: if so the rise and fall of the forts reflects their changing fortunes. It is tempting to see, in the large number of early forts and the comparatively few developed forts of the later period, a stage of active competition and a striving for power followed by a stabilization based on more widely dispersed power centres. Evidence of burning at a number of sites, including Danebury and Bury Wood Camp, the occurrence of quantities of sling stones, and battle wounds on skeletons, show that at times competition could flare up into open aggression. This would be all the more understandable if, as we have suggested, the Iron Age was a period of population growth. One could even go so far as to suggest that endemic warfare provided the context for frequent raiding and that it was in this way that the warrior elite maintained and enhanced their prestige.

Finally, what of larger confederacies or tribal groupings? The pottery evidence shows that three broad geographical zones can be recognized in the Early Iron Age and that by the Middle Iron Age a similar pattern, but with one of the groupings now sub-divided, continued in evidence. If we accept that distinctive pottery styles are one of the ways in which societies display their ethnic identity then it is quite possible that these ceramic style-zones reflect tribal entities. Some support for this is given by the fact that several of the boundaries recognizable as early as the sixth century BC coincide with tribal boundaries known to have existed at the time of the Roman invasion. Thus the entities which became the Durotriges in Dorset and southern Somerset, and the southern Dobunni in central and northern Somerset, may well have come into existence at this time. In Wiltshire, Berkshire and Hampshire the situation is more complex with three distinct but related groupings evident by the end of the Middle Iron Age. By the first century AD new tribal configurations – the Belgae and the Atrebates – had emerged but these names, which derive from immigrants in the first century BC, bear no relationship to the earlier tribal entities upon which they were grafted.

Although much remains obscure it is fast becoming clear that the social transformations of the eighth–sixth centuries heralded a major change in the history of Wessex. Thereafter the tribal geography, which was to influence subsequent developments up to the Norman Conquest, had come into being.

Chapter 6

The Coming of Rome: 100 BC–AD 80

The Expansion of Roman Entrepreneurial Activities

Throughout the latter part of the second century BC, Rome's involvement in the affairs of the tribes occupying the Mediterranean coast of France intensified. This was in part the result of the need to protect the overland routes between Italy and the rapidly developing Roman provinces in Spain but it also reflected the desire on the part of Roman entrepreneurs to create new markets in barbarian Gaul and beyond where surplus products from the Italian estates, such as wine, could be off-loaded in return for a variety of raw materials and, in particular, slaves.

By 120 BC Rome had annexed a large part of the Mediterranean coastal zone of Gaul and in about 118 BC a major urban settlement – a *colonia* – was established at Narbo Martius (Narbonne). With the old Greek city of Massilia (Marseilles) commanding the river route northwards along the Rhône into the centre of Gaul and Narbo controlling the westwards route, via the Carcassonne Gap, the Garonne and the Gironde to the Atlantic, Italian traders were now able to exploit the potential markets not only of Gaul but of southern Britain beyond.

The earliest manifestations of Roman-inspired trade in Britain are distinctive amphorae, known as Dressel type 1A, manufactured in western Italy between Etruria and Apulia to serve as containers for the locally produced wine. These vessels and their contents were probably transported by sea to Narbo, overland and by rivers to the Gironde and by sea again, via Brittany to the south coast of Britain. The main port of entry at this time seems to have been Christchurch Harbour – an almost land-locked expanse of water protected by the high promontory of Hengistbury Head (Fig. 6.1 and Plate 6.1). Here on the southern shore, in the lee of the headland, an extensive harbour settlement developed from about 100 BC or a little before.

The archaeological evidence from Hengistbury is particularly informative (Cunliffe 1987). Imports from abroad include considerable quantities of Dressel 1A amphorae, blocks of raw purple and yellow glass and figs – all

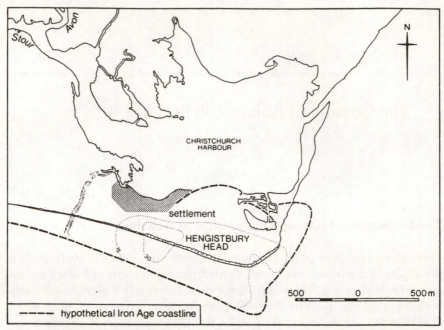

Figure 6.1 The Late Iron Age port at Hengistbury Head, Dorset. (From Cunliffe 1987: Fig. 42)

presumably originating in the Mediterranean. In addition large numbers of pottery vessels of Breton origin were recovered together with coins of the western French tribes, especially the Coriosolites who inhabited the region of the Côte du Nord centred on the river Rance. This Breton material and its general distribution (Fig. 6.2) provides a valuable insight into the direction of the trade route, suggesting that the last haul linked the Breton port of Alet, at the mouth of the Rance; via the Channel Islands, to Hengistbury. In all probability the cargoes, transported in Breton boats to Britain, were mixed, containing both Mediterranean and local products. How the Mediterranean wine and other luxury commodities reached the north Breton coast is less certain but the most likely way would have been in a series of short-haul operations along the Atlantic coasts conducted by native ship owners using transshipment points at intervals. There is no need to suppose that Roman vessels regularly put into Christchurch Harbour though a few may have made the journey (Cunliffe 1982, 1984c; Galliou 1984).

The Hengistbury excavations have produced some evidence of the range of materials collected together for export. These include iron, copper alloy, gold, silver, Kimmeridge shale and grain. There is also less tangible evidence to suggest that cattle may have been brought to the site to be slaughtered, their hides and salted meat adding to the cargoes. The list is interesting when compared with the exports from Britain noted by the Greek

Plate 6.1 Hengistbury Head, Dorset, from the air. The headland and spit protect the harbour scoured by the rivers Stour and Avon. (Photo: K. Hoskin)

geographer Strabo (Strabo IV.5.2.) 50 years later 'corn, cattle, gold, silver, hides, slaves and clever hunting-dogs.' Strabo's list reminds us of the importance of slaves to the ancient economy and there can be little reasonable doubt that one of the main exports passing through Hengistbury would have been captive manpower.

Hengistbury, therefore, served as a port-of-trade – a single location through which quite complex patterns of exchange were articulated. Materials produced in widely flung regions of central and western Britain were accumulated, refined and may have undergone some degree of manufacture, and were exchanged for luxury products from abroad which then passed into the hands of the British elite. Some indication of this is provided by the discovery of Dressel amphorae at a number of settlements in Wessex (Fig. 6.3). Another reflection of the local exchange processes at work can be seen in the distribution, in Dorset and the Mendip region, of wheel-made cordoned bowls, probably manufactured in the Hengistbury region in imitation of north-western French types (Fig. 6.2). This pattern is in all probability the result of the reciprocal exchanges by means of which silver-rich lead from the Mendips was transported to Hengistbury where the silver was extracted by cupellation.

It is impossible, from the archaeological evidence, to judge the intensity of the trade or to assess its effects on the local Wessex economy. On the one hand we could be dealing with a few boatloads of goods bought in in a single season, on the other with regular trade spread over half a century or more; on balance the available evidence would suggest an extended period of contact. If so the impact of this overseas trade on the Wessex community must have been quite considerable: the new demand for locally produced surpluses, including manpower, would have caused a major reorientation in productive systems; a totally new range of prestige goods suddenly became available for

Figure 6.2 Distribution of black cordoned ware made in northern Brittany. (From Cunliffe 1987: Ill. 219)

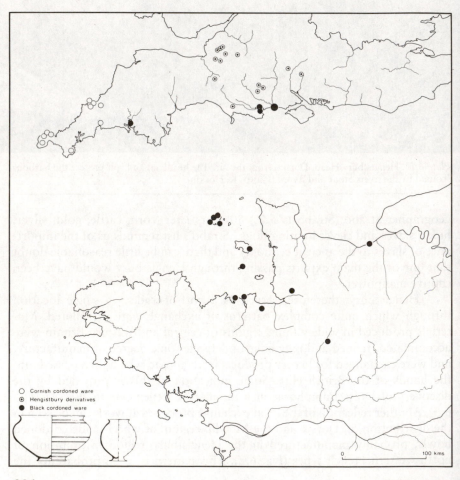

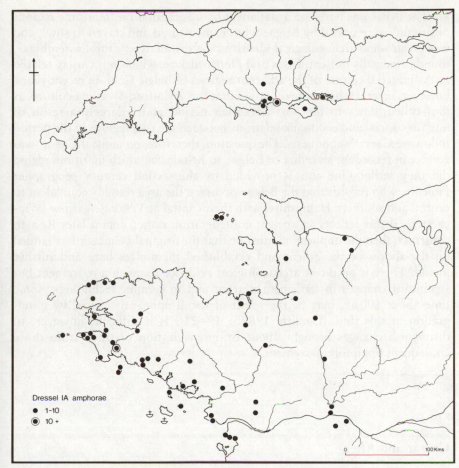

Figure 6.3 Distribution of Dressel 1A wine amphorae deriving ultimately from Italy. (From Cunliffe 1987: Ill. 234)

the elite; and new technologies, including the wheel-turning of pottery and shale, were introduced. The result of all this happening together some time about 100 BC or soon after cannot have failed to have caused major dislocations in traditional systems. The effects will be considered throughout this chapter.

The Question of the Belgae

It has long been believed that southern Britain experienced an influx of settlers from the Belgic areas of Gaul in the late second or early first century

BC. The belief was based on a statement by Caesar that the 'maritime regions of Britain' were settled by Belgae who 'came to raid and stayed to sow', and was given some archaeological identity by a distinctive cultural assemblage, found principally in Kent, Essex and Hertfordshire, which was closely related to the material culture of the adjacent regions of Belgic Gaul. In recent years, however, several scholars have shown that this Aylesford-Swarling culture, as it is called, dates to the post-Caesarian period and is largely a result of intensive social and economic relations between the two regions in the period following Caesar's conquests. The question, therefore, remains: if Caesar was correct in recording an influx of Belgae to Britain, in which maritime region did they settle? One clue is provided by the second century geographer Ptolemy, who records that the Belgae occupied the area roughly equivalent to central and southern Hampshire, with their capital at *Venta Belgarium* (Winchester). If this reflects an ancient confederation rather than a later Roman construct, then the implication must be that the original Belgic settlers landed on the shores of the Solent and established themselves here and further inland. There is no direct archaeological evidence for such a movement but significant changes in settlement pattern and in ceramic technology, some time about 100 BC, may be the result of social upheavals caused by immigration at this time (Cunliffe 1984b: 19–21). It is difficult, however, to distinguish changes brought about by intensification of trade from those consequent upon folk movement.

Caesar and After

In 55 BC and again the next year Julius Caesar campaigned in Britain at the head of a substantial military force. His activities were confined to the east of the country and did not impinge directly on Wessex but the long-term effects of his campaigns on southern Britain were far reaching.

One direct result was the flight to Britain of the Atrebatic king Commius, one-time friend of Caesar but latterly his sworn enemy. Commius and his entourage narrowly escaped Caesar's troops in 51 or 50 BC and sailed to Britain 'to join their people already there'. Within a few years he had established his authority in northern Hampshire and southern Berkshire, and had set up his principal base at *Calleva Atrebatum* from which coins stamped with his name were soon issued. It is tempting to read into this something of the political geography of the time. If we are correct in supposing that the earlier Belgic settlers had established themselves in central and southern Hampshire then it would have been quite understandable for their kinsman to have made for the same Solent landfall confident of a friendly reception. It

Plate 6.2   Coins of the Durotriges (1), the Dobunni (2) and the Atrebates (3). (Scale 2:1.)
(Photo: Institute of Archaeology, Oxford)

would have been equally logical for him to have proceeded northwards through his allies' territory, to carve out a new kingdom for himself just beyond their northern borders. The subsequent cultural similarity of the two areas and widespread use over the entire region of Atrebatic coinage implies a degree of unification under Commius and his successors.

A second result of Caesar's campaigns in Britain and his establishment of Roman control throughout Gaul, was in the economic field. The vigorous trading links which had been in operation for half a century or so along the Atlantic sea-ways declined rapidly after the middle of the first century BC though the few Italian and Spanish amphorae which found their way to the old port at Hengistbury showed that it was not completely dead. This may in part be explained by Caesar's deliberate suppression of the Breton tribes after their revolt in 56 BC, but it is more likely to be the result of the growth of a new exchange system which developed between the tribes of eastern Britain and their neighbours occupying the coastal region of Belgic Gaul, encouraged by the establishment of an infrastructure of engineered roads running from the Gaulish Channel ports north to the Rhine frontier and south, via Lyons, to the Mediterranean. The commodities which Rome required could more easily be transported along these routes: moreover Caesar had established friendly relations with the Trinovantes and possibly other tribes in eastern Britain and these treaties would have been strengthened by the granting of trading monopolies. In any event, as the trade with eastern Britain increased so that with the Dorset ports dwindled leaving Wessex as something of a cultural and economic backwater.

The Tribal Kingdoms

In the previous chapter we were able to recognize a number of ceramic style-zones which, we suggested, may have reflected ethnic entities (pp. 191–3).These broad divisions, established by the Middle Iron Age, were maintained throughout the Late Iron Age thus showing a degree of continuity. That the ceramic distribution may indeed represent tribal groupings is given further support by the coin evidence which becomes available in profusion after the beginning of the first century BC. For the Wessex region it is possible to recognize three distinct series which can be ascribed to three tribes: the Durotriges, the Atrebates and the Dobunni (Fig. 6.4). All three tribes were

Figure 6.4 The tribes and oppida of the Late Iron Age

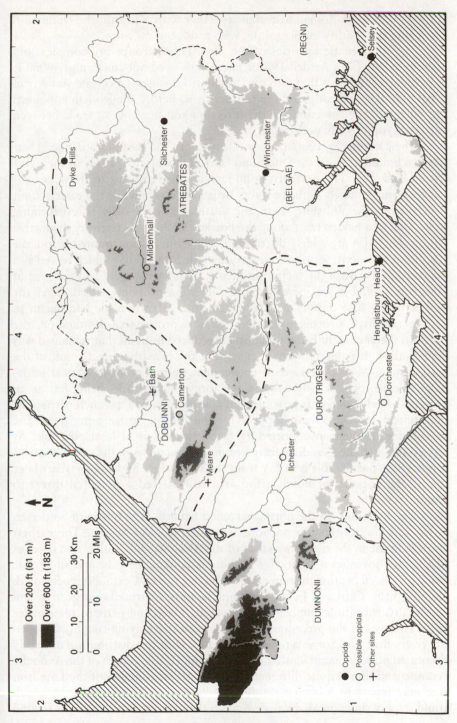

known to the later Roman historians together with a fourth, the Dumnonii, occupying the south-west peninsula, who produced no coins.

The numismatic histories of the three tribal groups are complex and open to debate (Van Arsdell 1989). The details need not concern us. What is of particular interest is that the coin distributions suggest a certain stability in tribal boundaries throughout the century or so before the Roman conquest: they also indicate something of the direction and intensity of trade between adjacent groups (Sellwood 1984).

The Durotriges, centred upon Dorset, are the easiest to define. Their western boundary with the Dumnonii lay roughly along the line of the rivers Parrett and Axe. The northern boundary is more difficult to draw but co-incides approximately with the rivers Brue and Wylye while the eastern limit is marked by the Wiltshire Avon, the heathland of the New Forest forming something of a barren tract along the border. Within this territory distinctive Durotrigan coins are widely distributed. The earlier coins, minted before the Caesarian invasions, seem to concentrate in the Stour valley which served as a major route between the metal-producing areas of the west and the port at Hengistbury and it was here that the elite were probably based. After the middle of the first century BC, by which time Atlantic trade had begun to decline rapidly, Durotrigan coinage shows a progressive devaluation, the precious metal content being successively reduced until all that remained was copper alloy. It is tempting to suggest that this was the direct result of the readjustment of trading systems consequent upon Caesar's political settle-ment, the Durotriges, originally in the forefront of trade, being left as an economic backwater. It is possible that Caesar intended as much perhaps as punishment for Durotrigan support for the Breton uprising in 56 BC. The speculation, though unsupported by firm evidence, is at least plausible. At any event when the Claudian army began its campaigns in the south in AD 43 it met with considerable hostility from the Durotriges and twenty years later during the uprising of Boudica the area still offered a potential threat to Rome.

The Dobunni, to the north, occupied what is now northern Somerset, Avon and Gloucestershire on both sides of the river Severn. The earliest coinage in use in the region was that of the Atrebates but within two decades of Caesar's invasion a distinctive Dobunnic coinage in gold and silver was being produced bearing the names of successive rulers, Corio, Bodvoc, Anted, Comux, Eisu, Catti and Inam. Dobunnic territory covered a large area and can be divided into a number of sub-regions, reflecting perhaps the smaller tribal enclaves of the preceding period. One of these, lying roughly between the rivers Brue and Somerset Avon, coincides with the distribution of highly decorated pottery manufactured in the Mendip region. North of the Avon the ceramic tradition is quite different. Thus the tribal coinages of the Late Iron Age may represent a confederation of smaller socio-economic units which could, at any time, break away or realign themselves. It is as well to remind ourselves that the situation was probably far more volatile than the coarse archaeological evidence allows us to appreciate.

The Dobunni occupied a favoured position with regard to trade routes, lying between the productive areas of the west and the trading interface of the east coast. The zone of interaction between them and the eastern tribes, the Catuvellauni/Trinovantes, roughly coincided with central Oxfordshire where coins from both areas are intermixed. Italian and Gaulish pottery, imported via the ports of Essex, also found its way into the homes of the Dobunnic elite. The coin evidence also suggests that the Dobunni engaged in exchange with the neighbouring Durotriges. However, unlike the Durotriges they do not seem to have maintained overt hostility to Rome. At the time of the Claudian landing the documentary sources record that a tribe called the Bodunni (presumably Dobunni) offered allegiance to the invaders.

The third tribe, the Atrebates, presents a more complex picture. Strictly speaking, the tribal name should not be used until after the arrival of Commius and his followers in about 50 BC but coin-issuing began twenty years before, the earliest types being based on the designs of imported Gallo-Belgic types. If we are correct in supposing that groups of 'Belgae' had established themselves in Hampshire some time around 100 BC then the pre-Commian coins circulating in the area may have been minted under their authority. From the time of Commius onwards Atrebatic coins bore the names of successive kings, Tincommius, Epillus and Verica, all claiming a filial relationship to the founder of the dynasty.

The limits of Atrebatic territory are not easy to define but the western boundary with the Durotriges and Dobunni seems to coincide with the Salisbury Avon, the Wylye and the upper reaches of the Bristol Avon; the northern limit extends to the Thames valley while to the east Atrebatic domination probably stretched as far as the rivers Mole and Adur. Significantly the distribution is broadly coincident with that of the distinctive saucepan pot pottery styles of the Middle Iron Age. The implication would seem to be that a high degree of territorial continuity had been maintained. However, within this broad and disparate region smaller socio-economic units no doubt existed. We have already seen that the saucepan pot continuum is divisible into several distinct style-zones. In the Late Iron Age similar divisions are discernible. It is possible to distinguish a distinct 'Southern Atrebatic' style of pottery manufacture extending from west Sussex through southern Hampshire, from a 'Northern Atrebatic' style which concentrates in Wiltshire. Once more we are reminded that the tribal groupings distinguished through coin distribution were in all probability loose confederations of much smaller socio-economic zones or *pagi*.

Finally we should mention the non-coin-issuing Dumnonii of the south-western peninsula, part of whose territory extends into the area of Wessex as it is here defined – the western part of Somerset. The extreme rarity of

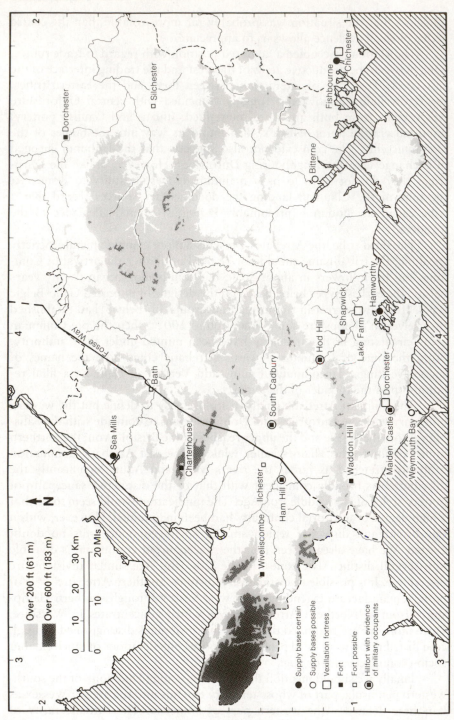

Over 200 ft (61 m)

Over 600 ft (183 m)

N

30 Km
20 Mls
0   10   20
0   10   20

Supply bases certain
Supply bases possible
Vexillation fortress
Fort
Fort possible
Hillfort with evidence
of military occupants

Dorchester
Silchester
Fishbourne
Chichester
Bitterne
Hamworthy
Shapwick
Hod Hill
Lake Farm
Bath
South Cadbury
Dorchester
Sea Mills
Charterhouse
Ilchester
Maiden Castle
Weymouth Bay
Waddon Hill
Wiveliscombe
Ham Hill
Fosse Way

Durotrigan or Dobunnic coins or pottery in this region suggests that they remained largely isolated from the affairs of their neighbours.

The Invasion of AD 43 and its Aftermath

In May of AD 43 an invasion force comprising four legions and detachments of auxiliary troops – in all some 40,000 – men landed in Kent to begin the conquest of south-eastern Britain (Fig. 6.5). After initial skirmishes and a major battle at the Medway the force reached the Thames, where they were joined by the Emperor Claudius before making a final thrust northwards to take the native capital of Camulodunum (Colchester). The initial stage satisfactorily completed, Claudius departed to enjoy his triumph in Rome leaving the troops, under the command of Aulus Plautius, to complete the subjugation of the territory which Rome intended to annex (Frere 1987: 48–80).

During the initial stage of the advance eleven native kings had offered their allegiance to Rome. One of these was probably a king of the Dobunni. Others among them may also have ruled in Wessex but of this we have no direct knowledge. Verica, king of the Atrebates, was in a rather different category. He had fled from Britain a year or so before, probably as the result of some local upheaval, to seek the patronage and protection of Claudius. It is conceivable that he may have been brought back to Britain with the invasion force and re-established in his former kingdom. The picture is confused by the appearance of another pro-Roman king, Cogidubnus, who, within a few years of the invasion, appears to have been ruling in much the same region. Cogidubnus had adopted the names Tiberius Claudius, indicating a grant of citizenship by the emperor; he also styled himself *Rex Magnus Britanniae* (Great King of Britain) and Tacitus recalls that he remained a faithful ally of Rome to within living memory – that is until the 70s of the first century AD (A. A. Barrett 1979; Bogaers 1979). While Cogidubnus was clearly a Roman appointee it remains a strong possibility that he was a member of the Atrebatic royal house and thus had a legitimate claim to succeed Verica, albeit as a client of the emperor. Tacitus also records that further *civitates* had been assigned to Cogidubnus as a reward for his unswerving loyalty.

To give geographical precision to all this is far from straightforward. A dedicatory inscription from a temple to Neptune and Minerva found in Chichester was erected under the authority of Cogidubnus and it has been suggested, though without proof, that the palatial building at Fishbourne

Figure 6.5 Early Roman military dispositions in Wessex

may have been a residence belonging to the king (Cunliffe 1971b: 72–6, 150–3). Thus the belief has grown up that the core of Cogidubnus' territory was focused on the Hampshire/Sussex coastal plain. In support of this the Roman name of Chichester, *Noviomagus Regnensium* (the new market of the kingdom), and Ptolemy's identification of the local tribe as *Regini* – both names ultimately derived from *regnum* (kingdom) – suggest that the core of Cogidubnus' domain coincided with the territory of the southern Atrebates (Rivet and Smith 1979: 445–6). This would be consistent with the observation that the northern part of Atrebatic territory, centred on *Calleva*, seems to have come under the authority of the Catuvellauni during the early decades of the first century AD. In giving further *civitates* to the care of Cogidubnus, the Roman authorities might have been restoring territories traditionally ruled by the Atrebates. The question is one of considerable interest but is impossible to untangle with any degree of certainty.

The chronology of these events is equally difficult to establish. It is, however, tolerably certain that the military authorities would have established the client kingships at the earliest opportunity to facilitate the subjugation of those areas which remained hostile. The kingdom of Cogidubnus, even if restricted at this time to southern Atrebatic territory, was ideally sited from a Roman military viewpoint; not only did it form a buffer between the initial theatre of operations in the east and the hostile west, but also it commanded excellent ports in the vicinity of Chichester which could be used as store bases for the western campaign when the moment came.

The task of subduing the west was assigned to *Legio II* under the command of the legate Vespasian, later to become emperor (Branigan 1974; Manning 1976). Suetonius records that he fought thirty battles, overcame two powerful tribes and the Isle of Wight and took over twenty native hillforts. Something of these campaigns can be reconstructed from the surviving archaeological evidence (Fig. 6.5). In all probability his advance began in 43 or 44 as a two-pronged attack mounted from a supply base in the Fishbourne–Chichester region, the army moving overland, first perhaps to secure the river crossing at Winchester before moving against the Durotriges and the southern part of the Dobunni, while the navy sailed westwards, accepting the submission of the Isle of Wight and establishing supply bases at intervals along the coast. There is some evidence to suggest a military base at Hamworthy on the north shore of Poole Harbour: another is likely in Weymouth Bay, probably at Radipole. Further west it is possible that a base was set up at Topsham on the Exe estuary in this initial period.

The brunt of Vespasian's attack was borne by the Durotriges. Hillforts,

---

Plate 6.3 Tombstone of a Roman cavalryman, Lucius Vitellius Tancinus trampling a conquered Briton. Tancinus died and was buried in Bath in the late first century AD. (Photo: Bath Archaeological Trust)

many of which may have been long abandoned, were put into defensive readiness. There is evidence at both Maiden Castle and South Cadbury for refortification at about this time. Several forts also bear witness to Vespasian's attacks. At Hod Hill it seems that the native settlement within the defences was softened up by ballista bombardment before the fort was stormed or capitulated (Richmond 1968). At Maiden Castle, within the massive earthworks of the east entrance a war cemetery was discovered the occupants of which bore the scars of a violent battle: skulls displayed sword slashes while in one back bone a Roman ballista bolt was found to be embedded (Wheeler 1943: 351–6). Less well controlled excavations at Spettisbury exposed military equipment and human bones thrown into the partially silted fort ditch (Gresham 1939). Here, then, are three candidates for the list of Vespasian's conquered hillforts.

To maintain control of this hostile landscape it was necessary to deploy troops in semi-permanent forts. The legion was divided into vexillations based on fortresses. One has been identified at Lake Farm in the Stour valley within easy reach of the supply base at Hamworthy (Webster 1960: 57), another probably lay in the vicinity of Dorchester, where several items of military equipment have been found, served by the supply base in Weymouth Harbour. Elsewhere smaller detachments of auxiliaries were strategically based to keep watch over recalcitrant natives. Forts were established within the old hillfort at Hod Hill (Richmond 1968) and on Waddon Hill near Bridport (Webster 1979). Large quantities of military equipment, from the now-destroyed site of Ham Hill, indicate the existence of another fort set up within an earlier hillfort (Webster 1960: 80–3). Further to the west an (undated) fort has been recognized at Wiveliscombe but this may belong to a slightly later phase in the conquest. The archaeological record is likely to be incomplete. Other forts of the conquest period no doubt await discovery but the bias of distribution of those known, to the territory of the Durotriges, may well be a fair reflection of where the main opposition lay in the first few years after the landing.

By 47, the year in which the term of office of Aulus Plautius came to an end, the south east of Britain had been brought under Roman control and a frontier zone, protected by a network of auxiliary forts, had been established across the country served by a rearward supply road, now known as the Fosse Way, which ran direct from Exeter to Lincoln. This system formed the *Limes* or frontier of the province of Britannia as it was conceived by the Claudian administration (Webster 1960). The frontier was not a single line but a zone of defence in depth, up to 30 km wide, between the Severn and the Fosse Way. As it became consolidated, more permanent military depositions were made and about AD 55 the vexillations of the Second Legion were gathered together in a fortress built at Exeter. Another fortress was established at Kingsholm near Gloucester in 49 and forts were probably sited at regular intervals along the Fosse Way. Military installations have been excavated at

Cirencester and there is circumstantial evidence to suggest a military presence at Bath and at Ilchester. It is possible that a supply base was established at Seaton, on Lyme Bay, at the end of one branch of the Fosse. Thus there would have been forts at intervals of 40–50 km, no doubt with lesser military posts between.

In advance of the Fosse Way roads were laid out to ports on the shore of the Severn estuary; one led to the mouth of the Parrett, another along the Mendips to the coast near Uphill, the third from Bath to Sea Mills at Avonmouth. We might reasonably suppose that these ports were an essential part of the supply system which served both the needs of the frontier forces and the economic aspirations of provincial governors. All were well placed to obtain metals and other commodities, such as slaves, from barbarian Wales. Little is known of their archaeology except for Sea Mills where some evidence for a military phase has been identified (Webster 1960: 89).

Behind the frontier zone a network of roads was laid out joining all the major urban and market centres and linking ultimately to London. It was probably at this stage that Cogidubnus was given additional territories to govern, his client kingdom now stretching in a swathe from the west Sussex coast to the Fosse frontier in the vicinity of Bath – the old territory of the Atrebates at its greatest extent. The Dobunni were now largely consumed within the military zone leaving the Durotriges, still a potential danger to Rome, isolated and surrounded.

In AD 60 a rebellion broke out in the east of the province led by Queen Boudica, wife of the recently deceased Prasutagus, client king of the Iceni. While the immediate cause was the ill treatment of Boudica and her family by Roman officials, underlying dissatisfaction with nearly twenty years of Roman rule enabled the incident to flare into a full-scale and exceptionally bloody revolt. The towns of Camulodunum, Verulamium and Londinium were destroyed within the opening days and 70,000 Romans and Roman sympathizers were slaughtered (Frere 1987: 70–7).

The full force of the rebellion focused upon the east of Britain and in particular the territory of the Trinovantes, Catuvellauni and the Iceni. How Wessex fared is less clear (Warmington 1976). In all probability Cogidubnus managed to keep much of his domain calm providing a valuable fire break across the centre of southern Britain but there are indications that further west the situation was far less stable. The Roman military commander, Suetonius Paulinus, marching from north Wales with his available force towards the heart of the insurrection, had sent a message to the Second Legion based at Exeter summoning them to join him. The legate was absent and the commanding officer, Poenius Postumus, the *praefectus castrorum*, refused to march. While this could have been cowardice, or inability to assume such a weight of responsibility, the strong possibility remains that the situation in the west was so volatile that he judged it to be necessary to keep the army in position to maintain order.

Hints of unrest are not entirely lacking. At South Cadbury hillfort a war cemetery tentatively dated to the Boudican period has been discovered (J. A. Campbell et al. 1979) and it is not impossible that the famous Maiden Castle cemetery also belonged to this event rather than to the invasion period seventeen years before. While the question cannot be resolved archaeologically the later dating would fit a little more comfortably with the archaeological evidence. In the same context we might mention traces of an extensive fire in the centre of Winchester dating roughly to the early 60s (Cunliffe 1964: 32). The possibility exists that it may have resulted from some act perpetrated during the Boudican uprising.

Towards the end of the summer the Boudican force was soundly beaten somewhere in the Midlands in a decisive engagement in which 80,000 British fell. Then followed months of reprisals leaving the war-torn province a shattered remnant of its former self.

In the decade to follow the social fabric and economy of occupied Britain was carefully rebuilt by a succession of governors chosen more for their administrative ability than for military prowess. It was not until 71, with the appointment of Petillius Cerialis, that a new military initiative was taken and the conquest of the Island began in earnest.

Throughout the decade of reconsolidation troops would have been withdrawn from the south to strengthen the military salient which thrust into the Welsh borderland to contain the tribes of Wales, and to add strength to the northern zone. The abandonment of the fort at Waddon Hill in the early 60s was no doubt part of this process of redeployment. But it was not until the early 70s, when the campaigns in Wales and the north were fully underway that the final troop withdrawals took place. The Second Legion Augusta was transferred from its fortress at Exeter to a new base at Caerleon in 74–5 and with it would have gone any remaining auxiliary detachments still left in the Dorset and Somerset countryside.

It was probably some time in the 70s or 80s that the client kingdom, ruled by Cogidubnus for so long, was finally incorporated into the Province, on the old man's death. When precisely this was we do not know but that the transition must have been a complex and delicate legal task is certain. It may be significant that a new post, that of *Legatus iuridicus*, was created by Vespasian in 79 and that the first two holders, C. Salvius Liberalis Nonius Bassus and his successor L. Iavolenus Priscus, were both noted legal authorities. Whether these appointments were occasioned by the problems consequent upon Cogidubnus' death is open to debate. What is clear, however, is that in the early 80s the civil systems of provincial government were being put into place in the south replacing the patchwork of temporary measures instigated in the wake of the invasion.

The Rural Economy

Although the period from 100 BC to AD 80 was a time of considerable political upheaval it is remarkable how little change can be recognized at the level of rural settlement. Where excavation has been carried out on a large enough scale continuity seems to have been the general rule. A few examples will suffice. At Winnall, Worthy Down and Gussage All Saints there is no evidence of any significant break in occupation from the Early Iron Age into the Early Roman period. The same sites were occupied and the structural evidence suggests that no significant change in status had occurred. The only recognizable difference is that old settlement forms – open settlements or the enclosed farmsteads of Little Woodbury type – had been replaced by a series of smaller conjoined ditched enclosures (Fig. 6.6). Similar settlement patterns dating to the Later Iron Age are widely known in Wessex, as for example at Rotherley and Casterley (Cunliffe 1973c: Fig. 44). It is tempting to suggest that the new enclosure pattern is a reflection of a greater emphasis on the control of livestock, but tangible evidence is lacking.

Continuity of occupation into the Roman period is also widespread. At Chalton a Late Iron Age settlement continued largely unchanged into the Early Roman period (Cunliffe 1977) while at Tollard Royal a small enclosed Durotrigan farmstead was replaced by what appears to have been a Roman settlement of village proportions (Wainwright 1968; Bowen and Fowler 1966: 46–8). Elsewhere, throughout Wessex, there is consistent evidence for the development of Roman farmsteads (*villas*) on sites previously intensively occupied in the Late Iron Age or earlier: among the dozens of sites which could be quoted we can mention Halstock and Tarrant Hinton in Dorset, Bramdean in east Hampshire and Balksbury, Chattis Hill, Rockbourne and Grateley South (Fig. 6.7) in the west of Hampshire. While it must be admitted that direct continuity, in social and economic terms, is difficult to prove, the patterns are so consistent over such a wide area that the general implication must be that systems of landholding and agrarian exploitation, already established by the Middle Iron Age, continued little changed into, and possibly throughout, the Roman period. The modest Roman villa of, say, the second century AD differs in no significant way from the round timber house of the second century BC: indeed the occupants of the former may well have been the direct descendants of the latter. The difference lies largely in the physical form in which their social prestige was expressed.

Having stressed the importance of legal, social and economic continuity throughout this transition period we must look at what changes can be detected in rural settlement. The most significant would seem to be the abandonment of hillforts as the seats of centralized power. This is not to say that all forts were totally abandoned but in those cases where the evidence is

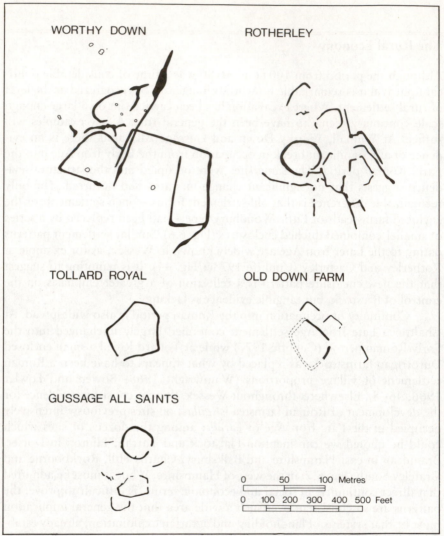

Figure 6.6 Comparative plans of Late Iron Age farmsteads. (From Cunliffe 1984b: Fig. 2.18)

sufficient there are clear signs of a rapid decrease in the intensity of occupation and a lack of concern for maintaining the defences. Some forts, however, for example South Cadbury, Maiden Castle and Hod Hill, were put into defensive readiness and reoccupied at the time of the invasion.

Various reasons may be offered for the decline of the hillfort: the question is best approached from the point of view of loss of function. We have argued that one function of the developed forts was to serve as redistribution centres for goods. With the development of increasingly intensive trading contacts with the Continent new centres for the articulation of trade and exchange arose at route nodes where the movement of goods could be more easily controlled. These locations became the oppida which we shall consider below (pp. 222–5). This reorientation in the exchange system could have been sufficient to have rendered hillforts obsolete. Another change, less easy to demonstrate, probably lay in the methods used to display prestige among the elite. In the Middle Iron Age raiding was probably the prime method by which an aspiring individual could broadcast his qualities of leadership and also acquire the goods needed to enhance his reputation as one able to bestow gifts. The advent of overseas trade, together with the development of coinage, provided a new method of display – the powerful could control the throughput of exotic commodities consolidating their wealth in easy-to-store coin. Thus raiding became obsolete and with it the physical manifestation of raiding societies – the hillfort. If this model is correct it would suggest that the aristocracy may have transferred their courts to the burgeoning oppida the better to control the movement of commodities.

What effect these changes at the elite level may have had on the food-

Figure 6.7 The Iron Age and Roman farm at Grateley South, Hants. (After R. Palmer 1984: Fig. 18)

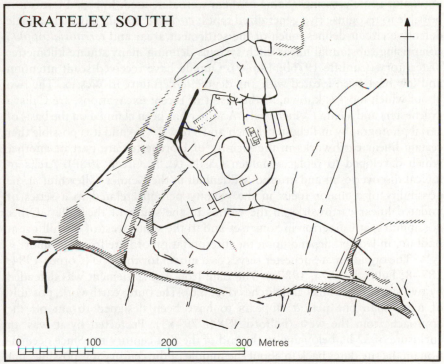

GRATELEY SOUTH

0   100   200   300 Metres

producing economy it is not easy to determine. Hard facts are difficult to come by. The diversification in crops – a trend already identified in the Middle Iron Age – seems to have continued and even intensified during the Late Iron Age. Some slight changes are also apparent in the livestock proportions. At Tollard Royal, cattle were more numerous than sheep while at Winnall Down cattle and sheep occurred in roughly even numbers. At Gussage All Saints, however, although there was an increase in the number of cattle present in the Late Iron Age, sheep still predominated. Too much should not be read into these observations, not least because the sample sizes are small, but there may have been a general shift towards cattle production. It should not be forgotten that hides were much in demand in the Roman world for manufacturing military equipment.

The Development of Urban Centres

In the last century or so before the Roman conquest a number of large nucleated settlements, or oppida, developed, quite often at points commanding major route crossings. Some of them were defended. In broad terms it is possible to recognize two generalized types: *enclosed oppida* in which a single defensive circuit defines much of the settlement area; and *territorial oppida* comprising substantial linear ditch systems defining many square kilometres of territory (Cunliffe 1976b: 145–9). Oppida have received scant attention and few have been located with any degree of certainty in Wessex. The two about which most is known, as the result of recent excavations, are Calleva (Silchester) and Venta (Winchester). Another has been claimed on the basis of aerial photography at Ilchester (Leach and Thew 1985) and it is possible that certain linear earthworks in the vicinity of Dorchester are part of another which developed to replace Maiden Castle (C. S. Green 1986). Archaeological discoveries in and around Mildenhall in the Kennet valley hint at the possibility of a major focus in the vicinity perhaps related to a series of undated linear earthworks in the woods to the south of the valley. Other possibilities, at Camerton in Somerset and to the south west of the hillfort at Badbury in Dorset, depend upon the interpretation of Late Iron Age finds.

The oppidum at Silchester serves as a model for the type (Corney 1984: 287–8; Fulford 1987a, 1987b). The Late Iron Age settlement was defended by two systems of banks and ditches (Fig. 6.8). The outer earthwork, possibly of more than one period, appears to have been designed to cut off the approach from the west (Fulford 1984: 79–83). Protected by it was an enclosure of 32 ha belonging to the end of the first century BC. Since occupation on the site dates back to about the middle of the century it is possible, but

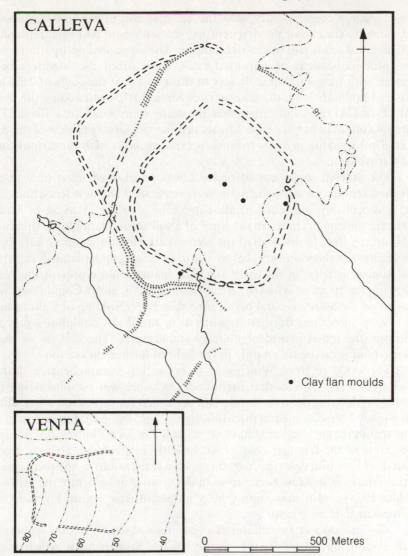

Figure 6.8 The Late Iron Age oppida at Calleva (Silchester) and Venta (Winchester). (Calleva, after Fulford 1984: Fig. 85; Venta, after Biddle 1983: Fig. 3)

by no means proven, that the outer defences were laid out at this time. If so it could well be that the first defences were the work of Commius soon after his arrival in the country.

An area excavation within the inner enclosure has exposed three distinct phases of occupation. The earliest, of mid first century BC date, consisted of a series of closely spaced round houses together with a well. In the second phase, roughly contemporary with the construction of the inner enclosure and dating to the end of the first century, the settlement had been replanned with metalled roads laid out at right angles. The associated occupation levels have produced sherds of imported table wares from the Mediterranean together with wine amphorae. It was to this phase that the coins of Tincommius and Epillus belong, the latter styling himself REX and adding the mark CALLE or CALLEV, indicating that the coins were struck at Calleva. The material culture in use in phase 2 bears distinct similarities to that of the east of England resulting perhaps from direct trading links with the Trinovantes and Catuvellauni.

The ordered settlement of phase 2 was refurbished some time in the early first century AD when the roads were remetalled and new fence lines laid out, and probably continued in use some time after the invasion of AD 43. There are some indications, in the form of a soil accumulation over the south road surface, that, in this area of the settlement at least, there may have been a brief phase of abandonment, before the town was again replanned, this time in a Roman manner, in the early 50s. The hiatus could represent the years following the invasion, when the Atrebatic leadership under Cogidubnus was focused on the Sussex coastal plain. If so then the rebuilding of Calleva may have begun after these northern regions were added to Cogidubnus' domain following the initial period of military stabilization. The validity of these interpretations can be tested only in the light of further excavation.

The evidence from Winchester is rather less comprehensive (Biddle 1983: 105–11). A substantial earthwork enclosure was established on the hillside overlooking the river flood plain in the first century BC on a site which had already been occupied in the Middle Iron Age (Fig. 6.8). Limited excavations within the enclosed area have so far failed to locate any *in situ* occupation layers of the late first century BC or early first century AD, but a coin 'mould' of Late Iron Age type, together with a scatter of Iron Age coins, many of them imports, indicate occupation in the century or so before the invasion (Biddle 1975) and it may simply be a matter of time before layers of the appropriate date are found.

The situation at Dorchester is even more obscure. Several lengths of ditch system are known in the vicinity of the Roman town which could conceivably be of Late Iron Age date (C. S. Green 1986), but aerial photography and limited excavation have brought to light a substantial area of cropmarks spreading across the undulating land north of Maiden Castle, between it and the Roman town. It could well be that the nucleus of the Late Iron Age settlement lay in this area. If so, unlike Silchester and Winchester, it would seem to have been unenclosed.

Finally we must mention the defended promontory of Hengistbury Head. Occupation here continued after the middle of the first century BC and it was during this time that metalled roads were laid out together with well-defined palisaded enclosures containing timber structures and pits (Cunliffe

1987: Ill. 95). The occurrence of a few Dressel 1B amphorae and amphorae of Dressel 1/Pascual 1 type from Spain indicate that the old Atlantic trade route was still functioning but on a much diminished scale. However, the presence of large quantities of Late Durotrigan cast bronze coins, suggestive of a mint, shows that the site continued to play an important role as a regional centre.

After the invasion the majority of the native oppida continued to develop as urban centres, the one notable exception being Hengistbury, which seems to have reverted to being little more than an agricultural village. The settlement at Badbury, if indeed it was of urban quality, also failed to become more than a roadside market.

Evidence for the early stages of Romanization are clearest at Silchester and Winchester where extensive excavations have been carried out over the years. Urban development was underway at Silchester in the 50s and 60s of the first century following what may have been a brief military interlude and that the programme was carried out with official encouragement is shown by the discovery of bricks stamped with the name of the Emperor Nero (54–68). Although the exact sequence of events cannot be reconstructed, the period 50–80 saw the construction of a regular grid of metalled streets defining insulae 400 by 400 or 400 by 275 Roman feet. In the centre was a large plot reserved for the administrative complex – the forum and basilica. The earliest of a sequence of buildings put up here was a timber structure, comprising a range of rooms 57 m long fronting onto a verandah or, more likely, an aisled hall (Fig. 6.9). In all probability this was the town's first basilica (Fulford 1987b).

Nearby were the public baths built in masonry to avoid risk of fire. They consisted of a simple range of rooms of graded temperature opening onto an exercise court, or *palaestra*, fronted by a colonnade. That the baths belong to an early phase in the town's history is shown by the fact that they pre-dated the layout of the street grid: the facade had to be modified when the streets were constructed (Boon 1974: 127–30).

Towards the periphery of the site an amphitheatre was created by excavating the elliptical area 2 m into the ground and using the spoil to build a sloping bank for seating all around: the periphery of the area was revetted with massive timbers.

Although little is known about early housing within the town one might suppose that it soon became cluttered with the shops and houses of the Atrebatic population who had been based on the native oppidum for decades. Thus within the first 40 years of the Roman occupation Calleva had acquired all the attributes of a thriving civitas capital.

The situation in Winchester is less clear. Very little is known of the Claudian or Neronian settlement though elaborate timber buildings with painted walls were in use. The first major impetus to urban growth seems to have come in the Flavian period (69–98) when a defensive circuit was erected

SILCHESTER BASILICA

AD50-85   AD85-Mid second century

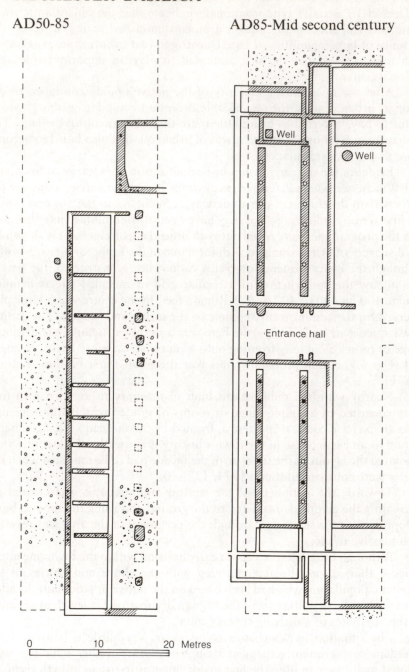

Figure 6.9   The early basilicas at Silchester. (After Fulford 1987b)

226

on the north, west and south side of the settlement. It comprised a turf-faced rampart in excess of 12 m wide and was presumably fronted by a ditch. A substantial timber gate was erected on the south side, later to be replaced in masonry. As part of the Flavian building programme it would appear that the first stage of the street grid was laid out (Biddle 1983: 110–11). On present evidence, therefore, it looks as though Winchester lagged behind Silchester in the early stages of its urban development but the construction of the Flavian defences singles it out from the rest of the towns of Wessex.

We have already suggested that the principal pre-Roman settlement at Dorchester lay to the north of Maiden Castle. Later, a military installation, possibly a fortress for a vexillation of the Second Legion, is likely to have been established in the vicinity perhaps on a site closer to the river beneath the town of *Durnovaria*. Once the military had moved away the population shifted to the river side site but very little is yet known of the early stages of urban development. The impressive aqueduct which winds its way along the valley from a spring to the north west of the town is dated to the latter part of the first century and may have been designed to serve a suite of public baths discovered in the grounds of Wollaston House. It was at about this time that the Late Neolithic henge monument, known as Maumsbury Rings, was modified to turn it into an amphitheatre. The exact dating of these three early amenities has not been closely established, but on present evidence they would seem to belong towards the end of the Flavian period. It is possible, therefore, that the advancement of the urban community was delayed, perhaps because of the hostility shown by the tribal leaders in 43 and again in 60. The same picture is repeated at Ilchester (*Lindinis*), the other major centre within the territory of the Durotriges, where no significant trace of urban development can be found before the last decade of the first century (Leach 1982: 6–7).

Of the growth of the other Wessex centres there is little yet to be said. The spa and sanctuary at Bath (Aquae Sulis) was certainly undergoing major redevelopment in the Late Neronian period but at this stage it could hardly be called a town. It may be that Camerton, 12 km south along the Fosse Way, had pretensions of becoming a market and administrative centre. Certainly timber buildings were being erected soon after the Fosse Way was built but the settlement failed to develop, eclipsed presumably, by the spectacular growth of Bath (Wedlake 1958).

In summary, the evidence for Early Roman urban growth in Wessex is at present patchy and inadequate and it would be wrong to draw firm conclusions from it, but it is tempting to suggest that the precocious development of Calleva, and also of Chichester (Cunliffe 1978c), both of which seem to have undergone major programmes of urban building under Nero, was due to the fact that both centres were within the client kingdom of Cogidubnus. It may have been as a result of the king's Romanizing policies or preferential treatment meted out by the Roman authorities (or a combination of the two), that his two towns began to enjoy the amenities of Roman urban planning while in the rest of Wessex the major market centres developed more slowly.

The Growth of Industry

There can be little doubt that the development of vigorous overseas trade at the beginning of the first century BC led to an intensification of production in certain parts of Wessex. It is nowhere more apparent than in the Poole Harbour—Isle of Purbeck region. Here the two traditional products – salt and Kimmeridge shale – began to be exploited on a greatly increased scale. The manufacture of shale bracelets and other trinkets also underwent something of a technical revolution with the introduction of the lathe (Calkin 1955; Woodward 1987). Bracelets were now produced in great numbers and traded widely, some of them reaching Brittany. Production continued throughout the Roman period at such a volume that shale bracelets became common-place on settlement sites of all kinds in the south.

In the same region, around the shores of Poole Harbour, pottery production began to take on an industrial intensity with the introduction of the wheel. The earliest vessels were made in imitation of black cordoned wares imported from Brittany in the early first century BC. They were used in local exchange systems and are found distributed sparsely throughout Dorset and Somerset. By the second half of the first century BC a wider range of types was being manufactured. These are the typical Durotrigan wares found widely distributed in Dorset in considerable quantity, occurring in smaller numbers as far afield as Devon and Hampshire. It was from this basis that, in the first century AD, the industry expanded still further to produce the so-called Black Burnished wares which flooded the Roman markets in the south and were eventually exported as far north as Hadrian's Wall (Williams 1977).

New demands created by the Roman building industry were also met from Purbeck where several different decorative stones were readily available. Much prized was the blue-grey fossiliferous Purbeck 'Marble' mined at Wilkswood, Langton Matravers, within a decade or so of the invasion (Calkin 1959: 121–2). Large amounts of the marble were used in decorative schemes at Fishbourne in the early Flavian period and the stone was widely favoured for inscriptions throughout the Province. Two other stones, a fine hard chalk and a grey siltstone, were also extracted and rough-worked at an industrial complex near Corfe Castle (Sunter 1987). Both were used for decorative inlay and for tesserae, the earliest occurrence being in the early Flavian period at Fishbourne.

Thus within comparatively short compass shale, pottery, salt, marble and stone were being extracted and worked for export on what must have been a substantial scale. It is difficult to resist the implication that by the 70s of the first century Purbeck and its harbours had taken on the aspect of an early industrial landscape.

Another industry of some significance to the Early Roman economy was the extraction of silver and lead from the galena deposits occurring in the carboniferous limestone of the Mendips. Lead was not widely used in the Iron Age but lead net weights found at the Somerset 'lake villages' point to limited extraction. Silver, on the other hand, was far more important especially after the middle of the first century BC when large quantities were used for the production of silver coinage and alloyed with gold and copper in gold coinage. Much of this silver may have come from the Mendips. At Hengistbury silver was extracted from silver-rich lead by the process of cupellation (Bushe-Fox 1915: 72–83) which involves the heating of the alloy in open hearths at temperatures in excess of 1100 °C. The lead oxidizes to lithage and can be removed as a scum from the surface of the molten metal. The process is repeated until only pure silver is left. If necessary the lithage can then be reduced to lead. Mendip lead had approximately 0.4 per cent silver. Another source of silver were the silver-rich copper deposits occurring around the fringes of Dartmoor. A large slab of ore probably from the Callington region was found at Hengistbury, brought in by sea for refinement and export.

The silver-rich lead deposits of the Mendips immediately attracted Roman interest (Elkington 1976) and a mining settlement grew up at Charterhouse at the head of Cheddar Gorge on the Roman road which led from the Fosse Way westwards to the port of Uphill. At least one fort can be identified and the community was also provided with an amphitheatre but little is known of the chronology of these structures. Other nearby settlements producing evidence of mining or smelting are Green Ore (Ashworth 1970), and Priddy together with Herriots Bridge in the Chew Valley (Rahtz and Greenfield 1977: 361–3).

The clearest indication of the Early Roman extraction of lead/silver is provided by stamped pigs of lead, of which nearly 30 have been found, though not all of Mendip origin (Elkington 1976). Two pigs are known dated to AD 49, one found at Wookey Hole (now lost), the other from Blagdon, Somerset. In the early years production was almost certainly under the control of the army – a fact borne out by the discovery of a pig at St Valéry-sur-Somme, near Boulogne, with an inscription recording that it was produced in Britain during the reign of Nero (54–68) by the Second Legion. The legion was at this time still in the West Country. Another Neronian pig dated to AD 60 was found at Bossington near Stockbridge in Hampshire. This pig, together with two of Vespasianic date found at Clausentum, on Southampton Water, indicates the probable route by which the ingots were transported for export, direct along the Roman road from Charterhouse to the crossing of the river Test and then down the river to the Solent port of Clausentum.

A stamp on the Bossington pig mentions that it came from the 'lead-silver works of Gaius Nipius Ascanius', who was probably an imperial agent or procurator's official charged with the oversight of the mines. By the Flavian period a variety of stamps and counterstamps suggests that production was now in the hands of civilian lessees like the Novaec[... partners (*societas*) who are mentioned on a pig found at Syde in Gloucestershire.

To what extent silver was extracted at source remains obscure. Several of the Mendip pigs were stamped EX ARG which probably means 'from the silver works' rather than pigs from which silver has been extracted. But the picture is complicated by the four pigs found hidden at Green Ore (L. Palmer and Ashworth 1957). Three had practically no silver, showing that they had been desilvered, but the fourth had a silver content equivalent to 18 oz per ton. Significantly, it was distinguished from the others in bearing four stamps of the lessee's name!

The principal modification to the industry brought about by the conquest lay in the change in value of the two products silver and lead. Silver was highly valued throughout but before the invasion lead had little use and there is no indication that it featured in exchange systems. After the invasion British lead was widely exported largely for use as a building material and may even have been used in Pompeii. In Britain itself the demand for lead would have grown steadily. The construction of bath suites during the Neronian period at Fishbourne, Silchester and Bath required considerable quantities and as the pace of urbanization intensified so the demand would have increased.

Lead from the Mendips and decorative stone from Purbeck contributed to the growing building industry which seems to have developed apace in the decade following the Boudican rebellion. Building stone and tiles and bricks — constructional materials virtually unknown before the invasion — came increasingly into general use particularly in the urban centres. To judge by the variety of tiles and bricks used in the Neronian 'proto-palace' at Fishbourne, production was on a large scale and was in the hands of specialists. The baths at Silchester and Bath required an equivalent array of products. Similarly the demand for stone increased — stone for both walling and flooring and for decorative fittings like the ornate Corinthian capitals from Fishbourne which were made of oolitic limestone. There can be little doubt that the quarries around Bath, where a high quality oolitic limestone was to be had, were already in active production by the early 70s.

Finally we should not overlook the demands of the ever-changing taste of the British elite as things Roman became increasingly desirable. It began with the import of Italian wine as early as the late second or early first century BC and as the century proceeded embraced Spanish wine, olive oil and fish sauce. Together with these commodities came the table vessels required for their display and consumption. After the invasion the quantity of imports greatly increased but so too did local production serving the increasingly sophisticated demands of the population. A number of specialist potters set up production centres to supply the local markets with vessels made in Roman style, like those who began producing flagons at Corfe Mullen in Dorset close to the fortress at Lake Farm. Metalworkers began copying Roman brooches and other trinkets while stone cutters – at first natives apprenticed to immigrant masters – provided the carved tombstones, the altars and architectural mouldings demanded by the alien Roman life style. New aspirations, new markets and a system of much improved communications radically changed not only the range of non-agrarian production but also its intensity, within the span of the single generation following the landing of the Claudian army.

Death, Burial and the Gods

The Late Iron Age was a time of major change in social attitudes towards death in southern Britain. Whereas before, we have argued, the disposal of the dead was usually by excarnation, only a small minority of the population being deposited in disused storage pits, the Late Iron Age sees the spread of new methods of careful burial. The picture is not entirely clear but in the south east of the country cremation and the disposal of ashes in containers set in small cemeteries became the norm. This rite spread to Hampshire, Berkshire and Wiltshire – that is the territory of the Atrebates – while in Dorset, among the Durotriges, extended inhumation in cemeteries became widespread though the boundaries between the two modes were not rigid. The Dobunni also appear to have adopted the inhumation rite.

Recognition of status is reflected in a class of well-furnished burials. Three male warrior burials, all inhumations, have been found in Wessex. At Owslebury in Hampshire the body was accompanied by a long iron sword in a wooden sheath associated with attachment rings and hook. By the side was a spear, broken to fit into the grave, while the body was covered by a shield, presumably of wood and leather, with a large central bronze boss (Collis 1968). At Whitcombe in Dorset the warrior was buried with legs flexed, together with his sword, spear, belt hook, brooch and an iron tool, possibly a hammer (Aitken 1968). The third warrior burial from St Lawrence in the Isle of Wight was provided only with sword and shield (Stead 1968: Fig. 19).

Females of rank were also distinguished by elaborate grave goods. The best known example is the burial found at Birdlip in Gloucestershire in 1879 (C. Green 1949). Three cist graves were recovered. Two contained males while the central cist housed the female. Her body had been buried in an extended position and a large bronze bowl had been placed over her face with a smaller bowl nearby. Other grave goods included an engraved mirror, a gilded silver brooch, bronze dress rings, a bronze amulet, a necklace of amber, jet and marble beads and a knife with an animal head terminal. Similar female burials with mirrors have been recorded from Bridport (Farrar 1954) and from elsewhere in southern Britain, from Cornwall to Essex, and it is possible that some at least of the stray bronze mirrors that have turned up may also have come from burials of this kind.

A few rich cremation burials have also been found in Wessex. At Marlborough, for example, the cremation had been placed in a wooden pail ornamented with bronze bands decorated in a lively repoussé style with running horses and human heads (Fox 1958: 69). Little is known of the burial circumstances. A similar grave was found beneath a small barrow at Hurstbourne Tarrant in Hampshire. All that remained of the bucket were bands of iron and plates of bronze and iron. Accompanying it was a brooch, fragments of a bracelet and thirteen pots constituting what can reasonably be regarded as a set of table ware. The vessels, some of which are Gallo-Belgic imports, suggest a date in the decade or two immediately before the invasion (C. F. C. Hawkes and Dunning 1931: 304–9). A third example was found during excavation on Ham Hill in 1923. Here the cremation was accompanied by a dagger with bronze anthropoid hilt.

The 'rich' burials are only part of a complex burial tradition which required grave goods to be buried with the dead according to the status of the deceased. More frequently the offerings were modest – little more than a pot or two and many were without even that. What is interesting is the change in belief pattern that the adoption of such a rite must imply. At the very least it means that attitudes to death and to the importance of the individual began to change quite dramatically some time soon after 100 BC.

The burial patterns once established in the Late Iron Age remained little altered throughout the first few decades after the invasion. While the Durotriges continued to inhume their dead, cremation, which was fashionable in the Roman world at the time, remained the norm across Atrebatic territory and was the practice used by the army. The persistence of inhumation among the Durotriges is a further demonstration of their individualism and their refusal readily to accept Roman manners.

Some disparity in wealth is also apparent in the Early Roman period although few rich burials of Claudian or Neronian date are known. Two well-furnished graves found at Grange Road, some 2 km south of Winchester, give some idea of the style of high status burials in the Flavian period. The first was comparatively modest with a set of table ware and a few trinkets. The second was more elaborate containing, besides a set of pottery, a glass vessel, a bronze jug, a trencher (or tray) made of Kimmeridge shale, together with a range of smaller items including counters from a board game (Biddle 1967). The range of grave goods is entirely within the tradition of rich burials established in south-eastern Britain from the middle of the first century BC and suggests that socio-religious patterns had changed little over a century and a half.

Much the same can be said of the sacred sites of Wessex. Direct evidence of continuity from the Iron Age into the Roman period is difficult to find but it is highly likely that many of the later Romano-Celtic temples in rural areas occupied sites of religious significance, some extending back at least into the Late Iron Age if not earlier. This is amply demonstrated by the religious complex on Hayling Island. Here a circular temple and its surrounding rectangular enclosure, built in masonry in the Flavian period, exactly copied the plan of its timber predecessor dating back to the first century BC (Downey, King and Soffe 1979). Similarly at Maiden Castle the circular masonry building which accompanied a rectangular Romano-Celtic temple exactly reproduced a building of similar plan dating to the Iron Age. In other cases continuity is implied. At Cold Kitchen Hill in Wiltshire, the site of a Roman temple has produced a wide range of Iron Age objects, going back to the seventh or sixth centuries, which might well have been deposited originally as votive offerings at a sacred location.

Finally we should briefly consider the sacred hot spring at Bath (Plate 6.4). Recent excavations have shown that a gravel causeway of pre-Roman date led to the water's edge and a number of coins of the Dobunni and the Durotriges were recovered from the mud filling the spring pipe (Cunliffe 1988: 1–4). It was only later, probably in the Neronian period, that the spring was surrounded by a masonry reservoir wall, lined with lead, and incorporated in a grandiose building scheme which turned Bath into one of the foremost healing sanctuaries in the western Roman provinces. The deity presiding over the spring was Sulis Minerva, a conflation of the Roman goddess Minerva with the Celtic goddess of the waters, Sulis, whose deep antiquity we can only suspect.

The transformation of Sulis' muddy spring into a spectacular religious complex within 30 or 40 years of the invasion could not have failed to have impressed on the natives of Wessex that Rome was here to stay.

Social and Administrative Changes

The Roman invasion imposed upon Wessex a new administrative structure but one based largely upon the political realities which the Romans found. To understand what emerged in the late first century AD it is necessary to try to untangle the complexities of the pre-conquest century. In essence we can distinguish three broad territorial groupings: the Durotriges occupying Dorset and parts of Somerset; the Dobunni (or more strictly the Southern

Dobunni) focusing on the Somerset Avon and a rather more amorphous group which we can refer to as proto-Atrebates or Atrebates stretching from Salisbury Plain to the Sussex coast. The definition of these territories is largely based upon an assessment of locally minted coins and the distribution patterns into which they fall.

The Durotriges and Southern Dobunni form tolerably cohesive groups which, superficially at least, seem to have maintained a consistency throughout the Late Iron Age. The Atrebates are more problematical and are better regarded as a confederation of three distinct pagi focused on Chichester/Selsey, Winchester and Calleva (Silchester). Judging from the coin distributions it would appear that while a degree of reciprocal exchange linked the Dobunni and Durotriges, the Atrebates remained largely outside this system buffered perhaps by the lightly inhabited 'wastes' of the New Forest and the chalk uplands of the central Salisbury Plain.

The tripartite division of Atrebatic territory may well have been partly the result of existing Middle Iron Age ethnic groupings intensified by the effects of immigrant elites (above, pp. 191–3). It is the distribution of the coinage of Commius and his dynasty which alone suggests a degree of political unity. Some time after the invasion the Roman administration formalized the old divisions by conferring on each a separate tribal identity – the Regni, the Belgae and the Atrebates – each with its own administrative centre. It is impossible to say when this divide was drawn up: the simplest scenario would be to suggest that it followed the death of Cogidubnus some time in the 70s or 80s and that until this time the client king was allowed to control the entire territory from the dual centres of *Calleva* and *Noviomagus* both of which he rapidly aggrandized. This would make some sense of the evidence from Winchester which suggests that little development happened until a major phase of urban reorganization began in the Flavian period occasioned, perhaps, by a period of political restructuring following the demise of the client king.

One puzzle remains: Ptolemy, a second century geographer, notes that Aquae Sulis was in the territory of the Belgae. While this is possible it seems highly unlikely since the spa lay centrally within the distribution pattern of Dobunnic coinage and there is no good reason why the whole of the Southern Dobunnic territory should have been amalgamated with the Atrebates. It is simplest, therefore, to accept that Ptolemy had made a misidentification.

The thirty years or so following the invasion was a period of gradual change for the communities of Wessex. With one part of the region under the control of the client king Cogidubnus and much of the rest under military authority, integration into the Province of Britain would have been slow and

---

Plate 6.4   The sacred spring in Bath during excavation. Bottom right is the gravel causeway of pre-Roman date. (Photo: Bath Archaeological Trust)

uneven, but with the death of the king probably in the 70s or 80s and the final withdrawal of the army from Exeter in 74–5, for the new fortress at Caerleon, the way was clear for the entire region to be systematically reorganized under the single unified administrative authority of the procurator.

How the native inhabitants of Wessex fared during this period of transition it is difficult to say in any detail. Those at the top of the social hierarchy, who were prepared to embrace the new order, would have benefited. The only individual known to us is Cogidubnus, whose spectacular success is an indication of the advantages which the pro-Roman aristocracy could and probably did enjoy.

With Romanization came change. Native systems of patronage and clientage could be absorbed with little need for modification, since they were mirrored in the Roman life style, but the expression of prowess and prestige now had new outlets. Some, like the war leaders Caratacus and Boudica, chose the archaic Celtic method of encouraging their entourages to battle. Other young aristocrats would have chosen to lead their followers as auxiliary troops within the Roman military system, while a few, men like Cogidubnus, used their wealth to monumentalize their homes and their towns. A series of rich villas sited along the Sussex coastal plains originated in the Neronian period and major public building works were being undertaken at this time in Silchester and Chichester. There can be little doubt that the personal wealth of the pro-Roman aristocracy lay behind this as indeed the inscription at the Temple of Neptune and Minerva in Chichester amply demonstrates. Such attitudes would have been highly acceptable to Rome and heralded the beginning of a new era.

Chapter 7

The Roman Interlude: AD 80–350

The painful aftermath of the Boudican rebellion which, in different ways, would have affected the entire Province was probably the last 'national' event to have impinged directly upon the lives of the inhabitants of Wessex for two centuries or so. During this time the movement of armies and the oscillation of frontiers was largely confined to Wales and the north. Yet these distant events cannot have failed, from time to time, to have had some indirect impact on the communities living in comparative safety in the south. From the beginning of the third century the North Sea shores and the Channel once more became the scene of increasing military activity as pirate raids and the comings and goings of usurping military leaders began to focus upon the southern estuaries and ports. To understand the social and economic changes so apparent in the archaeological record of Wessex during this period, it is necessary to survey, if only in outline, the salient points of the history of the period.

From Vespasian to Magnentius

The empire-wide crisis which followed the death of Nero was finally brought to an end in 69 when Vespasian emerged triumphant founding the Flavian dynasty. Under the Flavian emperors a succession of governors were appointed, who, chosen for their military skills and given expansionist briefs, were able to advance the frontiers of the Province absorbing first the Pennines, then Wales and finally much of Scotland. This increasing military concentration in the north led to the abandonment of all military bases in the south except for detachments of marines, who were left guarding the Channel ports, and a resident garrison at London.

The last stage in the Flavian campaign to conquer the Island was commanded by Julius Agricola, whose governorship in Britain lasted from AD 78 to 84. While spending much of this time on military expeditions, Agricola devoted the winter months to civil matters. In the second winter of his term of office his biographer, Tacitus, tells us that

> with private encouragement and public aid he pressed forward the construction of temples, forums and town houses, praising those who were keen and censuring those who were not. Thus, competition for his favour was as effective as compulsion. The sons of leading men were educated in the liberal arts. ... The result was that refusal to learn Latin was replaced by a desire to excel in it. In the same way Roman dress came into fashion and the toga was everywhere seen.

Although such a eulogy was required by literary convention when presenting the ideal governor, this by no means precludes the probability that Agricola offered strong incentives to the civitates of the south to adopt a more Romanized way of life. A generation had passed since the Boudican revolt, the south was stable and it must have been clear to all that Britannia was now firmly a part of the Roman empire. Thus we might expect to find an upsurge in civic development during the 80s.

The northern frontier remained in a state of unstable equilibrium for the next forty years and it was not until the visit of the Emperor Hadrian in AD 122 that the 'final solution' – a permanent linear frontier – was begun. Hadrian spent many years of his reign visiting provinces, putting their defences into good order and initiating and inspiring a variety of civil works. It is highly likely that his visit to Britain provided a further spur to civic development which may by now have been languishing after the initial Flavian impetus. The possibility is one which can usefully be tested against the sparse archaeological evidence available (below, p. 246).

Hadrian's Wall was by no means the answer to the problems of Britain's northern frontier and throughout the rest of the second century and the early years of the third there was unrest sparking occasionally into widespread rebellion. It is unlikely, however, that these distant rumblings had any significant effect on the south. But in 196 Britain was drawn into the wider sphere when, following the assassination of Commodus, Clodius Albinus, the governor of Britain, made a bid for the throne and departed for the Continent with the army in support of his claim. His defeat and death at Lyon in 197 at the hands of Septimius Severus ended the period of uncertainty, but Severus' retribution on Albinus' supporters was heavy and would have included the widespread confiscation of estates. This is likely to have had a dramatic effect on the more prosperous regions of Britain though confiscation may not be archaeologically detectable.

The early years of the third century saw the construction of two coastal fortifications, one at Brancaster protecting the Wash, the other at Reculver guarding the approaches to the Thames estuary. The implication of the new installations is that the North Sea was now becoming the haunt of pirates. By the 270s the threat of raids from the sea seems to have increased. It was probably at this time that an earth fort was constructed at Richborough around an old monumental arch now used as a look out point and it may be that the masonry forts at Burgh Castle near Yarmouth and at Dover were now built. These preparations and those on the adjacent coast of France show that the defence of the Channel, at its narrowest point, was of prime concern and that the aim was now to prevent the pirate threat from spreading west along the south coast.

In 286 a new turn of events brought southern Britain into the forefront of history. It was in this year that a Belgian sailor, M. Aurelius Mausaeus Carausius, fled to Britain to escape execution, which had been ordered by the emperor to punish misdeeds. In Britain Carausius set himself up as sole ruler styling himself *Restitutor Britanniae*. The existing system of shore defences augmented by a new fort at Portchester Castle, Hants., would now have provided a front line of defence against threat of Imperial attack. Carausius maintained his control of the Island for seven years until, in 293, he was killed by Allectus who replaced him.

In 296 the Emperor Constantius at last launched an invasion to recover Britain. One arm of the Imperial force, led by Asclepiodotus, seems to have sailed up the Solent to land somewhere in Southampton Water, evading and outflanking the garrison based at Portchester under cover of a convenient mist. Having disembarked, the boats were burned and the force moved off northwards through Hampshire towards London. At a decisive battle, fought somewhere near Silchester, Allectus was killed. Meanwhile Constantius leading a second army had crossed the Channel and had managed to reach London before the remnants of Allectus' troops could fall back on it. Such momentous events cannot have failed to have dislocated the lives of the communities of Hampshire and there is some evidence of damage in the town of Silchester which may be attributable to this campaign. Lasting disruption is, however, unlikely and in the restoration which followed the south enjoyed a period of peace and prosperity lasting throughout much of the first half of the fourth century.

The visit of the Emperor Constans in the winter of 342 suggests that all was not well and it may be that the pirates were once more threatening the coasts. At any event soon after this visit a new shore fort was built at Pevensey in Sussex and there is evidence of heightened activity at the forts of Portchester and Richborough at this time.

In 350 Constans' throne was seized by Magnentius, a barbarian by descent whose father may have been a Briton. Drawing military support from Britain, where he was evidently popular, Magnentius marched to Pannonia, only to be beaten by Constantius II in 351. He was killed two years later. In the aftermath Constantius took harsh reprisals against the supporters of

Magnentius in Britain – reprisals which would no doubt have involved the widespread confiscation of estates and other property causing another dislocation in the countryside and towns alike.

Barely had the Province settled down when the barbarian raids, which were to lead to the rapid disintegration of the Province, began in earnest.

The historical background, so briefly sketched, provides a framework against which to compare the development of the Wessex communities. We should, however, guard against using national and international events as a straitjacket within which to fit and constrain the archaeological evidence.

Civic Administration, Taxation and Money

The province of Britannia was ruled by a governor on behalf of the emperor. To help him in his tasks a number of officers were employed: the *Legatus iuridicus* to assist in legal matters, the *Legati Augusti* or legionary commanders and the *Procurator Augusti provinciae Britanniae*, who was solely responsible for the financial affairs of the Province. The procurator's office was established in London but many of his staff of junior procurators were probably outstationed at the ports, state-owned mines and Imperial estates.

Throughout most of the period two means of taxation produced revenue from the Province: the *tributum capitis*, a poll tax which included property, and the *tributum soli*, or land tax based on productivity. In the fourth century an additional levy on corn, the *annona*, was introduced to feed the army.

The Roman presence, then, for the first time in the history of Britain, applied a unified system of government and taxation across the country. In making individuals answerable to the state, and removing a high percentage of society's surplus in the form of taxation, it greatly undermined the power and prestige of the native nobility. Thus, in spite of its rigid hierarchical structure, the Roman system led to a degree of democratization. A significant percentage of the money raised by taxation would have been spent in the province as pay for the army and the civil officials, and would in turn have been used to buy goods and services supplied by craftsmen and workers of low social status. With a money economy, however rudimentary, in operation, those providing services would have been in a position to acquire and hoard cash for later investment. Whereas in the old 'Celtic' system surplus was distributed down the social system by mechanisms based on patronage and clientage alone, under the Roman system the individual had an earning capacity and thus an increased buying power. This change is strikingly demonstrated by comparing the range of artefacts found on typical downland peasant sites dating to before and after the invasion. In the pre-conquest period the range of ceramics and other artefacts is usually limited to what could have been locally produced. After the invasion it is not at all unusual to find quantities of imported pottery, including terra sigillata, together with personal trinkets such as brooches, bracelets and rings, acquired from the local markets. Such a change, while clearly reflecting the increased availability of consumer goods, must also indicate the enhanced ability of the peasant to acquire.

The number of Roman officials in the Province would never have been great and much of the administrative load would have been devolved to the local communities based on the towns. At what point the Wessex communities took on the burden of self-government it is difficult to say but if it is accepted that the building of the basilica and forum represents the point at which self-government was first attained then for the Wessex area the crucial transition seems to have been in the early Flavian period during the governorship of Frontinus or Agricola. By the end of the first century civitas capitals were flourishing at Chichester (*Noviomagus Regnensium*), Winchester (*Venta Belgarum*), Silchester (*Calleva Atrebatum*) and Dorchester (*Durnovaria*) and at some stage, possibly in the second century, a second Durotrigan centre at Ilchester (*Lindinis*) seems to have been upgraded to self-governing status (Fig. 7.1; C. E. Stevens 1952; Wacher 1974: 407–8).

It is likely that the organization of these civitates was based on the model of the colonia and municipium which in turn mirrored the government of Rome. Each would have been governed by a council of decuriones known as the Ordo. As their name implies there would have been about 100 men selected on the basis of a property qualification. Leadership of the Ordo was in the hands of two *Duroviri iuridicundo* assisted by two aediles responsible for maintaining the town's infrastructure of buildings and services. This system replaced traditional Iron Age hierarchies based on aristocratic kinship but it was not dissimilar in that wealth and prestige were still prerequisites for power. The old tribal nobility would have been absorbed directly into the Roman system of local government with little discomfort. In their role as decuriones the Celtic elite could continue to exercise control and to reaffirm their status through acts of lavish patronage channelled now into funding monuments and facilities to aggrandize their towns.

The Towns of Wessex

The development of the civitas capitals of Wessex is still surprisingly ill-known in spite of decades of archaeological endeavour, but Silchester, uncluttered by medieval and later development, presents a cohesive picture (Fulford

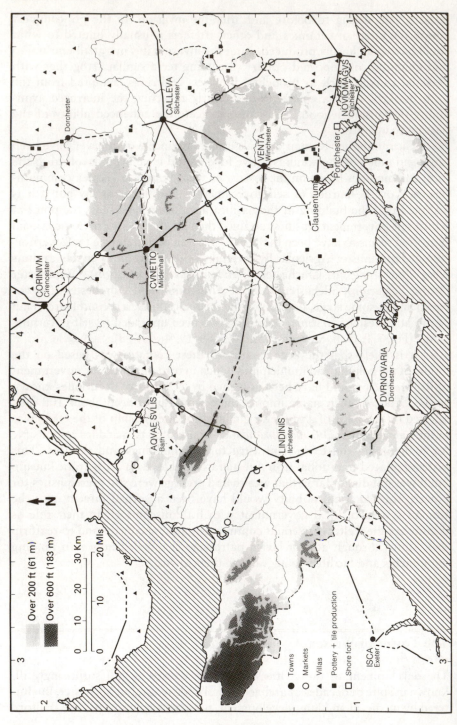

1984, 1987b). We have already seen that in the period AD 50–85 a substantial timber building was erected in a central position its plan suggesting that it may have been an early version of the forum and basilica with the basilica, at this stage, across the northern side of the open forum area. In the 80s of the first century the early building was demolished and replaced by a substantial basilica, also built of timber (Fig. 6.9). The sheer scale of the enterprise leaves little doubt that it was a major event in the development of the community and is in all probability the result of the Agricolan encouragement to the civitates to embrace Romanization. By this stage the town already had an amphitheatre of timber, built on the edge of the urban zone between AD 50 and 70, and a bathing establishment erected in the 50s. With its imposing street grid extending across and beyond the slighter Iron Age enclosure earthworks Silchester possessed all the accoutrements of a flourishing urban centre before the end of the first century.

The situation at Winchester is less clear but unlike Silchester it seems to have been provided with an earthen defence built in the Neronian or Flavian period by which time some at least of the streets had been laid out (Biddle 1983). The construction date of the forum and basilica has not been established with any precision though there is some suggestion that it may have been built in masonry before the end of the first century.

The archaeology of Dorchester is no more revealing of the town's early history, but there are some hints of rapid first century development. The old Neolithic henge monument of Maumbury Rings was converted into an amphitheatre before the end of the century and the aqueduct which brought water from the river Frome, 18 km away, was dug in the late first century (Wacher 1974: 315–26) and this could have coincided with the first phase of the large bathing establishment on the site of Woolaston House.

The evidence, scanty though it is, suggests, therefore, that the three civitas capitals of Wessex had acquired all the main attributes of urban status well by the end of the first century.

The second century was to see a further consolidation. At Silchester this is most dramatically exemplified by the total reconstruction of the forum and basilica in masonry in the middle of the century. The new building complex (Fig. 7.2) covered 0.8 ha and was adorned by a row of massive columns with elaborately carved Corinthian capitals. At Winchester the discovery of a fragment of monumental inscription with letters 0.3 m high, probably dating to the mid second century, may well represent the rebuilding or rededication of the basilica at that time. In all three towns the second century was the time when the predominantly timber-framed houses and shops were gradually replaced with masonry-built structures, the more affluent being provided with mosaics and private bath suites.

Figure 7.1 Roman Wessex. (After Ordnance Survey map of *Roman Britain*)

SILCHESTER BASILICA
Mid second century

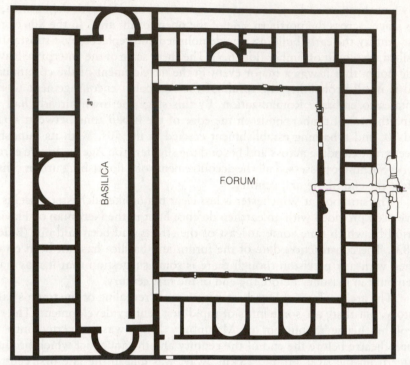

BASILICA

FORUM

Figure 7.2   The second century forum and basilica at Silchester. (After Fulford 1987b)

Towards the end of the second century there was a widespread phase of rampart building around many of the towns of Britain. This has been clearly demonstrated at Silchester where the rampart of dumped earth and rubble, fronted by double ditches, enclosed an area of 42 ha and at the same time the four main gates were built of masonry (Fulford 1984). Ramparts of a similar type and date have been recognized at Winchester, Dorchester and Ilchester; the last having probably acquired self-governing status by this period. It may be that this province-wide phase of defence was occasioned by unrest created when Clodius Albinus took the British army to the Continent to fight Severus in 196–7, but the defences show no sign of having been hastily erected and the masonry gates with their dual carriageways are monumental structures. A more reasonable alternative might be to regard these works as acts of civic pride occasioned either by the visit of the Emperor Severus in 208 or the grant of citizenship to all free-born provincials made in 214. The archaeological evidence, available at present, is insufficient to allow for precise dating.

Many of the towns of Britain later enhanced their defences with masonry-built walls inserted into the fronts of the earlier ramparts. Such a sequence is clear at Silchester, Winchester, Dorchester and Ilchester and at Silchester the event can be dated to some time between 260 and 280, the period when the pirate raids on the east and south coasts were intensifying. This, combined with a noticeable increase in coin hoarding, suggests that it was a time of unrest. The advent of city walls, then, might be taken as an indication of a change in the status, the towns now being regarded as safe havens for the local populations in time of danger.

Whether or not the whole urban concept was changing at this time it is difficult yet to say but one piece of evidence from Silchester is intriguing. The excavation of the basilica showed that in about the middle of the third century the hall was given over to a range of metalworking processes and this activity continued throughout the fourth century. Clearly the building could no longer be used for administrative and judicial purposes. Whether these civil functions were carried out elsewhere in the town, or whether the town had ceased to be a centre of local government by this date, it is impossible to say but in any event the change must signal a major reorientation in urban life. That this may be more than a local phenomenon is suggested by similar evidence from Leicester and the apparent failure to complete the rebuilding of the forum at Wroxeter.

Small Towns, Markets and Spas

Within the larger civitates were smaller administrative units called pagi and vici each of which is likely to have had its own settlement focus ranging from a cluster of buildings of village-like proportions to small towns. The map (Fig. 7.1) gives some idea of the spread of these smaller settlements but in its simplicity it obscures the very considerable variety which exists (Todd 1976; R. H. Leech 1976). Nor is their chronological development well known. Each is likely to have evolved along separate lines but one general observation is worth making – that the main period of development began in the middle of the third century and several appear not to have existed before then. It is tempting to link this observation with the disuse of public buildings in the civitas capitals. Together the evidence could be taken to suggest the fragmentation of the power and responsibilities of the civitates and the emergence of smaller self-governing units in the countryside. If such were the case it would be easy to understand why the huge urban basilicas, some now nearly two centuries old, were no longer maintained as civic buildings.

The status of the smaller settlements may well have changed over time.

Ilchester (*Lindinis*) for example seems to have been elevated to become a civitas capital in the second or third century (Leach 1982) while Mildenhall (Annable 1959) and Gatcombe (Cunliffe 1967; Branigan 1977) were both provided with substantial defensive walls in the fourth century. The position of Bath (*Aquae Sulis*) is of some interest. It occupies an important position on a route node where the Fosse Way crosses the Avon and other roads converge but the prime reason for its foundation was the spring of hot water which emerged at this point and was believed to have been presided over by the goddess Sulis. In the early years following the invasion the sacred site was adorned with a sanctuary of some splendour which included a huge bathing establishment where pilgrims could swim and be treated with the curative waters (Cunliffe and Davenport 1985). The initial buildings probably date to the early Flavian period and may provide another example of Agricola's policy of Romanization. Extensive modifications and additions were made in the early second century including the provision of a highly decorated circular temple or tholos. It is tempting to see the hand of Hadrian in this (Cunliffe 1989).

Throughout the first and second centuries the focus of the settlement was the sanctuary and its clutter of associated shrines and service buildings but immediately to the north, at the main river crossing, a more secular settlement developed. By the middle of the fourth century, after the buildings of the sanctuary had been enclosed within a temenos wall, this settlement grew considerably in extent.

The simplest explanation of the available evidence from Bath would be to see it beginning as a sanctuary which by virtue of its nodal location drew to itself a range of ancillary functions including those of providing a market in an area bereft of major towns. By the mid to late third century it may well have assumed responsibility for local government the occasion, perhaps, being marked by the separation of the religious area by an enclosing wall.

The importance of religious sites as locations for markets should not be under-estimated. Temples, like that on Cold Kitchen Hill close to a major road crossing in an area many kilometres from the nearest towns, would have been obvious meeting places for the rural community and travelling traders – places where local produce could be exchanged for consumer durables. Similar markets must have grown up at all the major road crossings especially where there was no convenient town in the vicinity. The great west road from London, through Silchester to Dorchester and beyond, ran for about 130 km across Wessex without going near a town but at each of the three major cross roads along its length *Leucomagus* (Andover), *Sorviodunum* (Old Sarum) (Stone and Algar 1955) and *Vindocladia* (Badbury) minor market settlements grew up. These nodes were about 30 km apart. Between them one might expect smaller markets like that which existed at Woodyates on Cranborne Chase. Once more the chronological evidence, insofar as it is available, suggests that these developments are a feature of the later Roman period.

The Spacing of Towns

A glance at the map (Fig. 7.1) is sufficient to stress the very uneven location of the civitas capitals in Wessex. Silchester, Winchester and Chichester form a well-spaced network in the east of the region with Dorchester and its daughter town of Ilchester serving the Durotriges in the west, but large areas of central Wessex are without any urban focus. One explanation which has been offered for this is that much of the region was an Imperial estate administered by bailiffs on behalf of the emperor and thus required no urban focus (Collingwood and Myres 1930: 323–4; C. F. C. Hawkes 1947: 27–81). A simpler explanation would be to see in this disparity little more than the reflection of the native tribal system with its traditional centres of power and concentrations of population determining where the Imperial authorities chose to establish the seats of local government. These civitas capitals were set up in the model of Rome. It could be argued that the system did not comfortably match the needs of the Wessex communities (or indeed the Province as a whole) and by the middle of the third century a more organic system had emerged – one that was smaller scale, dispersed and polyfocal. The civitas capitals continued to exist but their roles had changed, or rather had failed to develop, their emphasis by the late third century, being less on the provision of administrative services and more on offering protection for the local elites. Silchester in the fourth century with its twenty-five or so comfortable town houses and its estimated population of 2000–5000 was little more than an overgrown village. The failure of the towns of Britain to retain their administrative ascendancy into and throughout the fourth century is one of the principal reasons why Roman culture failed to maintain itself here in the face of the fifth century immigrations. In this Britain is in stark contrast to Gaul where a strong thread of continuity existed.

Rural Settlement

The study of rural settlement in Roman Britain has been distorted by the widely held belief that Roman villas, however they may be defined, can be regarded as a phenomenon in their own right separate from the other types of settlement densely spread across the landscape and that the development of the rural economy can be written in terms of the development of villa buildings. This is equivalent to saying that the history of the rural economy in post medieval Britain can be deduced from the study of grand country houses — clearly such a view is nonsense. It is understandable that villa studies should bulk large in the literature — walls, mosaics and bath buildings are more dramatic than post-holes and house platforms. Of the 400 or so known villas in Wessex a high percentage have been dug into and a few have been excavated on a reasonable scale. Yet of the many thousands of non-villa rural settlements only a handful have received any archaeological attention. In other words the database is heavily biased towards one class of rural settlement.

Whenever the full spectrum of rural settlement has been considered free from preconception it is clear that continuity from the Late Iron Age is a comparatively common occurrence. A classic case is provided by the settlement complex on Berwick Down, Tollard Royal, Wilts. (Bowen and Fowler 1966: Fig. 2). Here a complex Roman settlement represented by upstanding earthworks developed barely a hundred metres from a Durotrigan farmstead (Wainwright 1968). While direct continuity cannot be demonstrated the close juxtaposition of the two sites would suggest that they formed part of a single continuum of peasant occupation.

A rather similar pattern is suggested by the programme of field-work and excavation carried out on the chalk downs at Chalton, Hants. (Cunliffe 1973a, 1977), where a number of locations were found producing pottery from Middle Iron Age to well into the Roman period. The one settlement sampled by excavation (site 16) seems to have begun in the Late Iron Age and continued to develop into the fourth century, by which time it had reached considerable proportions and might reasonably be called a village (Fig. 7.3). The Chalton survey showed that three such 'villages' existed, spaced at intervals of one to two kilometres from each other in a densely farmed landscape. Apart from the clay-capped hilltops, which were left as pasture or scrub, the entire landscape was divided into small fields served by a network of trackways which linked the minor settlements together (Fig. 7.4). Within the survey area, measuring some 20 sq km, three 'village settlements', fourteen farmsteads and four masonry buildings were identified. Nor is there any reason to suggest that this pattern is in any way unusual. We should not, however, suppose that all the settlement units identified were in use together throughout the entire Roman period.

The picture of landscape continuity implied by the Chalton survey seems to apply quite widely in other areas of Wessex. In Dorset, for example, many of the Roman 'peasant' sites identified in the Royal Commission reports have produced Durotrigan pottery suggesting an origin in the first century BC or early first century AD. Moreover Pitt-Rivers' excavations at the sites of Rotherley and Woodcuts have demonstrated continued (though not necessarily continuous) use from the Late Iron Age into the fourth century AD. Many of the sites so far mentioned retained their peasant status throughout, but a few acquired some of the trappings of Romanization like factory-made tiles and even simple masonry buildings augmenting the native timber vernacular. A few of the sites, like Chalton site 16, grew substantially in size but were still largely native in form and, presumably, economy. The Chalton

Figure 7.3 Roman village and its fields at Chalton, Hants. (From Cunliffe 1977: Fig. 3)

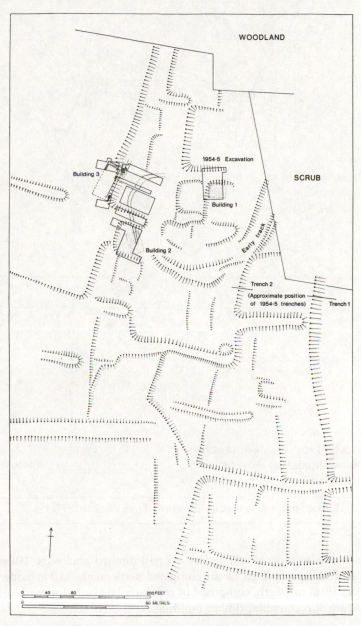

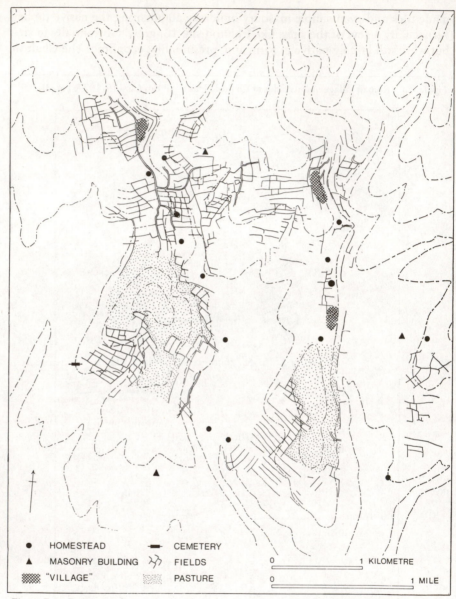

Figure 7.4　Roman settlement in the Chalton region. (From Cunliffe 1977: Fig. 2)

'village' seems to have originated as a small ditched enclosure 100 m or so across and to have grown to an elongated settlement, 150 m wide and in excess of 300 m in length, composed of regularly laid out plots some of which enclosed small rectangular timber buildings.

Similar 'villages' have been recognized on the chalk uplands of Wiltshire. One of the most impressive of these is at Chisenbury Warren (Bowen and Fowler 1966: Fig. 5) where surface features survive of an elongated cluster of more than 80 hut platforms spread out along a village street, covering an area of 6 ha (Fig. 7.5). Immediately next to the village is a regularly laid out field system of some 80 ha. Other villages of comparable form and size are known on Knook Down and Overton Down (Bowen and Fowler 1966: 56–7). A rather different form of village – agglomerated rather than linear in plan – can also be recognized at, for example Hamshill Ditches (Bonney 1967) where surface survey has demonstrated a large number of hut platforms within a multiple ditched enclosure of 16 ha (Fig. 7.6). Similar complexes are found along the Grovelly ridge at Stockton Earthworks and Hanging Langford Camp. In the absence of adequate excavation it is impossible to discuss the origins and growth of these villages but the field evidence does suggest that the agglomerated type may have begun in the pre-Roman period. There is archaeological evidence for this at Chalton, and at Hamshill the earliest earthworks appear to be banjo enclosures of Late Iron Age form. The linear villages, on the other hand, could well be Roman creations.

Continuity of a rather different kind is demonstrated by a number of Wessex sites which began as native, pre-Roman settlements and became Roman villas. An impressive example of such a site is provided by Grateley South, Hants., known largely from aerial photographic evidence (Fig. 6.7; R. Palmer 1984: Fig. 18). The settlement begins with a banjo enclosure of Late Iron Age type but developed a complex of rectilinear ditched enclosures linked to trackways. At some undefined date, around the original nuclear enclosure, four masonry buildings were constructed, evidently constituting the three ranges of a typical villa: one was the main domestic accommodation, one an aisled barn while the third range was composed of two simple barns or sheds. In the absence of direct archaeological evidence it is impossible to demonstrate continuous development but equally it would be perverse to argue that the site had not been the focus of a farming unit throughout much of the Late Iron Age and Roman period.

Grateley South appears to be typical of a particular class of site beginning with ditched enclosures of Iron Age date and subsequently becoming Roman villas. Other examples which may be quoted are Bramdean, Hants., where the villa developed on a site first occupied in the Middle Iron Age, and Houghton Down, Hants., where a Roman villa with attached bath building was preceded by a ditched enclosure of Iron Age form not seen by the excavators but subsequently identified by aerial photography. In all probability this pattern of continuity was widespread: 'stray' finds of Late Iron Age and Early Roman date have been found on many villa sites, but villa excavators in the past have seldom paid much attention to pre-villa features. Where work has been on an adequate scale, as for example at Rockbourne, Hants. (RCHM(E) 1984), Halstock (Lukis 1985), Bucknowle (Collins, Field

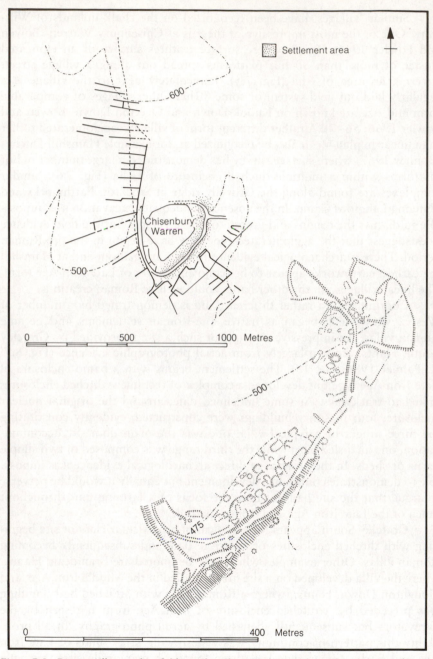

Figure 7.5   Roman village and its fields at Chisenbury Warren, Wilts. (After Bowen and Fowler 1966: Figs 4 and 5)

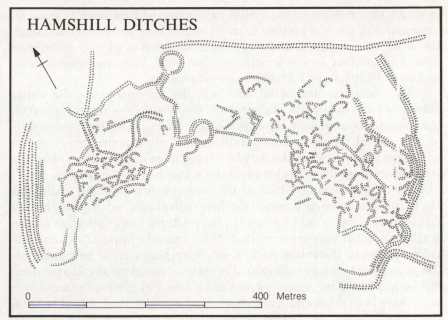

HAMSHILL DITCHES

0   400 Metres

Figure 7.6 Late Iron Age and Roman settlement at Hamshill Ditches, Wilts. (After Bonney 1967: Fig. 1)

and Light 1984, 1989), and Tarrant Hinton, Dorset (Giles 1982, 1983), traces of the earlier phases, going back to the pre-conquest period, have been noted. Thus, it may fairly be argued that a significant (but undefined) percentage of the elaborate Wessex villas of the third and fourth centuries emerged as a result of a process of gradual aggrandizement from humble origins going back several hundred years. In other words not only were many of the farming units of the pre-conquest period maintained well into the Roman era, an observation which argues forcefully for a continuity of land ownership, but also the families who inherited them were able to acquire sufficient wealth to invest in providing increasingly comfortable accommodation which, in a few cases, could verge on the luxurious.

The factors which distinguished successful farms (i.e. those that became 'villas') from the unsuccessful – those which ceased to be occupied, or were maintained on a peasant level – were no doubt many and are for the most part beyond recovery but one way to approach the question is by considering villa distribution. As the map (Fig. 7.1) shows, the great majority of the Wessex villas lie close to towns. The simplest explanation of this is to suppose that the ease with which goods could be got to a major market centre for sale endowed certain favourably located farms with an advantage. It was easier for them to convert surplus products into credit or cash which could then be reinvested in the estate. The fact that a very high percentage of the villas are within a 25 km radius of a town tends to support the view since 25 km is the maximum distance it is possible to travel to and from the market in a single day. A few villa clusters fall outside those limits, such as a group in the Stour valley and another in north Somerset, but both have convenient minor markets at Badbury and Charterhouse to depend on.

Two further points stand out from the distributions – the virtual absence of villas over much of central and south Wiltshire and the unusually dense distributions around the towns of Ilchester and Bath. The dearth of villas in central Wessex is usually explained in terms of the area being one vast Imperial estate. While this may be so (and there is no strong evidence for or against) an equally plausible explanation can be framed in terms of productivity and marketing. Much of the area consists of fragile chalk soils which had been intensely occupied for three millennium and may well by now have been showing signs of exhaustion. But probably more important was the fact that the entire zone lay more than 25 km from the nearest town and thus had no access to the major markets where surpluses could be turned into cash. Rural markets may have existed at the road junctions at Old Sarum and at Woodyates and the sanctuary on Cold Kitchen but in such places barter would have been the norm. A more appropriate model, then, would be to see the Wessex landscape divided between productive land close to major markets and less productive land distant from them. In the Roman capitalist system those who owned land within the productive zone were in a position to accumulate wealth.

The unusually dense distributions of villas around Bath and Ilchester cannot entirely be explained in this way. Moreover a detailed consideration of the, admittedly sparse, dating evidence has suggested that a significant number of these villas may have been built on unoccupied sites no earlier than the late third century. It has been suggested that the apparent rash of rich villas emerging at this time resulted from an influx of wealthy immigrants, fleeing the troubled lands of northern Gaul at the time when successive waves of barbarians were attacking, to seek the relative calm of western Britain, there to reinvest their capital (Rivet 1969: 207–9; Applebaum 1966: 104; Branigan 1976a: 82–95). Such a view is plausible if not proven. It could, moreover, explain the sudden appearance of several distinct schools of mosaicists, who may have set themselves up to serve the new market: it could also account for the concentration of Gallic deities in the region. Had such an influx of rich immigrants settled around Bath and Ilchester then it would explain why these two minor centres began to take on a range of service functions more appropriate to the civitas capitals. An alternative reason for these concentrations of rich villas might, however, be sought in the sheer productivity of the land around Bath and Ilchester. The variety of rich soils in the vicinity of each villa would have ensured a high level of yield, well in excess of the downland soils. The key to the question rests upon foundation date. If a significant number of these villas were, indeed, built on new sites over a short period of time in the third century then foreign investment may well have been the catalyst.

Our knowledge of the form, development and function of the Wessex villas though plentiful is based more on the anecdotal than the systematic (Branigan 1976b; Johnston 1978). Unlike the south east of the country, where substantial first century villas are known, in Wessex masonry buildings were rare in the countryside before the end of the second century and even then they were relatively simple. Elaborate buildings seem to have been begun in the late third century (Fig. 7.7) and by the early decades of the fourth

Figure 7.7 Roman villas: comparative plans

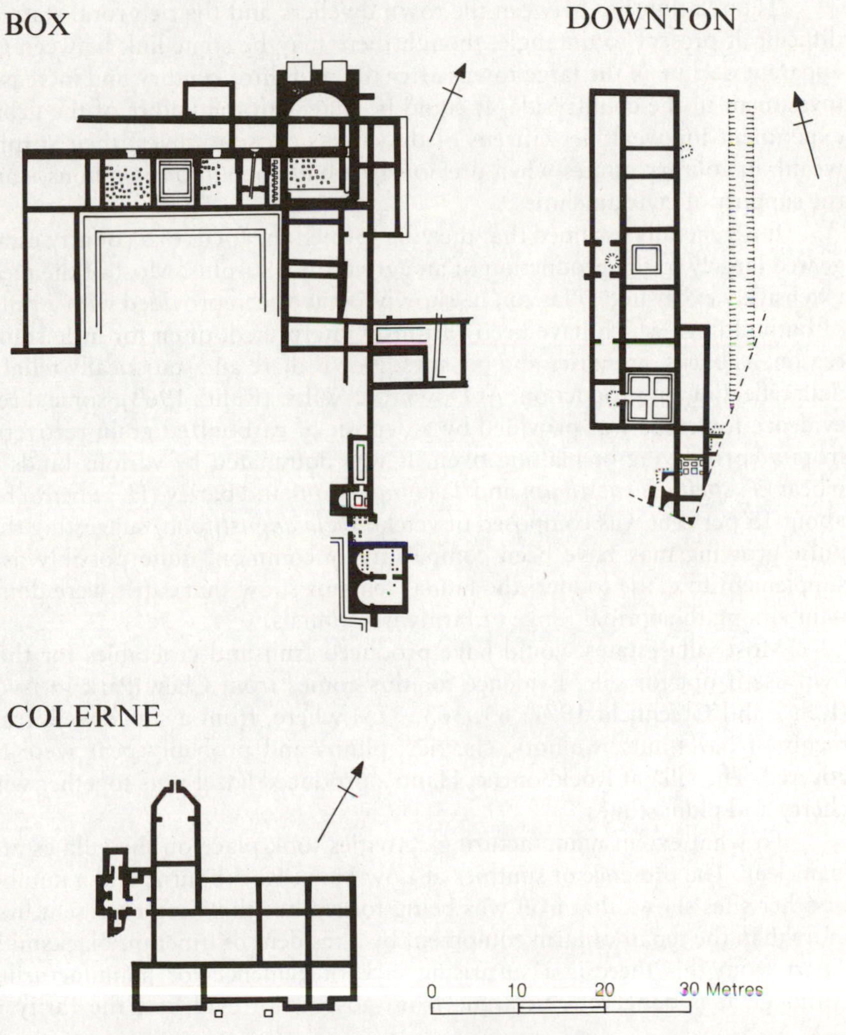

BOX   DOWNTON

COLERNE

0   10   20   30 Metres

255

century luxuries, like figured mosaics, were proliferating. Some of the compositions incorporating classical scenes, like the famous floors from Frampton and Hinton St Mary in Dorset, and Pitney and Low Ham in Somerset, suggest a clientele who not only could afford such things but also thought them socially desirable in proclaiming their *Romanitas*. Whether or not the owner of Low Ham knew the story of Dido and Aeneas, scenes from which adorned the floor of his principal room, is irrelevant. The significant point is that by the fourth century the Wessex aristocracy, whatever their origins, felt the need to be seen to embrace Roman culture. While this is often interpreted as an indication of peace and security in the Province it could equally well imply an underlying and growing insecurity which called for outward and visible symbols to provide some redress.

The relationship between the town dwellers and the rich rural states is difficult at present to untangle, though there may be some link between the apparent decline in the large towns after the mid third century and increased investment in the countryside. It could be that with the failure of the urban experiment the wealthier citizens of the civitas chose to invest their surplus wealth in country estates when previously it had gone into town houses and the support of civic amenities.

It is generally assumed that the villa formed the focus of a country estate geared largely to the production of an agricultural surplus. Most of the more extensively excavated villas can be shown to have been provided with a range of outbuildings which have been variously interpreted, often for little sound reason, as barns, granaries and pig sties. Nor is there any statistically reliable data reflecting on production. At Downton, Wilts. (Rahtz 1963), some direct evidence for crops was provided by a deposit of carbonized grain recovered from a corn drying or malting oven. It was dominated by various kinds of wheat (*T. spelta*, *T. aestivum* and *T. compactum*) and barley (*H. vulgare*) but about 15 per cent was composed of vetch (*Vicia angustifolia*) suggesting that pulse growing may have been comparatively common, quite possibly as a supplement to cattle fodder: the faunal remains show that cattle were dominant among the normal range of farmyard animals.

Most villa estates would have produced fruit and vegetables for their own use if not for sale. Evidence for this comes from Chew Park in Avon (Rahtz and Greenfield 1977: 63, 363, 375) where, from a single well, fragments of hazel-nuts, walnuts, cherries, plums and probably pear were recovered. The villa at Rockbourne, Hants., produced hazel-nuts together with cherry and plum stones.

To what extent manufacturing activities took place on the villa estates is unclear. The presence of smithies at Low Ham, Rockbourne and a number of other sites shows that iron was being forged but this need represent little more than the repair of farm equipment by a resident or itinerant blacksmith. Apart from this there is a surprising lack of evidence for manufacturing. Although it is dangerous to argue from absence of evidence, the rarity of loom weights may fairly be taken to suggest that wool, which must have been produced in bulk, was not turned into cloth on the estates. Instead it must have been transported either as yarn or as raw wool in bales to manufacturing centres elsewhere. Lead seals, probably from wool bales, have been found at Coombe Down, in Avon, where an inscription suggests the presence of an Imperial estate and by the fourth century an Imperial weaving mill, mentioned in the *Notitia Dignitatum*, was in existence in Winchester.

While it may be fairly assumed that the principal surpluses produced were corn, cattle and wool, the actual systems of production, their geographical variation and changes with time, are at present beyond recovery. Yet some generalizations can be made. We have already argued that in the Late Iron Age the proximity of the Roman consumer market encouraged an intensification in production since the Roman world was eager to receive selected surpluses, particularly corn and cattle. Once Britain was conquered further intensification would probably have taken place not least because the producers were now taxed. Heavier soils like those fringing the Vale of Blackmoor were brought under cultivation and a greater range of cropping regimes introduced to allow for their exploitation. It has also been suggested that parts of the coastal alluvial flats of Somerset were drained at this time and given over to mixed farming (Leech 1981). The more southerly marshes, south of Brent Knoll, seem to have remained subject to flooding at high tide but may well have been used periodically or seasonally as pasture for flocks and herds based on the drier upland fringes.

The chalk downland may also have seen agrarian expansion. A village like Chisenbury Warren, Wilts., with its regularly laid out fields, has the appearance of having been planted on a hitherto uncluttered landscape while recent field-work on the downs to the south of Sidbury has shown that considerable areas of fields were laid out in the Roman period (Richard Bradley, pers. comm.). Agricultural expansion into the Wessex chalk uplands would necessarily have been accompanied by an increase in the flocks of sheep so essential to manure the fragile downland soils. In the huge ditched enclosures like Rockbourne Down and Soldier's Ring (Plate 7.1) we may be seeing the accompanying facilities needed for flock control (C. F. C. Hawkes 1947; C. C. Taylor 1967).

Extractive Industries

The extractive industries, which were already underway by the early Flavian period, continued to develop as the pace of Romanization increased. Mendip lead would have been much in demand particularly in the late first and early

second centuries when public bath suites were being installed in all the major towns. To floor the Great Bath in Bath alone would have taken many tons. Once the urban building boom was over by the middle of the second century the level of demand would have been maintained by those building private bath suites in their town and country houses.

Towards the end of the third century and throughout the fourth, pewter vessels became fashionable, probably as an inexpensive substitute for silver table ware. Ease of access to Mendip lead and to Cornish tin brought in by sea to one of the ports along the Bristol Channel, gave rise to a series of production centres established in nucleated settlements along, or within easy reach of, the Fosse Way. Quantities of the stone moulds in which the vessels and other trinkets were cast have been found at the roadside settlement at Camerton (Wedlake 1958: 82–93) and at Lansdown just north of Bath. Pewter vessels were widely used on rural sites as well as in the towns of Wessex.

The demand for stone was maintained throughout the Roman period. The Isle of Purbeck, which had already begun to be exploited in the years immediately following the Invasion continued to produce high quality decorative stones especially the Purbeck marble which was widely employed for inscriptions and for wall inlays and mouldings. The 'marble' together with the coarser burr stone quarried nearby was also used to make the mortars and pestles, popular in the south. The Kimmeridge shale industry also flourished. Bracelets were made in very considerable quantity on many of the rural settlements, like Rope Lake (Woodward 1987), sited amid their fields on the limestone plateau within easy reach of the coastal outcrops. The only real differences to pre-Roman production in the same area were the elaborate luxury goods now being produced for an increasingly sophisticated market – items like trenchers and animal-headed table legs (Plate 7.2).

In addition to decorative and ornamental stone, durable building stone became increasingly in demand as urban building programmes and, later, villa development got underway. Many areas of Wessex were able to supply the need. Purbeck and Portland limestone from the Isle of Purbeck, Upper Greensand from various sources especially near Chilmark, Ham stone from the Ham Hill area, Lias limestone from various Somerset quarries and Pennant grit for roofing slabs from the vicinity of Keynsham, all provided high quality building materials for their local regions, while from the chalk downland vast quantities of flints were collected. The highest quality building stone was an oolitic limestone from south east of Bath. This bathstone was widely used in Bath and the countryside around but as a fine-grained free stone it was also popular for sculpture and architectural detailing well outside

---

Plate 7.1 Soldier's Ring, Hampshire. A Late Roman enclosure possibly to corral flocks and herds. (Photo: RCHM(E))

Plate 7.2 Table leg from Dorchester carved of Kimmeridge shale. (Photo: Dorset Natural History and Archaeological Society in the Dorset County Museum, Dorchester, Dorset)

its local area. It was used for the capitals of the great Corinthian columns of the Silchester basilica built in the second century and much of the sculpture found in Wessex is carved from stone which comes from the oolitic limestone ridge.

The working of the major quarries like those near Bath was probably in the hands of full-time quarry men and it is highly likely that sculptors had set up their workshops nearby but there is no reason to suppose that the smaller quarries were anything more than convenient outcrops worked sporadically by building contractors to serve the needs of a particular job.

The upsurge in building activity also required the production of considerable supplies of lime and bricks. The production of these commodities would have been sporadic, lime kilns and tile clamps being built as and when they were required since supplies of clay and limestone or chalk were never far away.

Other raw materials mined or quarried included coal, for which there is evidence of its use as fuel on a number of sites, and iron ore which could be had from various deposits in north Wiltshire, but details of their extraction are wanting.

The Pottery Industry

The pottery industry underwent a gradual intensification during the Roman period. Several centres of production can trace their origins back to the early years of the occupation if not before. The Black Burnished ware production on the south shores of Poole Harbour (Williams 1977), the Savernake production in north Wiltshire (Annable 1962) and the Alice Holt potteries of north-eastern Hampshire (Lyne and Jefferies 1979) were all turning out wares derived from native types by the middle of the first century AD and all three centres continued to develop as the Roman period progressed. By the early second century the Poole Harbour works were generating enormous quantities of plain kitchen wares and a significant part of the product was being transshipped to military installations in the north. Production continued on a massive scale throughout the third and fourth centuries and there is hardly an area of Wessex which did not receive at least a few vessels: on many sites in Dorset, as one might expect, Poole Harbour products were used almost to the exclusion of any other kitchen ware.

In the Brue valley, in Somerset, evidence of salt production has been discovered in the form of mounds of burnt material associated with briquetage from evaporation vessels. These mounds have also produced large quantities of Black Burnished pottery typologically identical to that made in the Poole Harbour region. This has led to the suggestion that an offshoot of the Poole industry established itself in the Brue valley in the third century (Farrar 1973: 93). Fabric analysis has, however, shown that the majority of the vessels analysed from the Brue mounds were Poole Harbour products (Williams 1977: 192–3). Nonetheless the dominance of Black Burnished pottery at the Somerset salt-working sites is interesting and deserves explanation. One possibility is that the Brue valley salt production was a seasonal activity and was in the hands of specialists coming from Poole Harbour, where salt works had been long established, who brought their domestic wares with them. The annual migration of specialists of this kind is not at all unlikely especially if tidal conditions in the Somerset Levels created optimum working conditions at a different time of year to those in Dorset.

The Alice Holt kilns near Farnham produced a similar range of coarse wares to the Poole Harbour centre but in a rather harder fired grey sandy fabric. Until the middle of the fourth century the distribution patterns of wares from the two centres did not significantly overlap, the Alice Holt products reaching no further east in Hampshire than Winchester, but after about 350 when the potteries began to expand their output, Alice Holt ware is found in northern Wiltshire, suggesting that the road from Silchester along the Kennet valley through Mildenhall was being used to serve the region on the northern fringe of the Black Burnished catchment area.

By the late third century two other pottery producing regions had begun to compete with the long established centres – the New Forest and Oxfordshire kilns (Fulford 1975; Young 1977). In addition to coarse wares made for essentially local consumption, both centres produced a range of fine wares which were widely distributed. New Forest wares dominated Wessex but even so significant quantities of Oxfordshire wares were finding their way into the southern markets (Figs 7.8 and 7.9). The range of vessel types produced by the New Forest potters was considerable including flagons,

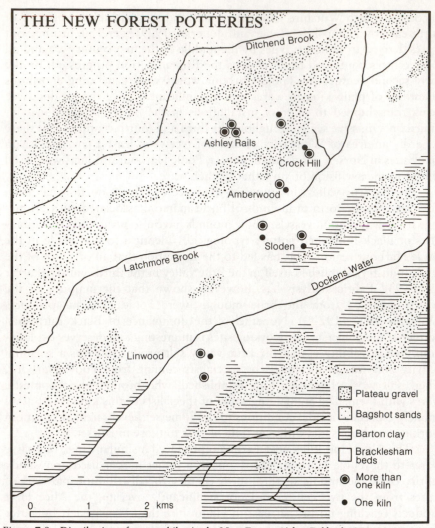

Figure 7.8 Distribution of pottery kilns in the New Forest. (After Fulford 1975: Fig. 3)

mortaria, red slipped bowls with painted or stamped decoration and a wide variety of beakers, bottles and flasks coated with coloured slip, and painted with white geometric motifs; these were often made to a hard metallic finish. The New Forest fine wares are found across the face of Wessex in concentrations which suggest that the markets at Winchester and Dorchester served as the main distribution centres. Significant quantities were also reaching Chichester whence they were distributed along the Sussex coastal plain.

No serious attempts have been made to quantify pottery production in Wessex during the Roman period but even a cursory glance at collections of site finds is sufficient to suggest that the sheer bulk of pottery available for use by the early fourth century was vastly in excess of that in circulation two centuries earlier. Clearly growing demand had led to an intensification of production and this in turn had encouraged the more favoured centres to develop to such an extent that they were able to capture most of the market. Few of the small producers of the late first and early second centuries were able to compete.

Some Dynamics

The archaeological record for the Roman period is sufficiently detailed to allow some of the trajectories of change to be recognized, albeit dimly. Perhaps the most important single factor is the dynamic created by changes in overall population size. Hard statistics are not available and at best we have to rely on guesses based on individual observers' impressions of soft data but the general consensus of opinion is that the population of Britain continued to increase from the Middle Iron Age or earlier until it reached a peak of between two and five million during the Roman period. If the Domesday figure of about a million can be accepted for the eleventh century, then there

Figure 7.9 New Forest pottery kilns at Amberwood. (After Fulford 1975: Figs 5 and 6)

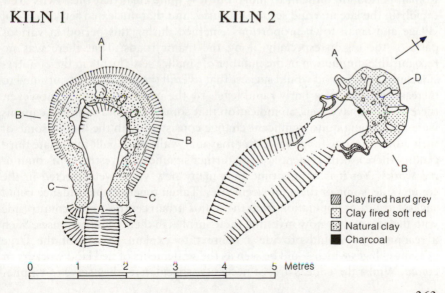

KILN 1

KILN 2

Clay fired hard grey
Clay fired soft red
Natural clay
Charcoal

0 1 2 3 4 5 Metres

must have been a decline after the Roman high. The question is at what point did the population of Britain begin to fall? Was it in the troubled times of the late fourth and early fifth centuries or was the peak reached earlier? There can be no firm answer to these questions. A number of villas seem to have been constructed for the first time in the late third century (Branigan 1976: 32–47) and newly constructed peasant sites also appear at about this time. At Butcombe, Somerset (Fowler 1970) a small farmstead was laid out in the late third century and at Bradley Hill, Somerton simple farm buildings were constructed on a virgin site in the mid fourth century (Fowler 1972: 39–41). In Wiltshire, on West Overton Down a group of cottages were put up in the later third or fourth century (Fowler 1967). At Chalton, Hants., we have seen that a small native site had, by the fourth century, grown into a considerable village (Cunliffe 1973a). Observations of this kind might suggest that the population was continuing to expand well into the fourth century but such an interpretation is not well founded. The West Overton cottages were built into the corner of disused fields and might simply result from the resiting of an existing peasant farm, while at Chalton the field evidence suggests that the development of villages may go hand in hand with a decline in the number of smaller peasant farms in the area and thus represent some form of social reorganization occurring in the late third or fourth century. The problem therefore is complex and cannot be solved by reference to the few excavations which have been undertaken. All that can safely be said is that there is no direct evidence of population decline before the middle of the fourth century and indeed what little data there is could be argued to be evidence of a late third century expansion.

The relative sizes of the urban to rural populations throughout the Roman period are difficult to judge but it is quite clear that the towns grew rapidly in the late first and second centuries and that nucleated settlements of village and small town proportions emerged during this period in various parts of the region especially along the major roads. That there was no recognizable diminution in the number of smaller settlements in the countryside during this period would suggest that overall the population continued to increase, possibly at a fairly rapid level. By the mid third century, however, there is, as we have seen, an indication that some of the old cantonal capitals were undergoing quite significant change consistent with the loss of some of their administrative functions. After masonry walls were built in the late third century there is little evidence of any further significant investment in communal works. Yet it is at this time that many new villas were erected in the countryside, some of them on virgin sites. Taken together the evidence could suggest a shift of population from the major urban centres to the countryside with the aristocracy now investing their surplus in their country houses. Such a readjustment would provide a context to explain growth of the large peasant villages which could be seen as the settlements of tied land workers or *coloni*. Whilst these ideas are, of necessity, speculative, they serve to emphasize that questions of population growth or decline can only be considered in terms of the entire settlement system and not just one part of it.

Standing back from the evidence reviewed in this chapter the overriding impression gained is that the Roman period in Wessex was one of change. The urban experiment, entered into with such enthusiasm in the first and early second centuries, failed. The Wessex native population was rural at heart and while the tribal aristocracy willingly embraced the concept of city along with other Roman attributes as a means of displaying their status, much as they had taken to wine drinking and Roman table ware in the century before the invasion, by the second half of the third century for many the novelty had worn off and the rural focus of life once more reasserted itself. Extraneous factors, such as an influx of wealthy immigrants and increasingly oppressive obligations imposed on the urban aristocracy by the state may well have exacerbated the trend.

In such a situation the rural markets flourished while the towns continued to provide readily accessible market centres for the estates within easy reach. That the system which had evolved by the late third and early fourth centuries was stable is amply demonstrated by the level of wealth manifest in the vivid figured mosaics of the large villas and the generally high level of production of consumer durables throughout the region. But this is not to argue that the socio-economic system of the fourth century AD was identical to that of the first century BC with a superficial overlay of *Romanitas*. The old bonds of clientage had been much weakened by Roman rule and in place of obligation repaying patronage, labour was now bought or was provided by the unfree. The classic Celtic system was in the throes of becoming feudal. In the villas, villages and rural markets of the early fourth century we are seeing the shape of medieval Wessex to come.

Chapter 8

Return to Tribalism: AD 350–685

The two centuries, from the revolt of Magnentius in 350 until Cynric's thrust into the heart of Wessex a traditional 'event' assigned to the year 552 – saw the most dramatic changes Wessex had ever known (Fig. 8.1). This brief and obscure interlude was a time of rapid transitions when the old prehistoric order briefly reasserted itself only to be overturned and replaced by new systems heralding the modern age.

The sources available for the study of this period are sparse and difficult to interpret. At the outset there are a few reliable Roman accounts which allow the principal historical events to be sketched up to about 409. Thereafter a broad chronological framework can be reconstructed from the works of Gildas, Bede and from the *Anglo Saxon Chronicle* but the reliability of these sources for this early period is very much in doubt. Few scholars are now prepared to accept the dates and events they list as an accurate record and much debate still surrounds the historical authenticity of the individuals whose exploits are chronicled (Sims-Williams 1983a, 1983b). It would, however, be wrong to regard these sources as complete fabrications. At the very least they are likely to reflect a view of the broad sweep of events and, used with care, they may throw some light on the transformations taking place.

The archaeological evidence is no less difficult to handle. At the beginning Roman pottery and coins occur in quantity but gradually coinage ceased to reach the province. Very little copper was minted after 402, gold continued to be imported until 406 and silver a year later in sufficient quantity to pay the army but after 409, when the last of the major field armies had been removed to the Continent to support the cause of Constantine III and there was no further need of bullion to pay the troops, supplies were halted. No doubt coins continued to circulate for some time but considerable quantities were removed and hoarded, and by about 430 coin-using in a market system was at an end. The collapse of the market economy in the first two or three

---

Figure 8.1 Early Anglo-Saxon Wessex. (After S. C. Hawkes 1986: Fig. 6)

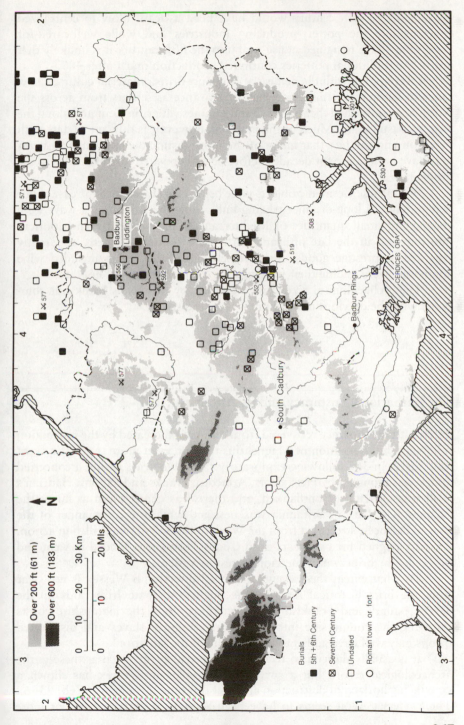

decades of the fifth century would have been a death blow to centralized concerns like the pottery-producing industries and while well-cared-for vessels may have remained in use well into the fifth century it is unlikely that any of the traditional potteries continued production much after 400.

Overlapping with the demise of Romano-British material culture a new range of Germanic items made their appearance as settlers from across the North Sea established themselves in the Thames valley, in Kent and along the Sussex coastal plain. Much of the material, however, is difficult to date with precision and the fact that many of the more distinctive and valuable items may have been in use for decades before being deposited in graves adds to the problem.

While these Germanic objects were being introduced into the east of our region, tenuous long-distance trading links along the Atlantic sea-ways were channelling small quantities of Mediterranean and western French pottery into the west in the late fifth and early sixth centuries, where, apparently regarded as prestige goods, these vessels (Fig. 8.2), which included wine amphorae, were finding their way into the courts of the local nobility.

The archaeological record is, therefore, by no means blank but compared with the previous millennium it is indeed sparse.

The Barbarian Conspiracy and its Aftermath: 367–370

Barely had the Province recovered from dislocation created by the retribution following the usurpation of Magnentius than an even more traumatic event took place. In 367 following exploratory raids two years earlier a concerted attack was mounted by Picts, Scots, Attacotti, Franks and Saxons. Hadrian's Wall was overrun, or outflanked, and there was chaos south as far as the Thames. The Dux of Britannia was besieged while the commander of the coastal defences, stretching from the Wash to the Solent, was killed in action. Anarchy reigned for two years until Count Theodosius landed in Kent and proceeded by bribery and coercion to restore order.

To what extent these events impinged directly on Wessex is not clear from the brief historical record. One might anticipate Irish raids up the Severn estuary and Frankish or Saxon raids along the Hampshire coasts throwing the countryside into confusion: runaway slaves and disaffected troops may well have added to the anarchy of the situation.

It is usually difficult to recognize historical events such as these in the archaeological record but a survey of the villas in Wessex has shown a convincing horizon of destruction at about this time (Branigan 1976b: 93–6). The Somerset Avon seems to have been a point of entry for one or more

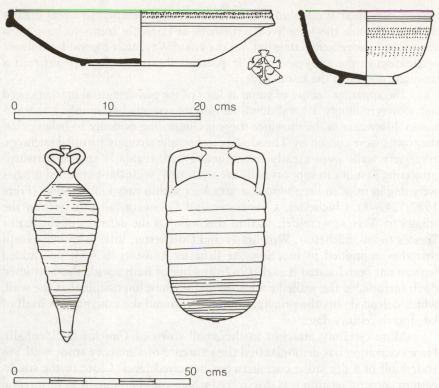

Figure 8.2 Pottery of the type imported into the west along the Atlantic sea-ways in the fifth and sixth centuries. Top row, A ware from the east Mediterranean; bottom row, B ware amphorae from the east Mediterranean

bands of sea-borne raiders, presumably Irish, who had penetrated along the Severn. Destruction levels have been located at a number of villas including Kings Weston, Brislington, Keynsham, Box and North Wraxall. At Brislington, skeletons of four or five individuals and a dozen cattle had been tipped down the well. Three bodies were also found in the well at North Wraxall. Although it is impossible to date these events precisely or to show that they relate to a single historical episode, the geographical proximity of the sites to the Avon adds to the possibility that their destruction may be linked to the attack of 367. Further, though less well dated, destruction horizons hint that the river Parrett may also have provided easy entry for raiders to the rich villa estates of southern Somerset.

The reconstruction of the Province following the landing of Theodosius in 369 was thorough. Villa life continued and in some cases flourished and several of the devastated villas were reoccupied. But widespread change can now begin to be detected. A number of the larger rural settlements, which may have functioned as markets, show signs of decline. At Woodyates, even though the Great West road remained open, activity after 367 was greatly diminished while the long-lived settlement at Catsgore seems to have been abandoned altogether. Camerton, on the Fosse Way, after a period of intense occupation in the early and middle parts of the fourth century suffered a dramatic decline in the last decades.

The apparent demise of some at least of the possible rural markets need not, however, imply a breakdown in trading systems but simply a reorientation. Elsewhere in the Province there is compelling evidence to believe that the towns were chosen by Theodosius to become strongly fortified enclaves. Some city walls were greatly strengthened with regularly spaced forward-projecting bastions to support ballistae while new, wide flat-bottomed ditches were dug in front to keep wouldbe attackers within easy killing range (Frere 1987: 247–8). Chichester, Cirencester and Caerwent, all just beyond the fringes of Wessex, were defended in this way. Of the defences of the major Wessex towns, Silchester, Winchester and Dorchester, little is known except that they continued to function. At Ilchester however at least one added bastion has been located (Leach 1982: 9) while at Bath a wide flat-bottomed ditch surrounded the walled enclosure and it is not impossible that the wall, which defended only the principal buildings around the sanctuary, is itself of late fourth century date.

More certainty attaches to the small town of *Cunetio* (Mildenhall). Here excavation has demonstrated the existence of a massive stone wall 5 m wide built of a dry stone core between mortared faces. Close to the south-eastern corner a bastion was discovered which could be shown to be integral with the wall. The discovery of a coin of *c.* 360 in a small ditch pre-dating the wall suggests that a Theodosian date is likely (Annable 1959). A closely comparable late masonry wall was erected possibly at about this time to surround the settlement at Gatcombe. No bastions have yet been noted but this does not preclude their existence. The dating evidence, such as it is, indicates a date some time in the fourth century (Cunliffe 1967: 130). Finally at *Clausentum* (Bitterne) on a promontory jutting into Southampton Water a long-established settlement was enclosed within a masonry wall which, anti-quarian accounts suggest, was defended with bastions (Cotton and Gathercole 1958). A coin of Valens, said to have been found in a context immediately preceding the construction of the wall (Waterman 1947: 157), seems to point to a Theodosian date for its construction. It has been customary in the past to regard Clausentum as a late addition to the system of shore forts. That it may have housed a militia is not unlikely but it is more appropriate to consider it in the context of the defended small towns.

Plate 8.1 Portchester Castle, Hampshire, from the air. The outer wall with bastions was built in the late third century as part of the coastal defence system. The Roman walls provided protection for the Saxon community and later for a medieval castle and monastery.

Plate 8.2   The Roman defensive wall at Portchester Castle.

The shore fort at Portchester (Plates 8.1 and 8.2), constructed in the Carausian period, continued in occupation throughout the fourth century and probably well into the fifth as we shall see below (Cunliffe 1975). Portchester, together with the newly fortified settlement at Clausentum and the town of Chichester, which had been strengthened with bastions and a wide flat-bottomed ditch, provided the communities of the exposed Solent coast with adequate and well-spaced refuges. Indeed it may have been one of the intentions of the Theodosian reorganization to create fortified places of varying kinds at regular intervals throughout the country. This raises the interesting question of the reuse of hillforts. A surprising number of hillforts in Wessex have produced Late Roman material (Fowler 1971). In some, like Maiden Castle and probably South Cadbury and Ham Hill, the archaeological material may have been associated with temples, but this by no means precludes a defensive role as well. The very existence of massive earthworks would have been inviting to rural communities in times of insecurity.

272

Thus it may be that after the Theodosian restoration, Wessex began to take on a rather embattled appearance. Not only were the walled towns and shore fort put into a state of defensive readiness but also smaller communities who could afford it now erected walls for the first time. Elsewhere the grass-grown ramparts of the Iron Age forts, enhanced perhaps with new timber breastworks, were being brought back to life.

To what extent this new scattering of fortification was manned by full-time military personnel is difficult to say but of some relevance is the discovery of 'Germanic-style' military equipment in or close to many towns (S. C. Hawkes and Dunning 1961). The earliest examples were probably used by regular soldiers recruited along the Rhine frontier region and brought over by Theodosius. Later types are most likely to be of British manufacture. Neither need imply the use of 'mercenaries', as was previously thought, but probably reflect the billeting of regular detachments, under the command of the Vicar of Britain, on selected towns of strategic value for the defence of the Province's communications. A number of individuals, equipped in this way, were found buried among the Romano-British population of Winchester in the Lankhills cemetery (G. Clarke 1979: 377–403): another group were found in a cemetery outside the Roman town of Dorchester-on-Thames just beyond the northern fringes of our region. In the context of resident urban militias these burials are readily understandable. More difficult to explain is the occurrence of military metalwork at villas, like Upper Upham and North Wraxall in Wiltshire. Regular troops are hardly likely to have owned villas but veterans might have been hired by villa owners to provide protection.

The End of Centralized Government: 370–410

The forty years or so following the Theodosian restoration was a time of growing insecurity exacerbated by the removal of armies, raised in the Province, to fight in support of their successive leaders in Continental campaigns. The first army left in 388 with Magnus Maximus, the second withdrew with Stilicho in 401, while the last followed Constantine III in 409. In theory they were regular armies protecting Britain from barbarian attack, in practice they were little more than paid mobs out for plunder. In each case the campaigns were failures and it is unlikely that anyone returned. Thus in the space of twenty years the Province was robbed of manpower at the time when the economic systems were beginning to fragment: moreover raids from across the North Sea were becoming more threatening and culminated in a serious Saxon attack in 408–9. The situation, not only in Britain but in Gaul as well,

273

was desperate as barbarian war parties from across the Rhine flooded into the empire.

The historian Zosimus (Zosimus IV.5) provides a valuable insight into the British situation at this time. 'The Britons', he writes,

> took up arms and, braving danger for their own independence, freed their cities from the barbarians threatening them, and all Armorica and the other provinces of Gaul copied the British example and freed themselves in the same way, expelling their Roman governors and establishing their own administration as best they could.

Taken on its face value the account of Zosimus leaves little doubt that the local civitates had decided to take control of their own destiny. When, in the next year, 410, the Emperor Honorius wrote to the urban communities telling them to look after their own defence he was simply legitimizing the status quo. 'From that time onwards', writes Procopius, 'Britain continued to be ruled by tyrants.'

The archaeology of these last decades is vague and ill focused but there is ample evidence from the Wessex villas to show that a high percentage of them continued to be occupied. Some of the small market centres were still in use in the fifth century, as is shown by the presence of coins minted after 395. Old Sarum, where 7.6 per cent of the coins recovered belong to this late period, was evidently flourishing. The towns, too, all produce evidence of continued occupation. But the problem is on what scale and for what function were these places maintained? Floors might be repaired and roofs patched but this says little of the strength of the local administrative system or of the well-being of the agrarian economy. At best the story of the last four decades of Roman rule is one of decline as, gradually, one support system after another ceased to work. In the countryside life would, of course, have continued but with consumer goods no longer being produced on an industrial scale and money supply becoming uncertain, the unified world fragmented as self-sufficiency and local barter became the norm.

In the towns, to which many of the local aristocracy would have gravitated for safety, some semblance of the old urban systems continued. The suggested strength of these urban communities in 409 indicates that many of them maintained their militias. Until that year such detachments were under unified control but after the urban revolt any remaining troops would have been in the pay of the individual towns.

One further point is worth considering. Zosimus tells us that the Armoricans 'followed the British example' and since it is known that in Armorica there was a peasant revolt against the urban communities, it has been argued that a similar rebellion took place in Britain in 409 (Thompson 1956). Such a scenario is entirely possible: indeed it would be surprising if some degree of alienation had not developed between town and country. By the first decade of the fifth century traditional bonds of clientage and service and even rights of ownership to land and its products would have been difficult to uphold in the growing anarchy: in such circumstances it is highly unlikely that the peasantry would have remained loyal and servile.

The Saxon Settlement in the East: 410–550

The history of the period following the letter of Honorius to the urban leaders is obscure in the extreme but that urban life continued, at least in some parts of Britain, is graphically illustrated by an account, in Constantius' Life of Germanus, which describes the saint's visit to Britain in 429 when he encountered a large assembly of Britons 'conspicuous for riches, brilliant in dress, and surrounded by a fawning multitude.'

Some broad outline of events can be pieced together from the works of Gildas, Bede and the *Anglo Saxon Chronicle* but it should be regarded as little more than a generalized model. In place of unified leadership there emerged a number of local leaders – tyrants as they are called – men like Vortigern, Ambrosius and Arthur, some or all of whom might have been actual historical personages. They came from the ranks of the urban aristocracy to lead local communities. Their aspirations varied. In the uncertain years of the early fifth century there was the expectation among many that Rome would once more establish centralized control: the name of Ambrosius is sometimes associated with this party. The alternative belief, ascribed to Vortigern, was that Rome was gone for ever and the only way to maintain order was to hire Germanic mercenaries to augment the local militias. Such a policy was little more than a continuation of the *status quo*.

Against this background must be seen the events unfolding across the North Sea, from the territory extending from western Holstein in the north to Dutch Friesland. In this densely settled land, communities had been coming under increasing stress since the early third century. The pressures on them were created in part by the disruption of trade with the Romann empire, caused by folk movements and war to the east, and in part by rising sea levels which began to drown once fertile land. Some of these 'Saxons' went south to join the Roman armies, others took to piracy and looked to Britain as a source of rich picking. In response the British authorities began to build coastal defences, the first of which, significantly, protected the Thames estuary and the Wash. By the fourth century the defences of the Saxon Shore, as it was known, stretched from the Wash to the Solent, and it was no doubt this tract of coast that was under attack in 365, 367 and 408/9 in which years Saxons are recorded as being among the barbarian bands pillaging Britain.

In the early fifth century, as their homeland became increasingly un-congenial, Saxons continued to pressure Britain and small groups were prob-ably allowed in to settle abandoned land to provide a buffer to further incursions. Such a policy had been adopted by the Romans for generations along the frontier zones of the empire. Soon, however, the tide of immigrants built up to such a degree that it came to be regarded as a threat to the indigenous inhabitants. This is probably what lay behind the traditional record of a Saxon 'rebellion' in 442, though whether it was a single uprising, precisely dated is doubtful. In any event the British leaders sent an appeal to the Roman commander, Aetius, who was campaigning in Gaul, in or soon after 446 seeking military help to stem the tide of Saxon settlers. In melo-dramatic terms Gildas records the message 'To Agitius (i.e. Aetius) thrice consul, the Groans of the Britons . . . the barbarians drive us to the sea, the sea drives us to the barbarians; between these two means of death we are either killed or drowned.' There was no known response and the British communities were left to their own devices.

The exact geography and chronology of the earliest Saxon settlement of Britain is still a matter of active debate but it is now generally accepted that, in the south of Britain, the earliest Saxon settlements, dating to the first half of the fifth century, lay in Kent and the Thames valley, in particular in Oxfordshire (Dickinson 1980; S. C. Hawkes 1982, 1986) and along the Sussex coastal plain (Welch 1983) – a distribution which neatly reflects the ease of penetration up the Thames and westwards along the Channel. It has been argued (Welch 1971) that the distribution of early fifth century cemeter-ies in Sussex echoes reflects two specific landfalls, one in the region of Bishop-stone, between the rivers Cuckmere and Ouse, and the other focused on Highdown between the rivers Arun and Adur. A third landing may have been made further west on the Solent coast (Cunliffe 1973b: 131–9). The evidence is controversial but within the walls of the old Roman Shore Fort at Portches-ter three sunken-floor huts (*grubenhauser*) were found along the Roman streets. One produced an assemblage of pottery best placed in the early fifth century together with a gilded bronze disc brooch (Plate 8.3) for which the closest Continental parallels are of the late fourth or early fifth century (Evison 1978 but for later dating Welch 1976). A similar brooch was found in a cemetery at Droxford in the Meon valley. If the early fifth century dating is accepted then here may be a pale reflection of an immigrant group, some of whom settled in the fort while others moved inland along the Meon. It is possible that the memory of some such group lay behind Bede's reference to a Jutish landing in the region. There is a certain neat logic in this three-pronged settlement of the south coast because each of the three supposed enclaves lies in an area well clear of the major Roman nucleated settlements (Cunliffe 1973b: Fig. 46).

By the 440s or 450, therefore, there is reason to believe that Wessex was flanked to the north east and south east by settled Saxon communities. If

Gildas is to be relied upon, there followed an uneasy period when Saxon raiding parties attempted a penetration of Wessex. But the Britons held their own winning a succession of battles, usually fought at river crossings, culminating with the great British victory at Mount Badon sometime about AD 500. If such a battle occurred its location is unknown: it may be the old hillfort of Badbury Rings in eastern Dorset (Jackson 1958) though various north Wessex hillforts have also been suggested (Myres 1986: 159–60). Southwards forays from the Oxford region might also have occurred and some writers have suggested, not unreasonably, that the massive linear earthwork of East Wansdyke, stretching for 20 km across the north Wiltshire Downs, just south of the river Kennet, may have been constructed by the British against the Saxon thrust from the north.

The *Anglo Saxon Chronicle* provides a terse account of events at this time which at best should be regarded as incomplete, inaccurate and garbled and at worst largely mythical. Scholars, while well aware of the problems inherent in dealing with texts of this kind, have been loath to reject the accounts of the formation of the West Saxon kingdom as entirely worthless and some have argued that a shadow of a narrative can be glimpsed through the fog (for one version see Myres 1986: 144–73) but more recently a new scepticism has emerged most cogently expressed by Barbara Yorke (Yorke 1989 and 1990: 128–56). The essence of the problem is that the *Chronicle*'s account of the early events in Wessex was not compiled until about 890 at the instigation of King Alfred when politically it was vital not only to establish the legitimacy of the ruling house but also to create a unified West Saxon ethnicity in the face of the Danish attacks (Bately 1978). The 'origins myth', if

Plate 8.3 Gilded bronze disc brooch of the fifth century AD from a grubenhaus at Portchester, Hants.

we can call it that, had therefore to be fabricated using whatever scraps existed in a style that was heroic, fitted the acceptable model of such accounts and provided Alfred with a legitimacy going back to the original landings. From 648, however, it seems that some contemporary records survived and were included providing an increasingly reliable account (F. M. Stenton 1926: 119). For the first crucial 150 years or so the *Chronicle*'s narrative shows all the signs of having adopted a standard 'foundation' model (Sims-Williams 1983b). It is also bedevilled by being a conflation of two similar traditions dislocated by a gap of nineteen years (F. Stenton 1971: 22–3; K. Harrison 1976: 127–30). These and other problems have been carefully assessed by Barbara Yorke (1989). The *Chronicle* for this period cannot therefore be accepted as history but it needs to be summarized if only to show how, four centuries later, the West Saxons chose to present their origins.

In 495, we are told, Cerdic and his son Cynric landed at *Cerdicesoru* and there fought with the Britons. Usually the site is identified with Stone on the Solent coast close to the mouth of the Beaulieu river but, as we shall see, it is more likely that a site further west, possibly at Christchurch Harbour at the mouth of the Avon, was intended. In 508 they fought a battle at *Natanleaga*, near Netley, and in 519 fought with the Britons again at *Cerdicesford*, probably Charford on the Avon south of Salisbury. The battle was decisive in establishing Cerdic's superiority and from it the *Chronicle* dated the origin of the Wessex lineage. In 530 the Isle of Wight was seized but four years later, on Cerdic's death, it was passed to the control of his kinsmen Stuf and Wightar. Cynric outlived his father for a further twenty-six years fighting against the Britons at Searoburg (Sarum) in 552 and in 556, in partnership with Ceawlin, he engaged the Britons on the North Wiltshire Downs at Barbury. In parallel with this, and unconnected by the chronicler, *Port* and his two sons landed at *Portesmupa* (Portsmouth) in 501 and fought a battle with a noble Briton. These were the principal events, whether fact or fiction, which the compilers of the *Chronicle* wished their audience to accept.

Bede, in his *Ecclesiastical History*, offers additional information which was probably provided for him by his correspondent, Bishop Daniel of Winchester, in the early eighth century when he was writing. He tells us that the Isle of Wight was occupied by Jutes of the same ethnic origin as the early settlers in Kent, and that the Jutish province extended to the mainland 'opposite the Isle of Wight'. A consideration of the basic geography of the area together with what little place name evidence survives suggests that Jutish territory extended from the New Forest across the lower reaches of the Test and Itchen to include the Hamble, the Meon and possibly the Portsmouth region (Yorke: 1989: 89–90).

What, then, can we make of it all? The simplest explanation would be to assume that the traditions concerning Port and his sons and Stuf and Wightar reflect a Jutish *Adventus* colonizing the territories on either side of the Solent probably during the fifth century and it may be to this context that the settlement at Portchester (and possibly Clausentum) and the cemetery at Droxford belong. There are elements of material culture in the early cemeteries on the Isle of Wight which clearly reflect links with Jutland (C. Arnold 1982).

The *Chronicle*'s geography of the Cerdic/Cynric adventure, whatever its validity, provides a more western focus for this series of episodes. If one accepts that the site of the landing at Cerdicesoru lay on Christchurch Harbour then the axis of penetration must have been the Avon. The cemetery evidence shows that there was considerable activity in the Salisbury area in the fifth and sixth centuries, some of the burials being of princely status. Here, evidently, was an early focus of aristocratic power whatever the origins and lineage of the leaders (Bonney 1973: 470–3).

The possibility emerges therefore of multiple landings along the Hampshire coasts with groups of Jutish origins claiming much of the territory in the fifth century, leaving the later Saxon immigrants to develop the more westerly landfall provided by the harbour at the mouth of the Avon. While Bede retains a memory of this complexity, the later West Saxon tradition conflates everything under the aura of Cerdic, a simplification suited to the political demands of the time.

The archaeological evidence, derived almost entirely from cemeteries, cannot be expected to mirror these ethnic differences and events with any degree of clarity but the distribution of early Anglo-Saxon cemeteries is informative (Fig. 8.1). Before the end of the fifth century cemeteries were already established in the Itchen valley north of Winchester and within the next 50 years a number had sprung up south and east of Sarum. Even without the documentary evidence it looks as though the major river valleys were the principal means of entry and it was here that the early settlements must have clustered. Whether or not the Winchester-centred communities derived from the Jutish incursion or from the groups who penetrated the Avon it is impossible to say. Another possibility, that they were a native enclave who simply adopted the alien burial rite, should not be entirely rejected.

The battle of Barbury recorded in the *Chronicle* for the year 556 introduces the name of Ceawlin into the story for the first time as the partner of the Wessex war leader Cynric. Ceawlin's origins are obscure. The chronicler evidently wishes us to believe that he was a relative of Cynric, possibly even his son, in order to legitimize the later Wessex lineage, but the strong probability remains that he was a member of the aristocracy which had established itself in the Oxford region in the fifth century and had grown to become powerful. The problem is a complex one frequently debated (Kirby 1965; F. Stenton 1971: 28; Myres 1986: 162–4; S. C. Hawkes 1986) but the simplest explanation would be that, in his brief record of the battle of Barbury, the chronicler deliberately conflated the Cerdic and Ceawlin lineages to create a single story line. At any event it is clear from what follows that the power now lay in the Thames valley and that Ceawlin was a war leader of some ability at a time of considerable expansion. After Cynric's death (traditionally 560) it is Ceawlin who is preeminent among the West Saxons, or Geuissae, as they probably called themselves at this time.

The *Chronicle* depicts Ceawlin and his associates as engaged in a programme of constant expansion around the borders of their middle Thames-based enclave. One of the most significant battles was fought at Dyrham, in the Cotswolds just north of Bath, in 577. It was here, according to the *Chronicle*, that Ceawlin and Cuthwine overcame British resistance and thus acquired control of the old Roman cities of Gloucester, Cirencester and Bath. The clear impression is that they were now involved in a westward thrust designed to annex the Cotswolds perhaps as far as the river Severn.

To what extent Ceawlin and his supporters were overlords of the enclaves based on Sarum and Winchester is unclear but the fact that the *Chronicle* records Ceawlin fighting and losing a major engagement at *Wodnesbeorge* on the downs south of East Wansdyke might suggest that the control of the south was not yet complete. By the end of the sixth century, however, some semblance of political unity had been established by the Geuissae over Oxfordshire, Berkshire, Hampshire, much of Wiltshire and the southern part of Gloucestershire. Dorset and Somerset remained largely untouched.

The conquest of Dorset was held back for a while by the massive defensive earthwork of Bokerly Dyke which runs for 10 km across the open chalkland of Cranborne Chase from the western forests to the heathland of northeast Dorset. The dyke was a long-established boundary, dating back originally to the Late Bronze Age but was finally reconstructed to sever the Roman road to the south west, and thus protect Dorset, in the fifth or early sixth century (C. F. C. Hawkes 1947; Rahtz 1961; Bowen 1990). It served to delay the Saxon advance until the middle of the sixth century when it was eventually overrun. It has been suggested (C. C. Taylor 1970: 43–4) that another defensive earthwork, Combs Ditch, crossing the Dorset Downs between the Stour and the North Winterbourne valley, held back the Saxons for a little longer but soon after 650 the penetration of the Dorchester region seems to have begun. We should not, however, think in terms of a replacement of population. The continuation of a strong British presence in the Isle of Purbeck is demonstrated by a collection of native inscriptions, carved on old Roman columns, found near the site of the Church of Lady St Mary, Wareham, the earliest dating from the seventh century. These stones are a vivid reminder that the Sub Roman population must have greatly outnumbered the Saxon war bands and the settlers who followed in their wake.

The advance into Dorset, reconstructed on the basis of topographic and cemetery evidence, was probably instigated by the Saxon population based on the Sarum region. The conquest of Somerset, on the other hand, may well have been mounted from the power-base in the Middle Thames. In 652, so the *Chronicle* records, the British were defeated at Bradford-on-Avon and another defeat followed in 658 at Penselwood in Somerset. The rest of the advance remains obscure but by 700 Exeter and probably most of the south west except for Cornwall was in the hands of the English. By this time the Anglo-Saxon inhabitants of Wessex were being converted to Christianity. The few pagan Saxon cemeteries found in Somerset and Dorset (Fig. 8.1) are a clear reflection of the late conquest of this region.

The Re-emergence of Tribalism in the West: 410–600

While the Saxon settlers were carving out territories for themselves in the east and north of the region the British inhabitants of western Wiltshire, Dorset and Somerset continued an existence at a cultural level that can best be called Sub Roman. The excavations at South Cadbury hillfort provide a glimpse of the period (Alcock 1972: 174–93). Here the old hillfort defences were refurbished with a new defensive work raised on top of the original inner rampart. The new work consisted of a setting of vertical timbers, forming a front face, tied back by horizontal beams to other verticals behind, the whole embanked with earth and rubble. The outer face was finished by a wall of dry stone work. The gate was also rebuilt in timber at this stage in the form of a simple rectangular structure with an inner and outer gate both of two leaves hung from sturdy verticals. While the gate shows vague similarities to much earlier Roman military structures the form of the rampart would not have been out of place a thousand years earlier – apart from the general crudeness of its construction. The dating evidence, such as it is, suggests that the redefence of the old fort should be placed in the late fifth century.

Within the defended area there are traces of occupation, the most impressive aspect of which was a substantial timber building, approximately 10 by 20 m which appears to have been constructed in the form of an aisled hall. The sheer size of the hall suggests that the settlement was of high status implying that South Cadbury may have been the residence of a local aristocrat. That Cadbury has been traditionally associated with the legendary King Arthur has given rise to much speculation.

One aspect of the archaeological record at Cadbury deserves further consideration. The site has produced a significant collection of imported pottery of the late fifth and early sixth centuries (Fig. 8.2). The most distinctive elements are fine red bowls decorated with rouletting (Class A ware) and sherds of large jars used to import wine or other commodities (Class B ware). Both types came ultimately from North Africa and are found together with bowls in a grey fabric with a blue/black slip which were made in western France (Class E ware). These imports evidently arrived by sea along the

Atlantic route and are characteristically found on sites of Dark Age date in the West Country, Wales, Ireland and Scotland (A. C. Thomas 1981). The range of imports and their distribution pattern provide an interesting echo of the long-established intercourse along the traditional Atlantic route which can be traced back to the third millennium BC.

Other hilltop settlements of the fifth and sixth centuries have been identified in Somerset. At Cadbury, near Congresbury, a substantial Iron Age hillfort was redefended in the fifth century and divided across the centre by a bank of stone and rubble. Just inside the new bank several timber-built structures were located. The discovery of imported Mediterranean pottery suggests that here too a local aristocrat may have set up his court (Fowler, Gardner and Rahtz 1970; Fowler and Rahtz 1970). Similar reoccupation has been demonstrated at the hillfort of Cannington just outside where a large cemetery of Sub Roman date has been excavated (Rahtz 1969). Finally, excavation on Glastonbury Tor has shown there to have been a phase of Sub Roman occupation possibly associated with an early monastic establishment (Rahtz 1971). Taken together the evidence for hilltop settlement in the fifth and sixth centuries in Somerset is impressive. The choice of hillforts raises the possibility that many if not most of these old earthworks may have been brought back into use as defensive enclosures and in this context we should remember that at least three of the battles fought by the Saxon war bands in the east of Wessex, at Badbury, Sarum and Barbury, were located at or close to hillforts. The incorporation of two hillforts within the defensive line of West Wansdyke (below, pp. 293–6), which must date to broadly this period, is a further indication of the significance of existing defensive enclosures (Burrow 1981: 80–4).

Outside Somerset evidence for the Sub Roman use of hillforts is slight but at Poundbury in Dorset a substantial settlement including at least eight timber buildings has been located above the site of a Late Roman cemetery immediately outside the hillfort defences (C. S. Green 1987: 71–92). It is tempting to regard it as a suburb to a settlement inside the defences (which show some sign of refurbishment at this time) but such a suggestion must remain pure speculation until excavation has told us more of occupation of this date (or of its absence) within the walled area of the Roman town.

The Introduction of Christianity

Christianity had become firmly established in Wessex in the fourth century and it is highly likely that the practice continued among many pockets of the

Sub Roman population throughout the succeeding centuries. The Wareham inscriptions, mentioned above, suggest a vigorous Christian enclave was encountered by the first Saxon settlers as late as the seventh century and in Somerset the Dark Age settlement on Glastonbury Tor may have been an early monastic establishment. The existence of other early Christian communities in the county is implied by traditional sources.

The Early Saxon settlers were, of course, pagan, and remained so until the middle of the seventh century. The conversion of Wessex was begun by a Christian from Italy, Birinus, who arrived *c.* 635 with the intention of converting the heathens of 'the remote inland regions of England where no teacher had preceded him.' By this Bede may well be referring to the Midlands. But on arriving in Britain, presumably via the Solent 'and coming first to the nation of the Gewissae (the West Saxons), where he found all to be extremely pagan, he thought it more useful to preach the word there, rather than to go further looking for people to whom he should preach' (Bede, *H.E.*, III, VII). His initial move, following the example set by other missionaries before him, was probably to make for the royal court in Oxfordshire and to convert the king, Cynegils. Cynegils was baptized in about 635 in the presence of Oswald of Northumbria who may have been his overlord and may have been at the court to marry Cynegils' daughter (Wormald 1983: 112). Thereafter Birinus was given Dorchester-on-Thames to serve as his episcopal see, where he succeeded in bringing 'many to the Lord by his pious labours' including Cynegils' son Cwichelm. It was at Dorchester that Birinus died and was buried. How far his ministry had extended is not recorded.

Cynegils was succeeded by his son Cenwealh in 641/2 at a time when the Mercians, occupying the territory immediately to the north, were beginning to cast covetous eyes on the middle Thames valley. Cenwealh, Bede tells us, 'was very often afflicted by his enemies with most serious losses in his kingdom.' To contend with this threat it is possible that he made his kinsman, Cuthread, under-king of the northern part of his Wessex kingdom – a territory including the Berkshire Downs and north Wiltshire, meanwhile moving his own power base to Winchester in the comparative safety of the Hampshire chalkland. It was here in 648 that he endowed the first Anglo-Saxon Minster. Twelve years later in 660, with Mercian pressure on the north still continuing, he further enhanced the position of Winchester by establishing a bishopric there, thus dividing the West Saxon diocese – an act possibly born of the realization that control of the northern territory was fast becoming untenable. In the next year he was proved right when Wulfhere, king of Mercia, devastated the West Saxon kingdom south to the Berkshire Downs. In the same entry the *Anglo Saxon Chronicle* records that he also took the Isle of Wight and handed it over to the control of the South Saxon royal house, ensuring that the people of Wight were baptized. Taken on its face value the *Chronicle* would seem to be suggesting a deep Mercian thrust through West Saxon territory bypassing the power base at Winchester.

Between the coming of Birinus in 635 and the events of Cenwealh's reign thirty years later Christianity was brought to most parts of the West Saxon kingdom, yet old burial customs lingered on. Cemeteries of this 'Final Phase' or proto-Christian cemeteries as they are more appropriately called (S. C. Hawkes 1986: 92–3), are quite distinctive. Grave goods are comparatively few and in place of the heavy jewellery of the past, needed to hold the loose female dress together, the new style in sewn garments allowed for lighter, more elegant adornment. The only functional items now were the pairs of chain-linked pins used to fasten the head-dress. One characteristic burial of this kind was that of a rich woman buried on Roundway Down in Wiltshire. She was adorned with gold jewellery of the kind in vogue among the Mercian aristocracy to the north, a reflection of style and fashion transcending political boundaries.

The best-known Wessex cemetery of this date is Winnall II on the outskirts of Winchester (Meaney and Hawkes 1970). It was founded on a new site a short distance from the old pagan cemetery, Winnall I, probably for a newly baptized Christian community some time about the middle of the seventh century. It remained in use for a century or so until the creation of churchyard cemeteries seems to have brought the early tradition of dispersed rural burial grounds to an end.

In the west, in Somerset, the residual Christianity rooted in the Roman system of the fourth century, was probably strengthened by the missionary zeal of wandering preachers coming mainly from Wales and Ireland in the fifth and sixth centuries, men like Cyngar, Decuman, Dyfrig, Petroc and Carantoc whose cults were later well established in the area (Radford 1963). The popular legend of the visit of Joseph of Arimathea to Glastonbury in the first century is without foundation. Little archaeological trace of these early Christian communities has survived, but at Glastonbury a boundary ditch dating to the sixth or early seventh century may have been associated with the Celtic religious establishment. At Wells the evidence is more convincing. Here an early post-Roman mausoleum was discovered which formed the focus of an eighth century cemetery and lies at the beginning of a long tradition of Christian use. It may have been preceded by even earlier Christian structures (Rodwell 1982).

With the coming of the Anglo-Saxons in the middle of the seventh century many of the Celtic Christian sites were taken over and developed. In the north of England in 670 St Wilfred claimed for the church 'Those holy places in various regions which the clergy of the Britons had deserted, flying before the wrath of the hostile sword in the hands of our people.' So it may have been in the west. Glastonbury was reendowed and at Malmesbury a poor establishment founded by the Irish monk Meldun in *c*. 630–50 was later provided for by one of his pupils, St Aldhelm, a member of the royal house of Wessex. His later fame and power allowed him to obtain a bull of privilege for the establishment from Pope Sergius I (687–701). In this way the established Christian communities of the Celtic west were brought under the patronage of the Anglo-Saxon elite.

Towns: 420–650

The fate of the Roman towns and other walled settlements in the fifth and sixth centuries is unclear but some scraps of evidence survive and may be briefly rehearsed. Within Wessex Portchester Castle provides the fullest picture partly because of the extent of the excavation but largely because within much of the enclosure there was comparatively little later destructive activity (Cunliffe 1976a). The Roman walls remained substantially intact throughout the Saxon period and the Land Gate was modified by retaining part of the original Roman gate house and building a timber structure in front of it (Plate 8.4). But apart from saying that these events were post-Roman and pre-Norman the dating remains imprecise. Within the fort, however, a sequence of phases has been recognized spanning the Saxon period. The earliest post-Roman structures were a group of sunken-floored houses and small post-built structures, located close to Roman streets, and provided with a well. While it is clear from associated finds that this early phase dates to the fifth century there is some doubt as to precisely when it began. Some specialists would argue for an early fifth century date, others for a date in the second half of the fifth century. On balance, the distinctive pottery and metalwork taken together with the complex stratified sequence would seem to point to occupation dating back to the first half of the century, thus raising the distinct possibility of continuity from Late Roman times. If so it is tempting to see the Portchester sequence as one reflecting the gradual 'Germanization' of the shore fort community – a process which began in the mid fourth century. By the mid fifth century the mixed population was now using a Saxon-inspired material culture rather than a Romano-British one.

Whether or not occupation was continuous throughout the sixth and seventh centuries is debatable but a scatter of pottery of sixth and seventh century type, and the fact that the well remained in use, suggests that the old fort continued to support a small population who may have been living in another part of the enclosed area and cultivating the zone occupied in the fifth century (Cunliffe 1976a: 302). At any event in the late seventh and early eighth centuries a new range of substantial timber buildings was erected marking the beginning of a phase of enhanced use which will be considered in more detail in the next chapter.

The impressive range of data from Portchester raises the possibility that

Plate 8.4 The land gate at Portchester, Hants. The wall to the right and chamfered stone blocks attached to it are Roman structures, the chamfered stones being the foundation of one of the two gate towers. In the Saxon period only the front wall of the tower remained with a new timber-built gate house attached in front. The post-holes of one side of this survive.

the fortified settlement of Clausentum (Bitterne) may also have continued in use into the fifth or sixth century. In support all that can be quoted is a disc brooch, similar to that found at Portchester (Plate 8.5) for which a late fifth or sixth century date is probable (Welch 1976: 205). Little is known of the other Roman towns. The presence of a Germanic element in the Late Roman population at Winchester and the discovery of at least one late fifth century cemetery nearby at Worthy Park suggest that here, as at Portchester, there may have been a continuous use of the old walled area throughout the fifth century and into the sixth century by which time Frankish pottery was being imported from the Continent (Biddle 1976: 325–6; 1983, 115–19). The

286

cluster of Saxon cemeteries around the town from the sixth century onwards demonstrates the growing significance of the settlement within the walls even though direct structural evidence is at present sparse.

The evidence from Winchester is in direct contrast to that from Silchester where Anglo-Saxon cemeteries of the fifth–seventh centuries are noticeably absent, nor is there any convincing trace for Saxon occupation within the walls. Instead what little evidence survives in the form of pins or other trinkets hints at a British presence with western Celtic contacts, well into the fifth century (Boon 1974: 74–82). The best known item of this period from Silchester is an Ogham inscription, carved on a Roman baluster pillar, recording the burial of one, Ebicatus, who was probably of Irish origin. Various dates have been proposed, the most likely being about AD 500 or soon after. These few scraps hint at the survival of some kind of Sub Roman community using the old defensive circuit throughout the period of Saxon penetration when Germanic enclaves were building up around Dorchester-on-Thames to the north and Winchester to the south. It was probably in this period that the Grims Bank – a major defensive earthwork – was constructed to the north west between the old town and the river Kennet, perhaps in an attempt to stem the southern advance of the Thames-based Saxon armies. The very existence of such a major construction (nearly 5 km long) suggests that a substantial community still used Silchester as a base. That it failed to develop in the sixth and seventh centuries may, in part at least, be due to the fact that Silchester lay in the zone of potential and actual conflict, first

Plate 8.5 Fifth century disc brooch from Portchester. A similar example was found at Clausentum. (Photo: Institute of Archaeology, Oxford)

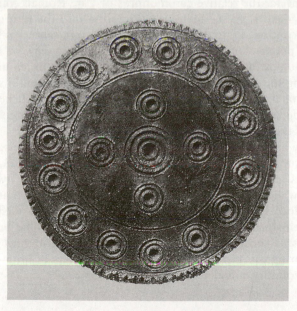

Plate 8.6   Penannular brooch of the fourth or fifth century found in the sacred spring in Bath. (Photo: Institute of Archaeology, Oxford)

---

between the southern and northern Wessex enclaves and later between Mercia and the West Saxons.

Of the towns in the west, we have already seen that a Sub Roman population occupied the old Roman cemetery to the west of Dorchester in Dorset and it is highly unlikely that the walled area was totally abandoned.

At Ilchester the relative commonness of Late Roman coins within the walled settlement suggests intensive occupation into the fifth century. That occupation continued into the late fifth or early sixth century is shown by the presence of pottery imported from along the Atlantic seaways (Rahtz 1974: 101–2). Two unstratified Byzantine coins of the mid sixth century could have arrived along the same routes. A pair of disc brooches and a squareheaded brooch, all of sixth century Saxon types, were brought to Ilchester either as trinkets traded across Wessex or with the earliest Saxon settlers, but nothing is known of their contexts (Leach 1982: 12).

Finally at Bath (Aquae Sulis) there is some structural evidence of continuous occupation throughout the fifth and sixth centuries. The temple precinct was reconsolidated with rough stone paving and at two other sites within the walled area, stratified levels show structural activity in the Sub Roman period. Throughout this time the hot spring continued to flow and may have remained the focus for worship. A fine penannular brooch of Irish inspiration was consigned to the waters, probably during this period (Plate 8.6). The spring was mentioned as one of the wonders of Britain by Nennius in his ninth century compilation *Historia Brittonum*.

In none of the towns summarized above is there any evidence of substantial populations nor do any traces of communal works survive. At best the Sub Roman and Early Saxon communities existing within the walls were living parasitically on the remnants of the Roman urban infrastructure. We are not, therefore, considering the continuity of urban life but simply the continued use of walled enclosures by communities of varying ethnic mix. Their size and degree of social organization is beyond recovery.

Settlement in the Countryside

The large number of cemeteries scattered across the face of Wessex implies a widely dispersed rural population made up of Sub Roman Britons, immigrant Saxons and communities of mixed ethnic antecedents. To what extent rural Romano-British settlements continued into the fifth century and later it is difficult to say but there is no sound reason to assume their disappearance in the early fifth century. A field survey in the region of Chalton, in eastern Hampshire, has shown that three of the Late Roman settlements produced sherds of grass-tempered pottery which elsewhere, at Portchester, can be shown to have spanned the fifth to eighth centuries (Cunliffe 1972: Fig. 2). Similar occurrences have been recorded in Wiltshire at Downton, Round Hill Down (Ogbourne St George) and Wellhead (Westbury) all on Roman sites (Fowler 1966) and at a number of other locations in Hampshire. The juxtaposition of Late Roman and grass-tempered wares at the same locations does not, however, prove continuity. Nevertheless grass-tempered pottery is a clear indicator of Saxon occupation and that so much of this excessively friable material has been picked up during casual field walking is an indication of the not inconsiderable density of Saxon rural settlement in Wessex.

Few settlements have been excavated on any scale but those which have are informative. At Old Down Farm near Andover, six sunken-floor huts of Saxon type were found on a settlement site occupied throughout the Iron Age and into the Early Roman period (S. M. Davies 1980) and the possibility remains that some at least of the postholes found during the excavation also belong to more substantial structures of the Saxon period. The associated pottery was all handmade in three basic fabrics, sandy, flint-tempered and grass-tempered. Dating was, of necessity, vague but no distinctive fifth century types were recovered. Finds were rare but included whetstones, fragments of bone combs and an iron arrow head. The exact nature of the settlement is difficult to assess but it may be only one element in a complex pattern of land use involving a large and apparently prolific site only a few hundred metres away at Charlton on the other side of the river (Dacre and

Warmington 1977) and the cemetery at Portway (A. M. Cook and Dacre 1985).

The field-work at Chalton, Hants., referred to above, brought to light an extensive settlement on a hilltop, Church Down. Excavation between 1971 and 1976 exposed an informative complex of buildings (Fig. 8.3). The details remain unpublished apart from interim notes (e.g. Addyman and Leigh 1973; Champion 1977). In all 61 structures were recovered, constituting the greater part of the total settled area, the majority being rectangular halls built of vertical posts set either in individual post-holes or in wall slots. The largest were 9 m in length. Only four sunken-floored structures were recovered varying from those of conventional size measuring 3 by 2 m to one big one 8.5 by 5.4 m. A sufficient number of buildings overlap to suggest that the settlement continued in use for some time and involved several phases of

Figure 8.3   The Anglo-Saxon settlement at Chalton, Hants. (After Champion 1977)

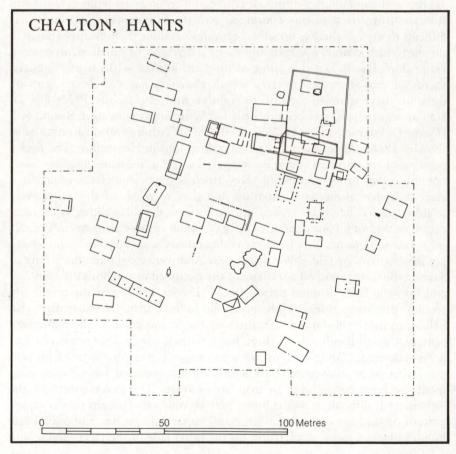

CHALTON, HANTS

0   50   100 Metres

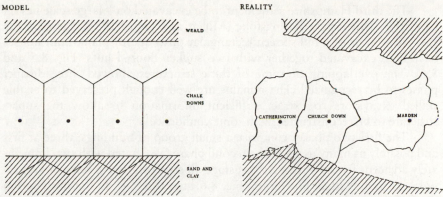

Figure 8.4 Anglo-Saxon settlement on the South Downs. The villages of Catherington, Church Down and Marden with parish boundaries and the spatial model which they suggest.

rebuilding. Some hints of social organization are given by the occurrence of fenced enclosures but differential preservation makes it difficult to be sure that the entire pattern has been recovered.

The economy of the site can be glimpsed from the comparatively small collection of associated material. Wool fabric production is indicated by loom weights, spindle whorls and thread pickers, iron was being forged and made into knives, other tools and nails; some limited bronze casting provided such trinkets as pins. The economic base of the settlement was, however, firmly agricultural and largely self-sufficient though oysters, presumably collected in Portsmouth Harbour, show that some food was brought in. The ability of the community to share in more extensive trade networks is demonstrated by the discovery of imported pottery possibly from northern France, glass and a decorated escutcheon from a hanging bowl.

The date of the Chalton settlement is difficult to establish: it probably lies largely within the seventh century but perhaps began a little earlier. How it fits in the local settlement pattern is obscure but, bearing in mind the possible continuity, from Roman into Saxon, shown by several neighbouring sites it is tempting to suggest that the Church Down village was established comparatively late in the Early Saxon period perhaps as the gradual coalescence of the more dispersed population, or the imposition of a central authority over them, at one location from which all the traditionally farmed lands could be reached easily. Five kilometres to the west, on a similar hilltop location at Catherington, there is some evidence of a settlement of broadly similar date. The configuration of the hundred boundary and later parish boundaries (Fig. 8.4) suggests that both settlements may have controlled elongated territories of comparable size stretching from the high chalk downs to the fringes of the Forest of Bere to the south (Cunliffe 1972). Subsequent changes in settlement pattern will be considered below (pp. 329–330).

The third Hampshire settlement to be excavated on a large scale lies on Cowdery's Down near Basingstoke (Millett and James 1983). Here on the east-facing spur of a hill sixteen rectangular post- and/or plank-built houses have been excavated together with two sunken-floored huts (Figs 8.5 and 8.6). The overlapping of some of these structures allowed three distinct phases to be recognized. The remains are well enough preserved to enable skilled excavators to extract sufficient information to allow the super-structure to be reconstructed with some confidence.

The first two phases comprise a small group of buildings, three at first and possibly as many as six in the second phase, associated with two immediately adjacent fenced yards. At this stage all structures were built of vertical posts set in individual post-holes (Fig. 8.6, structure B4). In the third period there was a major change in the alignment and structure of the houses of which there was now an increased number, up to a maximum of ten, stretching out along the ridge well to west of the early nucleus. The houses of this phase (Fig. 8.6, structures C8 and C12) were built of thick planks set vertically in continuous foundation trenches with wattle and daub infilling. The dating of Cowdery's Down settlement, based entirely on radiocarbon assessments, suggests a range in the sixth and seventh centuries.

The status of the settlement is not easy to assess but the high quality of the structural carpentry together with the virtual absence of occupation debris might suggest that we are dealing with a high status settlement, possibly the homestead of a lord and his entourage. If so then the fact that the roofed area of the settlement more than doubled with each phase of building

---

Figure 8.5 The Anglo-Saxon settlement on Cowdery's Down, Hants., showing buildings of all phases. (After Millett and James 1983: Fig. 31)

COWDERY'S DOWN

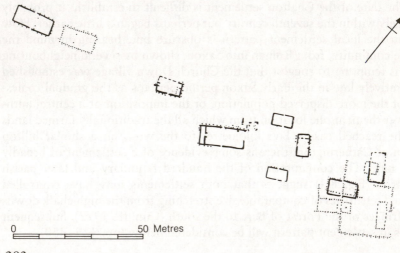

0   50 Metres

COWDERY'S DOWN

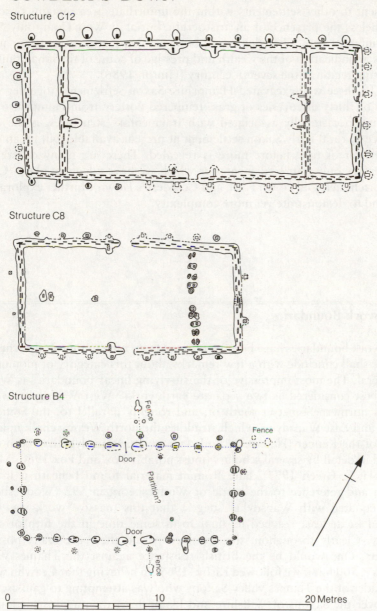

Figure 8.6 Saxon buildings from the settlement on Cowdery's Down, Hants. (After Millett and James 1983: Figs 37, 39 and 46)

is suggestive of the increasing status of the lineage. The relationship of this settlement to other settlements within the immediate area remains obscure. Nonetheless the presence of an aristocratic burial at West Ham, only 5 km away, interred with a hanging bowl, bone gaming-pieces, iron spears and a knife is an indication of the wealth and prestige of some of the inhabitants of the Basing region in the seventh century (Hinton 1986).

The three well-excavated Hampshire Saxon settlements together with twenty or thirty discoveries of grass-tempered pottery from Hampshire and Wiltshire, occasionally associated with fragmentary structures, is the only evidence of rural Early Saxon settlement at present available, but it can only be a matter of time before more is revealed. There are many differences between the only four settlements for which we have adequate plans (Chalton, Portchester, Old Down Farm and Cowdery's Down); further exploration is bound to demonstrate yet more complexity.

Earthwork Boundaries

Earthwork boundaries have been mentioned from time to time in this chapter and we shall conclude with a few remarks about this category of monument in general. The most impressive of the surviving linear boundaries is Wansdyke, best considered as two separate earthworks: West Wansdyke, which crosses northern Somerset south of, and roughly parallel to, the Somerset Avon, and East Wansdyke, which straddles the north Wessex chalk uplands south of the Kennet (Plate 8.7). Both face north. Wansdyke has been considered in detail by several scholars (most notably Fox and Fox 1960; Myres 1964; H. S. Green 1971). Late Roman material found beneath it in one section and reference to the battle of Wodnesbeorg in 592 (Wodnesbeorg being equated with Wansdyke) suggest that this massive work was constructed or at least reached its final form some time in the fifth or sixth century. Clearly throughout this troubled period there are many possible contexts. One would be the British resistance against the Thames valley Saxons *c.* 500 but if we followed Kirby (1965) in believing that Ceawlin was a war leader of the Thames valley Saxons who was attempting to gain ascendancy over the Saxons of Wiltshire and Hampshire, then a construction (or refurbishment) date some time after 577 (Ceawlin's campaign against the Britons occupying the old Roman towns of the Cotswolds) would seem most

Plate 8.7   Aerial view of West Wansdyke. (Photo: Mick Aston)

likely and the entire dyke would fall into place as a linear barrier to Ceawlin's southward advance. It is tempting to have the best of both worlds and argue for an initial construction of some part of the system (East Wansdyke?) *c.* 500 with sporadic reconstructions culminating in the extended system 80 years or so later. Archaeological evidence is unlikely ever to allow such precision.

Grims Ditch, which protects the approaches to Silchester, has, as we have seen, a good claim to being of late fifth century date, protecting the Sub Roman enclave using the old town from attack from the direction of the Thames valley. It is not unreasonable to suppose that this earthwork, together with East Wansdyke and the Bedwyn dyke, are a reflection of a British response, not necessarily unified, to the attentions of the Early Saxon settlers in the Thames valley. At a later date Bokerly Dyke and Combs Ditch, crossing Cranborne Chase, may also have been refurbished to serve as a British defence against the advance of the Sarum-based Saxon enclave into the south west.

This brief summary by no means exhausts all the linear defences in Wessex, which might prove to have an Early Saxon date. The Devils Ditch, north of Andover and the Froxfield entrenchments near Petersfield, deserve mention but they are at present totally undated.

Early Saxon linear defences show the political instability and war-like nature of this formative period. Yet their scale indicates something of the power of rulers and their capacity to unite societies in self-defence.

The three centuries 350–650, perhaps more than any other period in British history, were a time of rapid and often violent change. The urban infrastructure, which had begun to develop in the Late Iron Age and whose growth was encouraged by the Roman administrators of the early centuries of occupation, totally collapsed and so did all the economic and social systems based upon it. The end came fast in a flurry of raids, uprisings and plague. A man born in the relative stability of the 350s might have lived to face the anarchy of the 420s. So violent a systems collapse would have been psychologically devastating. Yet gradually over the next two centuries a new order was established and by the middle of the seventh century a degree of equilibrium had been reached leading to a situation, probably not unlike that enjoyed by the communities of the first century BC. From this base the state of Wessex was to emerge.

Chapter 9

The Ascendancy of Wessex: 685–1000

In the century following the death of Ceawlin in 588 Wessex (including the Thames valley) was ruled by a succession of kings all of whom, according to the *Anglo Saxon Chronicle*, could claim descent from Cerdic. Their origins are obscure and all that can safely be said is that each man must have been born into, or could claim to have been born into, the ranks of the royal lineage from which kings, by virtue of the individual's prowess as well as his ancestry, would be chosen. Direct succession of father to son was not a characteristic of early German kingship. The list, insofar as it can be reconstructed, is here given (Fig. 9.1) with dates based on those revised by David Dumville (1985). Fig. 9.2 is an attempt to display pedigree.

The events of this period are little known. Such battles as are recorded concentrate in north Wiltshire, north Somerset and southern Gloucestershire but not all were against Britons. Mercia, which lay to the north, was becoming an aggressive power in its own right and border disputes were inevitable. In 628, for example, Cynegils fought the Mercian king Penda over possession of Cirencester and in 661 Penda's son, Wulfhere, was conducting campaigns on the Berkshire Downs in the centre of what was then Geuissian territory. It was pressure from the north that encouraged Cenwalh to establish the new West Saxon see at Winchester in 660: the original location at Dorchester-on-Thames was now uncomfortably close to the disputed territories between the two kingdoms.

In this age of expansion, with their northern borders under pressure, the kings of the Geuissae looked to the south west and the south east for new territories to conquer. The south west was easy prey and within a few decades had fallen to the English kings. This much is shown by the fact that St Boniface received his education at a monastery in Exeter in about 680 and before that Cenwalh and Centwine had made benefactions to the British monasteries at Sherborne and Glastonbury. The south east, controlled for two centuries by Germanic kings, was a less easy target.

Cerdic 538-554

Cynric 554-581

Ceawlin 581-588

Ceol 588- 594

Ceolwulf 594-611

Cynegils 611-642

Cenwalh 642-673

Seaxburh 673-674

Æscwine 674-676

Centwine 676-685/6

Cædwalla 685/6- 688

Ine 688-726

Æthelheard 726-740

Cuthred 740-756

Sigebert 756-757

Cynewulf 757-786

Beorhtric 786- 802

Egbert 802-839

Æthelwulf 839-855(8)

Æthelbald 855-860

Æthelbert 860-866

Æthelred 866-871

Alfred 871-899

Figure 9.1   List of the kings of Wessex. (After Dumville 1985)

The Rise of Wessex: 685–840

In 685 Caedwalla, a descendant of Ceawlin, came to power. In the previous years, during a brief period of exile from Wessex, he had gathered a force and led an unsuccessful attempt to gain control of the kingdom of the South Saxons in Sussex. This experience as a war leader was put to good use when, in 685, Centwine abdicated and Caedwalla became king of the Geuissae. His

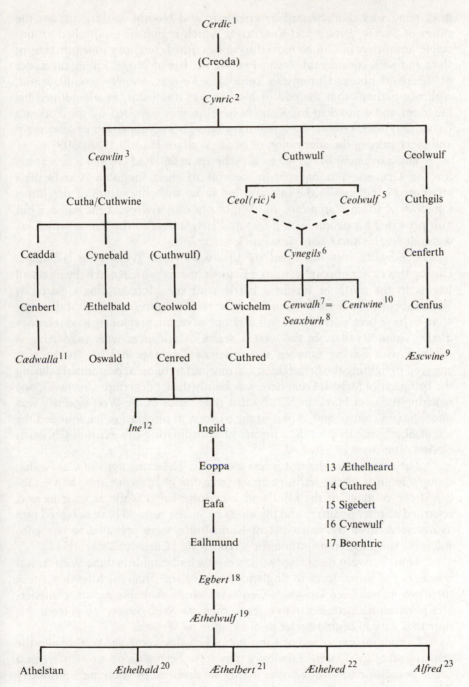

Figure 9.2 The genealogy of the West Saxon kings. The numbers give the order of succession. (After Yorke 1990: Table 16)

brief reign was characterized by energetic and bloody warfare against the rulers of Surrey, Sussex and Kent, over which region he established an unstable authority. In 686 he moved to annex Jutish territory in south Hampshire and with considerable savagery took the Isle of Wight, killing the males of the royal house. During this campaign he was severely wounded and, realizing perhaps that the end of his life was imminent, he abandoned his kingdom and embarked for Rome where he was baptized by the Pope on Easter Day 689, only to die a few days later, his combination of leadership and piety gaining the admiration of Bede (Wallace-Hadrill 1988: 309).

The movement of the see to Winchester *c.* 660 had created a new focus for the Geuissae but one hardly central to their kingdom. Caedwalla's attempted conquests in the east and his successful annexation of the Jutish kingdom of south Hampshire and Wight not only redressed the balance but also provided his people with direct and easy access to the Solent which, as we shall see, his successors were quick to exploit.

Caedwalla was succeeded by Ine, who ruled Wessex for 37 years. During this rather obscure period of English history we learn of fighting on all fronts. In the north he fought a battle with the Mercian king Ceolred at Wodnesbeorg (on Wansdyke) in 715. The result is unrecorded but it does not seem to have been part of a serious attempt to regain previously held territory in the Thames valley. In the west a series of advances were made. Ine is credited with having founded the town of Taunton and in 710 he was engaged in fighting the British king Geraint of Dumnonia, presumably during the conquest of Devon. From here war bands thrust deep into Cornwall, one reaching the river Hayle in 722. By this time much of the West Country was under Saxon control and as part of the process of integration Ine founded the see at Sherborne to provide a means of coordinating the existing Christian communities west of Selwood.

The situation in the east is less clear cut. The campaigns of Caedwalla, though acquiring little territory apart from the old Jutish lands, had established the primacy of the Geuissian kingdom: for a while at least he was regarded as ruler of Surrey and the kings of Sussex seem to have accepted him as overlord. Even the more distant Kentishmen were prepared to pay considerable sums in compensation for having killed Caedwalla's brother.

Thus, between them Caedwalla and Ine had established the West Saxon house as the prime force in England south of the Thames. In earlier times their people had been known as *Geuissae*, which probably meant 'confederates', henceforth Bede began to refer to them as 'West Saxons'. It is from this time that we can begin to refer to our region as Wessex.

During the long reign of King Ine old rivalries emerged to threaten the growing stability. Queen Æthelburg may have been a dissident member of a cadet branch of the royal house acting in defiance of the king's authority when she destroyed Taunton. In 705 we hear of West Saxon exiles being received by the king of Essex and the next year another nobleman, Ealdberht, fled to Surrey, only to be sought out and killed in 725. While it may be overstating the case to suggest that Ine was systematically removing rivals, the long reign of such a powerful king as he would have encouraged contenders to show their hands, if only in exasperation. At any event when eventually, in 726, the old man resigned and departed for Rome to die, the kingdom passed without conflict to Æthelheard.

Ine, the creator of Wessex, was also its consolidator. The setting up of a new see at the old British monastery at Sherborne and the installation of Aldhelm as the first bishop, together with considerable benefactions given to the abbey at Glastonbury, would have been part of a programme designed to integrate the disparate Christian communities of the newly acquired west. But his principal act of innovation was the formalization of a code of law, preserved in a later code of King Alfred's.

> I, Ine, by the grace of God, King of the West Saxons, with the advice
> and with the instruction of my father Cenred, and my bishop Hoedde
> and my bishop Eorcenwald, along with all my ealdormen and the chief
> councillors of my people, and also a great assembly of the servants of
> God, have been inquiring about the salvation of our souls and about
> the security of our kingdom, that true law and true statutes might be
> established and strengthened throughout our people, so that none of
> the ealdormen or of our subjects might afterwards pervert these our
> decrees.

The laws are fairly comprehensive, covering a wide range of human behaviour, but say little of land, and are composed, as the prologue makes clear, with the assistance, and by implication the acceptance, of the church and aristocracy. The laws of Ine mark a significant threshold in the history of Wessex – the end of tribalism and the beginning of the state. It is no coincidence that as part of this new outward-looking philosophy a trading port was set up at Hamwic, on Southampton Water, integrating Wessex, for the first time since the Romans, with the exchange systems of the Continent. By the beginning of the eighth century Wessex was poised to take over the leadership of the south.

The ascendancy of Wessex was, however, delayed for a century. Ine was followed by a succession of five apparently ineffective kings at just the time when the power of Mercia was growing. Somerton was lost by Æthelheard in 733 to the Mercian king Æthelbald and with it much of Somerset passed under direct Mercian leadership, greatly weakening the power and prestige of Wessex.

For eighty years Mercia was ruled by two strong kings Æthelbald (716–757) and Offa (757–796) and gradually their power extended throughout the south though not without sporadic opposition from the kings of Wessex. Cuthred rebelled against Æthelbald in 752 and retained some semblance of independence until his death four years later. The next Wessex king,

Sigeberht, was deposed within a year and was succeeded by Cynewulf (758–786) who, while paying lip service to Offa's superiority, seems to have recovered most of the old West Saxon territory lost thirty years earlier and was even contesting ownership of land north of the Thames with Offa until he was forced to withdraw in 779.

On Cynewulf's death in 786, in a local dynastic squabble, Offa once more regained control of Wessex by helping to prop up the next king, Beorhtric, against the claims of Egbert, a direct descendant of Ine's brother. While Beorhtric continued his subservient rule Egbert bided his time in the Frankish kingdom and on Beorhtric's death in 802 he returned to England to become king of the West Saxons, a reign which was to last for thirty-seven years. It was a turning point in West Saxon history and a return to the expansionist policies begun about a century earlier by his kinsmen Caedwalla and Ine.

For twenty years Egbert's authority was confined to Wessex but with the fall of King Ceolwulf of Mercia in 823 the power of Wessex's great northern rival was in decline. In 825 at Ellendun (probably Wroughton, south of Swindon) Egbert defeated the Mercian king in a decisive battle and so the tide turned. Immediately afterwards he sent his son Aethelwulf at the head of a large army into Kent where he received the submission of not only the men of Kent, but of those of Essex, Surrey and Sussex as well, as all the Mercian dependencies in the east threw off their old overlords. Four years later Mercia itself was conquered and at Dore, near Sheffield, Egbert received the submission of the Northumbrians.

For a brief moment the unity of England was foreshadowed but it was illusory: by 830 Mercia had broken free again and later Essex was to pass under the domination of the Vikings. South of the Thames, however, the rule of the West Saxon kings remained. Even the Cornish, who had remained free for so long, were finally brought to order between 815 and 838. Thus, by the time of Egbert's death in 839, the many little kingdoms which had been such a feature of the political geography of southern England in the past had disappeared and only the giants – Wessex, East Anglia and Mercia – remained. Gone too were the many cadet branches of the royal households whose rival claims to power had been a divisive and weakening factor: all the Saxon kings of Wessex for the last two hundred years or so before the Norman conquest were descendants of Egbert.

The Danish Invasions: 840–880

The story of the Danish invasions, insofar as they affected Wessex, must be briefly told. The first intimation of what was in store came in the last decade of the eighth century, when three Viking ships landed on the Dorset coast, probably in Weymouth Bay. The reeve, somewhat ill-advisedly, and apparently unaware of the danger, tried to compel the occupants to go to the royal vill in Dorchester and was slain for his pains. It was an isolated incident and not to be repeated for thirty years.

In 835 the raids began in earnest with an attack on Sheppey marking the beginning of thirty years of almost annual attacks on the southern coasts of Britain from Cornwall to East Anglia. In addition to attacks on the West Country, Portland, Hamwic and Winchester all suffered along with Sandwich, Canterbury, Rochester and London. For the most part these attacks, and no doubt others that have gone unrecorded, were hit and run affairs – flotillas of between 30 and 350 ships sailing in the summer to land the gangs of young men at some promising location where they could pillage and collect booty and be away again. Only occasionally did a force over-winter.

But all this changed in 865 when the Great Army, led by two sons of Ragnar Lothbrok, Halfdan and Ivar the Boneless, made an autumn landing in East Anglia and there remained. After a series of campaigns lasting fifteen years they had assumed control of most of eastern England.

In the winter of 866 the Viking force took York after bringing the kingdom of Northumbria to an end. The next year they turned their attention on Mercia, setting up winter quarters at Nottingham. The Mercian king Burgred, who was married to the sister of Æthelred, at that time king of Wessex, appealed to Wessex for help. A force was sent but the Vikings refused to do battle, and returned to York for the winter of 868–9. The next year they were back in East Anglia wintering at Thetford and it was from here, later in 870, that they set out on their first concerted attack on Wessex: the base they chose from which to launch the offensive was Reading.

The first engagement was a small-scale affair involving the rout of a Danish raiding party by a local force led by an ealdorman. Then followed a more substantial confrontation between the Danish army base and a Wessex force led by King Æthelred and his brother Alfred. The Danes won and encouraged by their victory decided to leave the safety of their fortifications at Reading and advance westwards onto the Berkshire Downs. It was here, in the open countryside, that the two armies met in out and out battle. Fighting continued into the night and many thousands were killed but the victory was for Wessex. The Battle of Ashdown, as it was called, was only a beginning. Then followed a series of engagements as the Danes penetrated deep into Wessex. The *Chronicle* records battles at Basing, *Maeredun* and Wilton but in summing up the year's events it tells us that nine major battles were fought as well as innumerable skirmishes. It must have been evident to all that the Danes had the advantage and so there was little that Alfred, who had now succeeded his brother as king, could do than to pay the Danes to leave Wessex in peace.

And so it was, for the next five years, that the Viking force contented itself with campaigns in the Midlands and the north. But having finally established themselves in Northumbria the Great Army moved south once again to Cambridge where they prepared for the second attack on Wessex.

To make sense of the rather garbled record of the years 876–7 it is best to assume that the Danes had planned a pincer movement by land and by sea to secure a foothold in southern Wessex. The land force evaded the Saxon army and reached Wareham in 876 but the anticipated sea-borne support was apparently delayed and the army agreed to submit to the West Saxons by giving hostages and promising to leave Wessex altogether. However, 'under cover of night the force's mounted troops stole away from them to Exeter.' It would seem, therefore, that the Viking strategy was to regroup further west along the coast and return later to the attack. However, the ploy went seriously awry when in 877 a fleet of some 120 ships, sailing to join the army in Exeter, was destroyed in a violent storm somewhere off Swanage. Meanwhile Alfred and his army made for Exeter, where the Danes again agreed terms. 'They gave him hostages, as many as he wished, swore great oaths and held a good peace' and in the autumn they left Wessex for Mercia.

One of the tactics used by the Danes was to bring up reinforcements by sea and river whenever possible. In 871 ships carrying troops had arrived at the Reading base. Alfred was well aware of the danger and had probably made good use of the interlude strengthening shore defences and building up his navy. Indeed in 875 the *Chronicle* records a successful sea battle though without telling us where it was.

In January 878 the Danes made their third and final attempt to conquer Wessex. In the previous year a substantial Danish force had been left at Gloucester, in Mercian territory, under the command of Guthrum: now they marched south to Chippenham to create a forward base for the onslaught on Wessex. Again it seems that a two-pronged attack was planned with a sea-borne force sailing around the Cornish peninsula and up the Bristol Channel. A landing was made on the north coast of Devon but at Countisbury Hill the Danish force was soundly beaten by the English. Meanwhile Guthrum's army was causing panic in the north. Alfred had retreated to the safety of the Somerset marshes where, at Athelney, he created a fortified base, from the comparative safety of which raiding parties could be sent out to harry the enemy. By May, his preparations completed, he marched east, through Selwood forest, to the Wessex chalk uplands to join force with levies from Wiltshire and Hampshire. The combined army then made for the Danish base at Chippenham, but fifteen miles to the south, at Edington, the two forces met and here Alfred achieved a decisive victory. Guthrum retreated to his fort at Chippenham and after suffering fourteen days of siege, agreed to terms with Alfred. Hostages were given, oaths were sworn and Guthrum submitted to Christian baptism. The formalities complete, the Great Army moved back to Gloucester and finally, in 879, to East Anglia, leaving Wessex in peace.

The Ascendancy of Wessex: 880–975

Alfred died in October 899 leaving Wessex both secure and powerful. By their support of the Mercians in 867 and the earlier marriage of a daughter of the Wessex royal house to the Mercian king, old rivalries were on the way to being healed and the Mercians, if reluctantly, recognized the reality of Wessex superiority. Alfred's agreement with the Danes, embodied in the document known as the *Treaty of Alfred and Guthrum*, also created a degree of stability in that it recognized, and therefore legitimized, the territory held by the Danes. Thus the threefold divide of southern England was formalized and the three power blocks developed an unstable (and brief) equilibrium.

Alfred was a realist. He had learnt two hard lessons from the Danes: the importance of controlling the sea and the need to create fortifications – burghs – at strategic intervals around the frontier of his kingdom. Once the new political map was drawn up and agreed and the defence of his Wessex realm was in place he could begin to relax and, at the age of 40, devote himself to literary pursuits. Only now did he learn Latin so that he could translate Latin works into Old English. When he died he was revered as both a saviour and a scholar.

Alfred was succeeded by his son Edward the Elder (899–925), his grandsons, Athelstan (925–39), Edmund (939–46) and Eadred (946–55) and his great grandsons, Eadwig (955–9) and Edgar (959–75) providing Wessex with a remarkable and necessary degree of stability for the next eight decades.

The early years of the tenth century were notable for the reconquest of Danish-held land east of Watling Street by Edward the Elder and his sister Æthelflaed, who had married a Mercian aristocrat. Edward's subsequent campaigns in the north, where he received the submission of the Scots, the Northumbrians and the Scandinavian rulers of York, established him as the foremost power in Britain. After Æthelflaed's death in 918 the whole of Mercia including Cheshire came under Edward's direct rule and at last Wessex and Mercia were united under a single king.

Athelstan, who succeeded his father in 924, spent much of his time campaigning in the north, his forces harrying the wilds of Caithness, and by the time of his death in 939 the political map of Britain had been totally redrawn – it was the climax of Wessex domination and paved the way for a period of comparative peace which was to characterize the latter half of the tenth century. In many ways the culmination of the era came in 973 when at Bath, significantly in the border between Wessex and Mercia, King Edgar was crowned in a ceremony presided over by the Archbishops of York and Canterbury. The presence of the senior clergy endowed the ceremony and the monarchy with a corporate existence which transcended the individuals who served it. The rituals enacted in Bath Abbey on that day, though possibly of earlier origin, formed the basis of the coronation service which has remained in use to the present day.

Mobile Kings and Royal Villas

A feature of Saxon (and indeed later) kingship was the mobility of the king and his court. To rule effectively the king had to see and be seen and this required a constant progression around his kingdom, he and his entourage staying for the most part in the royal villas dotted throughout the four home shires of Somerset, Dorset, Wiltshire and Hampshire. Each shire was named after one of the settlements surrounding such a royal villa – Somerton, Dorchester, Wilton and Hampton – but within each shire there were many villas usually attached to royal estates. In Wiltshire for example, in addition to Wilton, villas have been identified at Amesbury, Bedwyn, Bradford, Calne, Chippenham, Ramsbury, Tilshead, Warminster and possibly at Westbury and Downton (Haslam 1984b: 137). Each would have been the nucleus for a settlement which might have taken on any of a range of functions including local administration and the redistribution of commodities both locally produced and imported. Around some, industrial production may have developed while others became ecclesiastical centres. In other words the royal villas provided nuclei for the early stages of urban growth.

Surprisingly little is known of the physical characteristics of such sites but the topography of three of the Wiltshire examples, Calne, Chippenham and Wilton, has been distinguished (Fig. 9.3) giving some idea of their general siting and layout in the eighth and ninth centuries (Haslam 1984b: 132–6). In each case the site chosen was well protected by rivers. The royal residential complex lay close to a church and its precinct and both were sited in a defined open area, served by approach roads. This designated space would have functioned as the market place. Around its fringes and along the radiating roads spread the dwellings of the local population.

In these three cases all elements of the proto-urban complex were co-located at a single focus but this was not always so. In Somerset the royal villa at Cheddar did not develop into a town but nearby, at Axbridge, a small commercial port grew up to serve as a trading centre. It was conveniently located for ease of access by road and river while at the same time serving as a defensive barrier blocking the approach to the palace at Cheddar (Aston 1984: 173–4). Another, more extreme, example of this kind of dual focus is to be found at Somerton, where the royal villa was based, with the port and fortification at Langport some 6 km away on the river Parrett (Aston 1984:

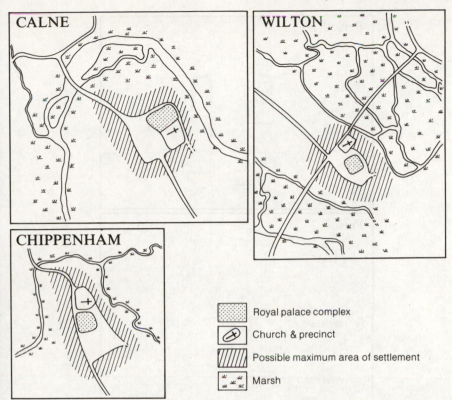

Figure 9.3 The topography of three Wiltshire towns in the eighth and ninth centuries showing the relationship of the royal villas and churches to the settlement layout. (After Haslam 1984b: Fig. 57)

181–3). The further potential complexity of the situation is hinted at by the dispositions at Dorchester in Dorset. Here there is some reason to believe that the royal villa may not have been located within the defences of the Roman walled town, where one might have expected it, but lay instead outside the wall to the east at Fordington close to the mother church of the royal estate (Keen 1984: 233). These examples illustrate something of the topographical variety displayed by Saxon royal villas.

The form which such an establishment could take is also likely to have varied. The only excavated example from Wessex is the palace at Cheddar, occupied from the ninth to the fourteenth century (Rahtz 1979). Here, the earliest arrangement (period 1) dates to the ninth and early tenth centuries and consists of a group of five buildings bounded on the north by a storm-water ditch and partially contained within fenced enclosures (Fig. 9.4). The main building was a long hall built of vertical timbers set in continuous foundation trenches, rectangular in plan but with slightly bowed sides in the

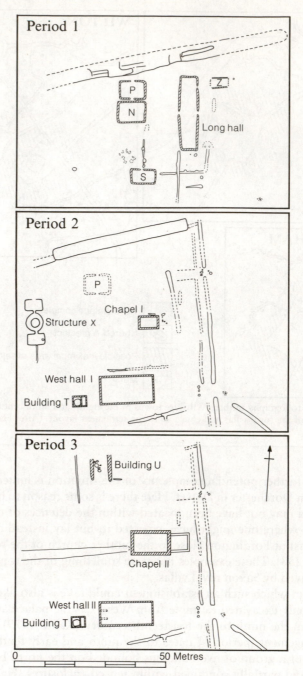

Figure 9.4 The development of the royal palace at Cheddar. Period 1, pre-*c*. 930; period 2, 930 to late tenth or early eleventh century; period 3, late tenth to eleventh century, probably pre-conquest. (After Rahtz 1979: Figs 10, 12 and 13)

centres of which were set the two, opposed, doorways. The hall was 24 m long and 6 m wide in the middle. The four smaller ancillary buildings around the hall were not all necessarily in contemporary use. The complex was evidently in existence during the reign of Alfred the Great, if not before, and it is tempting to see it as a royal residence at this early stage though whether the king actually stayed there is a matter of debate. He was, however, present nearby at Wedmore in 878 when Guthrum was baptized and it must have been somewhere in the vicinity that the famous treaty with the Danes was drawn up (Rahtz 1979: 373–4).

The major rebuilding of the palace in period 2 took place during the reign of Athelstan, some time about 930, and the complex remained in use, largely unchanged, for the rest of the century and possibly into the early eleventh century. An entirely fresh layout was imposed. The new hall was comparable in size to its predecessor though shorter and wider. It was strictly rectangular in plan and was constructed on a basis of vertical timbers set in individual but widely spaced post-holes. Nearby to the west was a small ancillary building, possibly a latrine, while to the north east lay a simple rectangular masonry-built chapel. Well away from the main buildings was a somewhat unusual tripartite structure interpreted by the excavator as a fowl house. The entire complex lay within an enclosure defined by ditches. The general lack of occupation debris accumulating during this period suggests that the site was kept scrupulously clean, a factor which probably reflects its high status.

At least three times during the tenth century the king met his *witan* (council) at Cheddar: in July 941 when Edmund was on the throne, in November 956 during the reign of Eadwig and in April 968 under Edgar. Among the king's entourage on this last occasion were the Archbishops Dunstan and Oscytel together with seven bishops, nine abbots, eight earls and nine thegns. The complex of buildings at present known could hardly have housed such a host: the assumption must therefore be that only a part of the palace complex has been uncovered.

The third period, which dates to some time after 991, saw little significant change in the layout but both hall and chapel were rebuilt on the same sites. These changes must have been instigated by Æthelred the Unready and may be a reflection of Æthelred's interest in developing the commercial potential of Somerset. There is no record, however, that he or the later Scandinavian kings ever used the palace, though the estate remained in royal hands until the thirteenth century.

The excavation at Cheddar provides a rare insight into life on a royal villa. That many such establishments were maintained throughout the length and breadth of Wessex is an indication of the wealth and prestige of the Wessex kings.

The Nobility

The land of Wessex was divided between the royal family, the Church and the lay nobility. Most of the last, generally known as *thegns*, were retainers of noble birth who in return for their services had received grants of land, usually from the king. By the eleventh century a thegn would be a man who owed the king a specific service and who possessed a fortified house with a kitchen, a bell house and a church together with land valued at five hides. Some, however, held more substantial estates spread over several counties. In 960, for example, King Edgar restored property to Wulfric consisting of eight villages in Berkshire, five in Sussex and two in Hampshire (F. Stenton 1971: 486–9).

Of greater seniority were the *ealdormen*, coming from the ranks of the nobility, sometimes from the royal household, and serving as royal officials. Normally the ealdorman's responsibilities were concentrated on a single shire: he had to lead the shire forces in time of war, control the business of the shire court and make sure that the king's commands were carried out. In return for these services he would enjoy wide-ranging privileges and hold vast estates rivalling those of the king, as did Godwine in Wessex when he died in 1053.

Very little is known of the homesteads of these nobles. The lesser thegns with only one estate were no doubt sedentary but those with many, like the king, may have travelled between them: the actual buildings of their courts would have differed only in scale and grandeur from those of the king himself.

Portchester provides an insight into what a noble establishment may have looked like (Cunliffe 1976a). Here, within the protection of the Roman walls, from the seventh to the late ninth century a succession of quite substantial rectangular timber buildings were maintained together with three wells (Fig. 9.5 and Plates 9.1 and 9.2). Associated finds, including decorated metalwork (Plate 9.3) and imported glass, suggest that the occupants may have been men of substance. The settlement seems to have come to an end by the late ninth century by which time the estate had passed into the hands of the Bishop of Winchester. In 904 it was acquired from him by the king. A possible context for this change of ownership may have been the requisitioning of the Roman fort for refurbishment as a burgh in the defence of the realm (see below, p. 325). During this time there is little evidence of buildings (at least within the area excavated) but large quantities of rubbish were tipped against the fort wall. The implication would seem to be that the occupation was of a more transitory nature.

However, by the mid to late tenth century a new complex of substantial buildings was in being, arranged around a courtyard containing the well.

PORTCHESTER CASTLE

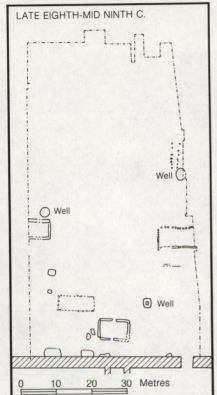
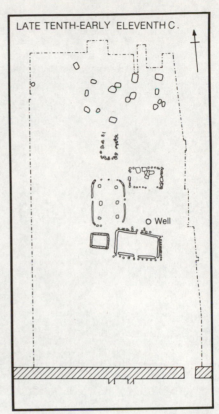

Figure 9.5 The developing settlement within the walls of Portchester Castle. (After Cunliffe 1976a: Fig. 100)

Some rebuilding occurred and by the end of the tenth or beginning of the eleventh century a masonry tower had been erected and later used as the focus for a small cemetery.

While the sequence at Portchester is clear enough and the dating is established within broad limits, the status of the community is not. That the land was held, at least from the end of the ninth century, by the Church and later by the king, would argue against the settlement being that of a member of the nobility after the late ninth century but it is not impossible that it was the residence of a minor noble before the Church acquired it. Certainly the style of the buildings and status of the finds indicate wealthy occupants. The later building complex, of the tenth–eleventh century, erected after the king had become owner, could be the residence of a favoured retainer who had not yet acquired estates of his own.

Plate 9.1   Late Saxon building found during the excavation of Portchester Castle.

The Church

The Christianization of Wessex took place throughout the seventh century (above, pp. 282–5). The principal events in this process are outlined by Bede in his *Ecclesiastical History* (completed in 731), to some of which dates, derived from later sources such as the *Anglo Saxon Chronicle*, have subsequently been attached. Compilations of this kind provided fertile ground for discussion and disagreement and the true sequence of events is unlikely ever to be known. However, it is generally agreed that the first bishop of the West Saxons was Birinus who was installed at Dorchester-on-Thames in 635 by the West Saxon king Cynegils. The origin of Winchester as an ecclesiastical centre is more obscure but it would seem that the see was created between 660 and 663, with Wine as its first bishop. The usual interpretation of the available documentary sources is that the first church to be erected in Winchester, the Old Minster, was founded as a monastery in 648 and later taken over by Wine as his cathedral. Doubt has, however, been cast on the reliability of the tradition and it is now argued that the Old Minster was built by Wine after his inauguration (Yorke 1982). The building continued in use with modifications and additions until the tenth century and was finally demolished in 1093–4 (Fig. 9.6). Whatever its exact date of construction the discovery and careful excavation of the seventh century building is one of the great achievements of Saxon archaeology in Britain (Kjølbye-Biddle 1986).

Plate 9.2   The water gate at Portchester Castle. The lower part is probably of Late Saxon date and is built on the foundations of a demolished Roman structure.

Plate 9.3   Decorated strap ends of Late Saxon date from Portchester Castle. (Scale 3:1.) (Photo: Institute of Archaeology, Oxford)

With the expansion of Wessex in the late seventh century, as Somerset was subdued and brought under control, the need to created a new see in the west became rapidly apparent, not least because of the requirement to integrate the enclaves of Celtic Christianity, strong in these remote areas, with the Roman Church of the east. Accordingly, in 705, King Ine created a new see at Sherborne to govern the area west of the Forest of Selwood and appointed Aldhelm, abbot of Malmesbury, as its first bishop.

These early arrangements served for two hundred years but by the time of Edward the Elder it had become clear that Wessex was too large to be organized effectively by only two bishops. Accordingly the Winchester diocese was reduced to Hampshire and Surrey while Sherborne became responsible only for Dorset. Two new sees were established: Berkshire and Wiltshire were governed from Ramsbury and Somerset by Wells. Thus it remained until 1058 when Ramsbury and Sherborne were united and twelve years later the episcopal seat was moved to Old Sarum.

The choice of Sherborne as the centre of the new bishopric created in

314

705 may well have been influenced by the presence of the earlier monastic establishment of *Lanprobus* which has been tentatively identified as occupying the site of the later castle. If so then Aldhelm, whose cathedral probably lies beneath or close to the present abbey, chose a new site for his church. Nevertheless, the estate granted to the earlier establishment by King Cenwalh some 30 years before, was taken over by the new foundation (Keen 1984: 209–12). Ramsbury was also a vigorous settlement. It probably grew up around an early royal villa and minster church. By the early ninth century it had developed an extensive iron-smelting industry, its commercial success

WINCHESTER OLD MINSTER

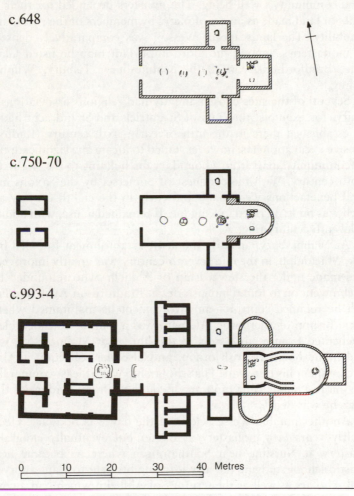

c.648

c.750-70

c.993-4

0   10   20   30   40   Metres

Figure 9.6   The development of the Old Minster at Winchester. (After Biddle 1986: Fig. 12)

being shown by exotic imports such as lava querns from Germany (Haslam 1984b: 96–7).

The establishment of a diocesan structure provided the Church in England with the means of regulating the religious life of the country. Although the diocese conformed largely to political boundaries, the broadly based organization of the Church transcended local, and often transient, political rivalries and thus provided a unifying force.

The seventh and eighth centuries saw the foundation of monastic establishments in many parts of the country. A minster comprised a group of monks and clergy who lived together communally and served a particular church. In physical terms the establishment would have consisted of one or more churches together with the residential and service buildings necessary for the community's well-being. The minsters depended for their livelihood on gifts of land made as an act of piety, by members of the royal family or by the nobility. The landscape of Wessex was comparatively densely packed with monasteries: among the more important may be listed Glastonbury, Frome, Bradford-on-Avon, Bath, Malmesbury, Tisbury, Wimborne and Nursling.

Several of the sites chosen already had religious associations. At Glastonbury, for example, the cults of St Patrick and St Indracht had probably been established there in the fifth or early sixth century (Radford 1963). Extensive excavation has, however, failed to locate any significant trace of the early community apart from a boundary ditch dating to the late sixth or early seventh century. With the conquest of Somerset by the Saxons in the 680s several benefactions were made and early in the eighth century a masonry church was built, ascribed to King Ine. It remained in use, with additions, into the eleventh century (Fig. 9.7).

At Malmesbury, an early monastic establishment founded by an Irish monk, Maeldulph, in the mid seventh century was greatly improved by royal grants made under the stewardship of Aldhelm who refounded the house. Aldhelm went on to found monasteries at Bradford-on-Avon and Frome over which he retained control – an involvement he maintained when later he became Bishop of Sherborne. Aldhelm was a man of considerable learning. He benefited from ready access to the library at Malmesbury, which contained many books of Irish origin, and also the collection at Canterbury, where he spent his last years. His scholarship was at least comparable to that of his more famous contemporary, Bede, and in his reading of the Roman classics he was Bede's superior.

Another notable Wessex cleric of the day was Boniface. He had spent his early years in a monastery at Exeter but eventually emigrated to the monastery at Nursling near Southampton where he became head of the monastic school studying the new learning brought to Canterbury by Continental scholars as well as the writings of Aldhelm which had a considerable influence on him. In 716 at the age of about 40 he set off on a mission to

GLASTONBURY

c.720AD

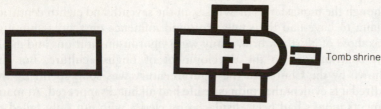

Tomb shrine

✝ Arthur's grave

c.760AD

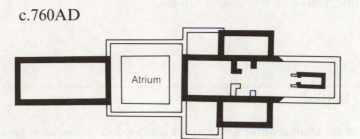

Atrium

c.1000 AD-St Dunstan

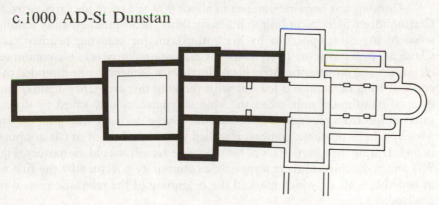

Figure 9.7   The development of the monastic church at Glastonbury. (After Aston 1982: Fig. 12.2)

Frisia returning for a while before leaving Britain finally in 718 for a life of missionary work among the Germans and the Franks. It was in Frisia that he and 50 companions were massacred in 754.

Although the monasteries of Wessex in the seventh and eighth centuries cannot claim to have had the same profound influence on scholarship and learning as those of Northumbria, many were vigorous institutions and made significant contributions to the development of English culture. But the energy shown by the Church in the eighth century was soon spent. By the time of Alfred it is evident that monastic life had all but disappeared. At many establishments monks had been displaced by clerics who not only failed to observe the usual orders but also were frequently ignorant of Latin. While the Danish raids and the uncertainty occasioned by them must have been a contributory cause the underlying reason was that the zeal and energy of that remarkable period, 680–720, had simply run out.

The Monastic Revival

By the middle of the tenth century a new spirit was abroad. Three men, two of them natives of Wessex, were to lead a virtual revolution ousting the decadence of the old monastic system and replacing it with a rigorous new order.

Dunstan was born in Somerset in about 909 and spent his early years at Glastonbury where, according to his biographer, he inspired hostility among some of his contemporaries by his enthusiasm for studying heathen (i.e. Classical) poets. A more likely cause of his unpopularity was his combined cleverness and intolerance. After his ordination at Winchester he attended the court of King Edmund but fell out with the king (his arrogance again?) and escaped banishment only when the king was miraculously saved by divine intervention from plunging down Cheddar Gorge during a stag hunt on the Mendips. In recompense Edmund installed Dunstan as abbot of Glastonbury in 944. During the fifteen years of his tenure he rebuilt the old monastery (Fig. 9.7) and re-established there a monastic community governed by the rule of St Benedict – an act which marked the beginning of the monastic revival in England.

Dunstan was ordained at Winchester on the same day as Æthelwold, a native of Winchester. Æthelwold later joined Dunstan at Glastonbury, where he learned the rigour of the rule of St Benedict before moving on, first to restore the monastery at Abingdon and later, in 963, to become Bishop of Winchester. By this time, after a brief exile abroad, Dunstan had been recalled to England and installed as Archbishop of Canterbury.

The third member of the triumvirate was Oswald. He came from a Danish family, with strong ecclesiastical roots (one uncle had been Archbishop of Canterbury). After studying and working abroad he returned to England to become Bishop of Worcester and later, in 972, Archbishop of York.

All three men were scholars and reformers. They had gained first-hand knowledge of the new ideas and innovations now rife on the Continent and, of no less importance, they had reached the peak of their powers under a powerful king, Edgar, himself an ardent reformer.

The changes brought about in the monastic movement in the second half of the tenth century were considerable. The situation in Winchester is revealing not least in that it demonstrates the importance of royal patronage in the changes which were then underway. The cathedral or Old Minster, founded by King Ine at the beginning of the eighth century, continued to function as the main ecclesiastical focus until the beginning of the tenth century when, early in the reign of Edward the Elder, traditionally in 903, the New Minster was built on a site immediately adjacent to the Old. Both buildings, however, continued in use together. Whereas the Old Minster had been the burial place of some of the earlier kings of Wessex the New Minster became the shrine of Alfred and his successors who could justly claim to be kings of England. Its foundation therefore could be interpreted as marking a deliberate break with the past and a reflection of the growing importance of Winchester as the principal city of Wessex and of England (Yorke 1984: 66–8).

When, in 963, Æthelwold became Bishop of Winchester his first act was to expel from both Minsters all the canons who were married or would not otherwise conform to the reformed rule. This done he created a vigorous monastic seat of learning at Winchester and it was here that the famous Winchester school of manuscript illustration came into being. In the latter years of his life, 980–4, he embarked upon an extensive restoration of the Old Minster where he set up a shrine for St Swithin. Further extensions were made under his successor Alphage (Quirk 1957; Biddle 1986: 22). It was at Winchester between 963 and 975 that Edgar summoned a synod to draw up a set of rules to govern the monks and nuns of the English nation. The *Regularis Concordia* as it was called was largely the work of Bishop Æthelwold and was widely adopted by the reformed monasteries.

From Minsters to Parish Churches

Beyond the great monasteries of Wessex lay the many small unreformed minsters remembered now in certain town names like Sturminster, Charminster, Yetminster and Warminster. They differed from the large establishments in a number of respects most notably in their lack of adherence to a strict order. The minsters were essentially communities of priests whose task it was to care for the spiritual life of the population often of a considerable region. They could own property and were allowed to marry (Blair 1988b: 1–2).

The origin of the minsters is obscure but in a detailed study of southern Hampshire it has been possible to demonstrate that the skeleton of the system was set up some time around 700, during the reigns of Caedwalla and Ine, and that each of the minsters' territories (*parochia*) coincided with a royal estate (Hase 1988: 45–8). The implication must surely be that the minster system was a deliberate creation designed to ensure that the social, political, judicial and religious life of the countryside had the same focus and that everything was ultimately under the king's oversight.

Within the *parochiae* of the minsters were many villages often considerable distances from the mother church. Priests would have travelled to the outdoor preaching crosses to minister to the rural communities and such arrangements sufficed for several centuries. But gradually many of these traditional locations were provided with more formal church buildings built under the patronage of local thegns in the centres of their estates. Such buildings not only were a convenience for the nobility and an outward and visible sign of their social standing, but also provided an income since their patrons retained the legal title. In this way the village church came into existence, each with its own priest, while the old mother churches began to decline eventually to serve only the needs of their own local communities.

Many of the early village churches would have been built of timber but by the middle of the eleventh century stone construction had become common. Something of the spirit of the time is captured in the words of Bishop Herman of Ramsbury who reported to Pope Leo IX in 1050 that England was 'being filled everywhere with churches, which daily were being added anew in new places; about the distribution of innumerable ornaments and bells in oratories; about the most ample liberality of kings and rich men for the inheritance of Christ.'

Hamwic, Overseas Trade and the Growth of Winchester

We have already seen how some at least of the royal villas provided foci around which markets could develop, providing facilities for trade and exchange which might in turn have encouraged local production. The larger monastic establishments may also have attracted a similar range of activities but no Wessex site before 700 can claim to have acquired urban character-

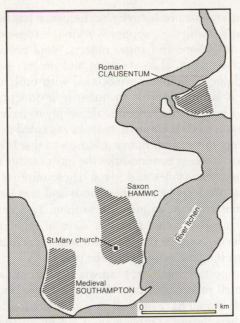

Figure 9.8 The location of the Saxon port of Hamwic on the peninsula in the upper reaches of Southampton Water.

istics. This makes the establishment of Hamwic on the west bank of the river Itchen at or soon after that date all the more remarkable (Andrews 1988; Brisbane 1988; Holdsworth 1980, 1984; Hodges 1981).

As a result of extensive excavations since 1946 Hamwic can now be seen to have been a planned trading settlement, occupying a site of at least 42 to 45 ha, on the peninsula now occupied by modern Southampton, at a point where the river Itchen widens to join Southampton Water (Fig. 9.8). As a port engaged in overseas trade it could hardly have been better sited to serve the heart of the kingdom of Wessex. The settlement was undefended but was delimited, at least along its western extremity, by a boundary ditch: at its eastern side it is likely that the buildings extended down to the strand along the shore of the estuary. The settlement was laid out from the start on a grid pattern with three north–south streets and more than six east–west streets, all of which were carefully maintained throughout the life of the port. One of the north–south streets showed ten separate phases of remetalling. Within this grid, usually close to the street frontage, the timber houses of the settlement were erected, the norm being 4–5 m wide and 12 m long. Associated with these were smaller sheds and workshops. Several graveyards have been identified but the possibility remains that the principal cemetery was focused upon the minster church, referred to in a charter of 1045, which probably lay on the site of the present Church of St Mary.

The community was a productive one. Evidence has been recovered for iron working (mostly smithying), copper working, lead working, gold working, the manufacture of bone and antler objects, wool processing and textile production, leather working, glass working and pottery production, in addition to normal domestic activities associated with building and food processing. Although it is very difficult to quantify production of this kind it would seem to have been on too large a scale simply to have provided for the resident community. If so then Hamwic must be regarded as a regional centre serving a much larger hinterland. But in addition to this Hamwic was a port of entry for a range of foreign commodities the most readily identifiable being pottery, quernstones, whetstones and glass. These imports were, no doubt, exchanged for local products like leather goods and textiles, as well as meat and cereals brought in from the countryside around. To facilitate the complex systems of exchange silver coins, *sceattas*, were in regular circulation and there is some evidence to suggest that a special series was minted for use in the closed system controlling the activities of the port.

The imported pottery found at Hamwic is predominantly of Frankish origin though a small percentage came from the Rhineland (Hodges 1981; Timby 1988). Some would have arrived as containers for commodities such as wine and oil, others for use as table ware. Lava quernstones from the Eifel region near Mayen, together with Rhenish glass and whetstones of Scandinavian schist, indicate the extent of the trading network. These commodities probably came through the Continental ports of Dorestad, in the area of the Rhine mouth, and Quentovic recently identified as Visemarest in the valley of the Canche, south of Boulogne, both of which maintained active contacts with Hamwic throughout the eighth century.

The creation of the trading port at Hamwic some time about 700 marked a significant threshold in the socio-economic development of Wessex. In all probability it was a deliberate act of policy belonging to the period of the expansion of Wessex under Caedwalla and Ine – an attempt to link the kingdom of Wessex firmly to the Continent and thus to benefit from the innovations taking place there. The choice of the site on the peninsula jutting into Southampton Water is informative. Clearly it was highly convenient in terms of communications but there may have been underlying political reasons. One strong possibility is that there already existed a royal villa in the vicinity: one is mentioned in a ninth century charter but it need not have preceded the development of the port. Another possibility is that the site was chosen because it was a 'no man's land' on an interface between the heart of traditional Wessex, the Jutish settlement of the Meon valley and the newly conquered Isle of Wight – a border situation not dissimilar to that of Hengistbury Head eight hundred years earlier. In any event the new port, by virtue of its command of the river Itchen, was well located to serve Winchester, which by this time was fast becoming an important ecclesiastical centre.

The port of Hamwic flourished until about 850 after which depopulation and decline set in. One reason for this was the vulnerability of the site to Danish raids. The first assault took place in 840 when 33 ships' companies were successfully repelled by the ealdorman, Wulfheard. Two years later the Danes returned, this time destroying Hamwic. The raid of 860, however, seems to have bypassed the port: the landing was made at 'Hamptun', an alternative name for Hamwic, but the attackers made for Winchester which suffered extensive destruction. The 'large army of pagans' fleeing with their booty were, however, intercepted by a West Saxon force.

Not only did the Danish raids devastate coastal settlements but also the presence of the marauders in the Channel totally disrupted the extensive systems of long-distance trade which had developed. Hamwic was vulnerable, and as a trading port it soon became redundant. Thus it was that the old settlement declined into insignificance, those of its population who remained moving to the greater security of a promontory site half a kilometre to the south west where, by about 900, defences had been erected to protect them. It was this settlement that was to grow into the medieval port of Southampton (Holdsworth 1984).

With the decline of Hamwic throughout the ninth century came the growth in importance of Winchester, which further escalated in the latter half of Alfred's reign following the defeat of the Great Army in 878. From this time forward Alfred began to invest Winchester with a legitimacy appropriate to a capital. The earliest reference to the king being in Winchester is provided by the *Anglo Saxon Chronicle* for the year 896 when a group of captured Vikings were brought there to the king and ordered to be hanged. By this stage Winchester was served by a town-reeve – a mark of its growing status – and coins were being minted here, perhaps for the first time. The royal presence implies the existence of a palace. Significantly Alfred's biographer Asser notes that the king moved royal palaces from ancient sites to more suitable places – a reference perhaps to the demise of Hamwic and the transfer of its administrative functions to Winchester. To further aggrandize Winchester, Alfred's wife founded the Nunnaminster and it is quite likely that Alfred was already making preparations for the building of the New Minster when he died, leaving the actual foundation to his son to complete in or about 903 (Yorke 1984: 66–7). Thus by the beginning of the tenth century Winchester had become the capital of Wessex in all but name.

The Burghs

An invaluable glimpse of the urban situation in Wessex in the late ninth and early tenth centuries is provided by a document known as the Burghal

Hidage. There is some debate as to when the text was written (Brooks 1964; Davis 1982) but it is generally agreed that it refers to a defensive system formalized by Alfred at the time of the Danish invasions. The document is a royal memorandum listing the fortified places, or *burghs*, of Wessex in roughly clockwise order starting in the east. To each stronghold a specific area of land is assigned (measured in hides) such that if each hide sent one man in times of need, each pole of the defences could be maintained by four men. In this way it is possible to compare the assessed length of the defensive circuit with the actual measured length today and to discover a high degree of correlation (Hill 1969). It will be seen from the map (Fig. 9.9) that, for the most part, the burghs follow the frontier of Alfred's kingdom. Along the south coast they were regularly spaced, seldom more than 50 km apart or more than a few kilometres from the sea. In the north they follow the Severn coast, the Bristol Avon and the Thames at an equivalent spacing. Within the heart of Wessex five inland sites, Winchester, Wilton, Shaftesbury, Chisbury and Eashing (Surrey), were included.

A variety of locations was chosen (Fig. 9.10). Chichester, Winchester, Exeter and Bath were all Roman towns with extant walls. Portchester and Clausentum (Southampton) were also Roman fortifications. Chisbury, a rather surprising addition in view of its isolated location, was an Iron Age hillfort. Wilton was a royal vill and shire town to which a new defence was added. Some like Wareham, Cricklade and Wallingford were major enclosures laid out for the first time in the Alfredian period and defended with timber-fronted ramparts and ditches (Haslam 1984b: 107–9; RCHM(E) 1959).

In Winchester a regular street system was imposed at about this time, that is *c.* 900 (Biddle 1986: 122). While it is likely that the creation of the street grid, one function of which was to provide ease of access to the defences, coincided with the bringing into defensive readiness of the Roman walls and gates, there is no compelling reason to date this phase to as late as the Alfredian period. Indeed, as the excavator has suggested, a case could be argued for these radical changes having been undertaken by one of Alfred's brothers a decade or so earlier in the wake of the early Viking raids on Hamwic (Biddle 1986: 122–6). In any event the concept of the regular street grid was probably developed by the surveyors of Winchester from the model already in use in the eighth century at Hamwic. By the time the Winchester streets were being laid out a standard system of measurements was in operation using the 4 pole = 1 chain = 66 ft. module (Crummy 1979).

The Winchester-style street pattern was adopted in many other of the Burghal Hidage towns though not always in such a highly developed form (Biddle and Hill 1971). Remnants of the original Saxon layouts are still

---

Figure 9.9   The major towns and Burghal Hidage fortifications of Wessex.

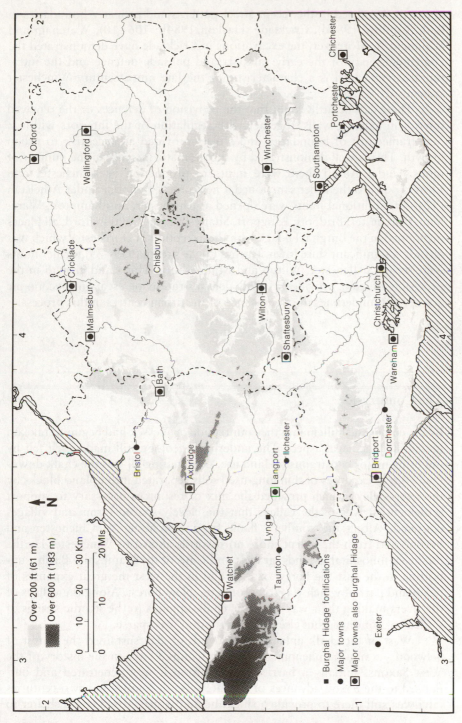

apparent, fossilized in the recent street patterns and property boundaries in Bath (Cunliffe 1984d), Cricklade (Haslam 1984b: 106–10), Wareham and Wallingford. Moreover, the excavations in Cricklade have demonstrated the contemporaneity of the early rampart and palisade defence and the intra-mural street which is a characteristic of the late ninth century Winchester system.

There can be little doubt that the provision of defences or the renewed interest in existing walls, together with regulation of the interiors within a new framework of boundaries and streets provided an incentive to urban growth. This is well demonstrated by the dramatic increase in the number of mints. Under Alfred there were mints in production at Winchester and Exeter: Edward the Elder sanctioned a new one at Bath but under Athelstan (924–39) additional mints were opened at Chichester, Southampton, Wareham, Dorchester, Bridport, Langport, Shaftesbury and Wallingford, all places mentioned in the Burghal Hidage with the exception of Dorchester which was already a significant shire town. During Edgar's reign (959–75) further mints were set up at Ilchester, Wilton and Malmesbury. This rapid growth in the provision of coin provides a vivid demonstration of escalating economic activity and underlines the significance of the urban centres in this process.

The Countryside

By the end of the millennium the countryside of Wessex had begun to take on its familiar medieval aspect. The underlying geology still made itself felt by imposing major constraints on land use. Dominating all was the chalk down-land – great expanses of thin long-used soils separated into upland blocks by the river valleys which provided the mix of resources necessary to support settlement. It was in the valleys that the closely spaced farms and villages clustered. Along the southern flank from Dorchester to Chichester and beyond and from the Solent shore northwards almost to Winchester lay the relatively inhospitable sands, gravels and clays of the Hampshire Basin, sup-porting in the east the Forest of Bere and in the west the great expanses of heathland part of which was to become the New Forest. Along the valleys of the rivers making their way from the chalk uplands to the sea the strings of settlement continued but elsewhere habitation was sparse.

West of the chalk uplands wide bands of clay sustained the Forest of Selwood – a natural phenomenon which featured large in the history of the West Saxons. Initially a barrier to expansion it was penetrated and out-flanked in the Saxon advances of the late seventh century but two centuries later was still there to provide a shield behind which Alfred could shelter to

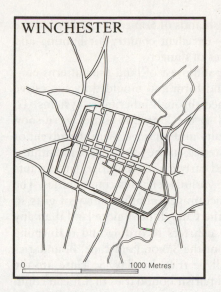

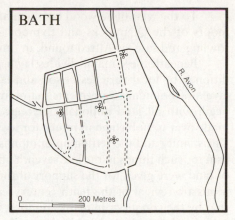

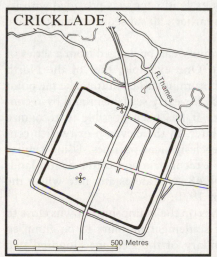

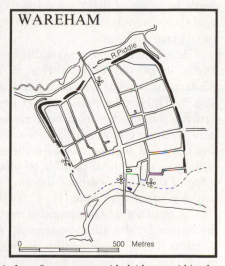

Figure 9.10 Four Wessex towns showing their Late Saxon street grids laid out within the defences.

prepare himself for the counter offensive against the Danes. Some sense of the mysteries and dangers of the forest is given by a seventh century West Saxon law code: a traveller passing through a forest off the main highway who does not shout and blow his horn may be assumed to be a thief and may thus be legitimately killed or ransomed. The forest was also protected. There were penalties for setting fire to trees, for felling large numbers and especially for destroying large trees that could shelter thirty swine.

To the west of Selwood lay the marshlands of Somerset and beyond the moors of the Quantocks and Exmoor – excellent country for hunting and fowling and safe, as Alfred found, in times of danger.

Beneath these major divides lay a palimpsest of land-use patterns conditioned by local varieties of soil and land form and moulded by successive layers of boundary agreements maintained through inheritance systems. To begin with all land notionally belonged to the king but estates were soon made over to noblemen in return for loyalty and services. With the advent of Christianity and the setting up of monasteries, in the initial spate of enthusiasm for such things in the late seventh and early eighth centuries, large grants of land were given for the support of the various religious communities. The monastic revival of the tenth century encouraged another flurry of gifts so that by the conquest, in many counties, the Church held more land than any other authority including the king. The charters recording and reaffirming these gifts provide a wealth of detail about the Saxon landscape. Boundaries were set out with precision and can still be traced today. So close are the correspondences with modern estate and parish boundaries that it can confidently be affirmed that the modern Wessex landscape was provided with its legal skeleton in the Saxon period (if not earlier): all subsequent changes have taken place within it.

Something of this remarkable continuity can be gauged from a series of studies in Dorset (C. C. Taylor 1970). One example, that of the North Winterbourne valley west of Blandford Forum, is sufficient to make the point (Fig. 9.11). Here by considering evidence for early settlement and by reconstructing boundaries from field evidence it has been possible to recognize eight separate estates which were only later, in the eleventh or twelfth century, grouped together to form three ecclesiastical parishes. Using similar techniques it has been possible to offer a reconstruction of the Saxon landscape of the Isle of Purbeck showing the 48 separate estates into which the land was originally divided (C. C. Taylor 1970: Fig. 7).

A similar study of a group of parishes on the Hampshire Downs close to the Sussex border allows something of settlement mobility to be glimpsed (Cunliffe 1972). Here, within the boundary of the Ceptune Hundred two middle Saxon settlements have been located, one at Catherington the other on Church Down, Chalton, both occupying hilltop locations. A north–south boundary, later formalized as a parish boundary, divided the two estates. By the Late Saxon period both estates had been subdivided into smaller units and these became the parishes which have persisted ever since (Fig. 9.12). The date of the subdivisions is obscure but if the abandonment of the Church Down settlement marks the change, then it must have been some time about 700. It is, however, possible that the settlement was moved to the more convenient site of the present Chalton village at this time and that the foundation of the estates of Blendworth and Idsworth came later, in the ninth or tenth century. This example illustrates in microcosm something of the reor-

PARISHES IN THE
NORTH WINTERBORNE VALLEY

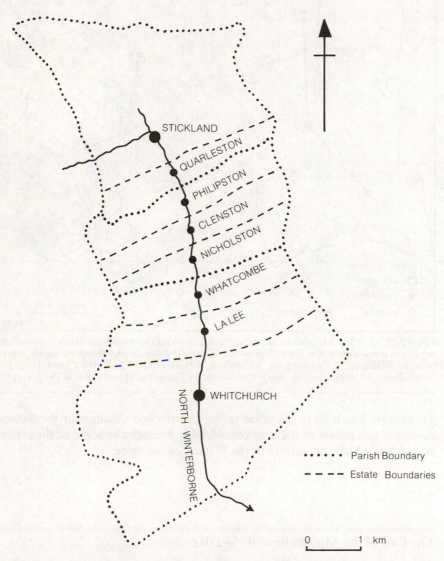

Figure 9.11 The valley of the North Winterborne, Dorset showing the Late Saxon estate boundaries in relation to the parishes which were probably organized in the twelfth century. (After Taylor 1970: Fig. 6)

329

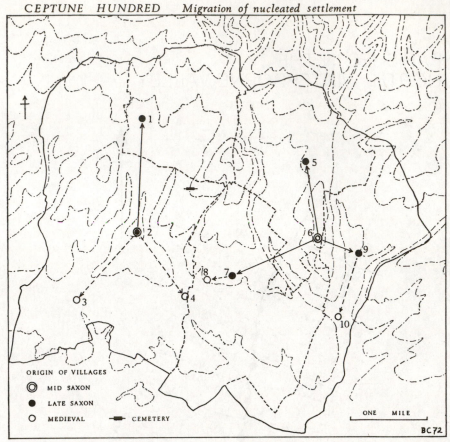

CEPTUNE HUNDRED   *Migration of nucleated settlement*

ORIGIN OF VILLAGES
◎ MID SAXON
● LATE SAXON
○ MEDIEVAL ■—■ CEMETERY

ONE   MILE

BC 72

Figure 9.12   The South Downs north of Portsmouth showing the estate boundaries surrounding the two major settlements at Catherington and Church Down and the subsequent parish development. 1 Clanfield; 2 Catherington; 3 Lovedean; 4 Horndean; 5 Chalton; 6 Church Down; 7 Blendworth (old); 8 Blendworth (new); 9 Idsworth; 10 Finchdean. (From Cunliffe 1972: Fig. 3)

ganizations which were going on in the countryside throughout the Saxon period: it also points to the very considerable antiquity of some of the estate boundaries which still survive in the Wessex countryside.

The End of the Millennium: 975–1016

King Edgar died in 975 and his son Edward, who succeeded him, was murdered three years later at Corfe, making way for the accession of Æthelred II,

330

known as the Unready. During his thirty-eight years on the throne England was attacked by successive Viking armies and finally succumbed in 1016 when Cnut of Denmark was crowned king.

The Danish threat, which began in 980, was quite different from that experienced more than a century before. Then the boatloads of people who arrived soon saw Britain as a place to settle and make their homes. The raiders who came now were a highly trained army of professional soldiers whose desire was to spend their lives fighting and amassing loot. It was a force far more difficult to contend with and for the most part the English response was ill-organized and, in the end, unsuccessful.

The Vikings came in two forces, from across the North Sea to ravage the east and south coasts and from Ireland to attack Wales and the south west. The raids began in 980 with an attack on Southampton which was severely damaged and the inhabitants either killed or enslaved. Later in the year Thanet was attacked and two years later it was the turn of Portland and London; meanwhile the Vikings from Ireland were raiding the west coasts. Devon and Cornwall were assaulted in 981 and Watchet on the north coast of Somerset was destroyed in 988.

These early raids, spread over a decade or so, were scattered and localized: they caused no widespread disruption. In 991 a much larger force arrived on the east coast and though they were halted at the battle of Maldon in Essex it was clear to the English that this was just the beginning: the next year both sea and land forces under Æthelred's command were ready and for two years engaged the enemy in the east of England. But in 994 the raids on the south coast and the south west began in earnest and lasted, with little let up, for the next fifteen years. The countryside was devastated, settlements burnt and the inhabitants slaughtered. All the while vast quantities of silver, known as Danegeld, were paid over by the English to buy off even greater excesses. It was the coastal region that bore the brunt of the attacks, not least because the Danes favoured the Isle of Wight as a convenient offshore base from which raids could in safety be mounted. Among the settlements devastated were Lydford, Tavistock and Watchet, between 995 and 997, Dean, Waltham and Teignton in 1001–2, Exeter and Wilton in 1003, Wallingford in 1006 and Oxford in 1009. The power of the Danish army to do as it pleased is vividly recorded by the *Anglo Saxon Chronicle* for the year 1006 when, it tells us, they obtained everywhere whatever they needed. After burning Wallingford and putting an English army to flight at a battle at the river Kennet they marched south, not even bothering to make a detour around Winchester, whose inhabitants 'could see the force, proud and unafraid, that went by their gates to the sea.' By 1012 most of southern England south east of a line from the Wash to Poole Harbour had been overrun.

The final stage in the drama came in 1013 when Swein Forkbeard arrived with his ships at Sandwich. After a rapid advance to the Humber,

Plate 9.4 Viking sword found in the city ditch just outside the Northgate of Bath. (Scale 1:3.) (Photo: Institute of Archaeology, Oxford)

where he received the submission of the people of Lindsey and the Five Boroughs (i.e. the East Midlands), he marched southwards. First Oxford submitted, then Winchester. London was defended by Æthelred and managed to hold out, so Swein left, passing through Wallingford to Bath, where he stayed with his troops receiving the western noblemen. 'They all bowed to Swein and gave hostages. When he had thus fared, he went north-ward to his ships, and all the nation had accepted him as full king.' Residual opposition lasted for a further three years focused in the western half of Wessex but on 30 November 1016 Swein's son Cnut was proclaimed king of England.

For ten years the land of Wessex had been ravaged and fought over. The disruption and dislocation which this caused cannot have failed to have made an impact. Burghs like Cricklade and Wareham were strengthened with stone walls inserted in front of their Alfredian ramparts and the old Iron Age hillfort of South Cadbury was redefended with new stone-built ramparts. Elsewhere items of military equiment, like the fine Viking sword found just outside the north gate of Bath (Plate 9.4), bear witness to the presence of the Danish armies. But when all is said and done events of this kind, bloody though they may have been, cause few significant changes. Struggles for power between a few avaricious aristocrats are seldom of sufficient moment to change the trajectories of history. Beneath it all the landscape of Wessex, gently moulded by hundreds of generations of its people, endured.

Appendix

Radiocarbon dates

A substantial number of radiocarbon dates have been obtained for prehistoric sites in Wessex and with careful manipulation they can be used to provide a valid chronological perspective for the social and economic developments we are considering in this book. But radiocarbon dates can be deceptive, not least because, to the unwary, they can give the appearance of spurious accuracy. Let us take a single example. In the Neolithic period one of the inhabitants of Wessex discarded a pick made of red deer antler in the bottom of the ditch dug to define a large circular enclosure within which the stones of Stonehenge were erected many centuries later. The pick was found in an excavation and taken to the British Museum Laboratory for dating and there given the sample number BM 1617. The published assessment is 4390 ± 60 bp. This means that there is a two to one chance that the date lies between 4450 and 4330 before the present (i.e. before AD 1950) measured in radiocarbon years. Radiocarbon years are not equivalent to calendar years and there is no simple formula for converting one to the other.

In recent years a great deal of effort has been expended on this problem and significant advances have been made by using high precision radiocarbon techniques to date tree rings from samples of known age thus providing a means of calibrating radiocarbon years to real years, distinguished as Cal BC. The results of this work are readily available and a computer programme exists for converting years bp to years Cal BC back to about 6100 bp (*c.* 5200 Cal BC).

Using these calibration techniques it is possible to arrive at two date brackets for our antler pick. There is 68 per cent chance (one sigma) that the date lies between 3097 and 2920 Cal BC and a 95 per cent chance (two sigma) that it falls within the range 3326 and 2910 Cal BC. Clearly to quote all this in the text would be cumbersome so the date will appear as '*c.* 3000 BC'. It is as well, however, to remember that such a citation is at best a very rough approximation.

Dates before about 6100 bp cannot at present be calibrated with any degree of certainty. As a *very rough* rule of thumb if you subtract 1000 years from the bp date you will get an approximation to the BC date but it is likely to be several centuries out!

To provide more detail for those who want it, some of the more useful dates are listed here in full giving their laboratory number, years bp and years Cal BC calculated for the standard one sigma standard deviation (i.e. 68 per cent chance). The list is by no means complete but it provides a framework of dates for much of the prehistoric period.

Two other lists may also be consulted. All dates for the Somerset Levels have been brought together in Volume 15 of the *Somerset Levels Papers* (1989) and a wide selection of first millennium BC dates will be found in the third edition of my *Iron Age Communities in Britain* (1991).

Those readers who have arrived at this point with their curiosity sharpened are recommended to read S. Bowman's extremely informative booklet *Radiocarbon Dating* published by British Museum Publications in 1990. It will explain what is here left unsaid and introduce them to further intricacies.

Upper Palaeolithic

Pickens Hole, Mendip
bp

Bone: layer 3	BM–654	34,265 (+2600 −1950)
: layer 5	BM–655A	26,650 (+1700 −1400)
	BM–655B	27,000 (+1850 −1500)

Sun Hole Cave, Mendip

Bone	BM–524	12,378±150

Gough's Cave, Mendip

Human bone GC2	OxA–2234	11,480±90
GC87/169	OxA–2795	11,820±120
GC3	OxA–2235	11,990±90
GC6	OxA–2236	11,700±100
M23	OxA–2237	12,300±100
GC87/190	OxA–2796	12,380±110
Antler baton	OxA–2797	11,870±110

Badger Hole, Mendip

Human bone BH1	OxA–679	9060±130
BH2	OxA–1459	9360±100

Aveline's Hole, Mendip

Human bone	Q–1458	9090±110
	BM–471	9144±110

Mesolithic Occupation Sites

Thatcham, Berks.

Wood from Zone IV	Q–651	9840±160
Wood from Zone V	Q–677	9780±200
	Q–650	9670±160
Wood from Zone VIa	Q–652	9480±160
Charcoal from hearth, site III	Q–659	10,367±170
Charcoal from another hearth, site III	Q–658	10,030±170

Oakhanger (Sites V/VII), Hants.

Hazel-nuts	Q–1489	9225±200
Wood charcoal	Q–1491	9100±200
Wood charcoal	Q–1493	9040±160
Wood charcoal	Q–1490	8995±200
Wood charcoal	Q–1492	8975±200
Wood charcoal	Q–1494	8885±165

Broom Hill, Hants.

Charcoal: base of pit 3	Q–1192	8540±150
	Q–1528	8515±150
	Q–1383	8315±150
Charcoal: top of pit 3	Q–1460	7750±120
Charcoal: above pit 3	Q–1191	7220±120
Charcoal: pit 2	Q–1128	6535±125

Wakefords Copse, Hants.

Charcoal	HAR–233	5680±120

Culver Well, Portland, Dorset

Charcoal from midden	BM–473	7150±135
	BM–960	7101±97

Blashenwell, Purbeck, Dorset

Bone from tufa: upper level	BM–1257	5750±140
: upper level	BM–1258	5425±150
: middle level	BM–89	6450±150

Wawcott, Berks.

Carbonized material from pit	BM–767	6120±134

Longmoor Inclosure, Hants.

Charred hazel-nuts	OxA–376	8930±100
	OxA–377	8760±110

Earlier Neolithic Occupation

Windmill Hill, Wilts.		bp	Cal BC (1 σ)
Charcoal pre-dating enclosure	BM–73	4910±150	3938–3526
Bone under outer bank	OxA–2405	4550±80	3371–3101
	OxA–2406	4870±70	3775–3543

South Street, Avebury, Wilts.

Charcoal beneath barrow	BM–356	4760±130	3700–3370

Marden, Wilts.

Charcoal beneath henge	BM–560	4604±59	3494–3206

Durrington Walls, Wilts.

Charcoal beneath henge	GRO–901	4584±80	3494–3135
	GRO–901a	4575±50	3371–3144
	NPL–191	4400±150	3340–2900

Cherhill, Wilts.

Occupation beneath colluvium	BM–493	4706±90	3629–3366

Hemp Knoll, Wilts.

Occupation	HAR–2997	4580±80	3493–3109

Coneybury 'anomaly' Wilts.

Animal bone	OxA–1402	5050±100	3980–3708

Maiden Castle, Dorset

Animal bone below bank	OxA–1336	4570±80	3375–3107

Rowden, Dorset

Charcoal from pit	HAR–5247	4940±70	3787–3689
Charcoal from pit	HAR–5248	4860±70	3774–3538
Charcoal from pit	HAR–5246	5250±140	4240–3828
Charcoal from post-hole	HAR–5245	4970±70	3931–3696

Neolithic: Long Barrows
Lambourn, Berks.

Charcoal from ditch bottom	GX–1174	5365±180	4360–3990

Wayland's Smithy, Berks.

Soil beneath barrows I and II	I–1468	4770±130	3700–3370

Fussell's Lodge, Hants.

Charcoal from mortuary house	BM–134	5180±150	4228–3790

Nutbane, Hants.

Charcoal from forecourt	BM–49	4680±150	3640–3147

Horslip, Wilts.

Antler from primary fill of ditch	BM–180	5190±150	4231–3814

South Street, Wilts.

Bone from ditch bottom	BM–357	4700±135	3640–3350
Antler from ditch bottom	BM–358a	4620±140	3615–3100
Antler from mound	BM–358b	4530±110	3370–3040

Normanton, Wilts.

Antler under mound	BM–505	4510±103	3370–3040

Beckhampton, Wilts.

Antler from buried soil beside inner face of revetment bank	BM–506b	4467±90	3344–2929

Worbarrow, Dorset

Antler from ditch bottom	BM–2284R	4740±130	3690–3360
Antler from primary fill of ditch	BM–2283R	4660±130	3626–3147

Thickthorn Down, Dorset

Antler beneath mound	BM–2355	5160±45	4031–3829

Arlington, Dorset

Bone from ditch	HAR–8579	4450±80	3335–2928

Neolithic Causewayed Camps
Windmill Hill, Wilts.

Bones from:
Outer ditch

Trench B primary fill	BM–2669	47405±0	3628–3381
Trench C upper primary fill	OxA–2401	4770±70	3643–3383
	OxA–2402	4665±80	3611–3352
Trench C tertiary fill	BM–2673	4310±60	3023–2896
Trench A top of primary fill	OxA–2399	4750±70	3637–3380

Middle ditch

Trench E under primary fill	OxA–2395	4730±80	3634–3374
	OxA–2396	4690±70	3616–3367
junction of primary and secondary fill	BM–2671	4550±50	3361–3109
Trench D primary fill	BM–2670	4670±90	3616–3350
secondary fill	OxA–2398	4715±80	3629–3372
	OxA–2397	4730±80	3634–3374

Inner ditch

Trench F primary fill	OxA–2394	4665±70	3602–3356
lower secondary fill	BM–2672	4370±50	3075–2918

Knap Hill, Wilts.

Bottom of ditch	BM–205	4710±115	3640–3360

Robin Hood's Ball, Wilts.

Bone from pit	OxA–1400	4740±100	3640–3370
Bone from pit	OxA–1401	4510±90	3361–3039

340

Maiden Castle, Dorset

Inner ditch:

primary fill – bone	OxA–1144	4550±80	3371–3101
– bone	OxA–1148	4810±80	3696–3389
– bone	OxA–1337	5030±80	3964–3708
– charcoal	BM–2449	5040±60	3958–3781
– charcoal	BM–2450	5030±60	3952–3722

Inner ditch:

pit cutting primary fill – antler	OxA–1145	4660±80	3607–3350

Inner ditch:

secondary fill – bone	OxA–1143	4730±80	3634–3374
– bone	OxA–1147	4690±80	3620–3363

Inner ditch:

secondary midden – bone	BM–2447	4800±45	3646–3522
– bone	BM–2448	4710±70	3623–3372
– bone	BM–2454	4830±60	3696–3529

Inner ditch:

final fill – bone	OxA–1141	4360±80	3094–2911
– bone	OxA–1142	4750±80	3640–3378

Outer ditch:

primary fill – bone	OxA–1338	4930±80	3787–3644
– bone	OxA–1339	4740±80	3637–3376
– bone	OxA–1340	4650±70	3511–3350
– bone	BM–2451	4860±70	3774–3538
– bone	BM–2452	4640±50	3503–3354

Hambledon Hill, Dorset

Bottom of ditch	NPL–76	4740±90	3640–3374
Internal pit	HAR–2041	4110±80	2878–2509
Main ditch (phase II)	HAR–1886	4840±150	3780–3382
Main ditch (phase II)	HAR–1882	4560±90	3375–3101
Main ditch (phase III)	HAR–2375	4670±100	3619–3350
	HAR–1885	4480±130	3360–2924
Outwork, ditch 1	HAR–2371	4680±110	3626–3350
	HAR–2377	4610±90	3505–3142
	HAR–2378	4820±120	3775–3384
	HAR–2379	4350±80	3091–2908
	HAR–2372	4630±80	3508–3340

341

Neolithic: Bank Barrows and Cursus Monuments
Maiden Castle, Dorset

Bank barrow:

primary ditch fill – bone	OxA–1146	4650±80	3597–3347
pit cutting primary fill – antler	OxA–1349	4460±80	3338–2929
early fill – bone	BM–2456	4720±100	3640–3370
middle fill – bone	BM–2455	3470±70	1889–1696
upper fill – charcoal	OxA–1341	4460±80	3338–2929

Dorset Cursus, Cranborne Chase

West Cursus ditch

– antler	BM–2438	4490±60	3342–3042
– animal bone	OxA–625/626	4575±77	3491–3109
– animal bone	OxA–624	4570±120	3502–3048

Stonehenge Lesser Cursus

Antler from ditch base (phase 1)	OxA–1404	4550±120	3496–3042
Antler from ditch base (phase 2)	OxA–1405	4640±100	3606–3200

Stonehenge Cursus

Antler from ditch	OxA–1403	4100±90	2878–2502

Later Neolithic: Henge Monuments and Related Structures
Durrington Walls, Wilts.

Midden	NPL–192	4270±95	3021–2705
Post-hole 92 – antler	BM–395	3900±90	2559–2283
– charcoal	BM–396	3950±90	2580–2343
– bone	BM–397	3850±90	2466–2147
Base of ditch – charcoal	BM–398	3927±90	2572–2308
– bone	BM–399	3965±90	2586–2365
– antler	BM–400	4000±90	2853–2459
Post-hole: north circle	NPL–240	3905±110	2571–2207
Hearth on primary silt	BM–286	3630±110	2183–1880
Hearth on secondary silt	BM–285	3560±120	2123–1750

Woodhenge, Wilts.

Primary ditch silt – antler	BM–677	3817±74	2456–2143
– bone	BM–678	3755±54	2283–2047

Coneybury Henge, Wilts.

Primary ditch fill – bone	OxA–1408	4200±110	2917–2615
Pit in interior – bone	OxA–1409	4370±90	3254–2911

Stonehenge, Wilts.

Phase 1:

ditch bottom – antler	BM–1617	4390±60	3097–2920
30 cm above bottom – antler	BM–1583	4410±60	3291–2924
primary silt – antler	I–2328	4130±105	2890–2508

Phase 2:

SE avenue ditch – antler	HAR–2013	3720±100	2290–1979
NW avenue ditch – antler	BM–1164	3678±68	2190–1972
– antler	I–2384	3570±110	2123–1760
Beaker burial in ditch	BM–1582	3715±70	2271–2033

Phase 3a:

ramp for trilithon – antler	BM–46	3670±150	2290–1880

Phase 3b: Y–hole – antler

Phase 3b: Y–hole – antler	I–2445	3190±105	1603–1400

Marden, Wilts.

Primary ditch silt

– charcoal	BM–557	3938±48	2557–2404
– animal bone	BM–558	3526±99	2023–1742
– antler	BM–559	3626±81	2135–1889

Maumbury Rings, Dorset

Bottom of shaft 1	BM–2282N	3970±70	2580–2457
Highest level in shaft 3	BM–2281R	3940±130	2600–2280

Greyhound Yard, Dorchester, Dorset

Charcoal from post–pits	HAR–6663	4020±80	2855–2466
	HAR–6684	4070±70	2865–2498
	HAR–6689	4140±90	2888–2583

Flagstones Causewayed Enclosure, Dorset

From ditch – bone	HAR–9158	4490±70	3345–3039
– antler	HAR–8578	4030±100	2863–2460
– antler	OxA–2322	4450±90	3338–2926
– bone	OxA–2321	4210±110	2919–2619

Mount Pleasant, Dorset

Pre-enclosure settlement – charcoal	BM–644	4072±73	2866–2498
Enclosure ditch (W),			
primary – antler	BM–645	3734±41	2201–2045
– antler	BM–646	3728±59	2272–2039
secondary – charcoal	BM–664	3410±131	1890–1530
Enclosure ditch (N) – charcoal	BM–793	4048±54	2856–2496
	BM–792	4058±71	2862–2494
	BM–791	3891±66	2470–2291
	BM–790	3619±55	2119–1911
	BM–789	3459±53	1881–1701
	BM–788	3506±55	1911–1749
Timber structure, primary			
– charcoal	BM–663	3911±89	2564–2289
– antler	BM–666	3941±72	2570–2352
– antler	BM–667	3988±84	2606–2458
Stone cove – charcoal	BM–668	3630±60	2131–1921
Palisade – antler	BM–662	3637±63	2133–1928
– charcoal	BM–665	3645±43	2130–1961
Palisade trench pit – bone	BM–794	3956±45	2565–2459

Conquer Barrow, Dorset

Ditch – antler	BM–795	4077±52	2863–2507

Silbury Hill, Wilts.

Primary core – unburnt vegetation	I–4136	4095±95	2878–2498
Secondary mound – turf	BM–841	3849±43	2456–2280
Secondary ditch – antler	BM–842	3752±50	2280–2047

West Kennet Palisades, Wilts.

Enclosure 1 – charcoal	BM–2597	3810±50	2345–2147
– charcoal	BM–2602	3620±50	2115–1920

Beaker Contexts from Settlements
Knap Hill, Wilts.

Upper fill in ditch of causewayed camp	BM–208	3790±130	2460–2040

Durrington Walls, Wilts.

Hearth above primary silt	BM–285	3560±120	2123–1750

Windmill Hill, Wilts.

Upper fill in ditch of causewayed camp	BM–75	3500±150	2030–1670

Stonehenge, Wilts.

Burial in ditch	BM–1582	3715±70	2271–2033

Mount Pleasant, Dorset

Primary silt in main ditch	BM–645	3734±41	2201–2045
	BM–646	3728±59	2272–2039
Occupation in silted ditch	BM–664	3410±131	1890–1530

Round Barrow Burials
Amesbury 39, Wilts.

Charcoal from pyre beneath barrow	HAR–1237	3620±90	2135–1885

Amesbury 51, Wilts.

Charcoal with burial	BM–287	3738±55	2275–2042

Amesbury 55, Wilts.

Charcoal from loam core of barrow	HAR–6226	3310±80	1731–1516

Amesbury 61, Wilts.

Cremation grave 2 charcoal	HAR–6225	3550±80	2028–1771
Burnt area – charcoal	HAR–6227	3520±100	2019–1740

Amesbury 71, Wilts.

Phase II (Beaker?) – charcoal	NPL–77	3960±110	2600–2330
Phase III (Food vessel) – charcoal	NPL–75	3590±90	2123–1787

Snail Down, Wilts.

Pyre under barrow with collared urn	NPL–141	3490±90	1937–1696

Bishops Canning 81, Wilts.

	HAR–2998	3540±70	2011–1772
	NPL–130	3745±135	2453–1970
	BM–1585	3766±60	2295–2048

Winterbourne Steepleton, Dorset

Wessex cremation	HAR–5620	3120±120	1520–1260

Edmondsham, Dorset

Wessex cremation	BM–708	3069±45	1414–1269
	BM–709	3477±52	1886–1741

Worgret Heath, Dorset

Bucket urn cremation	NPL–199	3690±90	2202–1959

346

Cowleaze, Dorset

Funerary enclosure	HAR–5622	3410±80	1875–1627
Wessex cremation 2	HAR–5620	3120±120	1520–1260

Milton Lilbourne, Dorset

Barrow 1 – SE grave	HAR–6471	3400±100	1878–1543
Barrow 2 – loam core	HAR–6456	3420±80	1878–1641
	HAR–6472	3590±190	2200–1696
Barrow 4 – loam core	HAR–6455	3380±80	1853–1542
– charcoal spread	HAR–6453	3580±80	2037–1787
– timber baulk	HAR–6454	3780±80	2344–2047
	HAR–6457	3590±90	2123–1787
	HAR–6458	3460±80	1889–1685
Barrow 5 – charcoal from ditch	HAR–6470	3410±80	1875–1627

Chilbolton Down, Hants.

Burial 1 with beaker and earrings	OxA–1072	3740±80	2290–2040
Burial 2 beaker	OxA–1073	3750±80	2340–2050

Later Bronze Age Burials
Simon's Ground, Dorset

Centre of barrow B	NPL–216	3200±90	1599–1411
Urn B 104	BM–697	2439±55	763–406
Centre of barrow C	BM–694	2867±55	1126–945
Urns C42 and C47	BM–696	2664±58	894–802
Urn F18	BM–698	2795±61	1016–898
Urn F47	BM–695	2854±63	1123–926
Urn G32	BM–699	2419±150	790–380
Urn G42	BM–697	2554±47	802–766

Knighton Heath, Dorset

II Burning off of old ground surface	BM–870	3155±49	1511–1409
III Primary burial Urn 54	BM–875	3098±34	1421–1322
Scatter of sherds	BM–871	3073±49	1417–1270
Urn 48	BM–872	3128±52	1446–1327
	BM–873	3139±50	1492–1399
V Urn 52	BM–874	3052±50	1408–1263
Urn 24	BM–875	3118±52	1440–1323

Hadley Barrow, Dorset

Urn: edge of cemetery	BM–1644	2710±40	906–822
Cremation 16	BM–1645	2840±35	1041–937
Cremation 18	BM–1646	2900±40	1160–1020
Cremation 32	BM–1647	2820±40	1023–920
Cremation 38	BM–1648	2810±60	1036–905
Cremation 46	BM–1649	2670±45	891–806

South Lodge, Dorset

Barrow 1	BM–1917R	3010±120	1420–1060
	BM–1918R	2900±150	1376–910
	BM–1919R	3140±120	1520–1269
	BM–2024R	2960±120	1395–1000
Barrow 2	BM–1920R	2890±120	1270–910
	BM–2023R	2900±110	1270–930

Kimpton, Hants.

Phase C (Barrel urns)	HAR–4316	3560±180	2182–1680
	HAR–4320	3470±110	1940–1680
	HAR–4317	2970±100	1389–1030
Phase D (Globular and bucket)	HAR–4572	3110±90	1507–1269
Phase F (Globular and bucket)	HAR–4319	3200±70	1526–1419

Later Bronze Age Settlements
Chalton, Hants.

Charcoal from floor of house	BM–583	3193±69	1524–1417

Shearplace Hill, Dorset

Charcoal from occupation	NPL–19	3130±180	1610–1165

Poundbury, Dorset

Occupation	HAR–993	3380±70	1750–1613
	HAR–994	3030±90	1416–1137

South Lodge Camp, Dorset

Enclosure phase, post–hole	BM–1921R	3240±120	1680–1420
	BM–1922R	3110±110	1510–1260

Rowden, Dorset

Storage pit 722	HAR–5548	2940±70	1266–1034
	HAR–5698	2920±80	1264–1003
Post–hole 841	HAR–5249	2920±80	1264–1003

Down Farm, Dorset

Lowest midden in ditch	BM–1851R	2950±100	1376–1010
Secondary midden in ditch	BM–1850R	2900±160	1382–900
Latest midden in ditch	BM–1853N	2980±50	1311–1130
	BM–2577	2980±50	1311–1130
	BM–1854R	3030±110	1420–1107

Rams Hill, Berks.

Double palisade – charcoal	HAR–228	3020±90	1412–1130
– ash	HAR–229	2960±80	1314–1043
Feature cutting primary entrance			
– charcoal	HAR–230	2690±70	910–805
	HAR–231	3000±90	1401–1099
Palisade packing – charcoal	HAR–232	3010±70	1395–1137

349

Settlements, etc.
Chalton, Hants.

Occupation	BM–583	3193±69	1524–1417

Shearplace Hill, Dorset

Occupation	NPL–19	3130±180?	1610–1165

Poundbury, Dorset

Occupation	HAR–993	3380±70	1750–1613
	HAR–994	3030±90	1416–1137

South Lodge Camp, Dorset

Enclosure phase post–hole	BM–1921R	3240±120	1680–1420
	BM–1922R	3110±110	1510–1260

Rowden, Dorset

Storage pit 722	HAR–5548	2940±70	1266–1034
	HAR–5698	2920±80	1264–1003
Post–hole 841	HAR–5249	2920±80	1264–1003

Down Farm, Dorset

Lower midden in ditch	BM–1851R	2950±100	1376–1010
Secondary midden in ditch	BM–1850R	2900±160	1382–900
Latest midden in ditch	BM–1853N	2980±50	1311–1130
	BM–2577	2980±50	1311–1130
	BM–1854R	3030±110	1420–1107

Wilsford Shaft, Wilts.

Wood from bottom of shaft	NPL–74	3330±90	1740–1518
Lower fill, 5 grouped dates	OxA(WS1)	3151±29	1446–1415
Upper fill, 4 grouped dates	OxA(WS2)	2413±32	751–405

Abbreviations

Ann. Rep. Univ. London Int. Arch.	Annual Report of the University of London Institute of Archaeology
Antiq. Journ.	Antiquaries Journal
Arch. Journ.	Archaeological Journal
Archaeol. Rev.	Archaeological Review
BAR Brit. Series	British Archaeological Reports: British Series
BAR Supp. Series	British Archaeological Reports: Supplementary Series
Berks. Arch. Journ.	*Berkshire Archaeological Journal*
BM Occ. Papers	British Museum Occasional Papers
Bull. B. Celtic Stud.	*Bulletin of the Board of Celtic Studies*
CBA Res. Rep.	Council for British Archaeology Research Reports
Current Archaeol.	*Current Archaeology*
DOE Archaeol. Rep. 10	*Department of Environment Archaeological Report Series*
Dorset Nat. Hist. and Arch. Soc. Mono.	Monograph of the Dorset Natural History and Archaeological Society
English Hist. Rev.	*English Historical Review*
Hants. Field Club Mono.	Monograph of the Hampshire Field Club and Archaeological Society
HBMC	Historic Buildings and Monuments Commission
Journ. Archaeol. Sci.	*Journal of Archaeological Sciences*
Journ. Celtic Studies	*Journal of Celtic Studies*
Med. Archaeol.	*Medieval Archaeology*
OUCA Mono.	Oxford University Committee for Archaeology Monographs
Oxford Journ. Archaeol.	*Oxford Journal of Archaeology*
Proc. Brit. Acad.	*Proceedings of the British Academy*
Proc. Dorset Nat. Hist. & Arch. Soc.	*Proceedings of the Dorset Natural History and Archaeological Society*

Proc. Hants. Fld. Club & Archaeol. Soc.	Proceedings of the Hampshire Field Club *and Archaeological Society*
Proc. IOW Arch. Nat. Hist. Soc.	Proceedings of the Isle of Wight *Archaeological and Natural History Society*
Proc. Prehist. Soc.	Proceedings of the Prehistoric Society
Proc. Somerset Arch. & Nat. Hist. Soc.	Proceedings of the Somerset *Archaeological & Natural History Society*
Proc. Univ. Bristol Spelaeol. Soc.	Proceedings of the University of Bristol *Spelaeological Society*
RCHM(E)	Royal Commission on Historical Monuments, England
Rescue Archaeol Hants.	*Rescue Archaeology in Hampshire*
Soc. Ant. Res. Rep.	Society of Antiquaries Research Report
Soc. Med. Archaeol. Mono.	Monograph of the Society for Medieval Archaeology
Sussex Arch. Coll.	*Sussex Archaeological Collections*
Wilts. Arch. Mag.	*Wiltshire Archaeological Magazine*
World Archaeol.	*World Archaeology*

Bibliography

Aaby, B. (1976) 'Cyclic climatic variations in climate over the past 5,500 yr. reflected in raised bogs', *Nature* **263**, 281–4.

Addyman, P. V. and Leigh, D. (1973) 'The Anglo-Saxon village at Chalton, Hampshire', *Med. Archaeol.* **17**, 1–25.

Aitken, G. M. (1968) 'Third interim report on excavations at Whitcombe, Dorset', *Proc. Dorset Nat. Hist. and Arch. Soc.* **89**, 126–7.

Alcock, L. (1972) *By South Cadbury is that Camelot* (London).

Allen, D. F. (1968) 'Iron currency bars in Britain', *Proc. Prehist. Soc.* **33**, 307–35.

Andrews, P. (ed.) (1988) *Southampton Finds Volume One. The Coins and Pottery from Hamwic* (Southampton).

Annable, F. K. (1959) 'Black Field Mildenhall', *Wilts. Arch. Mag.* **57**, 233–5.

Annable, F. K. (1962) 'A Romano-British pottery in Savernake Forest. Kilns 1–2', *Wilts. Arch. Mag.* **58**, 143–55.

Applebaum, S. (1966) 'Peasant economy and types of agriculture', pp. 99–107 in Thomas, A. C. (ed.) 1966.

ApSimon, A. M. (1950) 'Gorsey Bigbury, the second report', *Proc. Univ. Bristol Spelaeol. Soc.* **6**, 186–99.

ApSimon, A. M. (1954) 'Dagger graves in the Wessex Bronze Age', *Ann. Rep. Univ. London Inst. Arch.* **10**, 37–62.

ApSimon, A. M., Gamble, C. S. and Shackley, M. L. (1977) 'Pleistocene raised beaches on Ports Down, Hampshire', *Proc. Hants. Fld. Club and Archaeol. Soc.* **33**, 17–32.

Arnold, C. (1982) *The Anglo-Saxon Cemeteries of the Isle of Wight* (London).

Arnold, J., Green, M., Lewis, B. and Bradley, R. (1988) 'The Mesolithic of Cranborne Chase', *Proc. Dorset Nat. Hist. and Arch. Soc.* **110**, 117–26.

Ashbee, P. (1960) *The Bronze Age Round Barrow in Britain* (London).

Ashbee, P. (1966) 'The Fussell's Lodge long barrow excavations 1957', *Archaeologia* **100**, 1–80.

Ashbee, P. (1970) *The Earthen Long Barrow in Britain* (London).

Ashbee, P. (1984) 'The excavation of Amesbury Barrows 58, 61a, 61, 72', *Wilts. Arch. Mag.* **79**, 39–91.

Ashbee, P. (1986) 'The Excavation of Milton Lilbourne Barrows 1–5', *Wilts. Arch. Mag.* **80**, 23–96.

Ashbee, P. (1987) 'Hook, Warsash, Hampshire, excavations 1954', *Proc. Hants. Fld. Club and Archaeol. Soc.* 43, 21–62.

Ashbee, P., Bell, M. and Proudfoot, E. (1989) *Wilsford Shaft: Excavations 1960–62* (London: HBMC Arch. Rep. 11).

Ashbee, P. and Simpson, D. D. A. (1969) 'Timber mortuary houses and earthen long barrows again', *Antiquity* 43, 43–5.

Ashbee, P., Smith, I. F. and Evans, J. G. (1979) 'Excavation of three long barrows near Avebury, Wilts.', *Proc. Prehist. Soc.* 45, 207–300.

Ashworth, H. (1970) *Report on Romano-British Settlement and Metallurgical Site, Vespasians Farm, Green Ore.*

Aston, M. (1982) 'The medieval pattern: 1000–1500 AD', pp. 123–33 in Aston, M. and Burrow I. (eds) 1982.

Aston, M. (1984) 'The towns of Somerset', pp. 167–202 in Haslam, J. (ed.) 1984a.

Aston, M. and Burrow, I. (eds) (1982) *The Archaeology of Somerset* (Taunton).

Atkinson, R. J. C. (1956) *Stonehenge* (London).

Atkinson, R. J. C. (1965) 'Wayland's Smithy', *Antiquity* 39, 126–33.

Atkinson, R. J. C. (1968) 'Old mortality: some aspects of burial and population in Neolithic England', pp. 83–93 in Coles, J. M. and Simpson, D. D. A. (eds), *Studies in Ancient Europe* (Leicester).

Atkinson, R. J. C. (1972) 'Burial and population in the British Bronze Age', pp. 107–16 in Lynch, F. and Burgess, C. (eds), *Prehistoric Man in Wales and the West* (Bath).

Atkinson, R. J. C. (1978) 'Silbury Hill', pp. 159–73 in Sutcliffe, R. (ed.), *Chronicle Essays from 10 Years of Television Archaeology* (London).

Barfield, L. H. (1991) 'Wessex with and without Mycenae: new evidence from Switzerland', *Antiquity* 65, 102–7.

Barker, C. T. (1985) 'The long mounds of the Avebury region', *Wilts. Arch. and Nat. Hist. Mag.* 79, 7–38.

Barker, G. and Webley, D. (1978) 'Causewayed camps and early neolithic economies in central southern England', *Proc. Prehist. Soc.* 44, 161–86.

Barrett, A. A. (1979) 'The career of Tiberius Claudius Cogidubnus', *Britannia* 10, 227–42.

Barrett, J. (1976) 'Deverel-Rimbury: problems of chronology and interpretation', pp. 289–307 in Burgess, C. and Miket, R. (eds), *Settlement and Economy in the Third and Second Millennia BC* (BAR Brit. Series 33: Oxford).

Barrett, J. (1980) 'The pottery of the Later Bronze Age in lowland England', *Proc. Prehist. Soc.* 46, 297–319.

Barrett, J. (1987) 'The Glastonbury Lake Village: models and source criticism', *Arch. Journ.* 144, 409–23.

Barrett, J. C. (1990) 'The monumentality of death: the character of Early Bronze Age mortuary mounds in southern Britain', *World Archaeol.* 22, 179–89.

Barrett, J. and Bradley, R. (eds) (1980a) *The British Later Bronze Age* (BAR Brit. Series 83: Oxford).

Barrett, J. and Bradley, R. (1980b) 'Later Bronze Age settlement in South Wessex and Cranborne Chase', pp. 181–207 in Barrett, J. and Bradley, R. (eds) 1980a.

Barrett, J., Bradley, R., Bowden, M. and Mead, B. (1983) 'South Lodge after Pitt Rivers', *Antiquity* 57, 193–204.

Barrett, J., Bradley, R. and Green, M. (1991) *Landscape, Monuments and Society. The Prehistory of Cranborne Chase* (Cambridge).

Barton, R. N. E. (1992) *Hengistbury Head, Dorset. Vol. 2 The Late Upper Palaeolithic and Early Mesolithic Sites* (OUCA Mono. 34: Oxford).

Bately, J. (1978) 'The compilation of the Anglo-Saxon Chronicle 60 BC–AD 890: vocabulary as evidence', *Proc. Brit. Acad.* 64, 93–129.

Bedwin, O. (1978) 'Excavations inside Harting Beacon hill-fort, 1976', *Sussex Archaeol. Coll.* 116, 225–40.

Bedwin, O. (1979) 'Excavations at Harting Beacon, West Sussex: second season', *Sussex Archaeol. Coll.* 117, 21–36.

Bell, M. (1990) *Brean Down Excavations 1983–1987* (HBMC Arch. Reps. 15: London).

Bender, B. (1978) 'Gatherer-hunter to farmer: a social perspective', *World Archaeol.* 10, 204–22.

Bersu, G. (1940) 'Excavations at Little Woodbury, Wilts.; part 1', *Proc. Prehist. Soc.* 6, 30–111.

Biddle, M. (1967) 'Two Flavian burials from Grange Road, Winchester', *Antiq. Journ.* 47, 224–50.

Biddle, M. (1975) 'Ptolemaic coins from Winchester', *Antiquity* 49, 213–15.

Biddle, M. (1976) 'Hampshire and the origins of Wessex', pp. 323–41 in Sieveking, G. de G., Longworth, I. H. and Wilson, K. E. (eds), *Problems in Economic and Social Archaeology* (London).

Biddle, M. (1983) 'The study of Winchester: archaeology and history in a British town, 1961–1983', *Proc. Brit. Acad.* 69, 93–135.

Biddle, M. (1986) 'Archaeology, architecture, and the cult of saints in Anglo-Saxon England', pp. 1–31 in Butler, L. A. S. and Morris, R. K. (eds) 1986.

Biddle, M. and Hill, D. (1971) 'Late Saxon planned towns', *Antiq. Journ.* 51, 70–85.

Bishop, M. J. (1975) 'Earliest record of man's presence in Britain', *Nature* 273 (5487), 95–7.

Blair, J. (ed.) (1988a) *Minsters and Parish Churches. The Local Church in Transition 950–1200* (OUCA Mono. 17: Oxford).

Blair, J. (1988b) 'Introduction: from minster to parish church', pp. 1–20 in Blair, J. (ed.) 1988a.

Bogaers, J. E. (1979) 'King Cogidubnus: another reading of RIB 91', *Britannia* 10, 243–54.

Bonney, D. J. (1964) 'Rybury Camp', *Wilts. Arch. Mag.* 59, 185.

Bonney, D. J. (1967) 'Hamshill Ditches, Barford St. Martin', *Wilts. Arch. Mag.* 62, 118–20.

Bonney, D. J. (1973) 'The pagan Saxon period c. 500–c. 700', pp. 465–84 in Crittall, E. (ed.), *A History of Wiltshire Vol. I part 2* (Oxford).

Boon, G. (1974) *Silchester, the Roman town of Calleva* (Newton Abbot).

Bowen, H. C. (1990) *The Archaeology of Bokerley Dyke* (London).

Bowen, H. C. and Fowler, P. J. (1966) 'Romano-British rural settlements in Dorset and Wiltshire', pp. 43–67 in Thomas, A. C. (ed.) 1966.

Bradley, R. (1976) 'Maumbury Rings, Dorchester: the excavations of 1908–1913', *Archaeologia* 105, 1–98.

Bradley, R. (1978) 'Colonization and land use in the Late Neolithic and Early Bronze Age', pp. 95–102 in Limbrey, S. and Evans, J. G. (eds) 1978.

Bradley, R. (1980) 'Subsistence, exchange and technology – a social framework for the Bronze Age in Southern England *c.* 1400–700 bc', pp. 57–75 in Barrett, J. and Bradley, R. (eds) 1980a.

Bradley, R. (1981) 'Various styles of urn: cemeteries and settlement in southern England *c.* 1400–1000 BC', pp. 93–104 in Chapman, R. W., Kinnes, I. and Randsborg, K. (eds), *The Archaeology of Death* (Cambridge).

Bradley, R. (1982) 'Position and possession: assemblage variation in the British Neolithic', *Oxford Journ. Arch.* **1**, 27–38.

Bradley, R. (1983) 'The bank barrows and related monuments of Dorset in the light of recent fieldwork', *Proc. Dorset Nat. Hist. and Arch. Soc.* **105**, 15–20.

Bradley, R. (1986) *The Dorset Cursus: The Archaeology of the Enigmatic* (CBA: Salisbury).

Bradley, R., Cleal, R., Gardiner, J. and Green, M. (1984) 'The Neolithic sequence in Cranborne Chase', pp. 87–106 in Bradley, R. and Gardiner, J. (eds) 1984.

Bradley, R. and Ellison, A. (1975) *Rams Hill: a Bronze Age Defended Enclosure and its Landscape* (BAR Brit. Series 19: Oxford).

Bradley, R. and Entwistle, R. (1985) 'Thickthorn Down long barrow – a new assessment', *Proc. Dorset Nat. Hist. and Arch. Soc.* **107**, 174–6.

Bradley, R. and Gardiner, J. (eds) (1984) *Neolithic Studies. A Review of Some Current Research* (BAR Brit. Series 133: Oxford).

Bradley, R. and Hooper, B. (1975) 'Recent discoveries from Portsmouth and Langstone Harbours: Mesolithic to Iron Age', *Proc. Hants. Fld. Club and Archaeol. Soc.* **30**, 17–27.

Bradley, R. and Lewis, E. (1974) 'A Mesolithic site at Wakeford's Copse, Havant', *Rescue Archaeol. Hants.* **2**, 5–18.

Branigan, K. (1974) 'Vespasian and the South-West', *Proc. Dorset Nat. Hist. and Arch. Soc.* **95**, 50–7.

Branigan, K. (1976a) 'Villa Settlement in the West Country', pp. 120–41 in Branigan, K. and Fowler, P. J. (eds) 1976.

Branigan, K. (1976b) *The Roman Villa in South-West England* (Bradford-on-Avon).

Branigan, K. (1977) *Gatcombe Roman Villa* (BAR Brit. Series 44: Oxford).

Branigan, K. and Fowler, P. J. (eds) (1976) *The Roman West Country. Classical Culture and Celtic Society* (Newton Abbot).

Brisbane, M. (1988) 'Hamwic (Saxon Southampton): an 8th century port and production centre', pp. 101–8 in Hodges, R. and Hobley, B. (eds), *The Rebirth of Towns in the West AD 700–1050* (CBA Res. Rep. no. 68: London).

Brooks, N. (1964) 'The unidentified forts of the Burghal', *Med. Archaeol.* **8**, 74–90.

Bulleid, A. and Gray, H. S. G. (1911, 1917) *The Glastonbury Lake Village* Vols 1 and 2 (Glastonbury).

Bulleid, A. and Gray, H. S. G. (1948) *The Meare Lake Village* Vol. 1 (Taunton).

Burgess, C. (1969) 'The later Bronze Age in the British Isles and North-Western France', *Arch. Journ.* **125**, 1–45.

Burgess, C. (1974) 'The Bronze Age', pp. 165–232 in Renfrew, C. (ed.), *British Prehistory: A New Outline* (London).

Burgess, C. (1980a) 'The Bronze Age in Wales', pp. 243–86 in Taylor, J. A. (ed.), *Culture and Environment in Prehistoric Wales* (BAR Brit. Series 76: Oxford).

Burgess, C. (1980b) *The Age of Stonehenge* (London).

Burgess, C. and Shennan, S. (1976) 'The Beaker phenomenon: some suggestions', pp.

309–31 in Burgess, C. and Miket, R. (eds), *Settlement and Economy in the Third and Second Millennia BC* (BAR 33: Oxford).

Burl, A. (1979) *Prehistoric Avebury* (London).

Burl, A. (1987) *The Stonehenge People* (London).

Burl, H. A. W. (1969) 'Henges: internal features and regional groups', *Arch. Journ.* 126, 1–28.

Burrow, I. C. G. (1981) *Hillfort and Hill-Top Settlement in Somerset in the First Millennium AD* (BAR 91: Oxford).

Bushe-Fox, J. P. (1915) *Excavations at Hengistbury Head, Hampshire in 1911–12* (Soc. Ant. Res. Rep. 3: London).

Butler, L. A. S. and Morris, R. K. (eds.) (1986) *The Anglo-Saxon Church* (CBA Res. Rep. no. 60: London).

Calkin, J. B. (1948) 'The Isle of Purbeck in the Iron Age', *Proc. Dorset Nat. Hist. and Arch. Soc.* 70, 29–59.

Calkin, J. B. (1955) 'Kimmeridge coal-money. The Romano-British shale armlet industry', *Proc. Dorset Nat. Hist. and Arch. Soc.* 75, 45–71.

Calkin, J. B. (1959) 'Some archaeological discoveries in the Isle of Purbeck. Part II', *Proc. Dorset Nat. Hist. and Arch. Soc.* 81, 114–23.

Calkin, J. B. (1964) 'The Bournemouth area in the Middle and Late Bronze Age, with the Deverel-Rimbury problem reconsidered', *Arch. Journ* 109, 1–65.

Calkin, J. B. and Green, J. F. N. (1949) 'Palaeoliths and terraces near Bournemouth', *Proc. Prehist. Soc.* 15, 21–37.

Campbell, J. A., Baxter, M. S. and Alcock, L. (1979) 'Radiocarbon dates for the Cadbury massacre', *Antiquity* 53, 31–8.

Campbell, J. B. (1970) 'The Upper Palaeolithic period', pp. 5–11 in Campbell, J., Elkington, D., Fowler, P. and Grinsell, L., *The Mendip Hills in Prehistoric and Roman Times* (Bristol).

Campbell, J. B. (1977) *The Upper Palaeolithic of Britain. A Study of Man and Nature in the Late Ice Age* (Oxford).

Care, V. (1979) 'The production and distribution of Mesolithic axes in Southern England', *Proc. Prehist. Soc.* 45, 93–102.

Case, H. J. (1969) 'Neolithic explanations', *Antiquity* 43, 176–86.

Case, H. J. (1977) 'The Beaker culture in Britain and Ireland', pp. 71–101 in Mercer, R. (ed.), *Beakers in Britain and Europe* (BAR Supp. Series 26: Oxford).

Catherall, P. D. (1971) 'Henges in perspective', *Arch. Journ.* 128, 147–53.

Chadwick, S. and Thompson, M. W. (1956) 'Note on an Iron Age habitation site near Battlesbury Camp, Warminster', *Wilts. Arch. Mag.* 56, 262–4.

Champion, T. C. (1977) 'Chalton', *Current Archaeol.* 59, 364–71.

Christie, P. M. (1967) 'A barrow-cemetery of the second millennium BC in Wiltshire, England', *Proc. Prehist. Soc.* 33, 336–66.

Churchill, D. M. (1962) 'The stratigraphy of the Mesolithic sites III and V at That-cham, Berkshire', *Proc. Prehist. Soc.* 28, 362–70.

Clare, T. (1986) 'Towards a reappraisal of henge monuments', *Proc. Prehist. Soc* 52, 281–316.

Clare, T. (1987) 'Towards a reappraisal of henge monuments: origins, evolutions and hierarchies', *Proc. Prehist. Soc.* 53, 457–78.

Clark, J. G. D. (1938) 'Microlithic industries from the tufa deposits at Prestatyn, Flintshire and Blashenwell, Dorset', *Proc. Prehist. Soc.* 4, 330–4.

Clarke, D. L. (1970) *Beaker Pottery of Great Britain and Ireland* (Cambridge).

Clarke, D. L. (1972) 'A provisional model of an Iron Age Society and its settlement systems', pp. 801–70 in Clarke, D. L. (ed.), *Models in Archaeology* (London).

Clarke, D. L. (1976) 'The Beaker network – social and economic models', pp. 460–77 in Lanting, J. N. and van der Waals, J. D. (eds), *Glockenbecher Symposion* (Bussum/Haarlem).

Clarke, G. (1979) *The Roman Cemetery at Lankhills* (Oxford).

Coles, B. J. and Coles, J. M. (1986) *Sweet Track to Glastonbury* (London).

Coles, B. J. and Coles, J. M. (1990) 'The Sweet Track date', *Antiquity* 64, 216–20.

Coles, J. M. (1987) *Meare Village East. The Excavations of A. Bulleid and H. St. George Gray 1932–1956 (Somerset Levels Papers* 13).

Coles, J. M. (1989) 'Prehistoric settlement in the Somerset Levels', *Somerset Levels Papers* 15, 14–33.

Coles, J. M., Hibbert, F. A. and Orme, B. J. (1973) 'Prehistoric roads and tracks in Somerset: 3 The Sweet Track', *Proc. Prehist. Soc.* 39, 256–93.

Coles, J. M. and Orme, B. J. (1976) 'The Sweet Track, Railway Site', *Somerset Levels Papers* 2, 34–65.

Coles, J. M. and Orme, B. J. (1984) 'Ten excavations along the Sweet Track (3200 bc)', *Somerset Levels Papers* 10, 5–45.

Collingwood, R. G. and Myres, J. N. L. (1930) *Roman Britain and the English Settlements* (Oxford), 323–4.

Collins, J., Field, N. and Light, A. (1984) 'Excavations at Bucknowle 1984', *Proc. Dorset Nat. Hist. and Arch. Soc.* 106, 116–17.

Collins, J., Field, N. and Light, A. (1989) 'Bucknowle 1989', *Proc. Dorset Nat. Hist. and Arch. Soc.* 111, 107.

Collis, J. R. (1968) 'Excavations at Owslebury, Hants.', *Antiq. Journ.* 48, 18–31.

Connah, G. (1969) 'Radiocarbon dating for Knap Hill', *Antiquity* 43, 304–5.

Cook, A. M. and Dacre, M. W. (1985) *Excavations at Portway, Andover, 1973–1975* (OUCA Mono. 4: Oxford).

Cook, J. (1982) 'Traces of Early Man 600,000–50,000 BC', pp. 5–9 in Aston, M. and Burrow, I. (eds) 1982.

Corney, M. (1984) 'Field survey of the extra-mural region of Silchester' pp. 239–97 in Fulford, M. (ed.) 1984.

Cotton, M. A. and Gathercole, P. W. (1958) *Excavations at Clausentum, Southampton 1951–1954* (London).

Crummy, P. (1979) 'The system of measurement used in town planning from the ninth to the thirteenth centuries', *Anglo-Saxon Studies in Archaeology and History* 1 (= BAR Brit. Series 72: Oxford), 149–64.

Cummins, W. A. (1979) 'Neolithic stone axes: distributions and trade in England and Wales', pp. 5–12 in Cummins, W. A. (ed.), *Stone Axe Studies* (CBA Res. Rep. 23).

Cunliffe, B. (1964) *Winchester Excavations 1949–60 Volume 1* (Winchester).

Cunliffe, B. (1967) 'Excavations at Gatcombe, Somerset, in 1965 and 1966', *Proc. Univ. Bristol Spelaeol. Soc.* 11, 126–60.

Cunliffe, B. (1970) 'A Bronze Age settlement at Chalton, Hants. (Site 78)', *Antiq. Journ.* 50, 1–13.

Cunliffe, B. (1971a) 'Some aspects of hillforts and their cultural environments', pp.

53–70 in Hill, D. and Jesson, M. (eds), *The Iron Age and its Hill-Forts* (Southampton).

Cunliffe, B. (1971b) *Excavations at Fishbourne 1961–1969* (Soc. Ant. Res. Rep. 26: London).

Cunliffe, B. (1972) 'Saxon and medieval settlement-pattern in the region of Chalton, Hampshire', *Med. Archaeol.* **16**, 1–12.

Cunliffe, B. W. (1973a) 'Chalton, Hants.: The evolution of a landscape', *Antiq. Journ.* **53**, 173–90.

Cunliffe, B. W. (1973b) *The Regni* (London).

Cunliffe, B. (1973c) 'The Late pre Roman Iron Age (in Wiltshire)', in Crittall, E. (ed.), Victoria County History of Wiltshire Vol. 1 part 2 (London).

Cunliffe, B. (1975) *Excavations at Portchester Castle. Vol. 1: Roman* (Soc. Ant. Res. Rep. 32: London).

Cunliffe, B. (ed.) (1976a) *Excavations at Portchester Castle. Vol. II: Saxon* (Soc. Ant. Res. Rep. 33: London).

Cunliffe, B. (1976b) 'The origins of urbanization in Britain', pp. 135–61 in Cunliffe, B. and Rowley, T. (eds), *Oppida: The Beginnings of Urbanization in Barbarian Europe* (BAR Supp. Series 11: Oxford).

Cunliffe, B. (1977) 'The Romano-British village at Chalton, Hants.', *Proc. Hants. Fld. Club and Archaeol. Soc.* **33**, 45–67.

Cunliffe, B. (1978a) *Hengistbury Head* (London).

Cunliffe, B. (1978b) *Iron Age Communities in Britain* (2nd edn.: London).

Cunliffe, B. W. (1978c) 'Chichester: the first hundred years', pp. 177–83 in Down, A., *Chichester Excavations Vol. 3* (Chichester).

Cunliffe, B. (1982) 'Britain, the Veneti and beyond', *Oxford Journ. Archaeol.* **1**(1), 39–68.

Cunliffe, B. (ed.) (1984a) *Danebury. An Iron Age Hillfort in Hampshire.* Vol. 1 *The Excavations 1969–1978: The Site.* Vol. 2 *The Excavations 1969–1978: The Finds* (CBA Res. Rep. 52: London).

Cunliffe, B. (1984b) 'Iron Age Wessex: continuity and change', pp. 12–45 in Cunliffe, B. and Miles, D. (eds) 1984.

Cunliffe, B. (1984c) 'Relations between Britain and Gaul in the first century BC and early first century AD', pp. 3–23 in Macready, S. and Thompson, F. H. (eds) 1984.

Cunliffe, B. (1984d) 'Saxon Bath', pp. 345–58 in Haslam, J. (ed.) 1984a.

Cunliffe, B. (1987) *Hengistbury Head, Dorset. Volume 1 The Prehistoric and Roman Settlement, 3500 BC–AD 500* (OUCA Mono. 13: Oxford).

Cunliffe, B. (ed.) (1988) *The Temple of Sulis Minerva at Bath. Volume 2: The Finds from the Sacred Spring* (OUCA Mono. 16: Oxford).

Cunliffe, B. (1989) 'The Roman Tholos from the Sanctuary of Sulis Minerva at Bath, England', pp. 59–71 in Curtis, R. I. (ed.), *Studia Classica* (New York).

Cunliffe, B. (1990) 'Before hillforts', *Oxford Journ. Archaeol.* **9**, 323–36.

Cunliffe, B. (1991) *Iron Age Communities in Britain* (3rd edn: London).

Cunliffe, B. and Davenport, P. (1985) *The Temple of Sulis Minerva at Bath. I(1) The Site* (OUCA Mono. 7: Oxford).

Cunliffe, B. and Miles, D. (eds) (1984) *Aspects of the Iron Age in Central Southern Britain* (OUCA Mono. 2: Oxford).

Cunliffe, B. and Orton, C. (1984) 'Radiocarbon age assessment', pp. 190–8 in Cunliffe, B. (ed.) 1984a.

Cunliffe, B. and Phillipson, D. W. (1968) 'Excavations at Eldon's Seat, Encombe, Dorset', *Proc. Prehist. Soc.* 34, 191–237.

Cunliffe, B. and Poole, C. (1991) *Danebury. An Iron Age Hillfort in Hampshire.* Vol. 4 *The Excavations of 1979–1988: The Site* (CBA Res. Rep. 52: London).

Cunnington, M. E. (1908) 'Oliver's Camp, Devizes', *Wilts. Arch. Mag.* 35, 408–44.

Cunnington, M. E. (1912) 'Knap Hill Camp', *Wilts. Arch. Mag.* 37, 42–65.

Cunnington, M. E. (1917) 'Lidbury Camp', *Wilts. Arch. Mag.* 40, 12–36.

Cunnington, M. E. (1923) *The Early Iron Age Inhabited Site at All Cannings Cross Farm, Wiltshire* (Devizes).

Cunnington, M. E. (1929) *Woodhenge* (Devizes).

Cunnington, M. E. (1931) 'The "Sanctuary" on Overton Hill, near Avebury', *Wilts. Arch. Mag.* 45, 300–35.

Cunnington, M. E. (1933) 'Excavations at Yarnbury Castle Camp, 1932', *Wilts. Arch. Mag.* 46, 198–213.

Currant, A. P., Jacobi, R. M. and Stringer, C. B. (1989) 'Excavations at Gough's Cave, Somerset, 1986–7', *Antiquity* 63, 131–6.

Dacre, M. and Ellison, A. (1981) 'A Bronze Age urn cemetery at Kimpton, Hampshire', *Proc. Prehist. Soc.* 47, 147–203.

Dacre, M. and Warmington, R. (1977) 'Saxon site at Charlton, Andover', *Hants. Field Club Newsletter* 7, 22.

Darvill, T. C. (1982) *The Megalithic Chambered Tombs of the Cotswold-Severn Region* (Highworth).

Davies, H. (1936) 'The shale industries at Kimmeridge, Dorset', *Arch. Journ.* 93, 200–19.

Davies, S. M. (1980) 'Excavations at Old Down Farm, Andover. Part I: Saxon', *Proc. Hants. Fld. Club and Archaeol. Soc.* 36, 161–80.

Davies, S. M. (1981) 'Excavations at Old Down Farm, Andover. Part II: prehistoric and Roman', *Proc. Hants. Fld. Club and Archaeol. Soc.* 37, 81–163.

Davis, R. H. C. (1982) 'Alfred's and Guthrum's frontier', *English Hist. Rev.* 97, 803–10.

Delair, J. B. and Shackley, M. L. (1978) 'The Fisherton Brick pits: their stratigraphy and fossil contents', *Wilts. Arch. Mag.* 73, 3–19.

Dennell, R. W. (1976) 'Prehistoric crop cultivation in Southern England: a reconsideration', *Antiq. Journ.* 56, 11–23.

Dickinson, T. M. (1980) 'The present state of Anglo-Saxon cemetery studies', pp. 11–33 in Rahtz, P., Dickinson, T. and Watts, L. (eds), *Anglo-Saxon Cemeteries 1979* (BAR 82: Oxford).

Dimbleby, G. W. (1962) *The Development of British Heathlands and Their Soils* (Oxford).

Dimbleby, G. W. and Evans, J. G. (1974) 'Pollen and land-snail analysis of calcareous soils', *J. Archaeol. Sci.* 1, 117–33.

Downey, R., King, A. and Soffe, G. (1979) *The Hayling Island Temple: Third Interim Report on the Excavation of the Iron Age and Roman Temple 1976–9* (duplicated).

Draper, J. C. (1968) 'Mesolithic distribution in South East Hampshire', *Proc. Hants. Fld. Club and Archaeol. Soc.* 23, 110–19.

Dumville, D. N. (1985) 'The West Saxon Genealogical Regnal List and the chronology of Wessex', *Peritia* 4, 21–66.

Dunning, G. C., Hooley, W. and Tildesley, M. L. (1929) 'Excavation of an Early Iron Age village on Worthy Down, Winchester', *Proc. Hants. Fld. Club and Archaeol. Soc.* 10, 178–92.

Elkington, H. D. H. (1976) 'The Mendip lead industry', pp. 183–97 in Branigan, K. and Fowler, P. J. (eds) 1976.

Ellison, A. (1980) 'Settlements and regional exchange: a case study', pp. 127–40 in Barrett, J. and Bradley, R. (eds) 1980a.

Ellison, A. (1981) 'Towards a socioeconomic model for the Middle Bronze Age in Southern England', pp. 413–38 in Hodder, I., Isaac, G. and Hammond, N. (eds), *Pattern of the Past* (London).

Ellison, A. (1982) 'Bronze Age Societies 2000–650 BC', pp. 43–51 in Aston, M. and Burrow, I. (eds) 1982.

Ellison, A. (1987) 'The Bronze Age settlement at Thorny Down: pots, post-holes and patterning', *Proc. Prehist. Soc.* 53, 385–92.

Ellison, A. and Rahtz, P. (1987) 'Excavations at Hog Cliff Hill, Maiden Newton, Dorset', *Proc. Prehist. Soc.* 53, 223–70.

Evans, J. G. (1968) 'Periglacial deposits on the Chalk of Wiltshire', *Wilts. Arch. Mag.* 63, 12–26.

Evans, J. G. (1971) 'Habitat change on the calcareous soils of Britain: the impact of Neolithic man', pp. 27–74 in Simpson, D. D. A. (ed.), *Economy and Settlement in Neolithic and Early Bronze Age Britain and Europe* (Leicester).

Evans, J. G. (1972) *Land Snails in Archaeology* (London).

Evans, J. G. (1984) 'Stonehenge – the environment in the Late Neolithic and Early Bronze Age and a Beaker burial', *Wilts. Arch. Mag.* 78, 7–30.

Evans, J. G. (1990) 'Notes on some Late Neolithic and Bronze Age events in long barrow ditches in Southern and Eastern England', *Proc. Prehist. Soc.* 56, 111–16.

Evans, J. G. and Smith, I. F. (1983) 'Excavations at Cherhill, North Wiltshire 1967', *Proc. Prehist. Soc.* 49, 43–117.

Evison, V. I. (1978) 'Early Anglo-Saxon applied disc brooches', *Antiq. Journ.* 38, 260–78.

Farrar, R. A. H. (1954) 'A Celtic burial with mirror-handle at West Bay, near Bridport', *Proc. Dorset Nat. Hist. and Arch. Soc.* 76, 90–4.

Farrar, R. A. H. (1973) 'The techniques and sources of Romano-British black burnished ware', pp. 67–103 in Detsicas, A. P. (ed.), *Current Research in Romano-British Coarse Pottery* (CBA Res. Rep. 10: London).

Fasham, P. J. (1985) *The Prehistoric Settlement at Winnall Down, Winchester* (Hants. Field Club Mono. 2: Winchester).

Fasham, P. J. (1987) *A Banjo Enclosure in Micheldever Wood, Hampshire* (Hants. Field Club Mono. 5: Winchester).

Fasham, P. J., Farwell, D. E. and Whinney, R. J. B. (1989) *The Archaeological Site at Easton Lane, Winchester* (Hants. Field Club Mono. 6: Gloucester).

Fasham, P. J. and Schadla-Hall, R. T. (1981) 'The Neolithic and Bronze Ages (in Hampshire)', pp. 26–36 in Shennan, S. J. and Schadla-Hall, R. T. (eds) 1981.

Field, N. H., Matthews, C. L. and Smith, I. F. (1964) 'New Neolithic sites in Dorset and Bedfordshire with a note on the distribution of Neolithic storage pits in Britain', *Proc. Prehist. Soc.* 30, 352–81.

Fleming, A. (1971) 'Territorial patterns in Bronze Age Wessex', *Proc. Prehist. Soc.* 37, 138–66.

Foster, J. (1980) *The Iron Age moulds from Gussage All Saints* (B.M. Occ. Paper 12: London).

Fowler, P. J. (1966) 'Two finds of Saxon domestic pottery in Wiltshire', *Wilts. Arch. Mag.* 61, 31–7.

Fowler, P. J. (1967) 'The archaeology of Fyfield and Overton Downs, Wilts. Third interim report', *Wilts. Arch. Mag.* 62, 16–33.

Fowler, P. J. (1970) 'Fieldwork and excavation in the Butcombe area, N. Somerset', *Proc. Univ. Bristol Spelaeol. Soc.* 12, 169–94.

Fowler, P. J. (1971) 'Hill-forts, A.D. 400–700', pp. 203–13 in Hill, D. and Jesson, M. (eds), *The Iron Age and its Hill-Forts* (Southampton).

Fowler, P. J. (1972) [Note on Bradley Hill, Somerton], pp. 39–41 in *Archaeol. Rev.* 6.

Fowler, P. J. and Evans, J. G. (1967) 'Plough-marks, lynchets and early fields', *Antiquity* 41, 289–301.

Fowler, P. J., Gardner, K. S. and Rahtz, P. A. (1970) *Cadbury-Congresbury 1968* (Bristol).

Fowler, P. J. and Rahtz, P. A. (1970) 'Cadcong 1970', *Current Archaeol.* 23, 337–42.

Fox, C. F. (1928) 'A Bronze Age refuse pit at Swanwick, Hants.', *Antiq. Journ.* 8, 331–6.

Fox, C. F. (1930) 'The Bronze Age pit at Swanwick, Hants. Further finds', *Antiq. Journ.* 10, 30–3.

Fox, C. F. (1958) *Pattern and Purpose: A Survey of Early Celtic Art in Britain* (Cardiff).

Fox, C. and Fox, A. (1960) 'Wansdyke reconsidered', *Arch. Journ.* 115, 1–48.

Frankenstein, S. (1979) 'The Phoenicians in the far west: a function of Assyrian imperialism', pp. 263–94 in Larsen, M. T. (ed.), *Power and Propaganda* (Copenhagen).

Frere, S. S. (1987) *Britannia: A History of Roman Britain* (3rd edn: London).

Froom, F. R. (1972) 'A Mesolithic site at Wawcott, Kintbury', *Berks. Arch. Journ.* 66, 23–44.

Froom, F. R. (1976) *Wawcott III: A Stratified Mesolithic Succession* (BAR Brit. Series 27: Oxford).

Froom, F. R. (1983) 'Recent work at the Lower Palaeolithic site at Knowle Farm, Bedwyn', *Wilts. Arch. Mag.* 77 (1982), 27–37.

Fulford, M. G. (1975) *New Forest Roman Pottery* (BAR Brit. Series 17: Oxford).

Fulford, M. (ed.) (1984) *Silchester Defences 1974–80* (Britannia Mono. 5: London).

Fulford, M. (1987a) 'Calleva Atrebatum: an interim report on the excavation of the Oppidum 1980–86', *Proc. Prehist. Soc.* 53, 271–8.

Fulford, M. (1987b) *Calleva Atrebatum: A Guide to the Roman Town at Silchester* (Gloucester).

Galliou, P. (1984) 'Days of wine and roses? Early Armorica and the Atlantic wine trade', pp. 24–36 in Macready, S. and Thompson, F. H. (eds) 1984.

Gardiner, J. (1985) 'Intra-site patterning in the flint assemblage from the Dorset Cursus 1984', *Proc. Dorset Nat. Hist. and Arch. Soc.* 107, 87–94.

Gardiner, J. (1987) 'Hengistbury and its region. Neolithic and Bronze Age', pp. 329–35 in Cunliffe, B. W. (ed.) 1987.

Gerloff, S. (1975) *The Early Bronze Age Daggers in Great Britain* (Prh. Bronzefunde Abt. VI BD 2: Munich).

Gerloff, S. (1981) 'Westeuropische Griffzungenschwerter in Berlin', *Acta praehistorica et archaeologica* **11/12**, 183–217.

Giles, A. G. (1982) 'Interim report for the excavation of Barton Field, Tarrant Hinton 1982', *Proc. Dorset Nat. Hist. and Arch. Soc.* **104**, 184–6.

Giles, A. G. (1983) 'Notes on the excavation of the Romano-British site at Barton Field, Tarrant Hinton for 1983', *Proc. Dorset Nat. Hist. and Arch. Soc.* **105**, 146–8.

Gingell, C. (1980) 'The Marlborough Downs in the Bronze Age: the first results of current research', pp. 209–22 in Barrett, J. and Bradley, R. (eds) 1980a.

Gingell, C. (1981) 'Excavation of an Iron Age enclosure at Groundwell Farm, Blunsdon St. Andrew, 1976–7', *Wilts. Arch. Mag.* **76**, 33–75.

Gingell, C. J. (1987) 'An earthwork near Badbury Rings in Dorset', *Proc. Dorset Nat. Hist. and Arch. Soc.* **109**, 65–78.

Gingell, C. and Harding, P. (1983) 'A field walking survey in the Vale of Wardour', *Wilts. Arch. Mag.* **77** (1982), 11–25.

Gingell, C. and Lawson, A. J. (1985) 'Excavations at Potterne, 1984', *Wilts. Arch. Mag.* **79**, 101–8.

Godwin, H. (1940) 'Pollen analysis and the forest history of England and Wales', *New Phytologist* **39**, 370–400.

Godwin, H. (1956) *The History of the British Flora* (Cambridge).

Gray, H. S. G. (1966) *The Meare Lake Village Vol. 3* (Taunton).

Gray, H. S. G. and Bulleid, A. (1953) *The Meare Lake Village Vol. 2* (Taunton).

Green, C. (1949) 'The Birdlip Early Iron Age burials: a review', *Proc. Prehist. Soc.* **15**, 188–90.

Green, C. S. (1986) 'Earthworks of Prehistoric and Early Roman date in the Dorchester area', *Proc. Dorset Nat. Hist. and Arch. Soc.* **108**, 193–4.

Green, C. S. (1987) *Excavations at Poundbury. Vol. I: The Settlements* (Dorset Nat. Hist. and Arch. Soc. Mono. 7: Dorchester).

Green, H. S. (1971) 'Wansdyke, excavations 1966 to 1970', *Wilts. Arch. and Nat. Hist. Mag.* **66**, 129–46.

Gresham, C. A. (1939) 'Spettisbury Rings, Dorset', *Arch. Journ.* **96**, 114–31.

Grigson, C. (1981) 'Porridge and pannage: pig husbandry in Neolithic England', pp. 297–314 in Bell, M. and Limbrey, S. (eds), *Archaeological Aspects of Woodland Ecology* (BAR Int. Series 46: Oxford).

Grinsell, L. V. (1958) *The Archaeology of Wessex* (London).

Harding, A. F. and Lee, G. E. (1987) *Henge Monuments and Related Sites of Great Britain* (BAR 175: Oxford).

Harrison, K. (1976) *The Framework of Anglo-Saxon History to AD 900* (Cambridge).

Harrison, R. A. (1977) 'The Uphill Quarry Caves, Weston-Super-Mare, a reappraisal', *Proc. Univ. Bristol. Spelaeol. Soc.* **14**(3), 233–54.

Hase, P. H. (1988) 'The mother churches of Hampshire', pp. 45–66 in Blair, J. (ed.) 1988a.

Haslam, J. (ed.) (1984a) *Anglo-Saxon Towns in Southern England* (Chichester).

Haslam, J. (1984b) 'The towns of Wiltshire', pp. 87–148 in Haslam, J. (ed.) 1984a.

Hawkes, C. F. C. (1939) 'The excavations at Quarley Hill, 1938', *Proc. Hants. Fld. Club and Archaeol. Soc.* 14, 136–49.

Hawkes, C. F. C. (1947) 'Britons, Romans and Saxons round Salisbury and in Cranborne Chase: reviewing the excavations of General Pitt-Rivers, 1881–1898', *Arch. Journ.* 104, 27–81.

Hawkes, C. F. C. and Dunning, G. C. (1931) 'The Belgae of Gaul and Britain', *Arch. Journ.* 87, 150–335.

Hawkes, S. C. (1961) 'Longbridge Deverill, Cow Down', pp. 18–20 in Frere, S. S. (ed.), *Problems of the Iron Age in Southern Britain* (London).

Hawkes, S. C. (1969) 'Finds from two Middle Bronze Age pits at Winnall, Winchester, Hampshire', *Proc. Hants. Fld. Club and Archaeol. Soc.* 26, 5–18.

Hawkes, S. C. (1982) 'The archaeology of conversion: cemeteries', pp. 48–9 in Campbell, J. (ed.), *The Anglo Saxons* (Oxford).

Hawkes, S. C. (1986) 'The Early Saxon period', pp. 64–108 in Briggs, G., Cook, J. and Rowley, T. (eds), *The Archaeology of the Oxford Region* (Oxford).

Hawkes, S. C. and Dunning, G. C. (1961) 'Soldiers and settlers in Britain, fourth to fifth century', *Med. Archaeol.* 5, 1–71.

Hawkins, A. B. and Tratman, E. K. (1977) 'The Quaternary deposits of the Mendip, Bath and Bristol Areas: including a reprinting of Donovan's 1954 and 1964 bibliographies', *Proc. Univ. Bristol Spelaeol. Soc.* 14(3), 197–232.

Henderson, J. (1981) 'A report on the glass excavated from Meare Village West, 1979', pp. 55–60 in Orme, B. J., Coles, J. M., Caseldine, A. E. and Bailey, G. N. (eds) 1981.

Higgs, E. S. (1959) 'The excavation of a Late Mesolithic site at Downton, near Salisbury, Wilts.', *Proc. Prehist. Soc.* 25, 209–32.

Hill, D. H. (1969) 'The Burghal hidage – the establishment of a text', *Med. Archaeol.* 13, 84–92.

Hinton, D. A. (1986) 'The place of Basing in Mid Saxon history', *Proc. Hants. Fld. Club and Archaeol. Soc.* 42, 162–4.

Hinton, D. A. and Hodges, R. (1977) 'Excavations in Wareham, 1974–5', *Proc. Dorset Nat. Hist. and Arch. Soc.* 99, 42–83.

Hodder, I. (1984) 'Burials, houses, women and men in the European neolithic', pp. 51–68 in Miller, D. and Tilley, C. (eds), *Ideology, Power and Prehistory* (Cambridge).

Hodges, R. (1981) *The Hamwih Pottery: The Local and Imported Wares from 30 Years' Excavations at Middle Saxon Southampton and their European context* (CBA Res. Rep. 37: London).

Holdsworth, P. (1980) *Excavations at Melbourne St, Southampton, 1971–76* (CBA Res. Rep. 33: London).

Holdsworth, P. (1984) 'Saxon Southampton', pp. 331–44 in Haslam, J. (ed.) 1984a.

Holgate, R. and Tyldesley, J. (1985) 'A handaxe from West Kennet', *Wilts. Arch. Mag.* 79, 225–6.

Howard, H. (1981) 'Ceramic production at Windmill Hill', in Howard, H. and Morris, E. (eds), *Production and Distribution: A Ceramic Viewpoint* (BAR S120: Oxford).

Hughes, M. and ApSimon, A. (1978) 'A mesolithic flint working site on the South

Coast Motorway (M27) near Fort Wallington, Fareham, Hampshire 1972', *Proc. Hants. Fld Club and Archaeol. Soc.* **34**, 23–35.

Jackson, K. (1958) 'The site of Mount Badon', *Journ. Celtic Studies* **2**, 152–5.

Jacobi, R. M. (1978) 'Population and landscape in Mesolithic Lowland Britain', pp. 75–85 in Limbrey, S. and Evans, J. G. (eds) 1978.

Jacobi, R. M. (1981) 'The last hunters in Hampshire', pp. 10–25 in Shennan, J. J. and Schadla-Hall, R. T. (eds) 1981.

Jacobi, R. M. (1982) 'Ice Age cave-dwellers 12,000–9,000 BC', pp. 11–13 in Aston, M. and Burrow, I. (eds) 1982.

Johnston, D. E. (1978) 'Villas of Hampshire and the Isle of Wight', pp. 71–92 in Todd, M. (ed.), *Studies in the Romano-British Villa* (Leicester).

Jones, M. (1980) 'Carbonized cereals from Grooved Ware contexts', *Proc. Prehist. Soc.* **46**, 61–3.

Jones, M. (1981) 'The development of crop husbandry', pp. 95–127 in Jones, M. and Dimbleby, G. (eds) 1981.

Jones, M. (1984) 'Regional patterns in crop production', pp. 120– 5 in Cunliffe, B. and Miles, D. (eds) 1984.

Jones, M. and Dimbleby, G. (1981) *The Environment of Man: The Iron Age to Anglo-Saxon Period* (BAR 87: Oxford).

Keef, P. A. M., Wymer, J. J. and Dimbleby G. W. (1965) 'A Mesolithic site on Iping Common, Sussex, England', *Proc. Prehist. Soc.* **31**, 85–92.

Keen, L. (1984) 'The towns of Dorset', pp. 203–48 in Haslam, J. (ed.) 1984a.

Kidson, C. and Heyworth, A. (1976) 'The Quaternary deposits of the Somerset Levels', *Quarterly Journal of Engineering Geology* **9**(3), 217–35.

Kinnes, I. (1975) 'Monumental function in British neolithic burial practices', *World Archaeol.* **7**, 16–29.

Kinnes, I. (1979) *Round Barrows and Ring-Ditches in the British Neolithic* (Brit. Mus. Occ. Paper 7: London).

Kirby, D. P. (1965) 'Problems of early West Saxon history', *English Hist. Rev.* **80**, 10–29.

Kjølbye-Biddle, B. (1986) 'The 7th Century minster at Winchester interpreted', pp. 196–209 in Butler, L. A. S. and Morris, R. K (eds) 1986.

Langmaid, L. (1971) 'Norton Fitzwarren', *Current Archaeol.* **78**, 116–20.

Lanting, J. N. and van der Waals, J. D. (1972) 'British beakers as seen from the Continent', *Helenium* **12**, 20–46.

Leach, P. (1982) *Ilchester. Vol. 1, Excavations 1974–5* (Bristol).

Leach, P. and Thew, N. (1985) *A Late Iron Age Oppidum at Ilchester, Somerset* (Western Archaeol. Trust).

Leech, R. H. (1976) 'Larger Agricultural settlements in the West Country', pp. 142–61 in Branigan, K. and Fowler, P. J. (eds) 1976.

Leech, R. H. (1981) 'The Somerset Levels in the Romano-British period', pp. 20–51 in Rowley, T. (ed.), *The Evolution of Marshland Landscapes* (Oxford).

Lewis, E. and Walker, G. (1976) 'A Middle Bronze Age settlement site at Westbury, West Meon, Hampshire', *Proc. Hants. Fld. Club & Archaeol. Soc.* **33**, 33–43.

Limbrey, S. and Evans, J. G. (1978) *The Effect of Man on the Landscape: The Lowland Zone* (CBA Res. Rep. 21: London).

Lukis, R. N. (1985) 'Halstock Roman Villa – 1985 excavation', *Proc. Dorset Nat. Hist. and Arch. Soc.* **107**, 163–4.

Lyne, M. A. B. and **Jefferies, R. S.** (1979) *The Alice Holt/Farnham Roman Pottery Industry* (CBA Res. Rep. 30: London).

Mace, A. (1959) 'An Upper Palaeolithic open-site at Hengistbury Head, Christchurch, Hants.', *Proc. Prehist Soc.* **25**, 233–59.

Macready, S. and **Thompson, F. H.** (1984) *Cross-Channel Trade between Gaul and Britain in the pre Roman Iron Age* (Soc. Ant. Occ. Paper 4: London).

Malone, C. (1989) *Avebury* (London).

Manning, W. H. (1976) 'The conquest of the West Country', pp. 15–41 in Branigan, K. and Fowler, P. J. (eds) 1976.

Meaney, A. L. and **Hawkes, S. C.** (1970) *Two Anglo-Saxon Cemeteries at Winnall* (Soc. Med. Archaeol. Mono. 4: London).

Mercer, R. (1980) *Hambledon Hill, A Neolithic Landscape* (Edinburgh).

Metcalf, D. M. (1988) 'The coins (from Hamwic)', pp. 17–59 in Andrews, P. (ed.) 1988.

Meyrick, O. (1973) 'Some Beaker habitation sites in North Wiltshire', *Wilts. Arch. Mag.* **68**, 116–18.

Millett, M. and **James, S.** (1983) 'Excavations at Cowdery's Down, Basingstoke, Hampshire, 1978–81', *Arch. Journ.* **140**, 151–279.

Moffett, L., Robinson, M. A. and **Straker, V.** (1989) 'Cereals, fruits and nuts: charred plant remains from Neolithic sites in England and Wales and the Neolithic economy', pp. 243–61 in Milles, A., Williams, D. and Gardner, N. (eds), *The Beginnings of Agriculture* (BAR Int. Series 496: Oxford).

Morgan, F. de M. (1959) 'The excavation of a long barrow at Nutbane, Hants.', *Proc. Prehist. Soc.* **25**, 15–51.

Morris, E. (1985) 'Prehistoric salt distributions: two case studies from Western Britain', *Bull. B. Celtic Stud.* **32**, 336–79.

Morris, E. (1987) 'Later prehistoric pottery from Ham Hill', *Proc. Somerset Nat. Hist. and Archaeol. Soc.* **131**, 27–47.

Myres, J. N. L. (1964) 'Wansdyke and the origins of Wessex', pp. 1–28 in Trevor-Roper, H. R. (ed.), *Essays in British History Presented to Sir Keith Feiling* (London).

Myres, J. N. L. (1986) *The English Settlements* (Oxford).

Norman, C. (1975) 'Four Mesolithic assemblages from West Somerset', *Proc. Som. Arch. Nat. Hist. Soc.* **119**, 26–37.

Norman, C. (1982) 'Mesolithic Hunter-Gatherers 9000–4000 BC', pp. 15–21 in Aston, M. and Burrow, I. (eds) 1982.

O'Malley, M. (1978) 'Broom Hill, Braishfield: Mesolithic Dwelling', *Current Archaeol.* **63**, 117–20.

O'Malley, M. and **Jacobi, R. M.** (1978) 'The Excavation of a Mesolithic Occupation Site at Broom Hill, Braishfield, Hampshire 1971–1973', *Rescue Archaeol. Hants.* **4**, 16–38.

Orme, B. J., Coles, J. M., Caseldine, A. E. and **Bailey, G. N.** (eds) (1981) 'Meare Village West 1979', *Somerset Levels Papers* **7**, 12–69.

Palmer, L. and **Ashworth, H.** (1957) 'Four pigs of lead from green ore', *Proc. Somerset Arch. Nat. Hist. Soc.* **102**, 52–88.

Palmer, R. (1984) *Danebury. An Iron Age Hillfort in Hampshire. An aerial photographic interpretation of its environs* (London).

Palmer, S. (1970) 'The Stone Age industries of the Isle of Portland, Dorset, and the utilization of Portland Chert as artifact material in Southern Britain', *Proc. Prehist. Soc.* **36**, 82–115.

Palmer, S. (1972) 'The Mesolithic industries of Mother Siller's Channel, Christchurch, and the neighbouring areas', *Proc. Hants. Fld. Club and Archaeol. Soc.* **27**, 9–32.

Palmer, S. (1976) 'The Mesolithic habitation site at Culver Well, Portland, Dorset: interim note', *Proc. Prehist. Soc.* **42**, 324–7.

Palmer, S. and Dimbleby, G. (1979) 'A Mesolithic habitation site on Winfrith Heath, Dorset', *Proc. Dorset Nat. Hist. and Arch. Soc.* **101**, 27–56.

Peacock, D. P. S. (1969) 'Neolithic pottery production in Cornwall', *Antiquity* **43**, 145–9.

Peacock, D. P. S. (1987) 'Iron Age and Roman quern production at Lodsworth, West Sussex', *Antiq. Journ.* **67**, 61–85.

Perry, B. T. (1974) 'Excavations at Bramdean, Hampshire, 1965 and 1966 and a discussion of similar sites in Southern England', *Proc. Hants. Fld. Club and Archaeol. Soc.* **29**, 41–77.

Petersen, F. F. (1981) *The Excavation of a Bronze Age Cemetery on Knighton Heath, Dorset* (BAR Brit. Series 98: Oxford).

Piggott, C. M. (1942) 'Five Late Bronze Age enclosures in North Wiltshire', *Proc. Prehist. Soc.* **8**, 48–61.

Piggott, S. (1930) 'Butser Hill', *Antiquity* **4**, 187–200.

Piggott, S. (1931) 'Ladle Hill – an unfinished hill-fort', *Antiquity* **5**, 474–85.

Piggott, S. (1937) 'The excavation of a long barrow in Holdenhurst Parish, near Christchurch, Hants.', *Proc. Prehist. Soc.* **3**, 1–14.

Piggott, S. (1938) 'The Early Bronze Age in Wessex', *Proc. Prehist. Soc.* **4**, 52–106.

Piggott, S. (1940) 'Timber circles: a re-examination', *Archaeol. J.* **96**, 193–222.

Piggott, S. (1952) 'The Neolithic camp on Whitesheet Hill, Kilmington Parish', *Wilts. Arch. Mag.* **54**, 404–10.

Piggott, S. (1954) *Neolithic Cultures of the British Isles* (Cambridge).

Piggott, S. (1962) *The West Kennet Long Barrow. Excavations 1955–6* (London).

Piggott, S. (1963) 'Abercromby and after: the Beaker Cultures of Britain reexamined', pp. 53–91 in Foster, I.Ll. and Alcock, L. (eds), *Culture and Environment* (London).

Piggott, S. (1973a) 'The beginnings of human settlement: the Palaeolithic and Mesolithic period', pp. 281–3 in Crittall, E. (ed.), *A History of Wiltshire Vol. 1 part 2* (Oxford).

Piggott, S. (1973b) 'The later Neolithic: single graves and the first metallurgy', pp. 333–51 in Crittall, E. (ed.), *A History of Wiltshire Vol. 1 part 2* (Oxford).

Piggott, S. and Piggott, C. M. (1939) 'Stone and earth circles in Dorset', *Antiquity* **13**, 138–58.

Pitt Rivers, A. L. F. (1898) *Excavations in Cranborne Chase, IV* (London).

Pitts, M. W. (1982) 'On the road to Stonehenge: report on the investigation beside the A344 in 1968, 1979 and 1980', *Proc. Prehist. Soc.* **48**, 75–132.

Preece, R. C. (1980) 'The biostratigraphy and dating of the tufa deposit at the Mesolithic site at Blashenwell, Dorset, England', *Journ. Archaeol. Sci.* **7**, 345–62.

Quirk, R. N. (1957) 'Winchester Cathedral in the tenth century', *Arch. Journ.* **114**, 28–68.

Rackham, O. (1977) 'Neolithic woodland management in the Somerset Levels: Garvin's Walton Heath and Rowland's Tracks', *Somerset Levels Papers* 3, 65–72.

Radford, C. A. R. (1963) 'The church in Somerset down to 1100', *Proc. Som. Arch. Nat. Hist. Soc.* 106, 28–45.

Radley, J. (1969) 'An archaeological survey and policy for Wiltshire: part II Mesolithic', *Wilts. Arch. Mag.* 64, 18–20.

Rahtz, P. A. (1961) 'An excavation on Bokerly Dyke, 1958', *Arch. Journ.* 118, 65–99.

Rahtz, P. A. (1962) 'Neolithic and Beaker sites at Downton, Near Salisbury, Wiltshire', *Wilts. Arch. Mag.* 58, 116–42.

Rahtz, P. A. (1963) 'A Roman villa at Downton', *Wilts. Arch. Mag.* 58, 303–41.

Rahtz, P. A. (1969) 'Cannington Hillfort 1963', *Proc. Som. Arch. and Nat. Hist. Soc.* 113, 56–68.

Rahtz, P. A. (1970) 'Excavations on Knighton Hill, Broad Chalke, 1959', *Wilts. Arch. Mag.* 65, 74–88.

Rahtz, P. A. (1971) 'Excavations on Glastonbury Tor', *Arch. Journ.* 127, 1–81.

Rahtz, P. A. (1974) 'Pottery in Somerset AD 400–1066', pp. 95–126 in Evison, V. I., Hodges, H. and Hurst, J. G. (eds), *Medieval Pottery from Excavations* (London).

Rahtz, P. (1979) *The Saxon and Medieval Palaces at Cheddar* (BAR Brit. Series 65: Oxford).

Rahtz, P. and **ApSimon, A.** (1962) 'Excavations at Shearplace Hill, Sydling St. Nicholas, Dorset, England', *Proc. Prehist. Soc.* 28, 289–328.

Rahtz, P. A. and **Greenfield, E.** (1977) *Excavations at Chew Valley Lake, Somerset* (London).

Rankine, W. F. (1952) 'A Mesolithic chipping floor at the Warren, Oakhanger, Selbourne, Hants.', *Proc. Prehist. Soc.* 18, 21–35.

Rankine, W. F. (1956) 'The Mesolithic of Southern England', *Surrey Archaeol. Society's Research Paper: no. 4.*

Rankine, W. F. (1958) 'Hampshire: Mesolithic excavation: interim report', *Archaeological News Letter* 6, 5, 122.

Rankine, W. F. (1960) 'The Warren Mesolithic sites, Oakhanger, Hants.: discovery and excavation of Site V/VII', *Archaeological News Letter* 6, 11, 260–2.

Rankine, W. F. (1961) 'Further excavations at Oakhanger, Selborne, Hants.: Site VIII', *Wealden Mesolithic Research Bulletin* (privately printed).

Rankine, W. F. and **Dimbleby, G. W.** (1960) 'Further excavations at a Mesolithic site at Oakhanger, Selborne, Hants.', *Proc. Prehist. Soc.* 27, 246–62.

RCHM(E) (1959) 'Wareham West Walls', *Med. Archaeol.* 3, 120–9.

RCHM(E) (1979a) *Long Barrows in Hampshire and the Isle of Wight* (London).

RCHM(E) (1979b) *Stonehenge and its Environment* (Edinburgh).

RCHM(E) (1984) 'West Park Roman Villa, Rockbourne, Hampshire', *Arch. Journ.* 140, 129–50.

Renfrew, C. (1973) 'Monuments, mobilization and social organization in Neolithic Wessex', pp. 540–58 in Renfrew, C. (ed.), *The Explanation of Culture Change* (London).

Richards, C. and **Thomas, J.** (1984) 'Ritual activity and structured deposition in Later Neolithic Wessex', pp. 189–218 in Bradley, R. and Gardiner, J. (eds) 1984.

Richards, J. (1978) *The Archaeology of the Berkshire Downs: An Introductory Survey* (Reading).

Richards, J. (1984) 'The development of the Neolithic landscape in the environs of Stonehenge', pp. 177–88 in Bradley, R. and Gardiner, J. (eds) 1984.

Richards, J. (1990) *The Stonehenge Environs Project* (HBMC Arch. Rep. 16: London).

Richards, J. (1991) *Stonehenge* (London).

Richardson, K. M. (1940) 'Excavations at Poundbury, Dorchester, Dorset, 1939', *Antiq. Journ.* **20**, 429–48.

Richardson, K. M. (1951) 'The excavation of Iron Age villages on Boscombe Down West', *Wilts. Arch. Mag.* **54**, 123–68.

Richmond, I. (1968) *Hod Hill. Vol. 2 Excavations Carried Out between 1951 and 1958* (London).

Rivet, A. L. F. (1969) *The Roman Villa in Britain* (London).

Rivet, A. L. F. and Smith, C. (1979) *The Place-Names of Roman Britain* (London).

Robertson-Mackay, R. (1977) 'The defences of the Iron Age Hill-fort at Winklebury, Basingstoke, Hampshire', *Proc. Prehist. Soc.* **43**, 131–54.

Rodwell, W. (1982) 'From mausoleum to minster: the early development of Wells Cathedral', pp. 49–60 in Pearce, S. M. (ed.), *The Early Church in Western Britain and Ireland* (BAR Brit. Series 102: Oxford).

Roe, D. A. (1968) *A Gazetteer of British Lower and Middle Palaeolithic Sites* (CBA Res. Rep. 8: London).

Roe, D. A. (1969) 'An archaeological survey and policy for Wiltshire: part I Palaeolithic', *Wilts. Arch. Mag.* **64**, 1–18.

Roe, D. A. (1975) 'Some Hampshire and Dorset hand-axes and the question of the Early Acheulean in Britain', *Proc. Prehist. Soc.* **41**, 1–9.

Roe, D. A. (1976) 'The evolution of the Acheulian in Britain', pp. 76–95 in Combier, J. (ed.), *Les Premières industries de l'Europe* (Colloque VIII, IXe Congrès de l'Union Internationale des Sciences Préhistoriques et Protohistorique: Nice).

Roe, D. A. (1981) *The Lower and Middle Palaeolithic periods in Britain* (London).

Roe, F. (1979) 'Typology of stone implements with shaft holes', pp. 23–48 in Clough, T. H. McK. and Cummins, W. A. (eds), *Stone Axe Studies* (CBA Res. Rep. 23: London).

Rowlands, M. J. (1976) *The Production and Distribution of Metalwork in the Middle Bronze Age in Southern Britain* (BAR Brit. Series 31: Oxford).

Rowlands, M. J. (1980) 'Subsistence, exchange and technology – a social framework for the Bronze Age in Southern England *c* 1400–700 bc', pp. 57–76 in Barrett, J. and Bradley, R. (eds) 1980a.

Ruggles, C. L. N. and Whittle, A. W. R. (1981) *Astronomy and Society in Britain during the Period 4000–1500 BC* (BAR Brit. Series 88: Oxford).

Russel, A. D. (1990) 'Two Beaker burials from Chilbolton, Hampshire', *Proc. Prehist. Soc.* **56**, 153–72.

Saville, A. (1983) *Uley, Bury and Norbury Hillforts* (Western Archaeol. Trust Exc. Mono. 5: Bristol).

Sellwood, L. (1984) 'Tribal boundaries viewed from the perspective of numismatic evidence', pp. 191–204 in Cunliffe, B. and Miles, D. (eds) 1984.

Shackley, M. L. (1972) 'Preliminary note on handaxes found in gravel deposits at Warsash, Hampshire', *Proc. Hants. Fld. Club and Archaeol. Soc.* **27**, 5–8.

Shackley, M. L. (1973) 'A contextual study of the Mousterian industry from Great Pan Farm, Newport, Isle of Wight', *Proc. IOW Arch. Nat. Hist. Soc.* 6(8), 542–54.

Shackley, M. (1981) 'On the Palaeolithic archaeology of Hampshire', pp. 4–9 in Shennan, S. J. and Schadla-Hall, R. T. (eds) 1981.

Shanks, M. and Tilley, C. 1982 'Ideology, symbolic power and ritual communication: a reinterpretation of Neolithic mortuary practice', pp. 129–54 in Hodder, I. (ed.), *Symbolic and Structural Archaeology* (Cambridge).

Sharples, N. (1986) 'Maiden Castle Project 1985: an interim report', *Proc. Dorset Nat. Hist. and Arch. Soc.* 107, 111–19.

Shennan, S. J. (1981) 'Settlement history in East Hampshire', pp. 106–21 in Shennan, S. J. and Schadla-Hall, R. T. (eds) 1981.

Shennan, S. J. and Schadla-Hall, R. T. (eds) (1981) *The Archaeology of Hampshire* (Hants. Field Club Mono. 1).

Simmons, I. G. and Dimbleby, G. W. (1974) 'The possible role of Ivy (Hedera helex L.) in the Mesolithic economy of Western Europe', *Journ. Archaeol. Sci.* 1, 291–6.

Simmons, I. G., Dimbleby, G. W. and Grigson, C. (1981) 'The Mesolithic', pp. 82–124 in Simmons, I. G. and Tooley, M. J. (eds) 1981.

Simmons, I. G. and Tooley, M. J. (eds.) (1981) *The Environment in British Prehistory* (London).

Simpson, D. D. A. (1968) 'Timber mortuary houses and earthen long barrows', *Antiquity* 42, 142–4.

Sims-Williams, P. (1983a) 'Gildas and the Anglo-Saxons', *Cambridge Medieval Celtic Studies* 6, 1–30.

Sims-Williams (1983b) 'The settlement of England in Bede and the Chronicle', *Anglo-Saxon England* 12, 1–41.

Smith, A. G. (1970) 'The influence of Mesolithic and Neolithic man on British vegetation: a discussion', pp. 81–96 in Walker, D. and West, R. G. (eds), *Studies in the Vegetational History of the British Isles* (Cambridge).

Smith, A. G. et al. (1981) 'The Neolithic', pp. 125–209 in Simmons, I. and Tooley, M. (eds) 1981.

Smith, I. F. (1965) *Windmill Hill and Avebury, Excavations by Alexander Keiller 1925–1939* (Oxford).

Smith, I. F. (1966) 'Windmill Hill and its implications', *Palaeohistoria* 12, 469–82.

Smith, I. F. (1971) 'Causewayed enclosures', pp. 89–112 in Simpson, D. D. A. (ed.), *Economy and Settlement in Neolithic and Early Bronze Age Britain* (Leicester).

Smith, I. F. (1974) 'The Neolithic', pp. 100–36 in Renfrew, C. (ed.), *British Prehistory: A New Outline* (London).

Smith, I. F. (1979) 'The chronology of British stone implements', pp. 13–22 in Clough, T. H. McK. and Cummins, W. A. (eds) *Stone Axe Studies* (CBA Res. Rep. 23: London).

Smith, I. F. and Simpson, D. D. A. (1966) 'Excavation of a round barrow on Overton Hill, North Wiltshire', *Proc. Prehist. Soc.* 32, 122–55.

Smith, K. (1977) 'The excavation of Winklebury camp, Basingstoke, Hampshire', *Proc. Prehist. Soc.* 43, 31–130.

Smith, M. A. (1959) 'Some Somerset Hoards and their place in the Bronze Age of Southern Britain', *Proc. Prehist. Soc.* 25, 144–87.

Smith, R. W. (1984) 'The ecology of Neolithic farming systems as exemplified by the Avebury region of Wiltshire', *Proc. Prehist. Soc.* **50**, 99–120.

Sparks, B. W. and West, R. G. (1972) *The Ice Age in Britain* (London).

Spratling, M. G. (1979) 'The debris of metalworking', Chapter 9, pp. 125–53 in Wainwright, G. J. (ed.) 1979a.

Stead, I. M. (1968) 'An Iron Age hill-fort at Grimthorpe, Yorkshire, England', *Proc. Prehist. Soc.* **34**, 148–90.

Stead, I. M. (1970) 'Excavations in Blagden Copse, Hurstbourne Tarrant, Hampshire, 1961', *Proc. Hants. Fld. Club and Archaeol. Soc.* **23**, 81–9.

Stenton, F. M. (1926) 'The foundation of English history', pp. 116–26 in Stenton, D. M. (ed.), *Preparatory to Anglo-Saxon England: Being the Collected Papers of Frank Merry Stenton* (Oxford 1970).

Stenton, F. (1971) *Anglo Saxon England* (3rd edn: Oxford).

Stevens, C. E. (1952) 'The Roman name of Ilchester', *Proc. Som. Arch. Nat. Hist. Soc.* **96**, 188–92.

Stevens, F. (1934) 'The Highfield pit dwellings, Fisherton, Salisbury', *Wilts. Arch. Mag.* **46**, 579–624.

Stone, J. F. S. (1933) 'Excavations at Easton Down, Winterslow', *Wilts. Arch. Mag.* **46**, 225–42.

Stone, J. F. S. (1937) 'A Late Bronze Age habitation site on Thorny Down, Winterbourne Gunner, S. Wilts.', *Wilts. Arch. Mag.* **47**, 640–60.

Stone, J. F. S. (1941) 'The Deverel-Rimbury settlement on Thorny Down, Winterbourne Gunner, S. Wilts.', *Proc. Prehist. Soc.* **4**, 114–33.

Stone, J. F. S. (1949) 'Some grooved ware pottery from the Woodhenge area', *Proc. Prehist. Soc.* **15**, 122–7.

Stone, J. F. S. and Algar, D. J. (1955) 'Sorviodunum', *Wilts. Arch. Mag.* **56**, 102–26.

Stone, J. F. S., Piggott, S. and Booth, A. St. J. (1954) 'Durrington Walls, Wiltshire: recent excavations at a ceremonial site of the early second millennium BC', *Antiq. Journ.* **34**, 155–77.

Stone, J. F. S. and Young, W. E. V. (1948) 'Two pits of Grooved Ware date near Woodhenge', *Wilts. Arch. Mag.* **52**, 287–306.

Stringer, C. B. (1985) 'The Hominid remains from Gough's Cave', *Proc. Univ. Bristol Spelaeol. Soc.* **17**, 145–52.

Sunter, N. (1987) 'Excavations at Norden', pp. 9–43 in Sunter, N. and Woodward, P. J. (eds) 1987.

Sunter, N. and Woodward, P. J. (eds) (1987) *Romano-British Industries in Purbeck* (Dorset Nat. Hist. and Arch. Soc. Mono. 6: Dorchester).

Taylor, C. C. (1967) 'Late Roman pastoral farming in Wessex', *Antiquity* **61**, 304–6.

Taylor, C. C. (1970) *Dorset* (London).

Taylor, J. J. (1984) 'The Potterne gold bracelet and its affinities', *Wilts. Arch. Mag.* **78**, 35–40.

Thomas, A. C. (ed.) (1966) *Rural Settlement in Roman Britain* (CBA Res. Rep. 7: London)

Thomas, A. C. (1981) *A Provisional List of Imported Pottery in Post Roman Western Britain and Ireland* (Redruth).

Thomas, J. (1984) 'A tale of two polities: kinship, authority and exchange in the Neolithic of South Dorset and North Wiltshire', pp. 161–76 in Bradley, R. and Gardiner, J. (eds) 1984.

Thomas, J. (1988) 'Neolithic explanations revisited: the Mesolithic–Neolithic transition in Britain and south Scandinavia', *Proc. Prehist. Soc.* **54**, 59–66.

Thomas, J. and Whittle, A. (1986) 'Anatomy of a tomb – West Kennet revisited', *Oxford Journ. Archaeol.* **5**, 129–56.

Thomas, N. (1964) 'The Neolithic causewayed camp at Robin Hood's Ball, Shrewton', *Wilts. Arch. Mag.* **59**, 1–27.

Thompson, E. A. (1956) 'Zosimus on the end of Roman Britain', *Antiquity* **30**, 163–7.

Thorpe, I. J. (1984) 'Ritual, power and ideology: a reconstruction of Earlier Neolithic rituals in Wessex', pp. 41–60 in Bradley, R. and Gardiner, J. (eds) 1984.

Timby, J. R. (1988) 'The Middle Saxon pottery (from Hamwic)', pp. 73–124 in Andrews, P. (ed.) 1988.

Todd, M. (1976) 'The Vici of Western England', pp. 99–119 in Branigan, K. and Fowler, P. J. (eds) 1976.

Tratman, E. K. (1964) 'Picken's Hole, Crook Peak, Somerset; a Pleistocene site: preliminary note', *Proc. Univ. Bristol Spelaeol. Soc.* **10**, 112–15.

Tratman, E. K. (1967) 'The Priddy Circles, Mendip, Somerset. Henge Monuments', *Proc. Univ. Bristol Spelaeol. Soc.* **11**, 97–125.

Tratman, E. K. (1976) 'A Late Upper Palaeolithic calculator(?), Gough's Cave, Cheddar, Somerset', *Proc. Univ. Bristol Spelaeol. Soc.* **14**, 123–9.

Tratman, E. K., Donovan, D. T. and Campbell, J. B. (1971) 'The Hyaena Den (Wookey Hole), Mendip Hills, Somerset', *Proc. Univ. Bristol Spelaeol. Soc.* **12**(3), 245–79.

Tubbs, C. R. and Dimbleby, G. W. (1965) 'Early agriculture in the New Forest', *Advancement of Science* June 1965.

Tucker, J. H. (1985) 'Upper Palaeolithic and Mesolithic sites in the Chippenham area', *Wilts. Arch. Mag.* **79**, 226–8.

Turner, C. and West, R. G. (1968) 'The subdivision and zonation of interglacial periods', *Eiszeitalter und Gengn.* **19**, 93–101.

Tyldesley, J. A. (1987) *The bout coupé handaxe* (BAR Brit. Series 170: Oxford).

Ucko, P., Hunter, M., Clark, A. J. and David, A. (1990) *Avebury Reconsidered: From the 1660s to the 1990s* (London).

Van Arsdell, R. D. (1989) *Celtic Coinage of Britain* (London).

Vatcher, F. de M. (1961) 'The excavation of the long mortuary enclosure on Normanton Down, Wilts.', *Proc. Prehist. Soc.* **27**, 160–73.

Wacher, J. (1974) *The Towns of Roman Britain* (London).

Wainwright, G. J. (1960) 'Three microlithic industries from South-west England and their affinities', *Proc. Prehist. Soc.* **26**, 193–201.

Wainwright, G. J. (1965) 'The excavation of a round barrow on Worgret Hill, Arne, Dorset', *Proc. Dorset Nat. Hist. & Archaeol. Soc.* **87**, 119–125.

Wainwright, G. J. (1968) 'The excavation of a Durotrigian farmstead near Tollard Royal in Cranborne Chase, Southern England', *Proc. Prehist. Soc.* **34**, 102–47.

Wainwright, G. J. (1969) 'A review of henge monuments in the light of recent research', *Proc. Prehist. Soc.* **35**, 112–33.

Wainwright, G. J. (1970a) 'An Iron Age promontory fort at Budbury, Bradford-on-Avon, Wiltshire', *Wilts. Arch. Mag.* **65**, 108–66.

Wainwright, G. J. (1970b) 'The excavation of Balksbury Camp, Andover, Hants.', *Proc. Hants. Fld. Club and Archaeol. Soc.* **26**, 21–55.

Wainwright, G. J. (1975) 'Religion and settlement in Wessex 3000–1700 bc', pp. 57–71 in Fowler, P. J. (ed.), *Recent Work in Rural Archaeology* (Bradford on Avon).

Wainwright, G. J. (ed.) (1979a) *Gussage All Saints. An Iron Age Settlement in Dorset* (DOE Archaeol. Rep. 10: London).

Wainwright, G. J. (1979b) *Mount Pleasant, Dorset: Excavations 1970–1971* (Soc. Ant. Res. Rep. 37: London).

Wainwright, G. J., Evans, J. G. and Longworth, I. H. (1971) 'The excavation of a Late Neolithic enclosure at Marden, Wiltshire', *Antiq. Journ.* **51**, 177–239.

Wainwright, G. J. and Longworth, I. H. (1971) *Durrington Walls: Excavations 1966–1968* (Soc. Ant. Res. Rep. 29: London).

Wallace-Hadrill, J. M. (1988) *Bede's Ecclesiastical History of the English People. A Historical Comment* (Oxford).

Warmington, B. H. (1976) 'Nero, Boudicca and the frontier in the west', pp. 42–51 in Branigan, K. and Fowler, P. J. (eds) 1976.

Waterman, D. M. (1947) 'Excavations at Clausentum 1937–8', *Antiq. Journ.* **27**, 151–71.

Waton, P. V. (1982) 'Man's impact on the chalklands: some new pollen evidence', pp. 75–92 in Bell, M. and Limbrey, S. (eds), *Archaeological Aspects of Woodland Ecology* (BAR Int. Series 146: Oxford).

Webster, G. (1960) 'The Roman military advance under Ostorius Scapula', *Arch. Journ.* **115**, 49–98.

Webster, G. (1974) 'Interim report on excavations at Lake Farm near Wimborne 1973', *Proc. Dorset Nat. Hist. and Arch Soc.* **95**, 86–7.

Webster, G. (1979) 'Final report on the excavations of the Roman Fort at Wadden Hill, Stoke Abbot 1963–69', *Proc. Dorset Nat. Hist. and Arch. Soc.* **101**, 51–90.

Wedlake, W. J. (1958) *Excavations at Camerton, Somerset* (Camerton).

Welch, M. G. (1971) 'Late Romans and Saxons in Sussex', *Britannia* **2**, 232–7.

Welch, M. G. (1976) [description of gilt bronze disc brooch], pp. 206–11 in Cunliffe (ed.) 1976a.

Welch, M. G. (1983) *Early Anglo-Saxon Sussex* (BAR 112: Oxford).

Wheeler, R. E. M. (1943) *Maiden Castle, Dorset* (Soc. Ant. Res. Rep. 12: Oxford).

White, D. A. (1982) *The Bronze Age Cremation Cemeteries at Simons Ground, Dorset* (Dorset Nat. Hist. and Arch. Soc. Mono. 3: Dorchester).

Whitley, M. (1943) 'Excavations at Chalbury Camp, Dorset, 1939', *Antiq. Journ.* **23**, 98–121.

Whittle, A. W. R. (1977) *The Earlier Neolithic of Southern England and its Continental Background* (BAR Supp. Series 35: Oxford).

Whittle, A. W. R. (1978) 'Resources and Population in the British Neolithic', *Antiquity* **52**, 34–42.

Whittle, A. (1980) 'Two Neolithics (parts 1 and 2)', *Current Archaeol.* **70**, 329–34; **71**, 371–3.

Whittle, A. (1981) 'Later Neolithic society in Britain: a realignment', pp. 297–342 in Ruggles, C. L. N. and Whittle, A. W. R. (eds), *Astronomy and Society in Britain during the period 4000–1500 BC* (BAR 88: Oxford).

Whittle, A. (1990a) *West Kennet 1990: Preliminary Report on Excavations of the Palisaded Enclosures* (duplicated).

Whittle, A. (1990b) 'A model for the Mesolithic–Neolithic transition in the Upper Kennet Valley, North Wiltshire', *Proc. Prehist. Soc.* 56, 101–10.

Whittle, A. (1990c) 'A pre-enclosure burial at Windmill Hill, Wilts.', *Oxford Journ. Archaeol.* 9, 25–8.

Whittle, A. (1991) 'A Neolithic complex at West Kennet, Wiltshire, England', *Antiquity*, 65, 256–62.

Whittle, A. and Smith, R. (1989) 'West Kennet', *Current Archaeol.* 118, 363–5.

Williams, D. F. (1977) 'The Romano-British black-burnished industry', pp. 163–220 in Peacock, D. P. S. (ed.), *Pottery and Early Commerce* (London).

Woodward, P. J. (1987) 'The excavation of an Iron Age and Romano-British settlement at Rope Lake Hole, Corfe Castle, Dorset', pp. 125–80 in Sunter, N. and Woodward, P. J. (eds) 1987.

Woodward, P. J. (1988) 'Pictures of the Neolithic: discoveries from the Flagstones House excavations, Dorchester, Dorset', *Antiquity* 62, 266–74.

Woodward, P. J. (1991) *The South Dorset Ridgeway: Survey and Excavations 1977–84* (Dorset Nat. Hist. and Arch. Soc. Mono. 8: Dorchester).

Woodward, P. J., Davies, M. and Graham, A. H. (1984) 'Excavations on the Greyhound Yard Car Park, Dorchester 1984', *Proc. Dorset Nat. Hist. and Arch. Soc.* 106, 99–106.

Woodward, P. J. and Smith, R. J. C. (1987) 'Survey and excavations along the route of the southern Dorchester by-pass 1986–7: an interim note', *Proc. Dorset Nat. Hist. and Arch. Soc.* 109, 79–90.

Wormald, P. (1983) 'Bede, the *Bretwaldas* and the origins of the *Gens Anglorum*', pp. 99–129 in Wormald, P. (ed.), *Ideal and Reality in Frankish and Anglo-Saxon Society* (London).

Wymer, J. J. (1962) 'Excavations at the Maglemosian sites at Thatcham, Berkshire', *Proc. Prehist. Soc.* 28, 329–61.

Yorke, B. (1982) 'The foundation of the Old Minster and the status of Winchester in the seventh and eighth centuries', *Proc. Hants. Fld. Club and Archaeol. Soc.* 38, 75–84.

Yorke, B. (1984) 'The Bishops of Winchester, the Kings of Wessex and the development of Winchester in the ninth and early tenth centuries', *Proc. Hants. Fld. Club and Archaeol. Soc.* 42, 61–9.

Yorke, B. (1989) 'The Jutes of Hampshire and Wight and the origins of Wessex', pp. 84–96 in Bassett, S. (ed.), *The Origins of Anglo-Saxon Kingdoms* (Leicester).

Yorke, B. (1990) *Kings and Kingdoms of Early Anglo-Saxon England* (London).

Young, C. J. (1977) *Oxfordshire Roman Pottery* (BAR Brit. Series 43: Oxford).

Index

Sites within Wessex are distinguished by county, thus: Avon – A, Berkshire – B, Dorset – D, Hampshire – H, Isle of Wight – IoW, Somerset – S, Wiltshire – W. Numbers in italics indicate a reference to a plate, figure or table.